Wealth and Poverty

WEALTH AND POVERTY

GEORGE GILDER

Basic Books, Inc., Publishers
New York

Parts of this book have appeared in different form in *Harper's Magazine, Forbes, The American Spectator,* and *Policy Review.*

Library of Congress Cataloging in Publication Data

Gilder, George F   1939–
  Wealth and poverty.

  1. Capitalism.   2.   Wealth.   3.   United States—
Economic conditions—1945–   4.   United States—Economic
policy.   I.   Title.
HB501.G46   330.12'2   80–50556
ISBN: 0–465–09105–9

For Rosamond Gilder

a Great, Great Aunt

and Grand Lady of Literature

CONTENTS

Preface   *ix*

PART I
The Mandate for Capitalism

1. The Dirge of Triumph   *3*
2. The Economy of Frustration   *9*
3. The Returns of Giving   *21*
4. The Supply Side   *28*
5. The Nature of Wealth   *47*
6. The Nature of Poverty   *64*
7. The Entrepreneurial Future   *75*
8. The Clashes of Class   *86*
9. The War Against Wealth   *96*

PART II
The Crisis of Policy

10. The Moral Hazards of Liberalism   *105*
11. The Coming Welfare Boom   *114*
12. The Myths of Discrimination   *128*
13. The Jobs Perplex   *140*

14. The Make-Work Illusion 153
15. Laffer and Liberal Economics 170
16. The Inflationary State 190
17. The Productivity of Services 206
18. The Imperatives of Growth 217

PART III
The Economy of Faith

19. The Kinetic Economy 235
20. The Bullheaded Brewer 247
21. The Necessity for Faith 259

Notes 271

Selected Bibliography 289

Index 297

PREFACE

WEALTH AND POVERTY are the prime concerns of economics, but they are subjects too vast and vital to be left to economists alone. Although economists have provided me with some of my most valued counsel—and I will be acknowledging them in numbers—this book is in part an essay on the limitations of contemporary economics in analyzing the sources of creativity and progress in all economies.

Sociologists, too, have contributed to this work, and I will be thanking several. But one of my major themes is the grave distortions of view that issue from the sociological practice of discussing society chiefly in segments to be studied separately and statistically: the poor, the rich, women, men, business, and labor.

This book sprang from an earlier work of mine, *Visible Man*, an essentially sociological venture that undertook to understand poverty by studying the poor. *Visible Man* became a nonfiction novel based on interviews with hundreds of poor people in Albany, New York, and Greenville, South Carolina. I learned much from these researches about the devastating impact of the programs of liberalism on the poor. But perhaps the most important lesson I learned was the inadequacy of any theory of poverty that did not embody a theory of wealth. So *Wealth and Poverty* began with the title "The Pursuit of Poverty" and ended as an analysis of the roots of economic growth.

The contributors to my earlier analyses have been acknowledged in earlier works. Let me merely say in passing that this book could not exist without the earlier works and previous researches, and that my immersion in the world of economics was made far more fruitful by my previous immersions in the literature of anthropology and social theory, from Margaret Mead's *Male and Female* to Steven Goldberg's *The Inevitability of Patriarchy*.

Nonetheless, this book gained its special reach and character from a study of economics that began ten years ago with Milton Friedman's *Capitalism and Freedom* and led over the years through the works of Schumpeter and Keynes into what has been described with some felicity as "the supply-side" school of contemporary economists.

Intellectual progress, like the creation of wealth, does not normally occur in the rational and incremental way preferred by professional departments. I have learned that like Milton Friedman, Fredrich Von Hayek, Ayn Rand, and William Buckley, who were widely derided at the time they shaped my early economic ideas, Arthur Laffer, Irving Kristol, and Jude Wanniski are unpopular figures even among the professional economists who have taught me most. It so happens that the kind of "good" or "sound" economists who contribute most to the development of the science tend both to exaggerate its scientific rigor and to present their ideas in a way that fails to capture the high adventure and redemptive morality of capitalism. Even Adam Smith put altogether too much stress on self-interest rather than altruistic creativity as the foundation of the system.

In any case, Kristol and Wanniski, both in their books and on the editorial page of *The Wall Street Journal,* together with Warren T. Brookes, in his brilliant columns in *The Boston Herald American,* gave me a feeling for a capitalist economics that banished forever my previous apprehensions about the dismal science. Although I share the misgivings of many on its "political model," Wanniski's book *The Way the World Works* is one of the great inspirational works of economic literature—in the tradition of Henry George's *Progress and Poverty*—and in many ways, my book follows the supply-side trail that Wanniski so boldly blazed. I also want to thank Jude Wanniski and Nathan Glazer for their valuable encouragement after reading a ramshackle first draft of the manuscript.

As all writers learn sooner or later, it is only their best friends or closest allies who are willing to offer the kind of tough and tenacious criticism that all authors need. Jeffrey Bell, whose impact on Republican politics is only just beginning, gave this book a going over that strengthened several of its weakest chapters, and it may well be that I should have followed even more of his trenchant (that is, cutting) advice.

Like many of those acknowledged here, David Warsh will receive with great enthusiasm my authorial assurance that the ideas (and errors) in this book are my responsibility alone. Nonetheless, some of his own themes are easily found in these pages, and other less visible contributions of advice and encouragement abound.

Although I have only known him for a few years, Tom Bethell already seems an old friend, and his editorial counsel and criticism have made a highly significant impact on virtually every chapter of this book. Other early readers and valuable critics include Paul Craig Roberts and Tom Bray, then both of *The Wall Street Journal;* Michael Brewer who has been teaching me economics for more than ten years and who I hope can take some small pride in the work of his pupil, however aberrant it may be; Larry Pratt of the American Institute of Economic Research in Great Barrington, Massachusetts, a shrewd and sophisticated reader who alerted me to pitfalls in my arguments more rapidly than I could fill them; and Christopher De Muth of the Kennedy School at Harvard.

I had the great good fortune of meeting David Stockman before dispatching this book to the printers. Representative Stockman is by far the leading intellectual in the U.S. Congress, and his incisive criticisms and cogent amendments to this work—despite the pressure on his time—are deeply appreciated. Neil Howe, who is collaborating on an important book with Stockman, also gave me crucial advice during the final editing of this work.

Other valuable readers of all or part of the manuscript include Bill Hammett and Lynne Middelveen, my close colleagues with Antony Fisher at the International Center for Economic Policy Studies in New York, which provided an exciting intellectual atmosphere for the final writing on the book.

Parts of this book appeared first in magazine articles and their reception encouraged me to continue. Lewis Lapham and Mathew Stevenson of *Harper's* played an especially crucial role in shaping the final chapters, and the responses of Jack Kemp and Ronald Reagan alerted me to the emergence in America of Republican politicians who crave and celebrate ideas.

Although the ideas in this book are regarded as "conservative," I gathered them through a political education in circles as "liberal" as *The New Leader* magazine and the Ripon Society, the Kennedy Institute of Politics, the senatorial offices of Charles Mathias and Jacob Javits, and the three presidential campaigns of Nelson Rockefeller, a great American leader and patriot, whose loss transcends all the usual categories of ideology and politics. Three Ripon presidents, Josiah Lee Auspitz, Bruce Chapman, and John Topping participated heavily in the debates from which this work arose, and Auspitz made key contributions to the final chapters. Richard Rahn and Mark Bloomfield, also of Ripon, preceded me on my supply-side course. I believe that the central theme of *Wealth and Poverty*—the need to extend to the poor the freedoms and opportunities, the values of family and faith, that are indispensable to all wealth and progress—is also a central theme of American liberalism. Yet today, in a great historic irony, Phyllis Schlafly, Connie Marshner, Edwin Feulner, Jack Kemp, and others on the "New Right" have become the best friends of the poor in America, while Liberalism administers new forms of bondage and new fashions of moral corruption to poor families.

Bruce and Sarah Chapman and their innumerable friends in Seattle, Washington, provided the settings, surrounded in the distance by sparkling waters and snow capped peaks—with either the savory cornucopia of the Pike Place Market below or the dark firs and friendly livestock of Vashon Island—for the writing of most of this book. I cherish their friendship and their generosity and hope that the product is not unduly embarrassing to them. I wish also to thank Mike and Edith Williams for putting me up on their exquisite farm on Vashon Island.

Rod and Mellie Gilder had to endure most of the ideas in this book presented in their most raw and unpalatable form, at dinner or breakfast or late into the night, while at the same time putting up with the vagaries of the author well beyond the call of familial duty. I am grateful as ever for more services than I can even remember, let alone repay.

David and Peggy Rockefeller have shown faith in me when I lacked it in myself—and their faith has given me a sense of standards and possibilities that has extended the boundaries and lifted the goals of my life. This book is most deeply a tribute to them and to David's friendship with my father, which lives on in my life—and in their unending love and generosity to me.

This was Midge Decter's last book at Basic; her work, as usual, was superb and her support inspiring. The typists were Sally Bergmans, who also served as an able editor, and Bernice O'Neill.

My family is the source of all I am and can become and I want to thank them, my mother and Gilly, for their example and their love; and my wife, Nini, for giving me a reason and a way to live and for giving me Louisa.

GEORGE GILDER

Tyringham, Massachusetts
July 20, 1980

PART
I

The Mandate for Capitalism

CHAPTER 1

The Dirge of Triumph

THE MOST IMPORTANT EVENT in the recent history of ideas is the demise of the socialist dream. Dreams always die when they come true, and fifty years of socialist reality, in every partial and plenary form, leave little room for idealistic reverie. In the United States socialism chiefly rules in auditoria and parish parlors, among encounter groups of leftist intellectuals retreating from the real world outside, where socialist ideals have withered in the shadows of Stalin and Mao, Sweden and Tanzania, gulag and bureaucracy.

The second most important event of the recent era is the failure of capitalism to win a corresponding triumph. For within the colleges and councils, governments and churches where issue the nebulous but nonetheless identifiable airs and movements of new opinion, the manifest achievements of free enterprise still seem less comely than the promises of socialism betrayed. If socialism is dead, in some sense intellectually bankrupt, morally defunct, as they say, why does the capitalist vision seem to teeter so precariously over the same ash can of history? Why do the same writers who most tellingly confute the collectivist argument sing the praises of free enterprise only in an almost elegiac tone, writing staunch conservative tracts that end in the cadences of a dirge for their favored beliefs?

The dirge is sung in varied harmonies and arrangements. But it is undeniably a dirge. It is a curious fact that the celebrated group of neoconservative intellectuals, heralded as saviors of business, discuss the nature and future of capitalism in the same dolorous idiom used by some of the chastened but still assured advocates of "socialism." Meanwhile the intellectuals of the Old Right have usually shunned altogether the challenge of reconciling their philosophies and their economics, and they are equally likely to confide a belief that capitalism is in decline. William F. Buckley's *National Review,* which for two decades has waged brilliant battle for the free economy, publishes anti-Communist and Christian "socialists," if they are culturally conservative, with much of the enthusiasm and frequency that it devotes to the cause and philosophy of private enterprise. Conservatives give Solzhenitsyn and Malcom Muggeridge, both impassioned critics of the works of business, a place in their pantheon equaled by no contemporary businessman or philosopher of capitalism. Both are great writers and inspired Christian voices, and perhaps there are moments when carping is beside the point. Still, it is important for conservatives to deny with some comparable passion that capitalism is a historic and moral failure.

Yet Daniel Bell could survey the writers of the Right over the last seventy-five years and conclude that "romantic or traditionalist, Enlightenment or irrationalist, vitalist or naturalist, humanist or racialist, religious or atheist—in this entire range of passions and beliefs, scarcely one respectable intellectual figure defended the sober, unheroic, prudential, let alone acquisitive, entrepreneurial, or money-making pursuits of the bourgeois world."[1] This statement must be qualified, since many important thinkers have defended capitalism. But Bell is right that the defenses have usually not resounded clearly; they have been almost always *faute de mieux,* praising free enterprise for the lack of an alternative that accorded more easily with the writer's religious and aesthetic convictions and with his sense of the way in which the world was going. Capitalism has been presented as a transitory and conditional compromise: The worst possible system, as Churchill once said of democracy, except for all the others.

This negative view allows to arise, without indignant refutation, something of a consensus among thinkers on both the Left and the Right that, for all its superficial virtues, private enterprise suffers from profound social conflicts and moral contradictions deriving from its continuing practical failures and lack of transcendent justification. Our rising affluence, it is said, springs from a consumer ethic with a hedonistic base, a continual whetting of appetites by advertising that is in the end destructive to the moral disciplines of capitalist production and distribution. Or capitalism leads inexorably to large bureaucratic structures that stifle the spirit of entrepreneurship that is the essence and rationale of private enterprise. Such contradictions may be relieved, for a while, by economic growth. But growth is dependent on a momentum of technology that creates a new elite and exalts a rationalist mind-set also incompatible with democratic and religious values.

This, with some reservations, is the essential message of the recent works of John Kenneth Galbraith and Robert Heilbroner, both professed socialists. And this, amid all the mazes of his learning, even the pedantry of his endless verbal distinctions, is the practical message of "neoconservative socialist" Daniel Bell. This, among their fierce denunciations of contemporary social and psychological science, is the thesis of cultural conservatives Christopher Lasch and Robert Nisbet. This, too, amid all his sparkling wit and wisdom, is a persistent theme of neoconservative and capitalist writer Irving Kristol, who holds a deserved but nonetheless ambiguous position as our leading apologist for private enterprise.

One might ask whether, for sympathetic but firmly dolorous reflections on the decline of the bourgeois ethic, on the cultural contradictions of capitalism, on the inexorable emergence of a technocratic and possibly stationary state, we really need a neoconservative revival. We still have, after all, in those of our libraries not altogether devoted to the dissemination of best-sellers and audiovisual aids, the works of Marx, Tocqueville, Veblen, and Schumpeter. All these writers eloquently celebrate the vigor and thrust and the immense historic role of the bourgeoisie, only to predict its decline and fall. All traffic in the same moral contradictions, technological imperatives, managerial transformations, material satiations, and social changes that animate the critique of capitalism now and that were at least partly evident even to the Swiss economist Simonde de Sismondi, a pioneer of dynamic analysis, who nonetheless "wondered what we could possibly do with more production now that we had already met the essential needs of man"—in 1815.[2]

Even Adam Smith, whose very name symbolizes the capitalist order, foresaw its eventual decrepitude, in which the devoutly wished-for achievement of general riches would dissolve the purposes and preconditions of the system. To other visionaries over the years it was an exhaustion of resources as population grew that portended the obsolescence of capital. But for whatever reason, wealth or poverty or mediocrity or inequality or some other bizarre conjunction of complaints, agitated seers for centuries have been predicting the death, decline, stagnation, doom, and decay of capitalism and the emergence of some sort of more stationary state, some kind of benign equilibrium, some surcease of the human struggle.

In fact, the current prophets of ambivalent capitalism are in such ample and various company, reaching so far back into the past that one may guess that the meaning of their analysis resides less in what it says about capitalism than what it says about the incapacity of great thinkers to believe that their own epoch is not the climax of the human story— when soon will be broken the seven seals of the revelation, shaking "the mountains and islands . . . from their places."[3] Both intellectuals and commercial "statesmen" show a persistent tendency, stemming perhaps from their own increasing disappointments before the mirror and on the stairs, to predict the decline and fall of the most permanent things, followed by some stationary Nirvana, much resembling the Aspen Institute. Divorcees predict the transformation of the family, aging intellectuals and businessmen the declining vigor of capital.

Sociology, however, does not recapitulate biology. Even though senescence may afflict great men on their paths of glory to final equilibrium, it is not a characteristic of nations, and capitalism, like the family, is not an institution that can become obsolete or decrepit as long as human societies persist. Human needs and numbers annually increase; science and technology provide their continuing surprises. The exigency, complexity, and multiplicity of life on earth become yearly more unfathomable to any tyrant or planner. No nation can grow and adapt to change except to the extent that it is capitalistic, except to the extent, in other words, that its productive wealth is diversely controlled and can be freely risked in new causes, flexibly applied to new purposes, steadily transformed into new shapes and systems. Time itself means continuous change of knowledge and conditions. Among all states it is the "stationary state" so favored by the prophets that is most sure of withering away.

The more important charge of the intellectual consensus is that capitalism is morally vacant. At the innermost reaches of the system, after crossing plush carpets and mincing down hushed halls, we enter the sacramental crypts, part the velvet curtains, and find, says Daniel Boorstin, only an empty sanctum. He is glad of this, regarding it a source of our freedoms. Other capitalist defenders agree. The great Austrian political economists Friedrich von Hayek and Ludwig von Mises, like Milton Friedman in *Capitalism and Freedom,* are all eloquent in their critique of collectivism and their celebration of liberty, but they are uncertain of what it is for: their argument tends to be technical and pragmatic. Freedom is good in itself and also makes us rich; collectivism compounds bondage with poverty. None of these writers sees reason to give capitalism a theology or even assign to its results any assurance of justice.

None of them cogently refutes the thesis that the greatest of capitalists—the founders of the system—were in some sense "robber barons." None convincingly demonstrates that the system succeeds and thrives because it gives room for the heroic creativity of entrepreneurs.

These capitalist writers have neither a satisfactory reply to Kristol's question: "Can men live in a free society if they have no reason to believe it is also a just society?" nor a response to his answer, "I do not think so. My reading of history is that, in the same way as men cannot for long tolerate a sense of spiritual meaninglessness in their individual lives, so they cannot for long accept a society in which power, privilege and property are not distributed according to some morally meaningful criteria."[4] It is the new consensus that capitalist freedom undermines capitalism both because freedom defines no moral basis for its results, and because its successes are really dependent not on liberty but on bourgeois disciplines and restraints—diligence, integrity, and rationality—all inconsistent with the drives and appetites of the unfettered consumer in a heat of commerce, who is believed to give impetus to the system's growth. Capitalist freedom, it is suggested, leads to a vulgar and decadent civilization, afflicted with libido for the ugly and the trivial, the shallow and the ungodly, and lacking the discipline and courage to survive or the values to be worth preserving.

The leftist critique includes such charges and goes beyond them. Capitalism is not only morally vacant, it also perpetrates gross immorality: racism, sexism, inequality, environmental abuse. It is a practical failure as well, because it brings inflation and unemployment, and it prevents the emergence of the large-scale planning that is indispensable in a time of world ecological crisis, resource scarcity, and rising expectations in the populous Third World. Above all, capitalism creates and perpetuates inequality—between the rich and the poor, rich countries and poor ones, men and women—and destroys balance—between man and nature, consumption and conservation, individual appetites and social needs. This argument does not contradict the conservative one. The radicals agree with the idea that the goods of America are materially shoddy and that the consumer society is morally erosive. But they add a series of further charges that conservatives regard to be overwrought or misconceived, and they propose corrective programs that conservatives perceive as futile, wasteful, and often perverse.

Nonetheless, I believe that the two themes of criticism of American life converge as much as they divide. Robert Heilbroner, Daniel Bell, Irving Kristol, Aleksandr Solzhenitsyn, and Tom Hayden have more in common than they suppose. Most crucially, they assume that capitalism is an edifice without an inherent foundation in morality and religion, and that therefore it engenders a shallow and dubious order of human life. None of these men, it would seem, could have done much better than the dumbfounded President Dwight D. Eisenhower when he was confronted with Nikita Khrushchev's charge that our system is immoral because it is based on greed.

What has happened, one might ask, to the dreams of *The Good Society*, firmly and necessarily capitalist, that Walter Lippmann celebrated in his masterpiece of the late 1930s? Then he could assert in the face of impending war and from the still bleak ruins of the Great Depression that our system was based on an ideal that "for the first time in human history" gave men "a way of producing wealth in which the good fortune of others multiplied their own," in which at long last "the golden rule was economically sound," and in which "for the first time men could conceive a social order in which the ancient moral aspiration of liberty, fraternity, and equality was consistent with the abolition of poverty and the increase of wealth."[5] Lippmann continued the theme: "Until the division of labor had begun to make men dependent on the free collaboration of other men, the worldly policy was to be predatory. The claims of the spirit were otherworldly. So it was not until the industrial revolution had altered the traditional mode of life that the vista was opened at the end of which men could see the possibility of the Good Society on this earth. At long last the ancient schism between the world and the spirit, between self interest and disinterestedness, was potentially closed."

Although a masochistic intelligentsia insists on seeing radical transformations and moral contradictions everywhere in the free world, the fundamental beliefs uttered by Lippmann in a far more perilous and impoverished epoch remain luminously true. In a time of abundance, haunted by specters of peril, we should try to recover the faith proclaimed by a great man in the truly desperate plight of the thirties and forties.

CHAPTER 2

The Economy of
Frustration

THE BELIEF that the good fortune of others is also finally one's own does not come easily or invariably to the human breast. It is, however, a golden rule of economics, a key to peace and prosperity, a source of the gifts of progress. It is the belief that finally confounded the predatory economics of mercantilism, in which nations used regulation and beggar-thy-neighbor trade campaigns to gather surpluses and bullion. It was this golden rule that inspired the first great book of economics, *The Wealth of Nations*. It was this belief that David Hume proclaimed in 1742, at the end of his essay, "Of the Jealousy of Trade:" "I shall therefore venture to acknowledge, that, not only as a man, but as a British subject, I pray for the flourishing commerce of Germany, Spain, Italy, and even France itself. I am at least certain that all nations would flourish more [with] such enlarged and benevolent sympathies toward each other."[1]

The golden rule finds its scientific basis in the mutuality of gains from trade, in the demand generated by the engines of supply, in the expanded opportunity created by growth, in the usual and still growing economic futility of war. On this foundation have arisen most of the world's economic gains since the times of Smith and Hume. Its abandonment during the tariff wars of the thirties precipitated, deepened, and prolonged the Great Depression. Its continuing survival is our greatest patrimony as a free people. But it is a belief that is always in danger of erosion and attack.

A prominent source of trouble is the profession of economics. Smith entitled Book One of *The Wealth of Nations,* "Of the Causes of Improvement in the productive Powers of Labour and the Order according to which its Produce is naturally distributed among the different Ranks of the people." He himself stressed the productive powers, but his followers, beginning with David Ricardo, quickly became bogged down in a static and mechanical concern with distribution. They all were forever counting the ranks of rich and poor and assaying the defects of capitalism that keep the poor always with us in such great numbers. The focus on distribution continues in economics today, as economists pore balefully over the perennial inequalities and speculate on brisk "redistributions" to rectify them.

This mode of thinking, prominent in foundation-funded reports, best-selling economics texts, newspaper columns, and political platforms, is harmless enough on the surface. But its deeper effect is to challenge the golden rule of capitalism, to pervert the relation between rich and poor, and to depict the system as "a zero-sum game" in which every gain for someone implies a loss for someone else, and wealth is seen once again to create poverty. As Kristol has said, a free society in which the distributions are widely seen as unfair cannot long survive. The distributionist mentality thus strikes at the living heart of democratic capitalism.

Whether of wealth, income, property, or government benefits, distributions always, unfortunately, turn out bad: highly skewed, hugely unequal, presumptively unfair, and changing little, or getting worse. Typical conclusions are that "the top 2 percent of all families own 44 percent of all family wealth, and the bottom 25 percent own none at all"; or that "the top 5 percent get 15.3 percent of the pretax income and the bottom 20 percent get 5.4 percent."[2] The statistician can make great play with medians (the centerpoint of a distribution, with half of the entries above and half below) and means or averages. The median income of individual Americans, for example, is zero (because a majority of Americans are housewives and children).

Statistical distributions, though, can misrepresent the economy in more serious ways. They are implicitly static, like a picture of a corporate headquarters, towering high above a city, that leaves out all the staircases, escalators, and elevators, and the Librium® on the executive's desk as he contemplates the annual report. The distribution appears permanent, and indeed, like the building, it will remain much the same year after year. But new companies will move in and out, executives will come and go, people at the bottom will move up, and some at the top will leave their Librium® and jump. For example, the share of the tobacco industry commanded by the leading four firms has held steady for nearly thirty years, but the leader of the 1950s is now nearly bankrupt. The static distributions also miss the simple matter of age: many of the people at the bottom of the charts are either old, and thus beyond their major earning years, or young, and yet to enter them. Although the young and the old will always be with us, their low earnings signify little about the pattern of opportunity in a capitalist sytem.

Because blacks have been at the bottom for centuries now, economists often miss the dynamism within the American system. The Japanese, for example, were interned in concentration camps during World War II, but thirty years later they had higher per capita earnings than any other ethnic group in America except the Jews. Three and one-half million Jewish immigrants arrived on our shores around the turn of the century with an average of nine dollars per person in their pockets, less than almost any other immigrant group. Six decades later the mean family income of Jews was almost double the national average. Meanwhile the once supreme British Protestants (WASPs) were passed in per capita earnings after World War II not only by Jews and Orientals but also by Irish, Italians, Germans, and Poles (which must have been the final Polish joke), and the latest generation of black West Indians.[3]

It is a real miracle that learned social scientists can live in the midst of these continuing eruptions and convulsions, these cascades and cataracts of change, and declare in a tone of grim indignation that "Over the last fifty years there has been no shift in the distribution of wealth and income in this country."[4] Yet sociologist Peter Edelman made that statement in 1977, echoing hundreds of his colleagues, and the Carnegie Council on Children, after years of costly ruminations involving Edelman's wife Marian Wright and a dozen other social scientists, headed by Kenneth Kenniston of Yale, published reports in 1977 and 1979 depicting the United States as a "caste system." The American economy, said Kenniston, is a "stacked deck" in which "the brilliant exceptions may systematically mislead us" [for they encourage us] "to believe that any child with enough grit and ability can escape poverty and make a rewarding life."[5] Carnegie certainly knows better than that. Its social scientists have taught it the new myth of a static America.

Even so sophisticated an observer as Herbert J. Gans, in his book *More Equality*, managed to hold his footing on the quaking earth of American society (perhaps by clinging tight to the solidity of distribution tables) and concluded that, "the opportunity to strike out on one's own, and perhaps strike it rich, is closing down. . . . Of course," he notes, rather impatiently, "there are still exceptions," but "their small number [as if exceptional riches could ever be commonplace] only proves the rule" of economic sclerosis.[6]

This mode of thinking also sometimes afflicts conservatives when they have been sufficiently trained in the social sciences. In the late 1970s, Martin Anderson, an economist who has written speeches for both President Nixon and Ronald Reagan, began his book *Welfare* by declaring: "The 'war on poverty' that began in 1964 has been won."[7] He quoted the conclusion of Alice Rivlin, head of the Congressional Budget Office, that the combination of expanded welfare payments and in-kind benefits had effectively lifted all but a very small proportion (6.4 percent) of Americans above the poverty line. *The Wall Street Journal*'s editorial writers enlisted their formidable eloquence to propagate the good news to its 6 million readers. Income distribution may indeed be skewed, conservatives could sing, but what other system in the history of the world—what system that continues to admit immigrants in huge numbers, what system that embraces some 210 million souls across a giant continent—could ever have succeeded in raising its lowest ranks of earners above a line of poverty that exceeds the median family income of the Soviet Union by perhaps $1,000 a year. Blacks may still be low on the pole of earnings, it is said, but even they have made great progress since the massive social programs of the 1960s were put into place. The war on poverty, we are to believe, has been won by income redistribution.

Yet here again we see the blindness of the social scientist to realities that are blatantly evident to the naked eye. What actually happened since 1964 was a vast expansion of the welfare rolls that halted in its tracks an ongoing improvement in the lives of the poor, particularly blacks, and left behind—and here I choose my words as carefully as I can—a wreckage of broken lives and families worse than the aftermath of slavery. Although intact black families are doing better than ever, and discrimination has vastly diminished, the condition of poor blacks has radically worsened. The fact that they have more income only makes the situation less remediable.

Conservatives surely, above all, have long known and warned that real poverty is less a state of income than a state of mind and that the government dole blights most of the people who come to depend on it. The lesson of the period since 1964—a lesson so manifest it cannot be gainsaid—is that conservatives, if anything, understated their argument. In the time since the war on poverty was launched, the moral blight of dependency has been compounded and extended to future generations by a virtual plague of family dissolution. The number of female-headed black families, already a cause for great alarm at the time of the famous Moynihan Report of 1965, has more than doubled, as has the number of black children brought up in these fatherless homes. About six out of ten black children in 1978 were being raised in one-parent families or in institutions (compared to less than two out of ten whites).[8] The disastrous potential of these trends and programs was already becoming evident in the late 1970s, as shown in rates of black youth unemployment and work-force withdrawal running as high as 60 per cent in inner city areas, and in the increase of black male joblessness, despite declining joblessness rates for whites and steadily expanding levels of overall employment.[9]

Anyone contemplating these statistics—or, as I did during two years of interviewing in the ghetto, anyone contemplating the lives that have been maimed and demoralized as a result—can only pray that he has been deceived by these appearances of tragedy. Social history is too full of surprises to permit any sure prophecies. But no one can view that wreckage of broken homes and lives and call it victory over poverty without depriving the word of all meaning.

As the 1980s began, a similar myopia distorted the vision of economists and social scientists appraising the condition of the middle and upper classes in the American economy. Again scrutinizing their distribution charts, they could maintain that the years of inflation since 1973 have brought "no significant shifts," as Lester Thurow wrote in *The Wall Street Journal*, "in the distribution of economic resources either across sectors (government, business, and labor) or among individuals (rich vs. poor, black vs. white, etc.)."[10]

The true source of the economic pain professed by upper- and middle-class Americans, Thurow contended, was the huge gap between the 8 percent rise in real incomes and the 50 percent increase in money incomes between 1973 and 1978. This difference creates "a severe money illusion . . . and may even make it possible to convince yourself that your real standards of living have fallen when objectively they have not."[11] Like the blacks who cannot see their gains from the war on poverty, the upper classes, too, are said to be suffering from illusions of pain.

Now it is certainly true that no catastrophe remotely comparable to the one that struck the blacks has troubled the upper and middle reaches of American society. But their decline in wealth and welfare is just as surely real. It is the statistics of rising gross national product and rising real household incomes that seriously misrepresent the conditions of American life.

Numerically most important are the middle classes. To understand their situation, it is helpful to comprehend the many fallacies of income growth as it is registered in Gross National Product or Income (which are accounting identities). Economists have long stressed the deceptiveness of a measure of progress that improves with every jet of toxic fluid released into a rural stream, every oil spill on a secluded beach, and every roar of racket from a new factory or airport near a city community, but remains unmoved as public museums overflow and millions of Americans breathe cleaner air.

The chief fallacy of rising GNP in the decade of the 1970s, however, was its source in the disruption of families. The most obvious factor—divorces—tend to expand the national income by increasing the use of housing, fast foods, day-care centers, and domestic help, and by expanding the number of job holders. Divorced men and women also drink far more, suffer much more from mental and physical illness, and spend more money on social services of every kind.[12] Between 1965 and 1979 the number of divorces a year rose from 479,000 to around 1 million,[13] thus imparting some dubious push to GNP. Marriages, meanwhile, as is shown by the familiar example of the man who weds his housekeeper, can be seen to diminish GNP. (In marriage, the money that was previously paid to the housekeeper as a reportable paycheck is normally enlarged and given voluntarily to the wife, thus escaping the national—and tax—accounts.) In the seventies, the great ferment of family transformation, with higher rates of divorce and remarriage and more prolonged singleness, has conferred a net upward impetus to income totals.

A more important factor is the effect of inflation and taxes on the number of women in the work force. Inflation lifts incomes into higher brackets without raising purchasing power. In effect, taxes become more progressive, taking increasingly more as incomes rise. As the 1980s began, the marginal tax rate (the rate applying to the next dollar earned above current income) was nearly 50 percent for the *average* American.[14] That means that half the money earned through additional work goes to the government, in one way or another, either through giving up welfare and other transfers or through payments of taxes on the federal, state, and local levels.

The result is to penalize the family that depends on a single earner who is fully and resourcefully devoted to his career. Two half-hearted participants in the labor force can do better than one who is competing aggressively for the relatively few jobs in the upper echelons. Exacerbating this trend has been a gross insufficiency of new capital investment of the sort that sustains high productivity employment. Instead of buying durable equipment, companies have tended to hire low-paid workers, often seasonal or part-time.

These conditions have overshadowed American family life and undermined our economy during most of the 1970s, causing a simultaneous expansion of the work force and a decline in productivity growth. The two-income family does have more real purchasing power than the family with one breadwinner: the gross national product rises by that measure as it is multiplied through the economy. The revenues of the government may even climb because its total take from two incomes, plus associated new spending for domestic services and their substitutes, exceeds the take from one large salary.

Nonetheless, these middle-class families, as Thurow observes, are claiming to suffer economic pain; somehow their incomes don't reach as far as they expect. Thurow maintains that their expectations have been greatly inflated by a "money illusion." Thurow, however, is afflicted by a different sort of money illusion—a statistical illusion—because unlike the two-income families, he cannot see the emotional losses that accompany the income gains and he misses the effects of demography.

As families forgo leisure and domestic life in favor of work, there is a point when the scarcest of resources becomes, quite simply, time. As time becomes more scarce, it also becomes more valuable and its loss becomes more costly, more destructive of welfare. The first effect of the woman's acceptance of full-time work is an emotionally stressful time pinch. The second and related effect is the impact on the woman's domestic services. The worth of the housewife's work in the home varies in proportion to the number of children and other considerations, but it has been estimated by many analysts to average about $12,000. Some of this work is performed by the wife and husband anyway, after doing their jobs; some is farmed out to domestic help; and some is left undone or replaced by restaurants, launderers, day-care facilities, and processed foods. Both husband and wife suffer new strains of pure fatigue, together with tensions over the change in formerly settled sex roles. These strains are no illusion, as is attested by an increasing body of census data that shows a sharply rising rate of divorces and separations after wives submit to full-time work responsibilities. The family may well be worse off unless the wife earns more than $12,000.[15]

All these calculations, however, miss the dynamic context of family life. The new development—deterring aggressive male careers in favor of two incomes—emerges at the very time that the postwar baby boom generation is forming families and bearing children. This generation—the great demographic bulge that overwhelmed the schools and colleges in the sixties and early seventies and inundated the job markets—hit the housing market in the late seventies and began its homemaking phase. Until they have children, these couples can thrive on inflation as their dual incomes rise and their living expenses consolidate. But the arrival of children causes a crunch for the two-earner strategy. According to the Labor Department, to maintain the same family standard of living after the birth of the first child, income must rise by 26 percent; after a second birth, it must rise by 47 percent over the childless level; and after the first child enters school, by 57 percent over the childless level. By the end of ten years the income of the two-child family will have to be more than double the childless level.[16] That is real income, needed at the very time when the woman's earnings suffer most from the demands of small children.

In the inflated dollars of the late seventies, these figures indicate the need to *quadruple* family income in ten years merely to stay even. This will be impossible for most husbands to do alone. If they try, they will find themselves falling constantly behind, with even apparent successes frustrated by the bracket creep and lurch of income taxes. The man unable to perform his role as breadwinner is being slowly unmanned.

The meaning of these statistics should not be exaggerated. Like the other government income data, they too are distorted by statistical illusions. No one who has children is likely to accept the idea that one's life is impoverished by their arrival, that one's standard of living declines when money is spent on them rather than on maintaining a childless person's schedule of outside entertainments. The chief problem is the anguish inflicted on both the husband and the wife and thus on their relationship when the woman is forced to work despite the intensely increasing need for her in the home.

Despite all the celebrations of working women, the earnings statistics show that most women prefer to avoid full commitment to the work force. Their work effort, measured in annual hours and earnings, declines rapidly as family income increases.[17] After age twenty-five, they are eleven times more likely to leave the labor force voluntarily than men.[18] Women tend to favor part-time jobs and informal services. The men's pattern contrasts dramatically. As their earnings capacity increases, so does their exploitation of it; they extend themselves to the limit when their opportunities for income improve. These findings, from an elaborate study of earnings capacity by Irwin Garfinkel and Robert Haveman of the Institute for Research on Poverty,[19] contradict the assertion of John Kenneth Galbraith, Lester Thurow, and others that men work less hard when their earnings rise and that lower taxes would deter effort. The institute monograph clearly shows that married women work harder and married men less hard when, for whatever reason, family earnings possibilities are reduced. Since highly paid married men are the paramount source of productivity growth in America, it is easy to see that our highly progressive tax rates, enhanced by inflation, are eroding productivity at the same time that they are expanding the work force.

What has been happening is a drive, conscious or not, on the part of the government, to flush the wife out of the untaxed household economy and into the arms of the IRS. Accompanying her in her emergence from the home are a host of previously private and untaxed expenses, for everything from food preparation to child care, increasingly including, so it would seem from the proliferation of massage parlors around most American cities, the ministrations of sex.

As the example of massage parlors suggests, however, the IRS drive has been only partly successful. A portion of the untaxed household economy has moved into the taxable sector. But at the same time, at least a comparable portion of taxable activity, by men and women alike, seems to have gone underground. As families break down under the pressure of taxes and welfare, moral constraints tend to dissolve, mobility and anonymity increase, economic transactions become less traceable, and the temptations grow for concealed and undocumented income. IRS and other income totals exclude the growth in criminal behavior, such as narcotics trade, gambling, and prostitution, and they largely miss or under-report activities such as bartering, moonlighting, employment of illegal aliens and others off the books, tips and other gratuities, capital gains in stamps, antiques, and other collectibles, and the ubiquitous double bookkeeping and skimming almost necessary for many small businesses in the current regulatory and taxing climate.

Economists estimate the size of the underground by charting the growth of cash holdings (in 1979, nearly $500 for every man, woman, and child in the United States), by comparing official income statistics with the more rapid expansion of estimated total transactions, or by examining audits of selected tax returns. By every means, they are concluding that the "irregular" economy is now somewhere between 10 and 25 percent of the GNP. Although economists have no clear idea of the extent of such behavior, they have no doubt that it is large and growing—or as the once skeptical Edgar Feige of the University of Wisconsin put it, "of staggering proportions and growing rapidly."[20] "In this area, the more you look, the more you find," New York University's Peter Gutmann has written.[21]

People do not like to conceal income or evade taxes. Although unreported earnings have relieved financial pressures on some families, many have suffered severe tensions and anxieties in this high tax environment, whether from paying imposts that they feel are unfair or avoided by others, or from violating their own sense of what is right.[22] Either way, the results are rage and demoralization.

Such experiences, happening to the fastest growing group of American families, explain much of the pain and protest of the ostensibly affluent middle classes. These problems also demonstrate why large tax cuts are needed both to reduce illegal and concealed activity and to help strengthen families. The problem is international as well. In Sweden, where progressive taxes and social programs are more advanced than under the American system, the divorce rate is 60 percent higher, illegitimacy exceeds ours by a factor of three, with one-third of Swedish children born out of wedlock,[23] and as famed socialist Gunnar Myrdal has said, "high taxes are making us into a nation of hustlers."[24]

The income distribution tables also propagate a statistical illusion with regard to the American rich. While the patterns of annual income changed rather little in the 1970s, there was a radical shift in the distribution of wealth. In order to understand this development, it is crucial to have a clear-eyed view of the facts and effects of inflation, free of the pieties of the Left and the Right: the familiar rhetoric of the "cruelest tax," in which all the victims seem to be widows and orphans. In fact, widows and orphans—at least the ones who qualified for full social security and welfare benefits—did rather well under inflation. Between 1972 and 1977, for example, the median household income of the elderly rose from 80 to 85 percent of the entire population's.[25] As Christopher Jencks of Harvard University and Joseph Minarek of the Brookings Institution, both men of the Left, discovered in the late 1970s, inflation hit hardest at savers and investors, largely the rich.

During the late 1970s, as the rate of productivity growth sank toward zero and oil payments poured overseas, the average American standard of living necessarily began to decline. Therefore, any group that kept up with rising prices actually improved its relative position in the U.S. economy. In fact, most families that stayed abreast of the rise in the consumer price index (CPI) made substantial real as well as relative gains, since the CPI has been exaggerating the actual impact of inflation by at least one-fifth.

The key error is to include the rising cost of home ownership, with its high component of interest payments, as nearly 30 percent of the CPI. Few homeowners incur these costs every year. Instead, they find their existing homes increasing in value and their mortgages declining as a real burden of debt. In addition, homeowners can deduct interest payments from taxable income, even though the bulk of these charges are not true interest at all but an inflation premium designed to compensate the bank for the impact of the declining dollar on the value of the mortgage principal. During the 1970s, in fact, home ownership gave some protection against inflation to much of the American middle class, as well as to 70 percent of the elderly. Even among households with incomes below $10,000 in 1975, more than half owned their homes.

More important, however, was the rapid spread of indexing: the linking of incomes to the cost of living. The many Americans with Cost of Living Adjustments (COLAs) or income-escalator clauses all made relative gains in the late 1970s by escaping the effects of the general decline in U.S. wealth. Social security recipients did especially well, since a legislative error, not corrected for five years, gave a double-indexed push to their benefits. Welfare recipients in most states kept up with inflation or improved their position through the tripling of food stamps and other in-kind supports. Steel workers, auto workers, teamsters, and other heavily organized segments of work force, together with postal workers, municipal unions, and other government employees, all fought free of the American bottom line of stagnation. All gained wage hikes, pensions, and fringes that kept them whole at the expense of the taxpayer or the competitive position of their industries in the world economy.

Of particular importance in relation to the distribution of wealth was the rise in social security payments. Social security represents some 7 trillion dollars in liabilities of the government, and in assets of the nation's workers. These assets comprise much of the real wealth of the American middle class. As Congressman David Stockman has written: "Rather than being embodied in financial assets intermediated by the markets [that is, banks and other institutions of savings and investment], a growing share of middle-class savings is now embodied in future claims on the state intermediated by politicians."[26] Though absent from the distribution tables, this real wealth climbed steadily during the 1970s and greatly shifted the distribution of real wealth in favor of the middle class.

The American upper classes, meanwhile, underwent another "Great Depression." If progressive redistribution, from the rich to the poor, without real growth, could relieve social stresses, the years from 1974 to 1980 would have been a time of milk and honey in overtaxed and inflated Western economies rather than a period of growing frustration and social unease, affecting winners and losers alike.

The process of redistribution, according to the Minarek study for Brookings, can grow more intense and destructive of wealth as inflation continues. Minarek compares census income tables—which tend to show that inflation marginally helps the rich and hurts the poor—with a more comprehensive measure that includes in-kind benefits (from food stamps to corporate fringes), wealth effects (such as real-estate appreciation and the decline of the real value of stocks and bonds), and the impact of taxation (bracket creep and levies on nominal profits that may be actual losses).[27] This approach represents a major conceptual breakthrough, implicitly refuting most of the conventional wisdom on the current distribution of American wealth.

While increases in the value of home ownership and in-kind benefits tend to compensate for the effects of bracket creep on the lower and middle classes, at an earnings level of about $25,000 annually the impact of income taxes begins to exceed the appreciation of housing and other assets. At still higher income levels, the reduced income and equity value of stocks, bonds, and other dollar denominated securities inflicts major reductions in wealth. Although these wealth effects are difficult to measure, Minarek estimates that just a 2 percent, one-year, increase in inflation diminishes real incomes by about 10 percent at the $100,000 level and by nearly 18 percent at $200,000 (a loss of nearly $40,000 attributable to inflation alone). Although the one-year impact on millionaires is proportionately somewhat less, sustained inflation over a six-year period—such as the 1974–1980 stretch in the United States—has the greatest effect at the highest levels.[28] While Minarek does not extend his findings to the double digit rates at the end of the decade, a similar analysis would suggest a one-year reduction of over one-third in the real income of rich families in 1979. The wealth changes were dramatic. Bond values, for example, dropped some 500 billion dollars between June 1979 and early 1980.

As the 1980s began, the effects of these developments on all the American income classes and on the prospects for the economy were devastating, with productivity growth coming to a halt and the savings rate plummeting to below 4 percent. The upper classes, normally the cutting edge of the economy—the source of most investment—fled to unproductive tax shelters and hoards of gold, real estate, and speculation. The demoralization of the elite, moreover, worsened the pains of the classes below.

All such considerations eluded the experts of income distribution, parsing their charts for crypto-Marxist insights and emergencies. But most of all their statistical view of the economy misrepresented the interrelated roles of wealth and poverty in a world that can still be governed, if we let it be, by the golden rule of capitalism.

CHAPTER 3

The Returns of Giving

CAPITALISM begins with giving. This is a growing theme of "economic anthropology," from Melville Herskovits's pioneering book by that name to Marvin Harris's *Cannibals and Kings*. The capitalists of primitive society were tribal leaders who vied with one another in giving great feasts. Similarly, trade began with offerings from one family to another or from one tribe to its neighbor. The gifts, often made in the course of a religious rite, were presented in hopes of an eventual gift in return. The compensation was not defined beforehand. But in the feasting process it was expected to be a return with interest, as another "big man," or *mumi* as he was called among the Siuai in the Solomon Islands, would attempt to excel the offerings of the first.

Harris describes the process:

A young man proves himself capable of becoming a *mumi* by working harder than everyone else and by carefully restricting his own consumption of meat and coconuts. Eventually, he impresses his wife, children and near relations with the seriousness of his intentions, and they vow to help him prepare for his first feast. If the feast is a success, his circle of supporters widens and he sets to work readying an even greater display of generosity. He aims next at the construction of a men's clubhouse in which his male followers can lounge about and in which guests can be entertained and fed. Another feast is held at the consecration of the clubhouse, and if this is also a success his circle of supporters—people willing to work for the feast to come—grows still larger and he will begin to be spoken of as a *mumi*. . . . Even though larger and larger feasts mean that the *mumi's* demands on his supporters become more irksome, the overall volume of production goes up. . . .[1]

Helen Codere describes potlatching, a similar sequence of work and saving, capital accumulation and feasting, performed among the Kwakiutl of the northwestern United States: "The public distribution of property by an individual is a recurrent climax to an endless series of cycles of accumulating property—distributing it in a potlatch—being given property—again accumulating and preparing."[2] The piles of food and other gifts and ceremonial exchanges could mount to dumbfounding quantities. One South Sea offering mentioned by Herskovits consisted of 16,000 coconuts and ten baskets of fish.[3]

These competitions in giving are contests of altruism.[4] A gift will only elicit a greater response if it is based on a understanding of the needs of others. In the most successful and catalytic gifts, the giver fulfills an unknown need or desire in a surprising way. The recipient is startled and gratified by the inspired and unexpected sympathy of the giver and is eager to repay him. In order to repay him, however, the receiver must come to understand the giver. Thus the contest of gifts leads to an expansion of human sympathies. The circle of giving (the profits of the economy) will grow as long as the gifts are consistently valued more by the receivers than by the givers.

What the tribal givers were doing, by transcending barter, was to invent a kind of money: a mode of exchange that by excluding exact contractual planning allowed for freedom and uncertainty. Money consists of liabilities, debts, or promises. By giving someone a dollar, you both acknowledge a debt to him of a certain value, and you pass on to him an acknowledgment of debt given to you by someone else. But the process has to start somewhere, with a giver and a gift, a feast and a *mumi*, an investment and an investor.

By giving a feast, the *mumi* imposed implicit debts on all his guests. By attending it, they accepted a liability to him. Through the gifts or investments of primitive capitalism, man created and extended obligations. These obligations led to reciprocal gifts and further obligations in a growing fabric of economic creation and exchange, with each giver hoping for greater returns but not assured of them, and with each recipient pushed to produce a further favor. This spreading out of debts could be termed expanding the money supply. The crucial point is that for every liability (or feeling of obligation on the part of the guest), there was a previous asset (meal) given to him. The *mumi*, as a capitalist, could not issue demands or impose liabilities or expand money without providing commensurate supplies. The demand was inherent in the supply—in the meal.

The next step above potlatching was the use of real money. The invention of money enabled the pattern of giving to be extended as far as the reach of faith and trust—from the *mumi's* tribe to the world economy.

Among the most important transitional devices was the Chinese *Hui*. This became the key mode of capital formation for the overseas Chinese in their phenomenal successes as tradesmen and retailers everywhere they went, from San Francisco to Singapore. A more sophisticated and purposeful development of the potlatching principle, the *Hui* began when the organizer needed money for an investment. He would raise it from a group of kin and friends and commit himself to give a series of ten feasts for them. At each feast a similar amount of money would be convivially raised and given by lot or by secret bidding to one of the other members. The rotating distribution would continue until every member had won a collection. Similar systems, called the *Ko* or *Tanamoshi*, created savings for the Japanese; and the West African *Susu* device of the *Yoruba*, when transplanted to the West Indies, provided the capital base for Caribbean retailing. This mode of capital formation also emerged prosperously among West Indians when they migrated to American cities.[5] All these arrangements required entrusting money or property to others and awaiting returns in the uncertain future.

That supply creates its own demand is a principle of classical economics called Say's Law. It has come to be expressed, and refuted, in many interesting technical forms. But its essential point is potlatching. Capitalism consists of providing first and getting later. The demand is implicit in the supply. Without a monetary economy, such gifts were arrayed in expectation of an immediate profit in prestige and a later feast of interest, and they could be seen as a necessary way to escape the constraints of barter, to obviate the exact coincidence of wants and values required by simple trading. In most cases, the feasts and offerings were essentially entrepreneurial. They entailed the acquisition of goods at a known cost with the intention of acquiring in exchange—in this case, over an extended period—goods of unknown value. As devices of savings and investment, they depended for success on the continued honesty and economic returns of all members.

The chief difference between money and other liabilities is its indefiniteness. Money bears a presumption of faith and a grant of freedom. Without money all exchanges must be partly predetermined. It is the willingness of man to give—or work—without a specific reward that allows liberty. Money in a planned economy tends to be a deceit or false promise because the purchases are mostly preordained. The ruble in Russia can be used only for a very limited list of consumer goods in essentially predetermined amounts.

Money demand consists entirely of acknowledgments of debt for goods and services. It is therefore more valuable than the supplies of goods only because it confers freedom; it does not have to be spent on any particular good. In a capitalist economy every worker and businessman knows in the marrow of his bones that his buying power consists of his supplying power, no more, no less. He goes to the store and buys this book, not in essence with money, but with work transmuted into money. He exchanges, if I am lucky, his work, his productive services, not only for mine but also for those of the editors, artists, copy readers, printers, truck drivers, construction workers, salesmen—the list is virtually endless in a complex modern division of labor—who in one way or another were paid for their part in producing and marketing the volume.

Any buyer, whether of a coconut, a haircut, or a steel guitar, pays not ultimately in the currency of demand that can be expanded or restricted by government, but in his own provision of goods and services. His demand arises and is most vitally expressed not in the market where he performs the perfunctory act of purchase, but in the factory or office where he takes risks and suffers hardships in his vital creation of supply. He values his money because his expenditure of funds is psychologically rooted in his earlier expenditure of effort.

A useful definition of inflation is the dissociation of demand from supply—the rise of the belief that one's buying power can long exceed one's supplying power, that one can get something for nothing, that one can continually take from others without giving. Particularly if the central bank funds these demands, all too soon the value of money, the instrument of demand, approaches nothing, which, as Voltaire observed, is the natural worth of such scraps of paper. Even if the government insures the scraps by making them convertible into gold, they will be worth very little if the moral fabric of production and exchange dissolves. In a collapsed economy, where trust everywhere fails, a man might trade an ounce of gold for a pound of corn. In a money economy, his gold might buy him half a ton.

Capitalist production entails faith—in one's neighbors, in one's society, and in the compensatory logic of the cosmos. Search and you shall find, give and you will be given unto, supply creates its own demand. It is this cosmology, this sequential logic, that essentially distinguishes the free from the socialist economy. The socialist economy proceeds from a rational definition of needs or demands to a prescription of planned supplies. In a socialist economy, one does not supply until the demands have already been determined and specified. Rationality rules, and it rules out the awesome uncertainties and commensurate acts of faith that are indispensable to an expanding and innovative system.

The gifts of advanced capitalism in a monetary economy are called investments. One does not make gifts without some sense, possibly unconscious, that one will be rewarded, whether in this world or the next.

Even the biblical injunction affirms that the giver will be given unto. The essence of giving is not the absence of all expectation of return, but the lack of a predetermined return. Like gifts, capitalist investments are made without a predetermined return.

These gifts or investments are experimental in that the returns to the giver are unknown; and whether gains or losses, they are absorbed by him. Because the vast majority of investments fail, the moment of decision is pregnant with doubt and promise and suffused to some degree with faith. Because the ventures are experiments, however, even the failures in a sense succeed, even the waste is often redeemed. In the course of time, perhaps even with the passage of generations, the failures accumulate as new knowledge, the most crucial kind of capital, held by both the entrepreneurs themselves and the society at large.

This new knowledge is a deeper kind than is taught in schools or acquired in the controlled experiments of social or physical science, or gained in the experience of socialist economies. For entrepreneurial experiments are also adventures, with the future livelihood of the investor at stake. He participates with a heightened consciousness and passion and an alertness and diligence that greatly enhance his experience of learning. The experiment may reach its highest possibilities, and its crises and surprises may be exploited to the utmost.

This motivational advantage will often decide the success or failure of enterprises or nations otherwise equally endowed. Harvey Leibenstein of Harvard has presented a large body of evidence which shows that the key factor in productivity differences among firms and between countries is neither the kind of allocational efficiency stressed in economic texts nor any other measurable input in the productive process. The differences derive from management, motivation, and spirit; from a factor he cannot exactly identify but which he calls X-*efficiency*.[6] He quotes Tolstoy in *War and Peace:*

Military science assumes the strength of an army to be identical to its numbers. . . . [In fact it] is the product of its mass and some unknown x . . . the spirit of the army. . . . To define and express the significance of this unknown factor . . . is a problem for science . . . only solvable if we cease arbitrarily to substitute for the unknown x itself the conditions under which that force becomes apparent— such as the commands of the general, the equipment employed and so on . . . and if we recognize this unknown quantity in its entirety as being the greater or lesser desire to fight and to face danger.[7]

In other words, measurable inputs, such as those that can be calculated in a planned economy, do not determine output. Leibenstein shows that productivity differences between workers doing the same job in a particular plant are likely to vary as much as four to one, that differences as high as 50 percent can arise between plants commanding identical equipment and the same size labor force that is paid identically. Matters of management, motivation, and spirit—and their effects on willingness to innovate and seek new knowledge—dwarf all measurable inputs in accounting for productive efficiency, both for individuals and groups and for management and labor. A key difference is always in the willingness to transform vague information or hypotheses into working knowledge: willingness, in Tolstoy's terms, transferred from the martial to the productive arts, "to fight and face danger," to exert efforts and take risks.

Without this x factor, most of the highest possibilities of an economy will remain latent; the lessons of success and failure will only very slowly coalesce as the capital of economic knowledge. As Leibenstein's data shows, observation suggests, and long history confirms, the spirit factor is best elicited by ownership. Ownership means exposure to the risks and benefits of productive property, whether it is one's own land and labor or IBM shares. It means, in a competitive economy in a changing world, that the owner lives on the crest of creation, continually informed and inspired, edified and motivated, by the flashes of surprising knowledge, about fashion, taste, and technology, that can radically shift the values—the future returns—of what is owned.

Socialism is an insurance policy bought by all the members of a national economy to shield them from risk. But the result is to shield them from knowledge of the real dangers and opportunities ubiquitous in any society. Rather than benefiting from a multiplicity of gifts and experiments, the entire economy absorbs the much greater risk of remaining static in a dynamic world. In a capitalist economy, with more of the risks borne by the individual citizens and entrepreneurs, and thus vigilantly appraised and treated, the overall system may be more stable.

The crucial difference, however, is that the capitalist, by giving before he takes, pursues a mode of thinking and acting suitable to uncertainty. The socialist makes a national plan in which existing patterns of need and demand are ascertained, and then businesses are contracted to fulfill them; demand comes first. One system is continually, endlessly performing experiments, testing hypotheses, discovering partial knowledge; the other is assembling data of inputs and outputs and administering the resulting plans.

Socialism presumes that we already know most of what we need to know to accomplish our national goals. Capitalism is based on the idea that we live in a world of unfathomable complexity, ignorance, and peril, and that we cannot possible prevail over our difficulties without constant efforts of initiative, sympathy, discovery, and love. One system maintains that we can reliably predict and elicit the outcomes we demand. The other asserts that we must give long before we can know what the universe will return. One is based on empirically calculable human power; the other on optimism and faith. These are the essential visions that compete in the world and determine our fate.

Under capitalism, the ventures of reason are launched into a world ruled by morality and Providence. The gifts will succeed only to the extent that they are altruistic and spring from an understanding of the needs of others. They depend on faith in an essentially fair and responsive humanity. In such a world, one can give without a contract of compensation. One can venture without the assurance of reward. One can seek the surprises of profit, rather than the more limited benefits of contractual pay. One can take initiative amid radical perils and uncertainties.

When faith dies, so does enterprise. It is impossible to create a system of collective regulation and safety that does not finally deaden the moral sources of the willingness to face danger and fight, that does not dampen the spontaneous flow of gifts and experiments which extend the dimensions of the world and the circles of human sympathy.

The ultimate strength and crucial weakness of both capitalism and democracy are their reliance on individual creativity and courage, leadership and morality, intuition and faith. But there is no alternative, except mediocrity and stagnation. Reason and calculation, for all their appeal, can never suffice in a world where events are shaped by millions of men, acting unknowably, in fathomless interplay and complexity, in the darkness of time.

The superficial strength and final disabling flaw of collectivism is its belief in the possibility of detailed rational knowledge of human affairs and their future effects. The man who seeks assurance and certainty lives always in the past, which alone is sure, and his policies, despite all "progressive" rhetoric, are necessarily reactionary. Certain knowledge, to the extent that it ever comes, is given us only after the moment of opportunity has passed. The venturer who awaits the emergence of a safe market, the tax-cutter who demands full assurance of new revenue, the leader who seeks a settled public opinion, all will always act too timidly and too late.

A nation's producers can never depend on preordained demand for their goods. The demand arises from the quality of the goods themselves, and the qualities demanded will continually change in a changing world. The man who shapes the future must live ever in doubt and thus thrive on faith. The future of Western democracy and capitalism depends on whether this faith in the future still prospers in the lands that gave it birth.

CHAPTER 4

The Supply Side*

THE SOURCE of the gifts of capitalism is the supply side of the economy. In the capitalist economies of the West, this simple recognition is the core of all successful economic policy. It is a principle sometimes as obscure to conservatives, with their often excessive preoccupation with the statistics of money and deficit spending, as it is to liberals, with their obsession for aggregate demand and consumer spending. Wisdom on the subject can sometimes be found in strange places. Even Karl Marx knew enough not to stress, as the crux and keystone of capitalism, control over the means of *consumption!* Or even of the supply of money.

Marx, however, erroneously located the means of production in the material arrangements of the society rather than in the metaphysical capital of human freedom and creativity. The problem of contemporary capitalism lies not chiefly in a deterioration of physical capital, but in a persistent subversion of the psychological means of production—the morale and inspiration of economic man—undermining the very conscience of capitalism: the awareness that one must give in order to get, supply in order to demand.

The trend seems to have begun in politics. In fact, our current situation recalls the world in which economic science gained its first triumphs. This was the age of mercantilism, a time of a similar hypertrophy of politics, when Adam Smith reproached the governments of Europe for believing that the power of demand, in the form of accumulated gold, constituted the source of wealth. In *The Wealth of Nations* Smith argued

* This is a chapter on the theory of supply-side economics, which may be safely passed over by readers who prefer a less abstract exposition of the subject.

that real riches came from the power of production and supply, not bullion collected through a trade surplus.

But during the two centuries since Smith won this initial victory for supply-side economics, the demand side has all too often triumphed. The problem begins in political philosophy: in the theory of politics and public opinion.

Democratic politics are founded on a group of formal equalities—legal and electoral—ultimately deriving from a religious belief in the equality of men before God. Nonetheless, these equalities, in a more immediate sense, are largely mythological. One man may be restricted to one vote, but some men by their energy and eloquence, or their command of the media, may sway the opinions of millions. An elected leader may be expected to represent the views and interests of his constituency. But he may also, during the course of campaigning and in the conduct of his office, deeply affect the beliefs and decisively interpret the interests of his public. A realistic analysis will show that leaders, to the extent that they bear real authority, tend to create the views of their larger constituencies more than they follow them, particularly on technical or complex matters.

The public—as Walter Lippmann demonstrated, one should have thought for all time, in his magisterial work *Public Opinion*—is largely a phantom. On many issues, public opinion, as the term is commonly used, does not exist. Polls, it might be plausibly said, often create their own opinion. Out of the shifting and shadowy shapes of largely amorphous sentiment, they contrive spuriously discrete and definite sums—aggregates of air. Political leaders, in a deeper way, forge their own majorities. In their campaigns, speeches, and consultations, in all the performance of their official duties, successful politicians are engaged not in passive response to public demand, but in the active supply and marketing of ideas. Supply can create its own demand, even in the political realm.

By analogy, leadership is supply and public opinion is demand. In a democratic system, a reversal of the appropriate direction of influence allows impressionable figments of mass sentiment to dictate to the powerful and permanent mechanisms of representative leadership. The result is a restive and alienated electorate, a failure of political authority, a sluggish and uncreative government, and a tendency toward national decline—many of the disorders of inverted hierarchy described by Ortega y Gasset in *Revolt of the Masses*. In economics, when demand is permitted to displace supply in the order of priorities, the result is a sluggish and uncreative economy, inflation, and a decline in productivity. Such disorders afflict both our politics and our economics today.

The problem is that demand, like public opinion, does not exist in any very definite and identifiable way; it is a flux of hungers and sentiments which assume particular forms chiefly in response to the flow of supplies. Because there is no demand for new and unknown goods, no demand for the unforeseeable fruits of innovation and genius, preoccupation with demand fosters stagnation. Egalitarianism in the economy tends to promote greed over giving. It downplays the various and specific sources of supply to favor the diffuse and sterile clamor of demand. To the ordinary mind, there is no reason for an assumption of equal importance for the two concepts. Demand attained parity only in our economic texts, and it achieved its deceptive supremacy only through our deluded politics.

In our texts its initial breakthrough was the theory of value: the determination of price by the intersection of supply and demand curves. These graphs and equations are the central images of economic learning, and they seemingly assert an equivalence of potency between demand and supply.

But the impression betrays two fallacious modes of reasoning. One is what philosophers call misplaced concreteness or reification (from the Latin word *res* meaning "thing"). In reification, objective substance, "thingness," is ascribed to an abstraction, such as public opinion, or to a subjective concept such as value (for example, in such contentions as "the real value of money lies in gold"). Psychologist Wilhelm Reich reached a famous extreme of reification when he decided that sexual energy was a real collectible substance, called it orgone, and created orgone collection boxes. The other mistake of the economic texts is nearly the opposite of reification—namely, false abstraction, turning things into concepts and manipulating them as such. Much utopian thought consists of such spurious abstraction, assuming that human beings are simply mutable bundles of ideas rather than specific and partly unchangeable biological and social creatures.

In the computations of classical or "laissez-faire" economists—with their models of perfect competition—demand tends to be reified and supply to be ideated. The elusive and subjective impulses of consumer demand are treated as definite and specific sums, while the definite and specific objects of supply, produced over long periods of time, are sometimes treated as instantly changeable ideas and numbers. Demand curves signifying the purely mental reactions of consumers to particular goods and prices are assigned the same weight and priority as supply curves registering the real efforts, sacrifices, and intentions of producers (which determined what and how much they were already producing). In the equations, moreover, these processes are assumed to occur simultaneously. Conceptions of cause and effect are continually jumbled.

The notion of perfect competition—a prime image of classical theory—is extremely useful in depicting the behavior of particular markets for existing goods. But it has little to do with the central activity of capitalism, which is the turbulent process of launching new enterprise. As has been often observed in academic analyses, perfect competition actually comes to mean no competition at all: an equilibrium in which all participants have perfect information and in which companies can change neither prices nor products and can essentially affect neither supply nor demand.

Perfect competition thus excludes most supply-side behavior: all the acquisition and manipulation of knowledge that is the main activity of real entrepreneurs. Free men and creative enterprise—all the secrets and surprises of actual competition—are banished in favor of a mechanism by which savings are automatically invested, supplies and demands are simultaneously reconciled, and the entrepreneurial role could be best performed by modern computers.

Despite its elegance and insights, moreover, the classical model is less useful to conservatives than their commitment to it would suggest. Though it seems to provide an argument for limited government, it in fact gives endless pretexts for state intervention to remedy the inevitable imperfections. Indeed, the perfectionist view has often served more as a way to discredit the messy dynamics of real capitalism than to illuminate its workings.

Demand, however, was not to reach its supreme triumph until the development of macroeconomics as a separate discipline and the ascendancy of the Keynesian school, largely misinterpreting the works of Keynes. Keynes began his *General Theory of Employment, Interest, and Money,* with an apparent refutation of Say's Law.[1] Then he proceeded with a complex and abstruse argument, which was interpreted as meaning that the level of output and employment responds chiefly to the rate of consumer demand.

The chief role of government in the economy, according to the followers of Keynes, was to maintain suitable levels of aggregate or total demand by fiscal and monetary policies. Since governments in capitalist countries could seemingly control the supply of money—the instrument of demand—politicians came to suppose they could thereby influence the supply of everything else. Demand, as manipulated by government, came to preoccupy bureaucrats and economists. In their computations and analyses, supply gradually became a derivative. Say's Law was not only refuted, it was implicitly reversed, with cause and effect hopelessly confused in the proposition that demand creates its own supply—"take and you will be given unto."

It may be said that the alleged refutation of Say's Law by Keynes was the crucial event of modern economics since it affirmed emphatically in the economics of the whole society (macroeconomics) the more insidious triumphs of demand in the economics of the individual and the firm (microeconomics). Yet the actual works of Keynes, even in relation to Say's Law and the role of supply, are far more favorable to supply-side economic policy than current Keynesians comprehend.

As Thomas Sowell has explained in two books (*Say's Law: An Historical Analysis* and *Classical Economics Reconsidered*), the theorem, associated with the name of French economist Jean-Baptiste Say, essentially maintains that the sum of the wages, profits, and rents paid in manufacturing a good is sufficient to buy it. This does not mean that the same people who make a thing will necessarily buy it, but that they could. The sum of money paid to the factors of production, chiefly in rents, wages, salaries, and profits, for the making and marketing of an automobile, for example, is precisely enough to purchase it. Therefore, across an entire system, purchasing power and producing power can always balance: there will always be enough wealth in an economy to buy its products. There cannot be a glut of goods caused by inadequate total demand. Producers, collectively, in the course of production, create demand for their goods. This idea is obviously simplistic in many ways, but it bears a number of key economic truths and implications never refuted by Keynes or anyone else. These truths are the foundation of contemporary supply-side theory.

Keynes saw the essential theory as a truism, but he stressed the problems that arise when some of the money earned in the course of production is *saved.* If these funds are then borrowed and invested, as the classical economists believed, the money would go to wages, profits, and other incomes in the capital goods industries, and the balance would be maintained. If, in the example, the savings of the auto workers were not borrowed by their bosses to purchase machinery for the auto plant, those funds might be loaned to U.S. Steel to acquire equipment for steel workers; and the makers of blast furnaces would receive enough income to make a down payment on a house, and the home builders would be paid enough to buy a new motor boat, and so on until some recipient of the funds decided to buy an automobile and Say's circle was closed. Keynes, however, argued that savings very well might not be borrowed or invested at all; the money might just sit there, in the bank or elsewhere.

According to Keynes there are many reasons why businessmen may not choose to invest the savings of the public. For example, the same kind of economic crisis that would prompt consumers to buy less and save more might also frighten businessmen into borrowing less and making fewer investments. Goods would pile up in shops and warehouses while savings accumulated in banks and mattresses and workers lost their jobs. This situation, surrounding Keynes at every hand as he wrote *The General Theory* in the England of the early 1930s, seemed to him a sure refutation of Say's law. Demand had apparently evaporated despite the presence everywhere of unsold supplies.

According to Keynes, whether savings are in fact requited by investment depends on the fickle intentions and "animal spirits" of the businessman and financier. Knowing Say's Law and its mathematical assurance of buying power, perhaps the businessman should invest. But, Keynes contended:

Enterprise only pretends to itself to be mainly actuated by the statements in its own prospectus, however candid and sincere. Only a little more than an expedition to the South Pole is it based on an exact calculation of benefits to come. Thus, if the animal spirits are dimmed and the spontaneous optimism falters, leaving us to depend on nothing but a mathematical expectation, enterprise will falter and die.[2]

Even in the absence of depression, said Keynes, there are many reasons for a faltering of the animal spirits.[3] Perhaps the key Keynesian argument is the paradox of thrift: one person can provide more for his future by saving more—that is, by forgoing consumption. But if most people decide to buy less goods and save more money, incomes will collapse because of a lack of consumer demand and a resulting decline in investment. In the end, people will have less money to save than they had in the first place. In Keynes's world of volatile business leaders, an act of saving or forgone consumption in no way assures a corresponding purchase of capital goods.

Keynes, in fact, sometimes leaves one wondering why there is *ever* enough investment to defray savings—why economies do not stall endlessly, as they did for much of human history, in a slough of depression caused by insufficient buying power, stagnant savings, and hoarded funds, all untapped by the magic wand of entrepreneurship. And so indeed it appeared to many in the wearied world of the thirties. Keynes and others did not fully understand that investment collapsed during this period not merely because of a decline of spirit, but because of a collapse of the international trading system as a result of the Smoot-Hawley Tariff Act, a severe contraction of the money supply as a result of bank failures and Central Bank errors, a sharp rise in real interest rates (that is, nominal rates adjusted for expected deflation), and a series of crippling tax-rate increases.[4]

Nonetheless, Keynes had to acknowledge that investment does happen sometimes, and he attributed it to two considerations beyond mere animal spirits. One he called the *"marginal efficiency of capital,"* and the other *"effective demand."* Eschewing a lot of needless Bloomsbury complexities, these two concepts reduce to an affirmation of Say's Law in yet another sense, a firm assertion of the primacy of supply.

Both effective demand and the marginal efficiency of capital depend on *anticipated* profits, on "the proceeds that entrepreneurs *expect* to receive."[5] Demand, we discover, even in the works of Keynes, is mostly in the mind of the supplier. He does not invest in a productive plant because he is assured of buyers for his goods; he cannot be certain that new inventions or changing tastes will not make his factory worthless. If his product is new, it may create demand, perhaps over time. But the demand does not already exist, except in the imagination of the entrepreneur.

Today Keynes is known as an advocate of expanded spending—of enlarged aggregate demand—as the answer to all economic distress. But, in fact, he believed that income earners would spend and save their money in relatively fixed proportions and that what mattered was assuring enough investment. With enough investment, the problems of income, consumption, and savings would take care of themselves. In this belief, he broke, in a rightward direction, from the classical assumption that if savings were sufficient, investment would take care of itself. As the key act of capitalism, he replaced the measurable and passive setting aside of money with the active and aggressive investment of it.

Keynes thus restored to a position of appropriate centrality in economic thought the vital role and activity of the individual capitalist. It is free men rather than abstract forces or mechanisms that impel the Keynesian economy. In his view, the key to material progress lies not in the workings of automatic accumulation or in passive thrift and savings or in a benign tendency toward general equilibrium, but in "skilled investment" designed "to defeat the dark forces of time and ignorance which envelop our future."[6] Because the Keynesian world is not rational and predictable, the true message of Keynes cannot be reduced to mathematics or a scheme of reliable planning.

As George Shackle, the leader of the British school of "epistemic" critics of modern Keynesianism, has written:

In *The General Theory,* the analysis of business life as a steady application of reason to changeable, but knowable and coherent circumstances, the analysis of business conduct as an informed, collected and undismayed response to a stream of understandable and largely forseen events, was destroyed, rejected, overthrown in ruin and contempt.[7]

Keynes knew the limits of social science and predictable rationality[8] and saw that beyond all systems was the originative force of the human mind responding to a flow of frequent surprises. Economics is possible because human beings are reasonable and seek rationally to pursue their interests. But the ark of reason sails in turbulent and fogbound seas.

When Keynes made the individual investor the central figure in economics, he overthrew not only the more simplistic classical models, but indeed all the systems and sciences upon which totalitarian schemes are founded. Investment is dependent on "changing views about the future," and "the outstanding fact," wrote Keynes, "is the extreme precariousness of the basis of knowledge on which our estimates of prospective yield have to be made. . . . The actual results of an investment over a long period of years very seldom agree with the initial expectation."[9]

In these circumstances,

The *state of confidence* [Keynes's italics] is a matter to which practical men always pay the closest and most anxious attention. . . . Businessmen play a mixed game of skill and chance. . . . If human nature felt no temptation to take a chance, no satisfaction (profit apart) in constructing a factory, a railway, a mine, or a farm, there might not be much investment merely as a result of cold calculation.[10]

The cold calculations of mathematical economics left out what for Keynes—and all realistic observers of economic life—are the most vital matters. This is the conservative germ of truth in Keynes's too negative view of saving: the inert piling up of liquid funds does not provide for the future without daring acts of entrepreneurship that cannot be taken for granted.

As disdainful of Marxism as of laissez-faire, Keynes rejected all systems that saw the economy as a mechanism, whether of dialectics or markets. He offered for the economy a hierarchical ideal. The creative center of the system was the skilled entrepreneur and the goal of policy was to cultivate his skills and ensure his inducement to invest. This today is the theme of the editorial page of *The Wall Street Journal* and the rhetoric, at least, of the Republican party in America.

AN ESSENTIAL APPRECIATION of the centrality of supply, ironically, also explains the plausibility and appeal of America's leading socialist intellectual, John Kenneth Galbraith. In his trilogy on the U.S. economy— *The Affluent Society, The New Industrial State,* and *Economics and the Public Purpose*— Galbraith's theme is actually an interesting though deeply flawed reformulation of Say's Law. Like Keynes, Galbraith dismisses Say's Law itself ("It would be hard, though not yet impossible, to find an American economist who still subscribes to the historic dictum.").[11] But in a broader sense Galbraith refurbishes it and names it first the *Dependence Effect,* and then in a later work *The Revised Sequence* (which merely puts supply before demand). "As a society becomes increasingly affluent," he writes, "wants are increasingly created by the process by which they are satisfied. . . . Or producers may proceed actively to create wants through advertising and salesmanship." He sums up: *"Wants thus come to depend on output."*[12]

Supply creates its own demand may be a more felicitous way of putting it. But the essential point is fruitless to deny. Producers play a leading and initiatory role in eliciting, shaping, and creating demand. Investment decisions will be crucial in determining both the quantity and the essential pattern of consumer purchases.

Perhaps impeded by a little known streak of modesty, though, Galbraith fails to tell the full range and implication of his discovery. He seems to believe that this proposition reflects a revolutionary change in the structure of modern industry and applies only to large corporations committed to long and technologically intensive modes of production. Such businesses must plan so far in advance, invest so heavily, and depend so much on intermediate suppliers that management is virtually forced to shape and manipulate its market, create its demands. But the Dependence Effect applies to small businesses as well. They also forge their own demands. The differing patterns of commerce in various communities reflect not only the existing patterns of consumer wants, but also the configuration of entrepreneurial skills and ideas. Great Barrington, Massachusetts, contains a Somali restaurant, a baroque music school, and an Outward Bound Youth Center not because of spontaneous need for these ventures, but because of the presence of men who chose to start them and succeeded in creating a demand for them. There are many obvious differences between large and small businesses, but Galbraith's Dependence Effect applies to both.

Nor are the passage of long periods of time and commitments of large amounts of capital novel characteristics of modern enterprise. Modern corporations are indeed far more complex than earlier firms. But contemporary businesses may often have less need to plan ahead. They benefit from far more elaborate and flexible capital markets, from more readily responsive consumers, from far more effective advertising and marketing, and from prodigiously more efficient modes of transport and communication. It is difficult to imagine contemporary businesses with greater requirements for early investment and planning or for complementary government aid than the worldwide trading companies of sixteenth-century England or the canal and railroad firms of the early industrial United States. The Dependence Effect is no mere peculiarity of modern corporations.

Galbraith maintains that businesses, far from giving without predetermined returns, actually seek to control their markets, often with the aid of government, to "administer" prices and quantities of production and exclude all rivals. This revelation is sometimes offered in the spirit of a child discovering that his parents indulge in sexual intercourse. But we must grant that the child is right. For all their ideological commitment to free enterprise, businesses are primarily devoted to successful enterprise, pursue it any way they can, and are delighted to benefit when government blocks the competition. In precisely the same way that many "liberal" economists can profess egalitarian socialism while waxing rich on the capitalist system, corporations can feed off of government while celebrating free markets.

Neither the profit-making socialists nor the business leaders are really hypocritical. Both honestly believe in their ideals but succumb to immediate temptations and demands, from stockholders, wives and children, or their own needs. But as was taught by Adam Smith, what is good for particular merchants is not, despite their nationalistic appeals, necessarily good for the country. The merchants, with their claim that every tariff is a patriotic duty, said Smith, "were by no means such fools as they who believed it."[13] Government officials who succumb to the demands of businesses for protection or subsidy have only themselves to blame. The responsibility for equal application of the laws rests on the public sector, not the private.

What Galbraith and his followers see as the revolutionary new powers of business are in fact the inevitable workings of capitalist supply. Few measures would so deflate the rhetoric of the Left as the simple acknowledgment that the very essence of capitalism is the competitive pursuit of transitory positions of monopoly. To the extent that the equilibrium theory has crystalized as a religion of the Right, such an acknowledgment might seem radical and disruptive. But no supply-side ideas are as disruptive to the classical vision as the dynamics of capitalism itself.

Capitalist creativity is guided not by any invisible hand, but by the quite visible and aggressive hand of management and entrepreneurship. Businesses continually differentiate their products, their marketing techniques, their advertising, and their retailing strategies in order to find some unique niche in the system from which they can reap, as long as possible, monopoly profits. Without the aid of government, protecting patents or otherwise excluding competitors, these monopoly positions tend to be short-lived. But they are the goal of business strategy, the focus of creative entrepreneurship, the motivation of original research and development.

The monopoly positions, moreover, are not at all unlimited, because they are always held—unless government intercedes to enforce them— under the threat of potential competitors and substitutes at home or abroad. To the question of how many companies an industry needs in order to be competitive, economist Arthur Laffer answers: one. It will compete against the threat of future rivals. Its monopoly can be maintained only as long as the price is kept low enough to exclude others. In this sense, monopolies are good. The more dynamic and inventive an economy, the more monopolies it will engender. The ideal of perfect competition, like the ideal of an economy without business power, translates into an economy without innovations. A rapidly developing system will be full of monopolies as new industries repeatedly crop up and have a lucrative run before the competition can emerge and catch up, benefiting from the advantages of imitation. Every now and then a company like IBM or Polaroid will get such a lead and exploit it so efficiently that it retains dominance for decades, to the great benefit of the country.

This form of "monopoly capitalism" does not readily or automatically result in the fulfilment of the preexisting desires of consumers, for consumers do not know what they desire until they have tried a sample at a specified price. Consumers respond to the creative experiments of business. Demand, as Galbraith points out, "does not arise in spontaneous consumer need. Rather the dependence effect means that it grows out of [depends on] the process of production itself. If production is to increase, the wants must be effectively contrived."[14] Exactly. The quality of capitalist society depends not on automatic mechanisms, but on the quality, creativity, and leadership of the capitalists.

The contemporary Left prefers economic leadership from government. But Say's Law, in general terms, is a rule of all organized human behavior. The will of the people is often no more "spontaneous" or free of elite initiative and manipulation in politics than in economics. Democratic masses cannot be generative or creative; they can merely react and ratify. They affirm or reject the creative offerings of entrepreneurs in both business and politics. Howard Jarvis was no less an enterpriser in launching the Proposition 13 tax cut movement in California than was Ray Kroc in launching McDonald's. Both gave specific form to the previously amorphous though finally sovereign wishes of the public.

An economy can be democratic chiefly in proportion to its diversity of choices—the proliferation of monopoly experiments—corresponding to the huge multiplicity of individual tastes and desires. In its cornucopia of choice the capitalist marketplace contrasts vividly with even the most democratic political marketplace with its near monopoly of power vested at every election and with the requirement that voters select a whole cluster of policies in order to get the one desired. Representative democracy is a better system than any other chiefly because it evokes the experimental competition of elites. There is little evidence, moreover, that capitalism corrupts democracy and much evidence that capitalism is essential to it. The widespread belief that capitalist societies, perverted by corporate power, show a persistent bias in favor of business goods and against public services has not stood up well under recent experience. Government has been growing faster than business in most democratic countries.

Nonetheless, the crucial source of creativity and initiative in any economic system is the individual investor. Economies do not grow of their own accord or by dint of government influence. They grow in response to the enterprise of men willing to take risks, to transform ideas into monopolies, and monopolies into industries, and to give before they know what they will get in return.

The essential thesis of Say's Law remains true: supply creates demand. There can be no such thing as a general glut of goods. There can be a glut of "bads," but in the world of necessary scarcity in which the very science of economics finds its meaning, an apparent glut of all goods merely signifies a dearth of creative production, a lack of new supplies and fresh demands. Private savings, moreover, in the current inflationary period, *are* invested. Saving, in fact, signifies a commitment to the future, a psychology of production and growth. Since World War II the countries that have saved most, preeminently Japan and other Asian capitalist lands, have grown fastest. The apparent gluts of goods have emerged chiefly in countries that fail to save.

This situation illuminates a central fallacy of demand-oriented economics. Like the politician in the thrall of "public opinion," who lives always in the past, demand-oriented businesses rarely create new goods, for there is no measureable demand for what is not already familiar. The market surveys are mute on most innovations. Without a flow of new products, the marketplace can be filled with stale items, produced with ever greater efficiency, continually redesigned in trivial ways, repackaged in brighter colors, and marketed with a more expensive and harder sell. *Jaws* III will be followed by IV and V; Cheerios become Sugar Cheerios; and corporations grow chiefly by purchasing proven firms. New businesses that provide new products, new hierarchies, new opportunities, new patterns of jobs and skills, more rarely emerge and acquire the resources for rapid growth. The employment market becomes more stratified, bureaucratized, and alienating; the consumer market seems less diverse and savory; advertising appeals grow more strident and clamorous. The public becomes jaded and pressures mount on government for further expansion of demand. It is a vicious circle that steadily erodes the creative forces of capitalism.

Originating in a liberal effort to respond to the popular will and relieve the pressures of poverty, demand-oriented politics ends in promoting unemployment and dependency and creating a less open and accessible economy and a more stratified and hierarchical political order. Government bureaucracies proliferate to furnish the services that overtaxed businesses no longer can provide and to subsidize the favored private interests of a depleted capitalism. As bureaucracy grows, moreover, industrial progress declines. For progress is always dependent on the creativity of suppliers.

Say's Law in all its variations is the essential enactment of supply-side theory. But its value does not reside in its mathematical workings. In economics, mathematical models, however elegant, must always defer to the behavior and psychology of persons with free will, who often act, and interact, in unexpected ways. The importance of Say's Law is its focus on supply, on the catalytic gifts or investments of capital. It leads economists to concern themselves first with the motives and incentives of individual producers, to return from a preoccupation with distribution and demand and concentrate again on the means of production.

This return is crucial to understanding the current predicament of capitalism. But it will be difficult for economists. Reversion to the supply side means leaving the comfort of rigorous models and computations and again entering the fray of history and psychology, business and technology. Economists should again focus on the multifarious mysteries of human social behavior and creativity which Adam Smith luminously addressed in *The Wealth of Nations,* which Marx stuffed into the maw of his theory, which Keynes treated in most of his writings, and which even Galbraith, in his often perverse way, delights in describing.

The mathematical dazzle of the theory of general equilibrium, launched by Léon Walras, and the scintillating novelties arrayed by his modern followers, should not distract the economics profession from the continuing sagas of cabbages and kings, bombs and beanstalks, silicon chips and business psychology. In this effort, it may be useful to return to Keynes, both because of his massive role in modern economics and because he is known as the leading apostle of the primacy of demand.

IN KEYNES'S PARADOX of thrift, he showed that intentions and declarations of individuals may be a quite unreliable guide to the effects of their behavior (one man may intend to save, but if too many do, the result may be less savings). This is the aggregative fallacy, and it can be found in many of the key issues of contemporary political economics, from the effects of taxes to the role of the state.

Paul Craig Roberts, the brilliant young pioneer of supply-side economics, long an editorial writer for *The Wall Street Journal,* used this Keynesian mode of thought to great advantage in an article entitled "The Breakdown of the Keynesian Model."[15] Roberts was responding to the thesis of liberal economists that tax cuts can reduce work effort and tax hikes can increase it. Such theorists believe that people have a target income, or a target level of savings. If a tax cut gives them more take-home pay, they will not have to work as long to reach their targets. Therefore, so these advocates of high taxes maintain, people may tend to take their tax cuts in the form of more leisure, working less rather than spending and saving more. Alice Rivlin, head of the Congressional Budget Office, made this argument against the Kemp-Roth tax-cut bill, as did Walter Heller and most of its other opponents.

Making an exemplary Keynesian argument, Roberts pointed out that one person could respond to a tax cut by working less and taking more leisure (less overtime, more vacations, and less extra work in seeking promotions). But if many people responded that way, the total income and production of the economy would fall and each person would tend to have less real income than he started with.[16]

Leisure is uncommitted time, forgone work. It is in a sense liquid time, time that can be converted to any purpose as the opportunity arises. The desire for leisure in that way resembles the desire for liquidity, which Keynes associates with hoarding or saving without investing. In all these cases, men hang loose; they refuse to commit themselves to productive activity or investment—or even to particular consumption goods—in order to be open to opportunities to consume or use time in an unspecified way in the future. They wish to retain the power to decide later. But if too few decide what to produce now, there will be little to buy later. If most people take extra income in leisure rather than in purchasing power, there will be no extra income. If most people keep their income liquid rather than investing or spending it, the money will eventually become nearly worthless. In all cases, the prolonged refusal to commit oneself to particular work, investment, or even consumption deprives the community of demand or productivity and thus reduces total income. A few people can do it, but an aggregate cannot do it without defeating its original goals. The unflagging initiatives of suppliers are indispensable to the system.

Living at a time when government and taxes were seen as a relatively minor force in capitalist economies, Keynes did not apply his mode of thinking to governmental activity. But Keynes's paradox of savings applies just as much to forced savings by taxation as to consumption voluntarily forgone by private citizens. Like any group of individuals, the government may *intend* to save, but if it cannot generate real investments, the result will be merely a decline in total incomes and a tendency toward stagnation.

Through the progressive tax structure, government revenue tends to come from funds that might otherwise have been invested. But Washington itself does relatively little productive investment. As the federal budget grows, much of it goes to transfer payments that are spent heavily on the bundle of goods in the rapidly rising consumer price index, from gasoline to hamburgers, and to federal pay and contracts that go to bid up the price of real estate in the District of Columbia. Some money does go to "investments" in public works of various kinds and in education, but many appropriations are motivated less by their economic and social benefits than by political pressures.

Furthermore, from Keynes's theory of the sources of poverty arise vital new reasons for concern about the nature of government growth. Throughout human history, he wrote,

The weakness of the inducement to invest has been at all times the key to the economic problem. . . . The desire of the individual to augment his personal wealth by abstaining from consumption has usually been stronger than the inducement to the entrepreneur to augment the national wealth by employing labor on the construction of durable assets.[17]

One reason for this gap, according to Keynes, has been the continual existence of *sumps* of wealth, *sinks of purchasing power,* which divert money from productive use. Like Henry George, the eloquent author of economics' leading best-seller, *Progress and Poverty,* Keynes believed that during many historic periods land played this role. Since mortgage rates were often higher than the yield of the land in farming, it often could be purchased only by people inexpert in using it, chiefly urban speculators. Other important sinks of purchasing power have been gold, jewelry, art, and collectibles, such as stamps and coins.

The purchase of such goods—the sinking of money into these sumps of wealth—does not itself directly reduce investment, production, or purchasing power. If I have an ounce of gold and you give me six hundred dollars for it, you have simply transferred your investing or buying power to me; no wealth is lost. The problem arises when throughout an entire economy an ever-increasing number of people choose to spend their money on gold or other sumps of wealth. Then the price of gold will continually rise, absorbing more and more purchasing power. A rising price means that there is a steady increase of buyers or demands over sellers or supplies. The problem becomes worse when the sellers (in this instance me with my six hundred dollars) spend it on other relatively nonreproducible objects—land, works of art, historic buildings, or durable consumer luxuries such as Rolls Royces and jewelry—and then the men who profit from these transactions also tend to refrain from creative investment and instead themselves bid up the price of gold and Van Goghs, antiques and old autos, Rembrandts and real estate. The result is a decline in the returns to productive capital and a rise in the profits of collection and speculation. The economy is reoriented away from productive enterprise and toward nonproductive activities, away from inventions and risks and toward Caribbean resorts and early retirements. The land, the precious metals, the works of art just sit there, growing more valuable for a while, but for the most part contributing little to the welfare of the people or the productive capital of the economy.

All these sumps benefit from a belief in their ultimate liquidity. Supplies of land and gold are inelastic; they cannot be easily enlarged. But they will always be highly prized. Their scarcity assures their value as population grows. Therefore, seeking safety and salability, people have often put far too much of their wealth into these unproductive forms; and kings and nobles down through the centuries have lived what today would seem impoverished lives amid their stores of gold and jewels and on their vast demesnes.

To Keynes, however, in the period in which he wrote, the greatest sink of purchasing power had been money—liquidity itself. Within stable modern economies, so Keynes believed, the desire to hoard has been directed more frequently to holdings of cash than to land or gold. It is *liquidity preference*—the desire to hoard for speculation or security, by corporations as well as by individuals, through excessive funds for "depreciation" as well as through excessive stores of ready cash from profits—that kept interest rates at a level often well above the expected yield of capital goods. Throughout *The General Theory*, Keynes stresses the insidious role of excessive interest rates in deterring investment—an impact always greater, he maintained, than their effect in expanding savings. Keynes even urged policies to assure that interest rates would be lowered every year to sustain the level of capital spending during recessionary years.

In the seventies, however, the interest rate may have declined as a deterrent to investors. Although it seems high, the rate actually consists largely of an *inflation premium* to compensate the lender for the declining value of his unrepaid principal. In addition, interest is tax deductible, and as taxes and inflation premiums rise with inflation, the interest rate does tend to become lower, in real terms, each year. In fact, in the late 1970s, interest rates, adjusted for inflation and taxes, were consistently negative. If the purpose of lowering interest is to enhance the inducement to invest, an appropriate Keynesian policy now is not to cut interest rates annually, but to cut taxes. High tax rates on income and capital presently play a greater role in deterring investment than did interest rates in the past, when government and taxation were often relatively small.

Inflation steadily erodes the attractions of money as a store of value and liquidity. Keynes's flirtation with a system by which all cash would have to be validated from one period to another by the purchase of stamps—government interest on its issues of cash—is now virtual reality. Inflation exacts a penalty on the hoarder just as regular and sure as any stamping system.

As a result, the hoarders are once again turning to real estate, gold, and jewelry. But the most important sump of investment and purchasing power—the new Keynesian sink toward the end of the seventies—was manifestly government: federal, state, and local, in the United States and throughout the West. It was government, not land or gold or money, that was providing profits well above the interest rate and the private yield of investments.

The government reward went to the displaced enterprise of bureaucrats. In the hands of the state, the return on capital seemed deceptively higher and surer than in the hands of authentic entrepreneurs, because it was guaranteed by the power of progressive taxation.

Over the decade, government steadily acquired most of the characteristics that Keynes listed as signs of a "limitless sink" of wealth. There is no obvious limit on governmental expansion or forced profitability through taxes, few supply-side constraints on its size, no tendency for demand for government to slop over onto other products, and little short-run tendency for government to decline when the economy fails. When people want the Keynesian "moon," which he described as liquidity but which is now better seen as security, they turn to Washington and its outland satellites.

During the seventies, these enterprising bureaucrats gathered, bringing all their human capital and entrepreneurial aggressiveness to the ventures of the state. Many of them were lawyers, because governmental expansion is best achieved through exploiting the fertile chinks and fissures in the tomes of federal regulation. They joined with congressmen in mobilizing constituencies of private interests that could be profitably served. The programs multiplied, the money supply grew, inflation raised taxes, and the spurious yield of federal programs—which often gave no valuable service—and of government bonds—which often financed waste—remained as high or higher than the real profits of private capital. In fact, one could say that the yield of government from inflation has risen to 60 percent, since each percent of increase in the price level results in a 1.6 percent jump in federal revenues.[18] As government expanded, in a vicious circle it also enlarged its tax receipts.

This is the new Keynesian source of stagnation and poverty in the nations of the West. What politicans are essentially selling—the new liquidity—is tenure and security, and there seems to be no end to the demand for these services. Yet security, too, like thrift, liquidity, and leisure, has its own paradox of aggregation. Some people can gain exemption from risk, and safety from inflation, by turning to the state. But when a majority does, the security and stability of the nation declines. In a perilous and changing world the best defense against risk is innovation and creativity, research and discovery, competition and enterprise, "skilled investment . . . to defeat the dark forces of time and ignorance which envelop our future."[19]

As the enterprising spirit is channeled increasingly into law and other professional schools, and thence into government, its lobbies, consultant groups, and organized clientele—as great tycoons arise more readily selling "security" in HEW than in selling securities in private firms, or selling real products to the public—the crucial inducement to invest once again sinks below the attractions of other wealth. People without access to the state buy gold and yachts, government bonds and foreign money, or parlay private housing—with its special government protections—into a trillion-dollar sump exceeding in nominal value all the assets of American corporations.

What has happened is emergence of a final corollary of Say's Law: subsidized supply destroys demand. Production without a willing market is a form of disguised consumption, and despite first appearances it does not stimulate an economy.[20] Nonproductive government spending, even when designed to spur demand, actually soon reduces it, regardless of any statistical increase in "purchasing power." The artificial stimulus, like an addiction, requires even greater injections to sustain the initial effect.

When government gives welfare, unemployment payments, and public-service jobs in quantities that deter productive work, and when it raises taxes on profitable enterprise to pay for them, demand declines. In fact, nearly all the programs that are advocated by economists to promote equality and combat poverty—and are often rationalized in terms of stimulating consumption—in actuality reduce demand by undermining the production from which all real demand derives. Buying power does not essentially "trickle down" as wages or "flow up" and away as profits and savings. It originates with productive work at any level. This is the simple and homely first truth about wealth and poverty. "Give and you will be given unto." This is the secret not only of riches but also of growth.

This is also the essential insight of supply side economics. Government cannot significantly affect real aggregate demand through policies of taxing and spending—taking money from one man and giving it to another, whether in government or out. All this shifting of wealth is a zero sum game and the net effect on incomes is usually zero, or even negative.

Even a tax cut does not work by a direct impact on total disposable incomes, since every dollar of resulting deficit must be financed by a dollar of government debt, paid by the purchaser of federal securities out of his own disposable income. Even in the short run real aggregate demand is an effect of production, not of government policy. The only way tax policy can reliably influence real incomes is by changing the incentives of suppliers. By altering the pattern of rewards to favor work over leisure, investment over consumption, the sources of production over the sumps of wealth, taxable over untaxable activity, government can directly and powerfully foster the expansion of real demand and income. This is the supply side mandate.

CHAPTER 5

The Nature of Wealth

IS SAUDI ARABIA RICH? Is Mecca Muslim? one might respond. With a third of the world's known petroleum reserves and nearly half of its estimated oil wealth (because Saudi oil is far cheaper to pump than most oil elsewhere), Saudi Arabia is clearly among the world's best endowed states, and indeed its measurable income and assets per capita fall short only of those of a few still smaller sheikdoms and such. If sheer income and power to consume are a satisfactory definition of riches, Saudi Arabians would seem close to leading the world.

Like many evidently simple economic concepts, however, wealth conceals below its shining, or unctuous, surface a swarm of perplexities. A country's wealth turns out to be a more slippery sum than the spending power of its citizens or the reservoir of its resources. In fact, there is a sense in which too much spending power is a sign of impending poverty, suggesting by surplus liquidity an absence of wealth in its more solid and unspendable forms. A country—like Great Britain or Saudi Arabia—whose rich squander their money in conspicuous displays probably has a problem: A self-indulgent plutocracy, a canker of fear about the future, a hostile climate for enterprise, a lack of opportunities for investment in the real capital goods that will yield a return in years to come.

Wealth consists in assets that promise a future stream of income. The flows of oil money do not become an enduring asset of the nation until they can be converted into a stock of remunerative capital—industries, ports, roads, schools, and working skills—that offer a future flow of support when the oil runs out. Four hundred years ago, Spain was rich like Saudi Arabia, swamped by a similar flood of money in the form of silver from the mines of Potosi in its Latin American colonies. But Spain failed to achieve wealth and soon fell back into its previous doldrums, while industry triumphed in apparently poorer parts of Europe.

A wealthy country must be able to save as well as to consume. Saving is often defined as deferred consumption. But it depends on investment: the ability to produce consumable goods at that future date to which consumption has been deferred. Saving depends on having something to buy when the deposit is withdrawn. For an individual it sounds easy; there must always be *something* to buy after all. But for a nation, with many savers, real wealth is hard work, requiring prolonged and profitable production of goods. The fate of Midas, whose touch turned all to gold until he had nothing to eat—like the fate of Spain, whose fleet delivered an El Dorado on the doorsteps of Cadiz—demonstrates that unrequited saving can be as barren and fruitless as unrequited love.

At present, individual Saudi Arabians can buy stock in productive facilities in other countries, and they can purchase gold, yachts, Rolls Royces, jewels, art, and other presumptive stores of value. The government can buy guns and planes and port facilities. But Saudi Arabia itself can only become a truly rich nation if it can transform the transitory streams of income from oil into capital goods at home, with a yield for the future. Material resources become durable wealth only when mixed with other resources in profitable combinations.

One problem of the Saudis is that such combinations are extremely perishable; factories do not age or travel well. Margins of profit are usually narrow and tend to dissipate in passage to desert kingdoms. Capital can dissolve rapidly as world conditions change. In addition, its value depends upon expectations about the future. In a politically unstable land it is difficult to evoke the human attitudes—the commitments and loyalties—on which long-term yields rely. There is a constant temptation to take the oil profits and run to Switzerland and Wall Street.

The situation in Iran before the 1979 revolution was very similar. The Iranians could buy anything, but somehow, on reaching the country, what they bought seemed to waste away. Savings and investments would melt down into involuntary consumption under the desert sun. Mercedes Benz cost far more in Iran, but without roads or places to drive they were less valuable, perhaps, than Pintos in Pasadena. Factories and office towers loomed over the sand, erected at prodigious expense, but, lacking workable telephones or efficient secretaries or literate labor or committed management, the buildings smacked more of industrial monuments than of real industry. Highly paid consultants still throng the oil-rich countries, but with plane tickets in their pockets and little confidence in the future, they may cost more than they are worth.

Perhaps the Middle Eastern oil barons are right in sending most of their money abroad, with plans to follow it in case of political emergency or depletion of their oil. They are rich, as was Ozymandias, but their nations—Saudi Arabia and similar states—may not, to assert a useful distinction, be wealthy, and their citizens may be living in a mirage of money.

The problem is not peculiar to the Middle East. The controller general of Venezuela described the similar plight of his own nation: "In many countries, being rich is a consequence of the efforts and work of the people. When you make something you can manage it. The creation and management of wealth are part of a process. We never have had such a process. The wealth came out of the earth. We have a consequence without a cause."[1] The question is, which is the real wealth, the consequence, possessed by the oil-rich lands like Saudi Arabia, or the cause, manifested for centuries, for example, by relatively barren islands like Japan and Great Britain, and now by Hong Kong and Taiwan? The question acquires high importance as Great Britain itself stumbles into its legacy of North Sea oil and threatens to squander it. Will this oil be seen later as a "curse in disguise," which prevents Britain from recovering from its real losses: the declining productivity of its work force and the slackness of its management? Oil, like a neutron bomb, could end by destroying the real wealth of the land—the morale and ingenuity of its people—and leave standing only the sterile structures of an advanced industrial economy, ruled by a bloated and increasingly oppressive bureaucracy, trained only in the barren arts of redistributing bonanzas.

In the United States, too, the role of rich men and the nature of wealth seem enigmatic to many. Legends of robber barons and oil kings contend in the public mind with images of Horatio Alger and Henry Ford, and with the continuing sagas of Rockefellers, Mellons, Kennedys, and Du-Ponts, while radical writers speculate on the meaning of Midas in America. Scarcely less than Arabs and Englishmen, Americans confound money with wealth and confuse the actively invested fortunes of rich families with the treasure chests and thronging servants of an Indian rajah or an Arabian prince. American wealth tends to be real. But real, too, is the hostility toward it, the envy and perplexity aroused by the rich, the mystery and the coarse misunderstanding of the role of wealth. The admiration for some wealthy people whose virtues are evident—the inventor or athlete—vies with resentment toward the apparently cavalier beneficiary of inheritance or luck.

Here among the rich is capitalism personified and caricatured; here are its heroic figures and most opportune demonologies. Here is the system's focus of aspiration and source of enterprise; here is its mercurial strength and Achilles heel. How the rich are regarded and how they see themselves—whether they are merely rich or also bearers of wealth— is a crucial measure of the health of a capitalist economy.

A capitalist system is chiefly a noosphere, a circuit of ideas and feelings. As Irving Kristol has pointed out, the very expression, "the economy" may be deceptive because it can lead people to treat the statistics of GNP, capital formation, employment, and other fashionable sums as if they had a life of their own. In fact, the meaning of such numbers transpires entirely in the lives and minds of businessmen. Economics can predict events only to the extent that it can explain the incentives and psychology of business.

Even the physical capital and natural endowment of a country tell very little about its economy. From the air an industrial complex in New Jersey looks much like one in Iran, and a nationalized factory scarcely differs from a private one. The workers and managers under socialism resemble their Western peers closely enough to give rise to theories of *convergence*—the notion that the two systems are becoming more similar as the years pass. But for all the recent decline in productivity growth in some Western nations, socialism and capitalism are not converging at all in their ability to provide food and shelter and higher living standards for their people or to develop new industry and technology for the future. On the contrary, in these vital areas the two systems are rapidly diverging, as any cursory comparison of conditions on the two sides of the iron curtain will demonstrate. The United States alone produces half the world's food exports and 40 percent of its wealth, while socialist countries still look to the West for sustenance and technological advances. The differences between the two sides come not from natural resources or industrial plant, but from ideas and attitudes.

Because capitalism is chiefly an intellectual and psychological arena, however, its far greater creativity is combined with less apparent stability. In a free economy, spontaneous trends of thinking can change facts, can shape things. The price of gold and other sumps of wealth seesaws against the value of productive assets and the belief in the golden rule. Commitment to the future battles against the reasonable notions of national decline. The attitudes of investors rise and fall as their expectations change. Ideas can shrivel a nuclear power plant or a steel mill, move the semiconductor industry to Singapore and South Korea, confound the most lavish and scientific schemes for marketing soap, transform barren land, by spirals of speculation, into a trove of treasure, and wither it with a rumor.

Wealth resides in resources, but not all resources are wealth. The market, as it generates the "news"—its ceaseless play of prices and ideas—passes its wand over the world of human possessions, conferring capital gains as some things become profitable in a new light of time and knowledge, and casting giant shadows of loss over the looming wealth works of the past.

Even the too solid flesh of "human capital" can melt all too fast in a contagion of fears. Jung has said that though a society can resist epidemics of physical disease, it is defenseless against diseases of the mind. Against "psychic epidemics" our laws and medicines and great factories and fortunes are virtually helpless. Growth depends on its own expectation, investment on the "animal spirits" of investors, capital on the morale of work, and working, too, can be as elusive as thinking.

Qualities of thought and spirit in an economy can overshadow all the quantities of capital and contracts of labor. Indeed, so much of what is important is absent from a typical labor contract that industry can be brought to a halt, airports paralyzed, and traffic stalled merely by a decision of workers to observe exactly the written rules of work. Work under free enterprise depends, like investment, on "animal spirits," because work freely rendered, beyond the specifications of contract, is indeed an investment. It is made in the hope of a return in raises and promotions, which is uncertain and depends in part on the prospects of the firm.

Work, indeed, is the root of wealth, even of the genius that mostly resides in sweat. But without a conception of goals and purposes, well-paid workers consume or waste all that they earn. Pop singers rocking and rolling in money, rich basketball stars who symbolize wealth to millions, often end up deep in debt with nothing solid to show for their efforts, while the poorest families can often succeed in saving enough to launch profitable businesses. The old adages on the importance of thrift are true, not only because they signify a quantitative rise in investible funds, but because they betoken imagination and purpose, which make wealth. Few businesses begin with bank loans, and small businesses almost never do. Instead they capitalize labor.

For example, ten years ago a Lebanese family arrived in Lee, Massachusetts, with a few dollars and fewer words of English. The family invested the dollars in buying a woebegone and abandoned shop beside the road on the edge of town, and they started marketing vegetables. The man rose at five every morning to drive slowly a ramshackle truck a hundred miles to farms in the Connecticut Valley, where he purchased the best goods he could find as cheaply as possible to sell that morning in Lee. It was a classic entrepreneurial performance, arbitrage, identifying price differentials in different markets, and exploiting them by labor. But because both the labor and the insight was little compensated, it was in a sense invisibly saved and invested in the store. All six children were sources of accumulating capital as they busily bustled about the place. The store remained open long hours, cashed checks of locals, and began to build a clientele. A few years later one had to fight through the crowds around it in summer, when the choice asparagus or new potted plants went on sale. Through the year it sold flowers and Christmas trees, gas and dry goods, maple syrup and blackberry jam, cider and candies, and wines and liquors, in the teeth of several supermarkets, innumerable gas stations, and other shops of every description, all better situated, all struggling in an overtaxed and declining Massachusetts economy.

The secret was partly in the six children (who placed the family deep in the statistics of per capita poverty for long after its arrival) and in the entrepreneurial vision of the owner, which eluded all the charts. Mr. Michael Zabian is the man's name, and he recently bought the biggest office building in the town, a three-story structure made of the same Lee marble as the national capitol building. He owns a large men's clothing store at street level and what amounts to a small shopping center at his original site; and he preens in three-piece suits in the publicity photos at the Chamber of Commerce.

As extraordinary as may seem his decade of achievement, though, two other Lebanese have performed similar marvels in the Berkshires and have opened competing shops in the area. Other immigrants in every American city—Cubans in Miami, Portuguese in Providence and Newark, Filipinos in Seattle, Koreans in Washington, D.C., and New York, Vietnamese in Los Angeles, to mention the more recent crop—have performed comparable feats of commerce, with little help from banks or government or the profession of economics.

Small firms, begun by enterprising men, can rise quickly to play important roles in the national economy. Berkshire Paper Company, for example, was started by Whitmore (Nick) Kelley of Glendale, Massachusetts, as a maker of scratch pads in the rural town of Great Barrington. One of an array of paper manufacturers along the Housatonic River, the firm endured repeated setbacks, which turned into benefits, and, by 1980, it was providing important capital and consumer goods to some of the nation's largest and fastest growing corporations, though Kelly himself had no inherited wealth or outside support.

From the outset, the company's capital consisted mostly of refuse. Like the copper and steel companies thriving on the contents of slag heaps, Berkshire Paper Company employed paper, machinery, and factory space rejected as useless by other companies. Berkshire Paper, in fact, was launched and grew with almost no recourse to resources or capital that was accorded any value at all in any national economic accounts. Yet the company has now entered the semiconductor industry and holds virtual monopolies in three sophisticated products. The story of its rise from scratch pads to semiconductor products shows the irrelevance of nearly all the indices of economic value and national wealth employed by the statisticians of our economy.

As a sophomore in college, Nick Kelley used to visit his stepfather at Clark-Aiken, a manufacturer of papermaking machine tools in Lee, Massachusetts. Within and around the factory, he noticed random piles of paper and asked his stepfather what was done with them. He was told they were leftovers from machinery tests and would be loaded into a truck and taken to the Lee dump. Kelley asked whether he could have them instead.

He took a handful of the paper to an office-supply store, Gowdy's in Pittsfield, and asked the proprietor what such paper was good for. Scratch pads, he was told. After long trial and error, and several visits to a scratch pad factory in the guise of a student, he figured out how to make the pads. With the help of his stepfather he purchased and repaired a broken paper-cutting machine, and he even found a new method of applying glue, replacing the usual paintbrush with a paint roller. He then scoured much of the Northeast for markets and created a thriving scratch pad business that, again with his stepfather's help, even survived Kelley's stint in Southeast Asia during the Vietnam War.

In every case, setbacks led to innovation and renewed achievement. Deprived of paper from Clark-Aiken, he learned how to purchase it from jobbers in New York. Discovering that it cost two cents a pound more in sheets than in rolls (nine cents rather than seven cents), he computed that the two pennies represented a nearly 30 percent hike in cost and determined to contrive a sheeter out of old equipment. Finally, his worst setback drove him out of the scratch pad business altogether and allowed him to greatly expand his company.

Attempting to extend his marketing effort to Boston, Kelley approached the buyer for a large office-supply firm. The buyer said he doubted that Kelley could meet the competition. Kelley demanded to know how anyone could sell them for less, when the raw materials alone cost some fourteen cents a pound, and he sold the pads for eighteen cents. He went off to investigate his rival, a family firm run by Italians in Somerville. Kelley found a factory in an old warehouse, also filled with old equipment, but organized even more ingeniously than Kelley's own. He had to acknowledge that the owner was "the best." "He had me beat," Kelley said. "I decided then and there to go out of scratch pad manufacturing."

Instead he resolved to buy pads from the Somerville factory and use his own marketing skills to sell them. He also purchased printing equipment and began adding value to the pads by printing specified lines and emblems on them.

This effort led to a request from Schweitzer, a large paper firm in the Berkshires, that Kelley print up legal pads, and then later, in a major breakthrough, that he cut up some tea bag paper that the Schweitzer machines could not handle. Although Kelley had only the most crude cutting machinery, he said sure, he could process tea bags. He took a pile of the thin paper and spent several days and nights at work on it, destroying a fourth of the sheets before his machine completely jammed and pressed several of the layers together so tightly that he found he could easily cut them. This accident gave Kelley a reputation as a worker of small miracles with difficult and specialized papermaking tasks, and the large companies in the area began channeling their most difficult production problems to him.

These new assignments eventually led to three significant monopolies for the small Berkshire firm. One was in making women's fingernail mending tissue (paper with long fibers that adhere to the nail when it is polished) for cosmetic firms from Avon to Revlon. Another was in manufacturing facial blotting tissue (paper that cleans up dirt and makeup without rubbing) for such companies as Mary Kaye and Bonne Belle. His third and perhaps most important project, though—a task that impelled Kelley to pour endlessly through the literature of semiconductor electronics, trafficking in such concepts as microns (one-thousandth of a centimeter) and angstroms (one-thousandth of a micron)—was production of papers for use in the manufacture of microprocessors and other semiconductor devices. This required not only the creation of papers sufficiently lint free to wrap a silicon wafer in (without dislodging an electron), but also a research effort to define for the companies precisely what impurities and "glitches" might remain. Kelley now provides this paper, along with the needed information, to all the leading semiconductor companies, from National Semiconductor to Intel and Motorola, and he continues research to perfect his product.

Throughout his career, Kelley has demonstrated that faith and imagination are the most important capital goods in the American economy, that wealth is a product less of money than of mind.

The official measures miss all such sources of wealth. When Heilbroner and Thurow claim that 25 percent of American households owned zero net wealth in 1969, they are speaking of families that held above 5 billion dollars' worth of automobiles, 16 billion dollars of other consumer durables, such as washers and television sets, 11 billion dollars' worth of housing (about one-third had cars and 90 percent TVs), as well as rights in Medicaid, social security, housing, education, and other governmental benefits.[2] They commanded many billions of dollars' worth of human capital, some of it rather depreciated by age and some by youthful irresponsibilities (most of these poor households consisted either of single people or abandoned mothers and their offspring). Their net worth was zero, because their debts exceeded their calculable worth. Yet some 80 percent of these people who were poor in 1969 escaped poverty within two years, only to be replaced in the distributions by others too young, too old, too improvident, or too beset with children to manage a positive balance in their asset accounts.[3]

Now it may be appropriate to exclude from the accounting such items as rights in government welfare and transfer programs, which often destroy as much human worth as they create. But the distribution tables also miss the assets of the greatest ultimate value. For example, they treated as an increment of poverty, bereft of net worth, the explosive infusion of human capital that arrived on our shores from Lebanon in the guise of an unlettered family.

Families of zero wealth built America. Many of the unincorporated businesses that have gained some 500 billion dollars in net value since World War II (six times more than all the biggest corporations combined)[4] were started in households of zero assets according to the usual accounts. The conception of a huge and unnegotiable gap between poverty and wealth is a myth. In the Berkshires, Zabian moving up passed many scions of wealth on their way down.

Even the statistics offered by the leading proponents of the myth of immobility belie their arguments. Thurow presents a table that he believes indicates that inheritance was "the dominant factor" in accounting for the top ranks of millionaires in 1962. "Among these families," he said, "57 percent reported inheriting a substantial proportion of their assets, and 66 percent reported some inheritance."[5] Meanwhile, as he tries to show later, of the still higher handful of *Fortune*'s superrich, 75 percent received substantial legacies. But Thurow's admittedly impressionistic 75 percent conflicts with other estimates, and like most such figures it may distort the relevant percentages by including women, almost invariably inheritors, within the totals. By 1978 only about one-third of the male supermillionaires had inherited a significant portion of their money.[6] The rest of Thurow's data is as good as the Federal Reserve statisticians could make it. What it shows conflicts with the image that he tries to convey.

In the second tier of wealth-holders, in which each member would average nearly 2 million dollars net worth in 1979 dollars, 71 percent reported no inherited assets at all, and only 14 percent reported substantial inheritance. Even in the top group of multimillionaires, 31 percent received no inherited assets, and 9 percent only small legacies.[7] Other studies indicate that among the far larger and collectively more important group of wealth-holders of more than $60,000 in 1969, 85 percent of the families had emerged since 1953.[8] With a few notable exceptions, which are always in the news, fast movement up or down in two generations has been the fate of the American rich.

How could this be, when distributionist experts contemplating the magic of compound interest can easily demonstrate that the rich must get richer, until eventually they own nearly everything? Why can they not pass the grail on down without spilling most of its contents? Well, as they say, there are many a slip, and death and taxes take their toll of potential heirs and their money; Howard Hughes left no heirs. Widows, who normally die about twelve years after their husbands, traipse off to Europe with their money and marry indigent dukes or such. Fortune hunters abound near the funerals of the rich.

When the money is actually passed on, the part that escapes charity and philanthropy often ends among large numbers of prodigal sons and daughters to whom the *average return on capital* is a concept easier to understand than to achieve, even in those cases where the children have some interest in keeping their wealth. The receipt of a legacy, it turns out, often erodes the qualities of entrepreneurship that are needed to perpetuate it. Spending turns out to be far easier than choosing and maintaining those select forms of capital with yields greater than their costs.

In recent years, moreover, the magic of compound interest has met its match in compound inflation and taxes. These two forces hit hardest at both the assets and the earnings of the rich, destroying about a tenth of their income whenever the price level rises 2 percent or more. Even such families as Mellons, Rockefellers, and Fricks, while remaining wealthy, are in steady decline, diffusing their assets among scores of descendants, dissipating it in collapsing securities or failing companies at home and abroad, incarcerating it in foundations, and selling off or donating to nonprofit institutions, or even to government, some of their principal holdings of land and personal property. Even the ancestral Rockefeller estate at Pocantico Hills, their venerable Westchester domain, was given to the National Trust for Historic Preservation. After the deaths of three of the brothers, the remaining two and their children had neither the motivation nor the available money to sustain the manorial symbols of family power.

In future years the members of such families will remain well off, but they will not command "the heights" of the system or constitute a significant concentration of wealth in a multitrillion-dollar economy. In

America, one can say with assurance, the scions of the rich only rarely themselves get richer, though they are often replaced by yet more success-ful families from lower echelons of income. Fears of a hereditary pluto-cracy are as groundless as hopes for a withering state.

In the noosphere of capitalism, all riches must finally fall into the gap between thoughts and things. Wealth is governed by mind but it is caught in matter. To be negotiable, an asset must afford an income stream that is expected to continue. The expectation may shift as swiftly as thought, but things, alas, are all too solid and slow to change. The galleries of pop art paintings, the railroad lines that grid America's rural villages, the factories that made the giant computers of the sixties or the best computers of last year, the warehouses that contain them, all the once bustling canals, remaindered towers of best-sellers, cornered markets of rubber trees, all the mighty textile mills of Massachusetts and ironworks of Pennsylvania, the spectral waterwheels and ghost farms of New Eng-land, the stockpiles of cyclamates and the plants that produced them, all the great printing presses and linotype machines and the machine tools that shaped them—the images abound of the evanescence of value in the most ostensibly massive and enduring physical forms. When facts or fashion change, the most imposing machines of production often must be sold at well below cost and used in far inferior ways.

The kaleidoscope of shifting valuations, flashing gains and losses as it is turned in the hands of time, in the grip of "news," distributes and redistributes the wealth of the world far more quickly and surely than any scheme of the state. Thurow's calculations of returns to capital in the seventies—by which he alleged its unchanging distribution—mostly omitted the collapsing value of stocks, the trillion-dollar boom in residen-tial buildings, the massive gains and losses in small business, the massive losses in money, the plummeting of bond prices, the ascent of gold and art, all of which by a flick of an Arabian wrist can shift into a new constellation of radically differing worth.

Between 1946 and 1975 the unadjusted capital gains to American citi-zens on all their wealth, whether or not "realized" by sales, were two trillion, six hundred and sixty-four billion dollars. Within this inconceiva-ble aggregate, specific fortunes and conceptions of wealth gyrated wildly from year to year. In 1973 and 1974 stocks alone plummeted by two-thirds of a trillion dollars, or about a quarter of all the preinflationary gains on all forms of land and capital over the previous thirty years.[9] At the end of that thirty-year period, after correcting for inflation, the total stock market gains to households—realized and unrealized by sales—dropped to a net of 26 billion dollars, less than a billion a year, before taxes, and became losses after IRS took its share.[10]

Once upon a time, before the invention of experimental capitalism, when wealth resided in land and other stable properties—and even now in socialist systems where wealth attaches to party offices often held in perpetuity—a distribution chart could capture a fixed reality. But in modern capitalism, wealth is a dilemma: its value on the one hand is embodied in ever more specialized, complex, and inflexible forms, and on the other is utterly subject to ever more rapid and unpredictable changes in knowledge. Both more solid and more pervious, capital is now a Maginot Line for any determined hoarder of it.

The only stable asset among the quakes and shadows is a disciplined brain. Matter melts, but mind and will can flash for a while ahead of the uncertain crowd, beam visions across the sky, and induce their incarnation in silicon and cement before the competition gathers. The best, most compelling, most original, and flexible minds constitute the most enduring gold. They deserve what they win, for a time, before they are passed by, as they surely will be. As soon as the works of imagination and mathematics become concrete—are invested—they are trapped. This is why the vast majority of America's fortunes are dissipated within two generations. This is why the abstract *average return on capital* is so rarely received by particular rich men for long, even if perchance they choose to settle for it, taking interest rate scoops of liquidity from the banks of the economy, rather than plunging into capital in quest of higher and more elusive yields.

In general, the more liquid wealth is, the closer it is to money, the less likely it is to grow fast, the more vulnerable it is to the changing money supplies. Savings accounts, after inflation and taxes, have lost money for decades. The less liquid an asset the more likely are large returns or losses. The least liquid and most promising of all is to build and own a company. If it goes public in the stock market, the owners can win paper fortunes beyond belief, but they can sell only 1½ percent of their shares every six months (unless they can find a buyer for the entire firm). In 1970 the streets of New York were filled with paper millionaires, floating high on debt, who soon found themselves bankrupt after the crash of the growth stocks.

In a partial sense, a rich man resembles a gambler betting against the house. The laws of probability declare that his chances to hold or enlarge his fortune depend on the relationship between the size of his fortune and the amount of money commanded by the house. The rule of gamblers' ruin dictates that his ultimate collapse is 90 percent certain if his opposition has ten times more wealth than he does and the game lasts for more than 900 plays. If he has only 1 percent as much as his opposition, his ruin is 99 percent certain within just 50 plays.[11]

The analogy to the house in a free economy is the total wealth of the other players: the wealth of the entire economy. If free enterprise were pure chance, and a zero-sum game like gambling (in which one man's gain is necessarily another's loss), very early ruin would be assured. Enterprise is only partly chance, so the businessman has a much better opportunity to preserve his winnings than a pure gambler. But rich families face over time a series of fortuities that are sure to bring them down rather rapidly. As the money is passed along, the laws of probability gain in influence and the capabilities of the managers tend to decline. In general, the great fortunes are certain to rise and fall more in accord with the laws of probability, and entropy, than with those of compound interest.

This process is the secret of capitalist ferment and creativity. New ideas gain resources and ride to the top while old wealth withers. The chief threat to this system is taxation with rates so progressive—graduated so steeply to capture increasing portions of larger incomes—that the rich refuse to risk their money. Wealth is withdrawn from productive uses, hoarded in gold or collectibles, or put in tax shelters (businesses of little economic value except in relation to the tax laws). The rich still lose their money, but they no longer contribute to the economy. The movement of elites, up and down, becomes more sluggish and the performance of the system less dynamic.[12]

This is the gravest peril of capitalism in our current inflationary period. As the wealthy consume more and invest less, resentment toward them increases and ignorant or demagogic politicians impose yet higher rates to punish them. The rich discover that it is easier and more gratifying to spend money than to earn it for the government, and they get a yen to travel and invest abroad. The problem becomes worse in a vicious spiral of taxation and capital flight, familiar in many underdeveloped countries as well as in Europe and the United States. Under these circumstances, the wealth of a country can revert to mere riches, and its citizens begin to consume its capital, the source of future wealth.

In attacking the rich, tax authorities make great use of the concept of "unearned income," which means the returns from money earned earlier, heavily taxed, then saved or invested. Inheritances receive special attention, since they represent undemocratic transfers and concentrations of power. But they also extend the time horizons of the economy (that is, business), and retard the destruction of capital. That inheritance taxes are too high is obvious from the low level of revenue they collect and the huge industry of tax avoidance they sustain. But politically these levies have long been regarded as too attractive to forgo at a time of hostility toward the rich.

Nonetheless, some of the most catalytic wealth in America is "un-earned." A few years before Michael Zabian arrived on our shores, Peter Sprague, now his Berkshire neighbor, inherited 400,000 dollars, largely from the sale of Sprague Electric Company stock. Many heirs of similar legacies have managed to lose most of it in a decade or so. But Sprague set out on a course that could lose it much faster. He decided on a career in venture capital. To raise the odds against him still further, he eventually chose to specialize in companies that faced bankruptcy and lacked other sources of funds.

His first venture was a chicken hatchery in Iran, which taught him the key principles of entrepreneurship—chiefly that nothing happens as one envisions it in theory. The project had been based on the use of advanced Ralston-Purina technology, widely tested in Latin America, to tap the rapidly growing poultry markets of the Middle East. The first unexpected discovery was two or three feet of snow; no one had told him that it *snowed* in Iran. Snow ruined most of the Ralston-Purina equip-ment. A second surprise was chicanery (and sand) in the chicken feed business. "You end up buying two hundred pounds of stone for every hundred pounds of grain." But after some seven years of similar setbacks, and a growing capital of knowledge, Sprague began to make money in Iran: growing a million trees fertilized with chicken manure, cultivating mushrooms in abandoned ice houses, and winding up with the largest cold storage facilities in the country. The company has made a profit through most of the seventies.

In 1964, three years after starting his Iranian operations, Sprague moved in on a failing electronics company called National Semiconductor. Sprague considered the situation for a week, bought a substantial stake, and became its chairman. The firm is now in the vanguard of the world-wide revolution in semiconductor technology and has been one of Ameri-ca's fastest growing firms, rising from 300 employees when Sprague joined it to 34,000 in 1980.

Also in the mid-sixties Sprague bought several other companies, includ-ing the now fashionable Energy Resources, and rescued Design Research from near bankruptcy (the firm finally folded in 1979). In 1969, he helped found Auton Computing Company, a firm still thriving in the business of detecting and analyzing stress in piping systems in nuclear and other power plants, and in 1970 he conducted a memorably resourceful and inventive but finally unsuccessful Republican campaign for the New York City congressional seat then held by Edward Koch (who is now mayor).

Then he entered the latest phase of his career rescuing collapsing compa-nies. A sports car buff, he indicated to some friends an interest in reviving Aston-Martin, which had gone out of business six months earlier, in mid-1974. Arriving in England early in 1975 with a tentative plan to investigate the possibilities, he was besieged by reporters and TV cameras. Headlines blared: MYSTERY YANK FINANCIER TO SAVE ASTON MARTIN. Eventually he did, and the company is now securely profitable, although it has encountered difficulties in the American market because federal regulators in their wisdom apply the new pollution and safety rules and red tape with majestic evenhandedness to General Motors and to Sprague's small British firm.

In 1975 Sprague also purchased Advent Corporation (the Aston-Martin of phonographic equipment), when it was two days short of receivership after losing 3.5 million dollars and still over a million dollars in debt to its suppliers. Again, after a brisk reorganization and a decision to concentrate on production of large-screen television systems, the firm prospered under Sprague's management. Although it went through a financial wringer during a tempestuous period in the stock market (with Advent shares selling from three to twenty dollars at various times as investors assessed and reassessed the prospects of major competition), the company approached the 1980s still in the lead in its chosen technology despite concerted challenges from several American and Japanese conglomerates.

A government counterpart of Sprague's investment activity was Wedgewood Benn's National Enterprise Board in England, which spent some 8 billion dollars attempting to save various British companies by drowning them in money. Before Sprague arrived in England Benn had adamantly refused to invest in Aston-Martin—dismissing the venerable firm as a hopeless case—and instead subsidized a large number of other companies, most of which, unlike Aston, still lose money, and some of which ended up bankrupt. The British, however, did find 104 million dollars—fifty times more than Sprague had to invest in Aston-Martin—to use in luring John DeLorean's American luxury car project to Northern Ireland and poured 47.8 million dollars into the effort to create Inmos, a British nationalized semiconductor firm that has yet to earn any money and technologically remains well in the wake of Sprague's concern. With 400,000 dollars inheritance and his charismatic skills, Sprague has revived many times more companies than Wedgewood Benn with the British Treasury. One entrepreneur with energy, resolution, and charisma could turn 400,000 dollars into a small fortune for himself and a bonanza for the economy, accomplishing more than any number of committee-bound foundations, while a government agency usually requires at least 400,000 dollars to so much as open an office.

Nonetheless, considering the sometimes unedifying spectacle of the humpty-dumpty heirs of wealth—and often focusing on the most flamboyant and newsworthy consumers of cocaine and spouses—it is all too easy to forget that the crucial role of the rich in a capitalist economy is not to entertain and titillate the classes below, but to invest: to provide unencumbered and unbureaucratized cash. The broad class of rich does, in fact, perform this role. Only a small portion of their money is consumed. Most of it goes to productive facilities that employ labor and supply goods to consumers. The rich remain the chief source of discretionary capital in the economy.

These are the funds available for investment outside the largely sterile channels of institutional spending. This is the money that escapes the Keynesian trap of compounded risk, created by the fact that a bank, like an entrepreneur, may lose most of its investment if an enterprise fails, but only the entrepreneur can win the large possible payoff that renders the risk worthwhile. Individuals with cash comprise the wild card—the mutagenic germ—in capitalism, and it is relatively risky investments that ultimately both reseed the economy and unseat the rich, as the iron rule of gamblers' ruin plays itself out in the arena of business.

Often most fertile are the experimental ventures that depart from the patterns of the past and increase the public capital of knowledge even when their failure depletes the private wealth of the rich. These are the ventures that try fundamentally new products and services, that break new ground for others, who can then be backed by banks and institutions.

It is discretionary capital that finances most of what is original and idiosyncratic in our culture and economy, that launches the apparently hopeless cause in business and politics, that supports the unusual invention, art, or private school, that founds the institutions of the future. Yet it is this kind of spending that is considered waste or recklessness by the mathematical economist and denounced as plutocratic by the leftist politician (as he petitions his banker friends for cash). It is this kind of discretionary wealth that the rationalistic reformer wishes, above all, to wring out of the American system, to replace in politics by "public-interest committees" and merit panels; in philanthropy by ever more thoroughly regulated and routinized foundations; in culture by councils on the arts or humanities and their nonprofit clients and satellites—all the clones and cousins of government agencies that in the end are indistinguishable from the State.

Worst of all, though, are the proposals to replace the rich as providers of venture capital—to institutionalize innovations, the special visions and experimental investments in new technology and growth. This effort to routinize and politicize creativity is epitomized by the weathervane allotments of the Department of Energy, determining the prospects for new power sources largely by their ability to fire and fuel new constituencies for congressmen. Solar one month, geothermal the next, tides and windmills to come, in a steady progression of fads and fancies that will end, it now appears, in a solemn resolution to bravely reenter the past and rely for dusky centuries on the most costly and toxic of all the real possibilities—namely, bituminous coal.

It is only individuals who can be original. Institutions shy away from unproven or unfashionable ideas. Therefore, they cannot afford to create new knowledge. It is the rich who by risking their wealth ultimately lose it, and save the economy. In the still booming year of 1970, some 90 percent of the gross incomes of millionaires came from businesses and partnerships and stocks; the business and partnership losses were 40 percent as large as the gains. In 1978, the 250,000 millionaires were still at it—though to a lesser degree—investing half their money in stocks, some 20 percent in private businesses, and only 14 percent in government bonds and other supposedly safe securities.[13]

The risk-bearing role of the rich cannot be performed so well by anyone else. The benefits of capitalism still depend on capitalists. The other groups on the pyramid of wealth should occasionally turn from the spectacles of consumption long enough to see the adventure on the frontiers of the economy above them—an adventure not without its note of nobility, since its protagonist families will almost all eventually fail and fall in the redeeming struggle of the free economy.

In America the rich should not be compared to the Saudi Arabians or be seen in the image of Midas in his barred cage of gold. The American rich hold not only riches but also wealth. It is in the Third World where the Midas myth bears its grim truth, where governments can make nothing but money and there is little to buy except from abroad, and where all surviving wealth tends to flee into portable baubles and gold. Under capitalism, when it is working, the rich have the anti-Midas touch, transforming timorous liquidity and unused savings into factories and office towers, farms and laboratories, orchestras and museums—turning gold into goods and jobs and art. That is the function of the rich: fostering opportunities for the classes below them in the continuing drama of the creation of wealth and progress.

This is a drama most essentially not of measurable money and machines, aggregates and distributions, but of mind and morale. Above the vast architecture of production, and surrounding it, is a statistically invisible atmosphere of moods and ideas, a phantasmagoria of images and visions of the future, which either admit, or eclipse, the sustaining light and power of the sun: the life-giving faith in the possibility that free enterprises can prevail among the unpredictable forms of wealth in the unknown world to come.

CHAPTER 6

The Nature of Poverty

LIVING in a world of wealth, the upper classes of Americans have long listened straight-faced and unboggled to the most fantastic tales from the world of the poor. Although inclined to accept Ernest Hemingway's assurances that the rich differ from us chiefly in having more money, we have been willing to suppose that the poor were some alien tribe, exotic in culture and motivation, who can be understood only through the channels of credentialed expertise.

It helped that many of the poor were black. They looked different; perhaps they were different. There came forth a series of authoritative fables: blacks are allegedly matriarchal by nature; like the Irish, the Jews, and other urban immigrants before them, their IQ's were shown to be genetically lower[1] (possibly, in the case of blacks, because of cramped cranial spaces); and they were found to be markedly prone to violent crime and slovenly living. Nonetheless, we could not judge them, it was said by those of liberal spirit, without being guilty of ethnocentrism or cultural imperialism. A propensity for violence, low intelligence, and fatherless homes, it was implied, constitutes a reasonable adaptation to poverty from which we may all learn much.

This attitude, however, required a spirit of cultural relativism so heroic that it could not serve for long, particularly in political formulations. So new approaches emerged, allegedly more enlightened, but with implications equally farfetched. Slavery, discrimination, and deprivation, it was said, have so abused the black psyche that all sorts of new ministrations and therapies are needed to redeem it; racism and unemployment still inflict such liabilities that vast new programs of public employment and affirmative action are required to overcome them. The reasonable inference arises that even though blacks are not genetically inferior, science proves them to be so damaged by racism and poverty that they are inferior now.

Not only do these notions cause serious strain to the spirit of liberalism when confronting specific specimens of this maimed but deserving race, but such attitudes also perpetuate the idea that the poor, for whatever reason, are still very different from us. This belief permits a series of new fables to arise, some explicit, most implicit in government programs.

For example, most of us work for money and enjoy leisure. The poor, it is implied, despite their generally more onerous jobs, do not. They so lust for labor, so they tell all inquiring scholars, that their willingness to work is unaffected by levels of welfare and in-kind support substantially higher than the available wage; they even clamor to enter the work force in the face of effective tax rates on work (through reductions in welfare payments) of nearly 100 percent.

All American ethnic groups in the past rose out of poverty partly by learning English and downplaying their own languages. The current foreign poor, mostly Hispanic, are thought to require instruction chiefly in their native tongue, for reasons of ethnic pride.

Middle-class Americans are demonstrably devastated by divorce and separation: they leave their jobs, income plummets, health deteriorates; they drink and philander; their children behave badly in school. But the poor and their children are assumed to be relatively unshaken by a plague of family breakdowns; at least any resulting lower income and employment levels are said to be due to discrimination, and the behavior of the children is regarded to be little influenced by the absence of fathers.

Most American men earn more money than their wives; men that don't tend to leave, or be left, in large numbers. Yet poor men are assumed to be unaffected by the higher relative incomes available to their wives from welfare and affirmative action, which are alleged to have no relationship to high rates of unemployment and illegitimacy.

Perhaps most important of all, every successful ethnic group in our history rose up by working harder than other classes, in low-paid jobs, with a vanguard of men in entrepreneurial roles. But the current poor, so it is supposed, can leapfrog drudgery by education and credentials, or be led as a group from poverty, perhaps by welfare mothers trained for government jobs. These views depict the current poor as a race so alien to the entire American experience, so radically different in motive and character from whites, that one can speak in terms of a new form of bigotry.

The notion of liberal racism is perhaps needlessly provocative. Liberals are not racists any more than all but a small, dwindling, and utterly uninfluential minority of other Americans are. But the response of the dominantly liberal media to the racial situation is so quixotic and peculiar as to be reprehensible in its own special way. For example, anyone who has spent any time at all among the American political and economic elite knows that it is desperately eager to appoint blacks to high positions whenever they are reasonably able to perform the duties. The more prestigious American universities avidly pursue black Ph.D.'s and pay them on average some two thousand dollars more than white professors with similar credentials and experience.[2] Yet every American newspaper and magazine treated the appointment of Franklin Thomas as head of the Ford Foundation as if it were some amazing triumph, a startling breakthrough, although Thomas had previously turned down a post in the U.S. cabinet, had already served as temporary chief of the Whitney Foundation, professed the same impeccably fashionable views as his predecessor, McGeorge Bundy, and was chosen with the highest possible enthusiasm by the board.

Similarly, it has been demonstrated many times in American politics that blacks can get elected to virtually any office, particularly in big cities, if they are sufficiently resourceful politicians. Yet the editorial pages of *The New York Times* and *The New York Post* explained both Percy Sutton's defeat in the 1976 Democratic mayoral primary and their own refusal to endorse him by labored implications that the city was "unready" for a black mayor "at this time." Actually, the newspapers refrained from endorsing Sutton and the people refrained from voting from him because, although a pleasant and intelligent man, he was an unimpressive campaigner who conducted a lackluster drive for the office. He did as well as he did chiefly by getting unanimous black support. His defeat had nothing to do with racism, despite his own hapless claims to the contrary, encouraged by *The New York Times*.

The refusal of American leaders to tell the truth about blacks is more important when it comes to black poverty. The prevailing expressed opinion is that racism and discrimination still explain the low incomes of blacks. This proposition is at once false and invidious. Not only does it slander white Americans, it deceives and demoralizes blacks. Not only does it obstruct the truth, it encourages, by its essential incredibility, the alternate falsehood, held in private by many blacks and whites, that blacks cannot now make it in America without vast federal assistance, without, indeed, the very government programs that in fact account for the worst aspects of black poverty and promise to perpetuate it. Finally, the liberal belief in bigotry as an explanation for the condition of blacks leads to still more preposterous theories about the alleged poverty of other groups, from women to Hispanics, and to a generally manic-depressive vision of the economy, in which poverty is seen both as more extreme and more remediable than it is.

The first thing to understand is that regardless of the affluence of the American economy, we live in a world full of poor people. Modern transport and communications ensure that increasing numbers will be both eager and able to reach our shores. Unless we wish to adopt an immoral and economically self-destructive policy of prohibiting immigration, there will be poverty in America for centuries to come. The policies and approaches we have adopted in our neurotic concern about blacks will likely be applied to many millions of others. The potential injury that could be inflicted on our economy and on the poor people in it is quite incalculable. But, on the basis of the long and thoroughly unambiguous experience of our government in blighting the lives of blacks and Indians, one can only predict that the damage will be tragically great.

To get a grip on the problems of poverty, one should also forget the idea of overcoming inequality by redistribution. Inequality may even grow at first as poverty declines. To lift the incomes of the poor, it will be necessary to increase the rates of investment, which in turn will tend to enlarge the wealth, if not the consumption, of the rich. The poor, as they move into the work force and acquire promotions, will raise their incomes by a greater percentage than the rich; but the upper classes will gain by greater absolute amounts, and the gap between the rich and the poor may grow. All such analyses are deceptive in the long run, however, because they imply a static economy in which the *numbers* of the rich and the middle class are not growing.

In addition, inequality may be favored by the structure of a modern economy as it interacts with demographic change. When the division of labor becomes more complex and refined, jobs grow more specialized; and the increasingly specialized workers may win greater rents for their rare expertise, causing their incomes to rise relative to common labor. This tendency could be heightened by a decline in new educated entrants to the work force, predictable through the 1990s, and by an enlarged flow of immigration, legal and illegal. Whatever the outcome of these developments, an effort to take income from the rich, thus diminishing their investment, and to give it to the poor, thus reducing their work incentives, is sure to cut American productivity, limit job opportunities, and perpetuate poverty.

Among the beneficiaries of inequality will be the formerly poor. Most students of the problems of poverty consider the statistics of success of previous immigrant groups and see a steady incremental rise over the years, accompanied by the progressive acquisition of educational credentials and skills. Therefore, programs are proposed that foster a similar slow and incremental ascent by the currently poor. But the incremental vision of the escape from poverty is mostly false, based on a simple illusion of statistical aggregates that conceals everything important about upward mobility. Previous immigrants earned money first by working hard; their children got the education.[3]

The rising average incomes of previous groups signify not the smooth progress of hundreds of thousands of civil-service or bureaucratic careers, but the rapid business and professional successes of a relative few, who brought their families along and inspired others to follow. Poor people tend to rise up rapidly and will be damaged by a policy of redistribution that will always hit new and unsheltered income and wealth much harder than the elaborately concealed and fortified winnings of the established rich. The poor benefit from a dynamic economy full of unpredictable capital gains (they have few capital losses!) more than from a stratified system governed by educational and other credentials that the rich can buy.

THE ONLY dependable route from poverty is always work, family, and faith. The first principle is that in order to move up, the poor must not only work, they must work harder than the classes above them. Every previous generation of the lower class has made such efforts. But the current poor, white even more than black, are refusing to work hard. Irwin Garfinkel and Robert Haveman, authors of an ingenious and sophisticated study of what they call *Earnings Capacity Utilization Rates,* have calculated the degree to which various income groups use their opportunities— how hard they work outside the home. This study shows that, for several understandable reasons, the current poor work substantially less, for fewer hours and weeks a year, and earn less in proportion to their age, education, and other credentials (even *after* correcting the figures for unemployment, disability, and presumed discrimination) than either their predecessors in American cities or those now above them on the income scale.[4] (The study was made at the federally funded Institute for Research on Poverty at the University of Wisconsin and used data from the census and the Michigan longitudinal survey.) The findings lend important confirmation to the growing body of evidence that work effort is the crucial unmeasured variable in American productivity and income distribution, and that current welfare and other subsidy programs substantially reduce work. The poor choose leisure not because of moral weakness, but because they are paid to do so.

A program to lift by transfers and preferences the incomes of less diligent groups is politically divisive—and very unlikely—because it incurs the bitter resistance of the real working class. In addition, such an effort breaks the psychological link between effort and reward, which is crucial to long-run upward mobility. Because effective work consists not in merely fulfilling the requirements of labor contracts, but in "putting out" with alertness and emotional commitment, workers have to understand and feel deeply that what they are given depends on what they give— that they must supply work in order to demand goods. Parents and schools must inculcate this idea in their children both by instruction and example. Nothing is more deadly to achievement than the belief that effort will not be rewarded, that the world is a bleak and discriminatory place in which only the predatory and the specially preferred can get ahead. Such a view in the home discourages the work effort in school that shapes earnings capacity afterward. As with so many aspects of human performance, work effort begins in family experiences, and its sources can be best explored through an examination of family structure.

Indeed, after work the second principle of upward mobility is the maintenance of monogamous marriage and family. Adjusting for discrimination against women and for child-care responsibilities, the Wisconsin study indicates that married men work between two and one-third and four times harder than married women, and more than twice as hard as female family heads. The work effort of married men increases with their age, credentials, education, job experience, and birth of children, while the work effort of married women steadily declines. Most important in judging the impact of marriage, husbands work 50 percent harder than bachelors of comparable age, education, and skills.[5]

The effect of marriage, thus, is to increase the work effort of men by about half. Since men have higher earnings capacity to begin with, and since the female capacity-utilization figures would be even lower without an adjustment for discrimination, it is manifest that the maintenance of families is the key factor in reducing poverty.

Once a family is headed by a woman, it is almost impossible for it to greatly raise its income even if the woman is highly educated and trained and she hires day-care or domestic help. Her family responsibilities and distractions tend to prevent her from the kind of all-out commitment that is necessary for the full use of earning power. Few women with children make earning money the top priority in their lives.

A married man, on the other hand, is spurred by the claims of family to channel his otherwise disruptive male aggressions into his performance as a provider for a wife and children. These sexual differences alone, which manifest themselves in all societies known to anthropology, dictate that the first priority of any serious program against poverty is to strengthen the male role in poor families.

These narrow measures of work effort touch on just part of the manifold interplay between family and poverty. Edward Banfield's *The Unheavenly City* defines the lower class largely by its lack of an orientation to the future. Living from day to day and from hand to mouth, lower class individuals are unable to plan or save or keep a job. Banfield gives the impression that short-time horizons are a deep-seated psychological defect afflicting hundreds of thousands of the poor.

There is no question that Banfield puts his finger on a crucial problem of the poor and that he develops and documents his theme in an unrivaled classic of disciplined social science. But he fails to show how millions of men, equally present oriented, equally buffeted by impulse and blind to the future, have managed to become far-seeing members of the middle classes. He also fails to explain how millions of apparently future-oriented men can become dissolute followers of the sensuous moment, neglecting their jobs, dissipating their income and wealth, pursuing a horizon no longer than the most time-bound of the poor.

What Banfield is in fact describing in his lower-class category is largely the temperament of single, divorced, and separated men. The key to lower-class life in contemporary America is that unrelated individuals, as the census calls them, are so numerous and conspicuous that they set the tone for the entire community. Their congregation in ghettos, moreover, magnifies greatly their impact on the black poor, male and female (though, as Banfield rightly observes, this style of instant gratification is chiefly a male trait).

The short-sighted outlook of poverty stems largely from the breakdown of family responsibilities among fathers. The lives of the poor, all too often, are governed by the rhythms of tension and release that characterize the sexual experience of young single men. Because female sexuality, as it evolved over the millennia, is psychologically rooted in the bearing and nurturing of children, women have long horizons within their very bodies, glimpses of eternity within their wombs. Civilized society is dependent upon the submission of the short-term sexuality of young men to the extended maternal horizons of women. This is what happens in monogamous marriage; the man disciplines his sexuality and extends it into the future through the womb of a woman. The woman gives him access to his children, otherwise forever denied him; and he gives her the product of his labor, otherwise dissipated on temporary pleasures. The woman gives him a unique link to the future and a vision of it; he gives her faithfulness and a commitment to a lifetime of hard work. If work effort is the first principle of overcoming poverty, marriage is the prime source of upwardly mobile work.

It is love that changes the short horizons of youth and poverty into the long horizons of marriage and career. When marriages fail, the man often returns to the more primitive rhythms of singleness. On the average, his income drops by one-third and he shows a far higher propensity for drink, drugs, and crime. But when marriages in general hold firm and men in general love and support their children, Banfield's lower-class style changes into middle-class futurity.

The key to the intractable poverty of the hardcore American poor is the dominance of single and separated men in poor communities. Black "unrelated individuals" are not much more likely to be in poverty than white ones. The problem is neither race nor matriarchy in any meaningful sense. It is familial anarchy among the concentrated poor of the inner city, in which flamboyant and impulsive youths rather than responsible men provide the themes of aspiration. The result is that male sexual rhythms tend to prevail, and boys are brought up without authoritative fathers in the home to instill in them the values of responsible paternity: the discipline and love of children and the dependable performance of the provider role. "If she wants me, *she*'ll pay," one young stud assured me in prison,[6] and perhaps, in the welfare culture, she can and will. Thus the pattern is extended into future generations.

In his concern with present and future orientation, Banfield was right about the role of time in upward mobility. "Capital," as the Austrian school of economists tells us, "*is* time"—the delay in consumption entailed by extended modes of production. In poor communities, it might be said, all time is present time, and capital—in its human form of work effort combined with education and savings—does not adequately accumulate to provide income and wealth. But a more fundamental way of defining the stagnant lower class is by its lack of family structure. The men's links to children and future are too often insufficient to induce work and thrift.

British demographer E. A. Wrigley has even argued that the emergence of these direct and exclusive links to children in the nuclear family was a prerequisite of the industrial revolution. In slow-developing areas of Eastern Europe and Asia, he maintains, marriage took place within the compass of extended families, and fathers were not expected to support their children alone. But as early as the Elizabethan period in England and in other industrially precocious parts of Western Europe, a couple normally could not marry until the man had demonstrated his ability to provide for an independent household. As I wrote in *Sexual Suicide,* "Sexual energies were directly tied to economic growth, and since strong sanctions were imposed on premarital sex, population growth was directly tied to economic productivity."[7]

As Wrigley wrote, "Preindustrial men lived their lives in a moving present," devoted to "short term prospects."[8] Such men could not find the time to make capital, could not bring themselves to work, save, and forgo rewards in the name of an unseen and unknowable future. It was firm links between work, wealth, sex, and children that eventually created a future-oriented psychology in the mass of Western European men. Wrigley concludes: "So often said to be the result of industrialization and urban living," the nuclear family, in fact, "preceded it by centuries" and facilitated the long-term development of the highly motivated industrial bourgeoisie and work force.[9]

Although this is an oversimplified account of both Wrigley and the industrial revolution, it expresses his crucial point: that "the act of marriage is necessarily one which stands centrally in the whole complex of social behavior."[10] In particular, it stands centrally to a man's attitude toward time, and thus toward saving and capital. Conversely, a condition of widespread illegitimacy and family breakdown can be a sufficient cause of persistent poverty, separating men from the extended horizons embodied in their children.

An analysis of poverty that begins and ends with family structure and marital status would explain far more about the problem than most of the distributions of income, inequality, unemployment, education, IQ, race, sex, home ownership, location, discrimination, and all the other items usually multiply regressed and correlated on academic computers. But even an analysis of work and family would miss what is perhaps the most important of the principles of upward mobility under capitalism—namely, faith.

Banfield understood this moral dimension better than he comprehended the role of families. One of the reasons why *The Unheavenly City* missed the importance of family structure, perhaps, was an earlier study Banfield had made of a completely stagnant Italian village riddled with nuclear families but devoid of faith.[11] Here the devotion to the interests of the family was so short-sighted and fanatical, fears of the future so paralyzing, and mutual suspicions so rife that all group endeavor failed, making impossible the kinds of large-scale organization necessary to a modern economy.

From his Italian experience Banfield developed a theory, anthropologically very dubious, that extended families represent an advance over nuclear ones. As nice as they are, extended families without a core of nuclear responsibility tend to thwart economic development. But Banfield amply proves his central theme: that family alone will not suffice.

Banfield has arrived at that point, eventually reached by every profound explorer of social and economic life, at which an appeal is made to a higher morality. He identifies it with secular concepts such as cooperation, public spirit, and long time horizons. Adolph A. Berle, contemplating the contrast between prosperous and dominantly Mormon Utah and indigent, chiefly secular Nevada next door, concluded his study of the American economy with the rather uneconomic notion of a "transcendental margin,"[12] possibly kin to Leibenstein's less glamorous X-efficiency and Christopher Jencks's timid "luck."[13] Lionel Tiger identifies this source of unexplained motion as "evolutionary optimism—the biology of hope,"[14] and finds it in the human genes. Ivan Light, in his fascinating exploration of the sources of difference between entrepreneurial Orientals and less venturesome blacks, resolved on "the spirit of moral community."[15] Irving Kristol, ruminating on the problems of capitalism, sees the need for a "transcendental justification."[16] They are all addressing, in one way or another, the third principle of upward mobility, and that is faith.

Faith in man, faith in the future, faith in the rising returns of giving, faith in the mutual benefits of trade, faith in the providence of God are all essential to successful capitalism. All are necessary to sustain the spirit of work and enterprise against the setbacks and frustrations it inevitably meets in a fallen world; to inspire trust and cooperation in an economy where they will often be betrayed; to encourage the forgoing of present pleasures in the name of a future that may well go up in smoke; to promote risk and initiative in a world where the rewards all vanish unless others join the game. In order to give without the assurance of return, in order to save without the certainty of future value, in order to work beyond the requirements of the job, one has to have confidence in a higher morality: a law of compensations beyond the immediate and distracting struggles of existence.

The nuclear families of Tuscany lacked this faith, and the polygynous company of Mormons possessed it. This faith sustained the overseas Chinese, working for years far from their wives. This faith roused and inspired thousands of American blacks in the pits of the Great Depression, when under the auspices of "Father Divine" they launched hundreds of successful businesses in America's inner cities. Between 1933 and 1937 God, Inc., as its eponymous leader called his effort, became Harlem's leading landlord, operated innumerable groceries, ran ten dry cleaners, sponsored twenty or thirty hucksters selling vegetables, fruit, and fish "at evangelical prices" from small wagons, and managed a coal business shuttling trucks between New York and Pennsylvania.

Meanwhile the group also sustained similar enterprises in Newark, Jersey City, Bridgeport, and Baltimore, and fed thousands of wholesome ten-cent meals—and even more free ones—to near starving blacks. Divine's Lieutenant Faithful Mary headed a kitchen in Newark that prepared food for some 96,000 people in one depression year. By 1953, when, unhappily, Divine absconded in ungodly circumstances, his empire embraced "peace garages," construction and painting firms, tailors, furriers, hotels and photographic studios, and an employment service for domestic servants.[17]

The employment service brought thousands of Father Divine's "angels" to serve in the kitchens and nurseries of white families in downtown Manhattan. Two of these domestics, Gratifying Love and Ezekiel, once took me, as a boy of eight, to Harlem, to visit the divine sanctum, appointed in ivory and velvet, and I fell to my tremulous knees before His then empty throne.

Father Divine is known as a fraud. But if God works in mysterious ways, and if the Black Panthers are to be praised for giving breakfasts to little school children, after extorting them from terrified small grocers, Father Divine deserves the gratitude of many, for giving meals and meaning to the lives of some million blacks. He demonstrated conclusively that blacks, like every other group in America's cities, can create and sustain enterprise even when their families fail. Faith, in all its multifarious forms and luminosities, can by itself move the mountains of sloth and depression that afflict the world's stagnant economies; it brought immigrants thousands of miles with pennies in their pockets to launch the American empire of commerce; and it performs miracles daily in our present impasse.

In general, however, upward mobility depends on all three principles—work, family, and faith—interdependently reaching toward children and future. These are the pillars of a free economy and a prosperous society. They are being eroded now in America by the intellectual and political leaders of perhaps the freest and most prosperous of all the world's societies.

CHAPTER 7

The Entrepreneurial Future

MOST CRITICS of capitalism now accept the crucial role of entrepreneurs in the earlier stages of the system. In their view, however, the nations of the West are now undergoing a vast and irreversible historic change. Driven by the imperatives of modern science and the growing scarcity and pollution of natural resources, capitalism is seen to be entering a new, "mature" phase. In this phase, so it is said, innovation and growth are elicited only by large bureaucracies: by corporations and government bodies, in various licentious but fruitful combinations, which leave no room for the individual inventors and investors of the past.

Financed more and more by their own cash flow and commercial paper, run by professional managers and technicians, largely beyond the control of stockholders or boards of directors, spreading their operations around the globe, modern corporations are seen as great multinational leviathans that require ever growing governmental power merely to keep them in line. The fabled entrepreneurs, cranky financiers, and small-scale inventors of early capitalism are regarded to be a dying breed, unimportant in the new world economy, the new industrial state.

This is the essential position propagated continually by John Kenneth Galbraith and his followers, and there is enough truth in it to disguise its essential falsity. Galbraith is right, for example, on the existence of a large commercial technostructure, somewhat divorced from the direct control of its owners. Modern corporations do have some sway over their own demands, are at least partly capable of fixing prices, and to some degree do give rise to countervailing powers and complementary services of government. Galbraith is also right that this sector of business, bestriding world markets and increasingly facing the subsidized competition of government firms abroad, is extraordinarily efficient and should not be broken up by the sweeping enforcement of antitrust laws against bigness itself. Galbraith's mistake is to follow Schumpeter—who knew better when he was a young economist rather than an aging Cassandra—in predicting the withering away of the entrepreneur. Galbraith, Schumpeter, and their many followers among world economists mistakenly believed that the technostructure would inevitably expand its sway over the economy and be assimilated by government in a socialist future.

These analysts see that the large corporations of "the planning sector" tend to be more efficient and productive than the small ones of "the market sector." Thus they predict that the planning sector will eventually dominate the entire economy and merge with government in a socialist state. Many economists welcome this development as both inevitable and good, subjecting the immense productivity of the technostructure to social control and making possible the creation of a less wasteful and anarchic system.

Such a prediction has been made by some eminent pundit every five years or so ever since the Industrial Revolution. But the theory springs from an error so simple and familiar that any schoolboy should be able to avoid it. The prophets of socialism are making static observations of dynamic phenomena. At any time in the history of a reasonably mature economy, the largest businesses will tend to be the most efficient. That's how they became large. They benefit from economies of scale and specialization. But only someone viewing the economy as a system of statistical quantities could imagine that size is the crucial fact about successful companies. That is like supposing that the crucial fact about professional football teams is huge stadiums filled with people yelling and drinking beer. The crucial aspects of big companies are not quantitative but qualitative: the nature of the product and the mode of manufacture and marketing.

In general, big companies have attained, in the jargon, a position near the top of their Kuznets curves: a place on the slowly rising upward slopes that follow the steep ascent of creative development in the slanted "S" (⌒) of business evolution. Successful firms typically start slowly as they make their initial investments in a new product, then enter a period of very rapid growth as markets are developed and productive methods are perfected. Finally they reach a stage of routinized mass production. In any economy, only a relatively small number of large companies ever arrive at this final phase, looming over the national and world economies. These firms have found such efficient ways to make their product that few competitors can arise. Invariably they dominate their fields, which tend to be old markets for relatively routine products. Their great efficiency derives from many years of making the same thing and incrementally improving it and perfecting the means of producing and selling it.

Such companies have become highly rigid and specialized, and in static terms, greatly productive. Many of them are now experiencing a new lease on life in the international realm. But from the point of view of overall economic growth and technological innovation, these leviathans are of little importance to the economy. They are efficient now only because they were dynamically inefficient and competitively aggressive during their earlier phases. To treat these companies as the epitome of a progressive economy and call for the launching of more of them is like urging the creation of a professoriat full of best-selling elder statesmen like John Kenneth Galbraith, rather than looking for hungry young economists of the sort represented by the tall young author of the little noticed *Theory of Price Control* in 1952.

The Left is also misled in the assumption that the largest companies are increasing their dominance of the economy. Government tax policies have done their best to deter innovation and promote mergers, creating a capital blight in which smaller companies that were attempting to expand suffered most throughout the 1970s. Nonetheless, both the top fifty and the two hundred largest manufacturers have failed to enlarge their share of nonfinancial assets or manufacturing shipments since 1937.[1] Reports to the contrary chiefly reflect the growing foreign assets of these companies as they struggle with subsidized national corporations in the ever more competitive world arena. There is no evidence that the large companies are squeezing out small entrepreneurs. The number of annual small business starts has increased from 93,000 to 450,000 since 1950, without any long-run rise in the proportion of failures.[2]

The root of the peculiar leftist perspective is not difficult to find. The prophets of a transition to socialism almost always seek the future by peering resolutely at the obsolescent. Just as Marx focused on industrial conditions that were already passing away at the time he wrote, the contemporary scholars focus on processes of production and organization that are rapidly undergoing change.

In analyzing the nature of modern technological progress, for example, they tend to neglect the most dynamic industries. They ignore the surge in informatics and telecommunications and the myriad new energy technologies. They pay little attention to the revolutionary developments in microbiology, the breakthroughs in the production of glass products, the innovations in copying, printing, and photography. The emergence of laser science, new diagnostic devices, and antiviral pharmacology play no significant role in their theories.

Reading the industrial analysis of the Left, in fact, one might believe that miners, migrant workers, and assembly line laborers in textiles and steel were the exemplary figures in the future economy of capitalism. Galbraith even presents to our view, as his prime example of new technology, the launching in 1974 of "what is now called," as he says, "a new automobile!" The futuristic thesis of *The New Industrial State* is actually founded on Ford Motor Company's nearly last gasp with a gas-guzzling car, the Mustang, at a time when automotive markets were about to turn swiftly toward smaller and more efficient vehicles. Ford's laborious adjustments in its plant are relevant only as an essay on the sclerosis and stagnation of huge corporations.

The theory of the Left applies chiefly to firms at the top of their S-curves of growth: the time when innovation dwindles and heavily bureaucratized companies seek minor new adaptations, packaging changes, and manufacturing efficiencies in order to wring the last gains of productivity from an essentially static industry that has already long passed its phase of "fast history." The American automotive industry had shaken itself down to three huge and immensely productive companies by the late 1930s, and neither rankings nor products have substantially changed since then. The big opportunity for a new breakthrough that arose in 1974 was not the Mustang, but the possibility of finding new ways to satisfy environmental standards. But the American companies left that chance to the Japanese and the Europeans. Instead of meeting the new requirements by developing new and better engines, the U.S. big three, under the shortsighted prodding of the Environmental Protection Agency, adopted the catalytic converter, which reduces some pollutants without requiring significant change in the engine itself.

It may be that this decision was inevitable. The auto companies had devoted themselves for so long to running the perfect industrial system for building and marketing a specific kind of automobile, based on internal combustion, that they were incapable of adapting to change. At the very pinnacle of productivity, they had lost all room to maneuver.

Burton Klein's brilliant book, *Dynamic Economics,* maintains that new developments almost never emerge from the leading companies in an industry. Even when a breakthrough is made at a large corporation (such as the transistor or photovoltaic solar cells invented at Bell Labs), the new item is usually launched commercially by smaller businesses, often started by breakaway teams of engineers and managers from the parent firm. Just as none of the carriage makers and buggy whip producers could create a salable automobile and the gaslight and candle businesses neglected the promise of electricity; just as new companies arose to dominate each of the new phases of aircraft and air-engine development; just as Kodak failed to pioneer the instant camera and the slide rule people at Keuffel and Esser succumbed without response to the hand-held calculator; just as IBM lagged behind other companies in adopting most major innovations in business machines, from copiers to word processors; and as even Texas Instruments finally became relatively rigid and uncreative in the microprocessor field, Ford and General Motors, whatever their marketing ability, could not be expected to jeopardize their established plant and equipment by radical changes in technology until other companies had proved them out. Indeed, it was a motorcycle company, Honda, that first created a car that could meet the emission standards without a catalytic converter.

Klein shows that this pattern of leadership lag applied, in varying degrees, to all fifty of the key twentieth-century breakthroughs he studied.[3] The very process of rationalization and bureaucracy by which a company becomes the most productive in an industry tends to render it less flexible and inventive. An exclusive preoccupation with statistical productivity— simple coefficients between inputs and outputs—can lead to a rigid, and in the long run, unproductive economy.

Nearly all of what Galbraith says about the nature of modern technology conflicts with our recent experience of it. While the professor chatted with Bob McNamara and Walter Murphy about the doings at Ford and GM, imagining himself to be right at the futuristic center of things in the "new industrial state," a real industrial revolution was, in fact, massively erupting behind his back. It happened in hundreds of smaller companies, led by men whom he had never met or heard of, and some of whom, stepping from university laboratories and scientific libraries into the vanguard of modern industry, had probably never even heard of him. These were the boffins, the callow geniuses of the semiconductor and microprocessor revolution, turning the world's most common matter, the substance of sand, into an incomparable resource of mind: a silicon chip the size of a fly, with computing powers thousands of times greater than a million monks adding and subtracting for millennia—an infinitesimal marvel that extends the reach of the human brain incomparably further than oil, steel, and machines had multiplied man's muscle in the industrial age.

There is no way to fathom the full potential of this technology, now in its Promethean infancy. In conjunction with other advances it is already transforming the world of work and forging at last the long predicted age of computers, just as the steam engine and the railroads inaugurated the industrial age. It is possible to disparage this development and to deride its enthusiasts, to point to the inevitable problems and to fantasize chimerical threats of "dehumanizing" machines and Frankensteinian robots. But this technology, coolly considered, bears no such menace at all, while it offers, to nations that pursue its promise, gains quite incalculable, even by the machines themselves.

The microprocessor shares an explosive logic with certain crucial technologies of the past, those transforming inventions—the printing press, the clipper ship, the steam engine, the electric generator, the railroad, the automobile, and the telephone—that transfigure an economy and extend the dimensions of the world. Like these key technologies, the microprocessor does not operate within the confines of the existing industrial structure, but makes possible a new one.

Unlike nuclear energy or jet propulsion or, debatably, television, for example, the chip does not simply improve an existing capability or create a self-limiting industry. It creates radical new capabilities applicable in all industries, including its own, making possible a vast diffusion of applied knowledge and technical logic. It effects a simultaneous animation and miniaturization of machines, making them cheaper, more portable, flexible, adaptable, powerful, systematic, self-adjusting, dependable, laborsaving, and energy efficient, and it multiplies and redistributes the means of production, possibly reducing the need to travel and restoring the home to its role as an industrial center. If small is beautiful, that mandate is fulfilled not chiefly in windmills and solar cells, but in California's vale of cubistic new factories across the bay from San Francisco—Santa Clara's Silicon Valley where worlds indeed unfold in grains of sand.

Anyone who predicts the technological future is sure soon to seem foolish. It springs from human creativity and thus inevitably consists of surprise. One can only point to the manifest powers and potentialities of a new development. Its applications will transpire in a complex interplay with other new or now undiscovered technologies, in ways that remain unfathomable. Perhaps the best reason for confidence in the future of the microprocessor is that it is, in a sense, a "breeder reactor," creating its own fuel of knowledge. It is not only a product but also a producer of science; not only a result of technical progress, with multifarious industrial and commercial uses, but also a uniquely fertile source of further progress in every field, from astrophysics to medicine, if not perhaps in economics.

This fabulous breakthrough is of little interest to most American liberals, however, except as an occasion for dolorous and surely false reflections on the computer's threat to individuality or for equally unfounded alarms about automation as a cause of unemployment. The entire history of economic progress attests to the fact that productivity simultaneously frees and empowers individuals and multiplies jobs and professions. Needless to say, material gains do not assure moral, spiritual, or aesthetic values or otherwise relieve the deeper predicaments of man. But if one is to traffic as an expert on technology and the economy, one must come to terms with the silicon chip.

The failure of the Left is quite understandable, though, for this development casts the gravest doubt on their predictions for the economy. If they had been right in their theory of the bureaucratization of invention and enterprise, the computer revolution presumably would have been launched by the leading computer company, imperial IBM, or at least by *one* of the leading computer companies, probably in league with government. Instead the revolution was started by a second-rank camera firm, Fairchild, was developed by scores of new businesses led by strikingly unwithered and unbureaucratized entrepreneurs, and achieved its crucial breakthrough in 1971 at a tiny firm, Intel. This company contrived the microprocessor just three years after it was formed with a staff of twelve, including the directors, Robert Noyce and Gordon Moore, and the inventor, E. H. Hoff. Five years later it was the world's leading producer of the devices, with eight thousand employees, from Silicon Valley to Singapore.

Washington bureaucrats—well primed to be panicked by good news from reading the ostrich school of liberal economics—see a giant firm, such as IBM, both as the epitome of innovative technological enterprise and as a dangerous monopoly. IBM is indeed the world's most resourceful and creative *big* company. But it largely missed out on the most important development in its field; it fumbled in its copier confrontation with Xerox, Kodak, Savin, and others; and it faces a continuing siege of trenchant competition from firms as small as Cray Research, which dominates the field of high-potency scientific computers, as large as Exxon, which has entered the fray in business machines through its subsidiary, Vydec, and as dynamic as Wang Labs and Digital Equipment, which already lead IBM in several areas of office apparatus and are advancing into others from their headquarters near Boston's Route 128. At the same time, IBM's old-line rivals in selling large mainframes—Control Data, Burroughs, NCR, Sperry Rand, and Honeywell—show few signs of fading away, and they have been joined by new ventures, however embattled, like Amdahl, and now a tiny firm called Cambex.

All this is not to deny that companies like IBM play an absolutely vital role in both the national and world economies. Large corporations both consolidate and rationalize the gains of others and act to countervail, as Galbraith himself showed long ago, the powers of other large firms, and even of the government itself. As *Forbes* magazine has observed, "[M]ore than the Anti-Trust Division of the Justice Department, it is IBM that breaks up existing monopolies."[4] Not only did it challenge the dominance of Xerox in the copying business and compete resourcefully against a series of state monopolies in nations around the world, but IBM has moved rapidly into the field of satellite networks and is now embroiled in a fierce rivalry with American Telephone and Telegraph in the realm of long-distance communications.

A possible danger is that the great publicity that always attends a battle of the titans will lead a new generation to accept the prevailing illusion that huge corporations form the cutting edge of most new technologies. Communications satellites aside, there is no evidence that technological development has fundamentally changed to favor large firms. (Large firms were needed in certain applications of old technology, too, particularly in transport and communications.) Indeed, the microcomputer may have exceeded previous breakthroughs in the number of small companies that contributed to it and the intensity of competition that continues among them in exploiting its new applications.

Barry Commoner, who cannot imagine anything good without the hand of government, has theorized that this industry was made possible in 1962 by large government purchases of integrated circuits (advanced transistors).[5] But by 1962 there were already scores of companies making semiconductor products and hundreds of patents had been awarded. Governments very rarely launch innovations. Even the space program failed to invent any new technology; its achievements were almost entirely based on the state of the art ten years before. Government laboratories have for many years been the most sterile part of the American scientific establishment, often more obstructive than creative of new technology. In 1962 the government somewhat accelerated semiconductor advances by buying a militarily useful product created by the private sector. But the industry was already irrepressibly on its way, in the same multifarious and highly competitive form that attended the early stages of the automobile industry before its thousands of machine shops were consolidated and the Big Three emerged to administer its less dynamic phases.

There is substantial evidence, moreover, that the microcomputer industry is not a special case, an exception to the essential modern rule of bigness and bureaucracy. On the heels of the microprocessor are coming two other new technologies, in lasers and microbiology. Both of them offer great but still largely undecipherable potentialities. The microbiologists are creating new organisms that may produce insulin, interferon, and hormones, clean up oil spills, and manufacture alcohol or other energy products, among many other possibilities. Lasers are already useful in many ways, from newfangled light shows, to construction measurement, and conceivably fusion energy. Both new technologies are still chiefly in the hands of scores of young scientists and entrepreneurs, pioneering in the classic way of capitalism, as Schumpeter celebrated it in his earlier works and even nostalgically described it in retrospective pages of *Capitalism, Socialism, and Democracy.*

Such entrepreneurs are fighting America's only serious war against poverty. It is small and high-technology businesses, not firms like Chrysler, that generate most of the employment in America. During the past decade, businesses on *Fortune*'s list of the one thousand largest companies have experienced virtually no job growth at all and have undergone a 26 percent decline in the real value of their equity. Meanwhile between 1969 and 1976 smaller firms created 7.4 million new jobs, nearly four times as many as the government.[6] A study for the Commerce Department showed that "young high-technology companies" have been growing in employment at a rate of 40 percent annually, about thirteen times faster than "mature firms."[7] In addition, small firms provide more than 80 percent of the jobs for young blacks and other "disadvantaged" citizens.[8]

Recent decades have seen a boom in entrepreneurship in America, with new businesses accounting for the vast majority of new jobs during that period. Even unincorporated businesses have experienced greater gains in asset value during this period than have the leviathans. The 1978 cut in capital-gains taxes, engineered by the late Congressman William Steiger of Wisconsin, has prompted a new surge in venture capital. In "Silicon Valley"—already the home of hundreds of new companies— more than a hundred new firms emerged in 1979 alone, and the pace of new business formations continued to accelerate into the eighties.

All these creative activities embody the same gift and genius of capitalism that was exhibited by the *mumis* in primitive tribes; by the traders in England and Holland, who elaborated a world market; by the venturers of the industrial revolution, who reshaped the possibilities of mankind; and by the pioneers of American enterprise, who launched the greatest capitalist economy. But the potentialities of invention and enterprise are now greater than ever before in human history.

The question, as the eighties began, was whether these possibilities would be fulfilled in the United States and assure U.S. leadership in the world economy or move to other countries in Europe and Asia. Some of the most creative industries, from semiconductor products to communications satellites, generate huge needs for capital, and no major capitalist country was creating savings so slowly and wasting them so wantonly as the United States. Many of these industries need a favorable regulatory climate, managed by men who are capable of comprehending the promise and complexity of modern science. Yet the United States was taxing and harrassing successful businesses more than any other capitalist country, regulating them as if they were dangerous conspirators against the public interest, and requiring new firms to offer impossible proof that their products cannot be abused.

Japan, once far behind in the microcomputer field, was saving at a pace almost six times the U.S. rate and making vast investments in microelectronics and other research and development. Most European countries were also exceeding the United States in both savings and research and development. As a result, the Japanese were moving toward the lead in microprocessor memories and Europe was making rapid gains in pharmacology and nuclear power, while the United States squandered resources on failing auto companies and worried about windfall profits in the increasingly capital hungry oil industry, a supreme national asset in an era of energy shortages.

Nonetheless, in the late 1970s in America entrepreneurs were bringing the forces of the future to a new prominence on the nation's stock exchanges. Most of the attention of press and public was focused on the continuing saga of a declining average of Dow Jones Industrials—thirty huge companies, led by General Motors and AT & T, whose equity value has collectively plummeted in real terms since the late 1960s and rose a nominal 4 percent in 1979. But meanwhile the smaller stocks, though scarcely running wild, rallied steadily since the crash of 1974. The Value Line Composite Index of some 1,675 stocks returned to its highs of the early 1970s, rising some 140 percent since 1974 and decidedly exceeding the rate of inflation. The American Exchange, with its mass of energy stocks, grew 260 percent since its 1974 low and rose 63 percent in 1979 alone. The largest index of all, published by the Wilshire Associates of Santa Monica, and covering nearly the entire universe of U.S. equities, rose in tandem with the Dow between 1974 and 1977 and then kept going up, even in real terms, while the Dow plunged. During 1979 the Wilshire Index rose 20 percent, to 1056, higher than it was in 1973 when the Dow reached its all-time high.

As a fully weighted measure, the Wilshire is heavily influenced by the Dow companies; it takes hundreds of small stocks to counteract a downward plunge by Exxon or IBM. Yet the needed hundreds, and thousands, of smaller firms did indeed emerge and rise up. As the U.S. economy moved into the 1980s—with portents and predictions of doom abounding in the world of the dominant firms and government bureaucracies—the smaller companies and their followers were issuing a defiant claim that the future can be mastered. As the world mobbed the markets for gold, these companies raised the banner of human creativity and new technology as the way to triumph over the trials of the day.

To fight inflation, they offered products with declining real costs. To increase productivity, they presented devices that vastly magnify the efficiency of men and machines. To protect the environment, they produced items that neither pollute nor employ scarce material resources. To conserve energy, they offered products that use scant fuel either in manufacture or operation, but which yield great energy savings and efficiencies for the entire economy. Many successful high technology companies, moreover, even economize on capital. As Warren Brookes has pointed out, their essential resource is ideas and men. These firms require about half as much capital formation per worker as heavy industries like autos and steel.

These new firms will inevitably triumph in the long run. But whether they can fulfill their promise to relieve our current problems in time depends largely on politics—on whether the dominant powers will allow the future to prevail, whether the politicians can comprehend the value of free men and free wealth. As the 1980s began, with the bailout of Chrysler and the imposition of new taxes on energy, the politicians were suggesting that they could not trust anything they could not predict and control.

CHAPTER 8

The Clashes of Class

DEMOCRACY is a system devoted to the expression of the sentiments and interests of the people—or, more precisely, as Chesterton put it, the views of that "small and arrogant oligarchy of those who merely happen to be walking about" at the time.[1] The interests and sentiments of the majority—the children of the future and our ancestors in the past—are little consulted. This inevitable limitation on the suffrage, as a result of the mere accidents of birth or death, does not distress many of us.

A more serious restriction on the fulfillment of our ideals arises from the character of the incumbent public—the people who, as the case may be, "happen to be walking about," or lurking in shadows with drugs and dangerous weapons, or conspiring to bomb the new federally financed school buses. Our ideals of liberty and equality and peace and comity have inspired the world. But the attempt to enforce them in detail will always founder on fallen flesh and blood, on the slow procedures of politics, and on the sure resistance and parochialism of family and community.

The goal of perfection may invite efforts to impose it on imperfect humans by means of compulsion and through the agency of undemocratic power. Inevitably failing to fulfill the impossible dream of a society without conflict and hierarchy, the supposed idealists often lash out at the very attitudes and institutions—social pressures and legal processes—that are indispensable to all social improvement in a democracy. Idealists, for example, always much abominate what they call hypocrisy. But hypocrisy—the insincere profession of unfulfilled ideals—is the means by which the influence of ideals is extended beyond the small circles of true believers. Hypocrisy is indeed the tribute paid by vice to virtue. A society that often and heavily exacts this tribute has arrived at one of the two most humane and beneficial forms of redistribution (the other is capitalism). Hypocrisy might also be described as manners or exalted as civilization. These are the ways of social sublimation: the means by which we at once protect one another from the rough edges of a perennial social struggle and indicate our hopes for something else. Hypocrisy can make us better than we are.

The mask of manners and hypocrisies grows necessarily densest in the realms of money and sex, where the edges of the struggle are the roughest of all. Norman Podhoretz observed in his important autobiography, *Making It,* that money has become the "dirty little secret" of American life, surrounded by as many taboos and proprieties as sex in Victorian society.[2] Steven Goldberg has made a similar claim for the superior aggressiveness of males, universally manifest in life, crime, and culture, but everywhere denied as a prime mover in the relations between the sexes and in the work place.[3] One might object that there remain plenty of "dirty secrets" in the realm of sex as well. There is, for example, a nearly complete taboo both on telling the sad truth about homosexuality and on discussing the sexual inferiority of males.

Yet Podhoretz is correct in stressing the money taboo as a central fact of capitalism. There are few rules of etiquette so firm as the ban on boasting about salary and income or on confessing the financial spurs and influences in our behavior. Because money so profoundly and intimately shapes the prospects of our lives, our position in the community, our attractiveness to friends; because money is a primary index of value in capitalist society; because it is the key arbiter of status, to flaunt our riches is to assert our superiority in a way beyond easy appeal. And never do we brandish our wealth so rawly as when we declare it means nothing to us, that "it's more trouble than it's worth," that all we really want is a nice home, good schools for the kids, a loving and understanding wife, time for reading and fishing, good health care, and "interesting work." In other words, we want it all, and to be one of the boys as well. We want to have everything, including freedom from the envy of others. But it can never be.

Confusion on these points often arises from failure to distinguish between men and women. Money is far more immediately decisive in the lives of men than of women, and women often fail to understand what is at stake among men at work. The man's earnings, unlike the woman's, will determine not only his standard of living but also his possibilities for marriage and children—whether he can be a sexual man. The man's work thus finds its deepest source in love.

Women are valued for their intrinsic worth far more than men. Men, most fundamentally, are measured by their performance of the role of provider and if they fail in it, there are few easy appeals to other criteria of success. But in accord with the crucial proprieties of capitalism, only other criteria are explicitly applied. She leaves him because "he drinks too much" or "we grew apart" rather than because he earns too little. He leaves her because of "incompatibility" rather than because her job is better than his and destroys his male role or because he has become rich and fantasizes he can recover his youth by remarriage to a younger woman.

Of course artists, cultural connoisseurs, pretenders to hereditary distinction, amateur athletes, public officials, members of Mensa, and sexual exhibitionists all make strong claims for other standards of status. But the very variety of the other claims, however valid they may be, merely mitigate the primacy of finance. Few intellectuals, indeed, can deny the rough trenchancy of the jibe: "If you're so smart, why aren't you rich?"

One response to the social pressures of money is a tendency by everyone to pretend to be "middle class" and from a "modest" background. This hypocrisy, for all its usefulness in softening envy and conflict, has the further effect of distorting many people's views of the very nature of the society. At Harvard, for example, an investigator will have to search far and wide to find anyone, beyond the offspring of Arabian royalty, who will admit to being wealthy, let alone "upper class." One mode of disguise is ethnic: Irish, Italians, Jews, Poles, and other "minorities" who collectively outnumber, and per capita much outearn, WASPs, all often posture as aggrieved outsiders scarcely free of Ellis Island, regardless of their objective standing in the economy. Andrew Greeley, the respected Jesuit sociologist, remains hot under the collar about "Boston Brahmins who look down their noses" at the Irish. *The Wall Street Journal,* Senator Daniel Patrick Moynihan, *The New York Times,* and other voluble institutions periodically denounce "discrimination" against Catholics, the most successful large religious group in the country, earning substantially more per capita than white Protestants.

White Protestants themselves, sometimes with trust funds or other pending moneys, claim to suffer like sharecroppers for being "black sheep" in their families, and thus presumably hardly even white. A morbid hatred of parents becomes a symbol of virtue, and a sign of sympathy for the wretched of the earth. Of course, many of the best-educated, most privileged, longest-living, healthiest, most socially esteemed, and financially secure of our citizens—holding the bulk of the nation's wealth and property—can parade themselves as members of an oppressed and disadvantaged underclass simply on the grounds of being female.

Nearly all politicians, athletes, business leaders, and other celebrities tell the inquiring reporter that they spring from impoverished and ethnically embattled stock. This is always true, inasmuch as nearly everyone in the world was poor in comparison to present-day American standards (and still is, for that matter), and even the WASPs at various times in their history have been embattled and beaten down by Romans, Danes, Frenchmen, and other invaders. In general, however, the "modest" backgrounds turn out, as in the celebrated case of James Earl Carter, to be wealthy in relation to any pertinent standards.

To put the claims of poverty into perspective, it is useful to remember that any American family earning more than $25,000 in 1979 was in the top fifth of all American households, and 60 percent of them made it only by having two or more earners. Any American family with a total income more than $35,000 was in the top tenth.[4]

The vast majority of Americans would seem abjectly poor to the average professor or student at a major American college, or to a poverty official at HEW (or HHS), or to a television producer anywhere. Applying "middle-class" (actually upper-class) standards to the realities of American life, both academic sociologists and federal officials create "poverty lines" or "moderate-income budgets" and estimate "essential human needs" and requirements for "decent" housing or employment—and entitlements to "adequate" income and dignity—that cannot possibly be fulfilled by more than a minority of hard-working and self-sacrificing families. Poor families who receive comparable value from welfare and other programs, plus time for leisure or undocumented work, are in fact getting a package of benefits as valuable as a middle-class job. They will seem hopelessly poor, however, to the middle class, because welfare fosters a slovenly and improvident way of life.

Such misconceptions are particularly acute in relation to jobs. There has been created a serious problem of youth unemployment. But the kinds of jobs that the average liberal bureaucrat or college professor regards as suitable for poor youths—entry-level work in relatively attractive circumstances, paying enough to support a family, and promising promotions and other benefits without any particularly arduous labor, overtime, supervision by domineering bosses, or other unpleasantness—scarcely exist for anyone (as professionals' sons and daughters are now discovering, often to their great surprise and sense of betrayal). The kinds of jobs that are expected by the average young upper-class college graduate— male or female—jobs granting autonomy, room for self-expression, lack of submission to higher authorities, and, most of all, adequate (that is, top one-fifth) pay are the objects of the most fanatical, even if carefully disguised and buffered, competition. They can be won only by those who are willing, with whatever artful grace or resort to discrimination suits, to compete fanatically. Many of these jobs, moreover, depend on subsidies earned by various disdained "wonks" and "workaholics" in regimented businesses and taxed away in a spirit of "distributive" justice by lawyers working for the government.

Like aristocracies in history, the current officialdom seeks a moral justification for its objective exploitation of others (in this case, businesses). Many in government-supported jobs try to suggest that commerce consists largely of rounds of martinis, golf, and collusions in restraint of trade. Contrary to all the fantasies of the affluent society and its leading beneficiaries, however, there is no such thing as an unenvied and uncompetitive upper-class job (and almost all professionals, by any standard of income, are really upper class in America).

The widespread incomprehension of such truths leads to broader social costs. Among the most noticeable is a corrupt and destructive egalitarianism in politics. Rather than redistributing their own money, the rich all too often discharge their sense of guilty unease by assuming postures of moral hauteur expressed in demands for a general redistribution of wealth. They support various policies that chiefly inhibit the emergence of new wealth without significantly threatening their own. College professors, paid mostly in leisure time and other perks, are in the forefront of the movement to "redistribute" other people's earnings of money (but when the IRS threatened to tax free tuitions for faculty children, the outcry shook the marble walls of Washington).

A more serious peril of denying the prevalence of economic motives is a tendency to ascribe far more importance to other influences than they deserve. Many of the apparent manifestations of racial and ethnic prejudice, for example, are in fact expressions of economic class—the natural reluctance of higher classes to expose their children to lower-class values. The problem of integrating the races and classes in America can be summed up in one principle: the more successful a society is in achieving equal economic opportunity, or so-called meritocracy, the more separate tend to be its economic classes. Integration and equal opportunity are inherently conflicting goals. There may have been more commingling of the races in Southern slave society and more association of different classes in medieval feudal England than there is in contemporary America.

When social status is settled or largely beyond challenge, rich and poor can live in close proximity without tension. But when men have comparable opportunities to achieve wealth, people tend to associate with their own economic class. In a society of rapid social mobility, all but the most supremely rich know they can plummet down, and the poor know that their condition is to a great degree their own fault or choice. The rich know, too, that the lowest classes have little to lose in challenging the claims of wealth. In order to escape such tensions, economic classes will seek out their own kind, whenever possible, and send their children to schools dominated by their own economic class. This rule applies with near perfect equality to liberals and conservatives, blacks and whites, senators and judges, socialists and libertarians. It is violated chiefly by unmarried youths (I myself long considered it chic to live in slums), and by families who are willing to sacrifice the interests of their children in order to increase their own disposable incomes. In most instances of serious court-ordered busing to schools in the inner city, the only white children who remain in the program are from broken families who lack the means or concern to make other provisions. Nearly all upper-class and many middle-class families, no matter how liberal their politics, send their children to private or safely middle-class public institutions.

By a strange "populist" twist these families are now charged with "hypocrisy" for failure to live by their integrationist ideals. They respond, with supreme irrelevance, by citing the presence of upper- or middle-class black children in the school. The presence of suitable blacks, in fact, has become a crucial asset of the best urban private schools—like soccer or classes in Latin—as if it were the race rather than the class of blacks that accounts for middle-class resistance to integration.

The real point is that it is highly moral and fully beneficial to the society for people to make sacrifices for their children. Nowhere is the continued vitality of families more dramatically expressed than by the inspiring willingness of millions of American parents to scrimp and save to assure a safe and disciplined education for their children. Moreover, this willingness is the highest sign of social responsibility. In their efforts to educate their offspring as best they can, whatever the cost, these families are making a major investment in the future of the country, in the human capital on which coming generations will depend, and on which currently child-free couples will rely for their pensions and social security.

What is reprehensible is the simultaneous effort of some liberals to force lower middle-class families, who love their children no less, to dispatch them to ghetto schools dominated by gangs of fatherless boys bearing knives. Racism has nothing to do with any of these attitudes. The worst thing that liberals do is depict as racist the desire of parents to protect their children from the schools that liberal policies have largely ruined, and that black parents flee as rapidly as white, and that liberal parents would themselves no more accept for their children than submission to the white slave trade. Integrated schools are desirable. But success cannot possibly be achieved without acknowledging the prevailing facts and functions of class.

These realities are customarily treated as "hypocrisy" and "prejudice," but they are crucial to the maintenance of a culture of upward mobility and economic growth. If a capitalist system is to expand, it must give social and educational rewards and reinforcements to "middle-class" discipline and morality. This means that successful families must take care in choosing their associates and those of their children. This process helps the poor by creating a distinctive culture of upward mobility which they may emulate, and it helps the rich by transmitting upper-class disciplines to their children. The breakdown of these disciplines hurts all classes.

Many a wealthy youth has been mulcted, blackmailed, sued, or otherwise afflicted for his noble impulse to flee his "stuffy" forebears. Many a wealthy ingenue has been fleeced and flummoxed by entrepreneurial admirers. Many a lower-class drug habit has been financed by rich kids desperate to be accepted as "one of the boys." Many a wealthy neighborhood has been robbed by the "friends" of generous teenagers with a *nostalgie de la boue.* Parents who fail to warn their children of these pitfalls and to protect them from them—who profess a morbid egalitarianism of leveling down rather than summoning up—should not be surprised if their children end up in the lower class.

For the upper classes to accept and pander to lower-class behavior is to betray the lower class and assign them to permanent poverty, erode the requirements of growth and opportunity, and foster processes of cultural and economic deterioration. Only people who have already made it can afford the self-indulgent styles of lower-class life.

Government housing policy suffers from the same illusions about the roles of money and class that bedevil educational policy. As any real-estate agent will tell you, with little exaggeration, the three decisive factors in housing values are "location, location, and location." The chief criterion of a good location, sad to say, is distance from the poor, most particularly from the broken welfare families that produce the bulk of America's violent criminals. Housing values—and particularly their potential for appreciation in an inflationary era—are the main assets of every middle-class community and are virtually the only assets of the lower middle class. This housing often is of no great inherent physical value; without upkeep such a community can become a slum in six months. The worth of the housing derives from the social values and disciplines of a familiar community and access to schools that are not dominated by the lower class. From this housing, moreover, are cantilevered out great wings of debt, accommodating automobiles, color televisions, and other consumer durables. Even a decline in the rate of appreciation of housing may drastically shake the very economic foundations of the American middle and lower middle classes.

To the upper-class (that is, the "middle-class") officials at the Department of Housing and Urban Development, these facts are seen chiefly as the effects of "racism" and thus irrelevant to policy. The two key goals of HUD are class and racial integration and the provision of "decent" homes for the poor. Housing in a welfare community, however, is never "decent." Because welfare clients receive their apartments free and value them commensurately, and because ghetto streets are full of fatherless youths, welfare housing is invariably "bad housing." Decent housing is an effect of middle-class values, not a cause. The housing of the poor can only be made "decent" by selling it to the nonpoor—that is, by the process disdainfully known in the halls of HUD as "gentrification."

The other prime housing goal of government is racial integration. This would be virtually no problem at all if it were not combined with the goal of class integration, which on any large scale is impossible and undesirable. Black government officials can live wherever they like, and indeed the movement of wealthy blacks into supposedly exclusive suburbs has been proceeding without much notice for the last decade. But the movement of welfare blacks into the communities of middle or lower middle-class whites or blacks is an act of social disruption, particularly if done by the subterfuge of rent or mortgage subsidies. These policies are self-fulfilling prophecies of racism. In a housing market distorted by rent controls, affirmative action, and other devices, the middle class, in defense of its chief financial and social assets, takes the safest course—hostility to all government projects threatening the neighborhood.

In the process, many apparent opportunities arise for journalists and TV reporters to "prove" the false liberal hypothesis that racism still prevails in American society. What prevails in the United States and in every other country—and notably prevails within the liberal and bureaucratic intelligentsia from the moment they have children—is the desire for economically homogenous communities, where there is no fear of being robbed, mugged, or balefully resented. In the context of HUD's impossible ideals, the only nonracists turn out to be those urban families who refrain from "burdening" the world with progeny.

The ideal of a homogenized egalitarian society has also obscured the continuing triumphs of the American "melting pot." Perhaps the metaphor would be less confusing if it were rendered in the plural. There are, in fact, as many melting pots as there are communities, and they are still transforming floods of immigrants into American citizens and bearers of American culture. With the possible exception of some Hispanic groups, whose disabling isolation is persistently fostered by HEW's bilingualism, the United States during the 1970s continued to assimilate its new minorities, including—in a major historic development—the latest generation of Chinese, Japanese, Filipinos, West Indians, and many Puerto Ricans. Intermarriage between members of these groups and native Americans has become increasingly frequent.

There is no alternative to assimilation in modern society. To reject the concept of a melting pot is to consign the continuing masses of immigrants to picturesque poverty—or seditious factionalism—in new American ghettos. Our precious diversity of ethnic cultures and communities will persist as new immigrants come to our shores and older immigrants give ceremonial tribute to their forebears. But cultural diversity does not mean rigid ethnic parochialism. The only effective form of segregation in modern-day America is the refusal of HEW to insist on literacy in English as the prime goal of education; it is a separatist technique more destructive than any system of Southern schooling. *E pluribus unum* must still be the theme of our social enterprise.

This theme is not merely a disguise for what is called "cultural imperialism." The United States is now dominated not by the WASP ethos but by an eclectic national culture. As Harvard's West Indian sociologist Orlando Patterson has written, even the English language has been irretrievably taken from its creators and "been adapted in a thousand ways to meet the special feelings, moods, and experiences of a thousand groups." Similarly, black jazz is "no longer a black American music,"[5] but the music of the universal culture of America; basketball is an expressive vehicle for the best in black athleticism; and pizza is as American as apple pie or chop suey. All are part of the American melting pot, as vital an ideal as ever. But as always it will continue to render not a smoothly homogeneous American gruel, but a rich and varied stream of national history and consciousness, with a dominant note of "middle-class values" and upward mobility.

All the studies of occupational mobility in America acknowledge that change is considerable over two or three generations. It is only by focusing on a single generation that the notion of sluggish movement can even be entertained. Yet the redistributive ideal, in its necessary implication that parents and families should be allowed to have little influence on the fate of their children, is, if one considers the consequences, altogether monstrous. It is a call for the repudiation of social history, ethnicity, religion, even gender (since in this view sex, too, should have no effect on earnings). The implication of the studies is that society as a whole is the only legitimate collectivity, that it should comprise a mass of amorphous individuals of nearly random endowments, performing almost randomly. Ethnicity and cultural diversity are always affirmed in a ritual way—as in the phrase "our cultural diversity is a great national asset"—but then it is effectively dismissed, except perhaps for clothing styles and dance steps, since this national asset, however great, is forbidden to have any significant impact, even on such impressionable matters as ambition and income.

The irony of this position is that the influences that the egalitarians would vitiate—home, family, church, and ethnic community—are, in fact, the only influences that work. The day-care centers, schools, and poverty programs that might replace them are mostly ineffective in promoting upward mobility. The egalitarian program is capable of destroying families and communities, taxing away the earnings of the successful, and penalizing ambition and productivity, but it is not capable of fostering upward mobility among the groups that lack strong community and familial cultures. It is no novelty, though, to discover that levelers can lend upward mobility only to the administrators of the leveling bureaucracy.

To justify these futilities, a truly perverse hypocrisy—a tribute of virtue to vice—is arising. While the usual hypocrisy consists of the insincere profession of unfulfilled ideals, the hypocrisy of secular socialism entails the insincere attribution of evils. American society is described as racist, sexist, exploitative, and corrupt, not because it is, by any relevant standard, but in order to vindicate sweeping new powers for government and its messianic new class. Its members discharge their repressed spirituality in millennial programs for the restructuring of all human life—from sex to economics—while living private existences of quite conventional motivation and character. This kind of hypocrisy has become something of a national disease: intelligent people, who know better, denouncing their fellows for crimes against humanity.

This attitude is conspicuous even in what, at first glance, would seen an unlikely place—the church. Under the stress of secular culture, many clerics suffer a loss of faith, undergo the most acute pains of unbelief, and compensate by issuing militant demands for secular redemption. The crisis of democratic capitalism is perhaps most peculiarly manifest in the religious institutions that disdain the concerns of spirit and instead seek to satisfy spiritual hungers through the barren intensities of radical politics. The church sometimes joins the academy and the state in an effort to overcome the clashes of class through a war against wealth.

CHAPTER 9

The War Against Wealth

ONE OF the little probed mysteries of social history is society's hostility to its greatest benefactors, the producers of wealth. On every continent and in every epoch the peoples who have excelled in creating wealth have been the victims of some of society's greatest brutalities. Recent history has seen, in Germany, the holocaust of Jews; in Russia, the pogroms of Kulaks and Jews; in northern Nigeria, the eviction and slaughter of Ibo tribesmen; in Indonesia, the killing of near a million overseas Chinese; in China itself, the Red Guard rampages against the productive; in Uganda, the massacre of whites and Indians; in Tanzania, their expropriation and expulsion; in Bangladesh, the murder and confinement of the Biharis. And as the seventies drew to a close, much of the human wealth and capital of both Cuba and Southeast Asia was relegated to the open seas.

Everywhere the horrors and the bodies pile up, in the world's perennial struggle to rid itself of the menace of riches—of the shopkeepers, the bankers, the merchants, the traders, the entrepreneurs—at the same time that the toll also mounts in victims of unnecessary famine and poverty. Everywhere nations claim a determination to "develop"; but everywhere, too, their first goal is to expropriate, banish, or kill the existing developers. At the United Nations, these contradictions reach a polyglot climax, as voices rise with alternating zeal against the blight of want and against the Americans and Zionists, creators of wealth.

There is something, evidently, in the human mind, even when carefully honed at Oxford or the Sorbonne, that hesitates to believe in capitalism: in the enriching mysteries of inequality, the inexhaustible mines of the division of labor, the multiplying miracles of market economics, the compounding gains from trade and property. It is far easier to see the masters of these works as evil, to hunt them as witches, favored by occult powers or Faustian links.

The fantasies take a lurid turn in the minds of the mob. A French sociologist tells of the furies called forth as recently as the 1960s by a group of Jewish dressmakers who opened shops in a small town in Provence. How could their prices be so low for fashions so elegant, for styles of Parisian design and grace? It must be a conspiracy. They were selling drugs, it was muttered at first; then darker rumors arose. Two young women left for Paris. They were victims of the white slave trade, it was said, and the dressmakers were its front! A mob gathered and stormed and burned the shops to the ground. Amid the smoldering ashes, the proprietors presumably reflected on the strange profits of efficient enterprise.

In American cities this mode of thought appears in milder form in the inevitable rumors surrounding any prosperous Italian businessman ("he is in league with the Mafia"), and in the notion that any thriving Chinese restaurant or laundry is a conduit for the opium trade. A convict once told me, with complete assurance, that everyone in his prison knew for a fact that John D. Rockefeller had acquired his money as a member of the gang of Jesse James, for which Standard Oil served as a convenient cover. The ideal that all wealth is acquired through stealing is popular in prisons and at Harvard.

Edward Banfield in his book, *The Moral Basis of a Backward Society,* maintains that this attitude is a crucial characteristic of an undeveloping economy.[1] In the small town in Italy that he studied in an effort to understand the sources of poverty, every businessman was assumed to be cheating his employees, every priest to be filching from the plate, every politician and policeman to be on the take. A teacher justified his laziness by confiding that the only use of education was to better exploit the poor. Any signs of prosperity were taken as evidence of peculation or crime. Needless to say, in such a town few such signs appeared.

In the American inner city, the suspicion of wealth arises still more virulently, with anti-Semitic overtones but ecumenical fire and plunder when the electrical power goes out. Orde Coombs has written poignantly of the schism among blacks that yawned over the rubble of the New York riots of 1977.[2] Two young black businessmen had opened a store to sell stylish fashions in Harlem, expecting to be happily received by their "brothers." Instead, their shop, though extremely successful, was frequently vandalized and finally burned during the long night of darkness and torches despite conspicuous signs in the windows telling of black ownership. The resentment of riches apparently emerges without regard to race, creed, or color, though it helps of course when the pogroms begin, to have a clearly identifiable class of victims.

Whether the controlling sentiment is racism or envy, throughout human history it has been deemed more respectable to hate another race or tribe than to hate the wealthy or successful. Most group resentments therefore took on an ostensibly ethnic character. But these expressions of the usual xenophobia did not often break out into ravages of mass violence unless the resented group also happened to be economically visible. Behind the scenes, moreover, one can often find the native wealthy trying to deflect hostility away from themselves and toward the competition of aliens.

In the past this strange struggle has often enlisted the services of lumpen intellectuals, contriving gothic rationales for racism and pillage: inventing tales of cabalistic Jewish financiers, conspiracies of Oriental shopkeepers, peculiar collaborations of usurious moneylenders. In more recent times the fashion has turned decisively against ethnic prejudice, which remains socially acceptable chiefly among the poor. But hatred of producers of wealth still flourishes and has become, in fact, the racism of the intelligentsia.

Replacing the ethnic conspiracy theories, therefore, have been fantasies that envisage a whole predatory system of oppressors—plutocrats, robber barons, bankers, speculators, bourbons, oil monopolists, establishments, nabobs, exploiters, imperialists, with, as an occasional fillip, a family of Rockefellers so potent as to seem an entire ruling class in itself. From this general animus and in this essential idiom arises much of the dense scholarship and obsessive polemics of Marxism. But whether crude or labyrinthine, seasoned with ethnic resentments or elaborated in computer printouts, the intellectual case against the rich reflects the same dumb disbelief in capitalism that seethed on the streets of Harlem and Provence, the same incomprehension of the mutality of gains from trade that has always animated the hysterias of protectionism, the same fantastic belief that the real cause of poverty is, yes, wealth! As young Abby Rockefeller, the most eloquent of radicals in the younger generation of the family, once put it: "The idea that riches and poverty were interwoven, that one fed on the other, that the many suffered because of the few; that good and bad fortune were inextricably linked—this was new to me. It was compelling."[3]

Wealth causes poverty—an idea to conjure with, an idea that has burst like blinding sunlight in the mind of many a young radical and still shines brightly for all who seek some alternative to hard work, inequality, thrift, and free exchange as a way of escaping want. How much easier it is—rather than learning the hard lessons of the world—merely to rage at the rich and even to steal from them. How much simpler than diligence and study are the formulas of expropriation! Property is theft. Hate is community. Violence is freedom. Reality is oppression.

Yet everywhere these ideas prevail, poverty persists and spreads. Rather than wealth causing poverty, it is far more true to say that what causes poverty is the widespread belief that wealth does.

It is thus an important irony that a chief American source of this impoverishing creed—much the same sad system of beliefs that Banfield detected in his backward society—is the public establishment of ideas: mainly through government officials, academic social scientists, and media leaders, with their theories of poverty focused on blacks. Blacks are told that the world is against them; that the prevailing powers want to keep them down; that racism and discrimination are ubiquitous except under the order and surveillance of the law; that jobs are unavailable in business; that slumlords gouge their tenants; that policemen are to be assumed guilty until proven innocent of bias and brutality; that Martin Luther King and the Kennedy brothers were killed by the white establishment; and that the only allies of the young black are the poverty lawyers, social workers, employment counselors, liberal politicians, and other agents of the state. If the average black fails to get the message through direct instruction, he can encounter it again on television, as each narrative tells a story in which the ultimate villains nearly always wear expensive suits, live in penthouses, work in the sleek office towers of corporate businesses, and hold their positions chiefly by benefit of violence and chicanery.

Such a view of the world had some remote validity in rural Italy, as depicted by Banfield, where the few local businessmen did seem corrupt and the Mafia preyed. But in the United States what this image of a racist and venal country achieves—just as surely as in Italy, the image of a corrupt and immobile society—is to incapacitate all of the poor who believe in it. Upward mobility is at least partly dependent on upward admiration: on an accurate perception of the nature of the contest and a respect for the previous winners of it. If we tell the poor that the system is corrupt, racist, and partly ruled by violence and can be beaten only through the attainment of college degrees and civil-service credentials, we give them a false and crippling view of society.

The fact is that the United States is probably the most mobile society in the history of the world. The virtues that are most valuable in it are diligence, discipline, ambition, and a willingness to take risks. Education and credentials are most important in government; elsewhere most skills are learned on the job. The best prospects for uneducated blacks are in small firms, where dedication and hard work serve better than any other assets. Although fewer Americans are self-employed than in the past, most of the decline derives from the eclipse of the small farmer. Some

400,000 new small businesses are started annually, and they provide over 80 percent of the new jobs for young blacks. In the thirty years between 1946 and 1975, unincorporated firms in America achieved a net of 500 billion dollars in capital gains,[4] realized or unrealized, after inflation, an amount greater than households earned in the stockmarket by a factor of twenty. Business is not only the best route to wealth in America; it is almost the only route for those without education. In business, moreover, the sky is the limit.

Why, then, is a contrary vision so popular in government and the media, in education and social service? One answer is that the picture of a static society of little opportunity and scarce room for risk and initiative—except for the corrupt and the predatory—is highly congenial to the offspring of the American upper classes who were taught to disdain business and have had to come to terms with secure but uninspiring jobs in bureaucracy. In choosing to eschew the great risks and great opportunities of enterprise in favor of work in government or the nonprofit sector, in the arts or education, or even in some of the professions, many millions of Americans gave up any real prospect of winning great wealth. Those from once upper-class families thereby accepted a career trajectory likely to run far below the pinnacles of their forbears. They made a deal with society, exchanging the possibility of great achievement for the assurance of security, and the solace of leisure and limited demands. It was not necessarily an unworthy exchange, but it left them reluctant to confront the spectacle of hundreds of thousands of sons and grandsons of immigrants moving into the commanding heights of the American economy; it left them loath to acknowledge that these usurpers are surely forming a new American upper class, consisting largely of Jews, Italians, Irish, Orientals, Germans, and Poles, many of short heritage on these shores.

This reluctance to come to terms with the new American social reality also has a darker side. The great secret of the American gentry is downward mobility. It is not discussed much when gather the scions of the displaced upper class. But it is everywhere in the air. Rich people who inherited and attempted to husband their wealth through the last five decades tended to see most of it wither away. Many who lived off of capital found their capital dwindling rapidly and their income from it shrivelled by inflation and taxes. Many saw their children enter the professions and live moderately and well. But then they had to watch their grandsons grow hair to their shoulders, drop out of expensive schools financed by disappearing family wealth, and dabble with careers in art and carpentry, interspersed with unemployment checks, before they grabbed a briefly open slot in a government bureaucracy from which to instruct the poor on the ways of upward mobility.

The best route to negotiate the rapids of the American capitalist economy over the last decades has been to own or work for a business in a
sector of growth, usually serving consumers directly or working with
advanced technology—firms small and large in insurance, real estate, fast
foods, retailing, electronics, computers, and energy. Such a position allowed one to benefit from incomes that rose with the price level, to
gain nonmonetary perquisites that one needed because of inflation, to
hide salaries as unrealized capital gains in small proprietorships, and to
hold assets that appreciated rapidly. Instead the American upper class
tended to eschew technical training and to alternate financially between
conservative securities that declined in value, bank accounts that sunk
with the rising price level, and occasional desperate gambles on "growth"
stocks purchased at their pinnacle. And whatever they did, most of them
did it far less well than the largely Catholic groups who, lacking inheritance and "culture," studied science and machines and entered business.

Hence all the usual upper-class caricatures of the new rich. Hence the
references to corruption and chicanery as the prerequisites of wealth.
Hence a refusal to believe that intelligence, resolution, hard work, and
a willingness to take risks are all it really takes to succeed in the American
economy. Such a belief would call all their cautions and credentialed
choices into agonizing question.

Yet the displaced upper classes did do one thing that the new ones
did not. They mastered the art of communication. They got elaborately
and expensively educated. They therefore had influence on the prevailing
imagery out of all proportion to their numbers. The result is the peculiar
American sense of defeat, propagated by the media and government and
communicated to the poor at a time of unprecedented opportunity and
mobility in our society.

The war against the rich thus continues in the world's wealthiest country. It is a campaign now led and inspired by the declining rich, to arouse
the currently poor against the insurgently successful business classes.
By their communicative skills and social refinements, the defecting upper
class can exert influence and mobilize support far beyond their own numbers. They can dominate the media and the foundations, the universities
and the government, all the secure but ultimately unenriching havens
for those who refuse to enter the real arena of upward mobility—the
businesses that are necessarily the prime source of wealth in still capitalist
America. The victims, though, of the war against wealth, even when
they are inveigled to join its ranks, are always and inevitably the poor,
the ones who still need a mobile society. The declining rich of all ethnic
groups are happy to stay put near the top, administering ideological benefits for those below and adopting the fashionable image of a progressive
"new class" to disguise the reality of the old class in decline.

PART
II

The Crisis of Policy

CHAPTER 10

The Moral Hazards
of Liberalism

"HE WILL not go far who knows from the first where he is going." So spoke Napoleon as he launched his brilliant, tempestuous, and catastrophic career from Versailles via Moscow to St. Helena's Isle. A heroic spectacle for a man, perhaps, but a less inviting trajectory for a nation. Countries in their foreign affairs cannot afford to learn by doing, cannot easily earn the rewards of enterprise and experiment; they must have a good idea of where they are going or they may end in catastrophe.

A central role of statecraft is managing and assigning risks. Politics is in great degree a science of insurance. In the international realm, leaders of great peoples must act with caution, for there is no effective insurer of nations, no policy for Napoleonic, much less nuclear, wars. But in its domestic affairs the state must take equal care to balance insurance with risk. The individuals and businesses of a society cannot know too well where they are going—outcomes cannot be excessively preordained—or the economy will become too inflexible to prosper in a world of uncertainty. Individuals may feel secure under such a failsafe system of comprehensive insurance (of incomes, jobs, equality, demand, health), but the entire society will suffer the grave and often irremediable risks of a failure to adapt to change.

At the same time, too much risk and uncertainty in domestic affairs will destroy the feeling of faith in the future that is the foundation of capitalism. Indeed, in capitalist systems the desire for security has often been as important to enterprise as the spirit of adventure. The heroic efforts of enterprise often begin in the humble pursuit of safety. These two impulses lead on the one hand to saving and on the other to investment. Though an identity in the national accounts, these two activities—setting aside funds for the future and purchasing productive assets—spring from different motives and are often performed by different persons and institutions. Investment embodies the risk impulse and savings the desire for insurance.

Perhaps the central secret of capitalist success is its ability to convert the search for security, embodied in savings, into the willingness to risk, embodied in enterprise. The financial markets enact this crucial alchemy, turning fear into growth, caution into creativity, timidity into entrepreneurship, and the desire to conserve into the drive to build and innovate. This is a key capitalist industry, processing the abundant raw materials of anxiety about the future into the rare assets of faith in it and provision of productive facilities for it. One role is performed chiefly by an elite of businessmen, the other by millions of savers, but the two impulses are indissolubly linked at the heart of capitalism; they are the systole and diastole of the production of wealth and the circulation of income.

In primitive societies, moreover, entrepreneurial skills themselves are often first applied to the creation of rudimentary insurance systems. Group survival often depends on inventing modes of cooperation in calamities, ways of redistributing the take to unsuccessful hunters, and rules for assigning responsibilities for support in case of death or illness. Acts of thrift in primitive life, as in modern society, are more often motivated by the need to survive trouble than by the desire to invest.

In America those immigrant groups, such as the Jews and the Orientals, with the most developed traditions of cooperation, also proved most able to compete in enterprise. The most lasting effect of slavery on blacks was the destruction of tribal patterns of mutual aid;[1] and when in the late nineteenth century black businesses finally did emerge in number, it was in the form of the insurance schemes of churches and fraternal groups that were later extended into the creation of great companies, such as Atlanta Life and Pilgrim Health and Life.[2]

This is the pattern in all capitalist lands. Insurance is necessary to promote trade. The key to extending markets is trust and credit, and neither can arise without systems to counteract the perpetual threat of ruin from natural disasters. During the first decades of independence, the United States chartered more insurance companies than any other kind of firm outside the field of transportation.[3] Many of the companies specialized in marine policies, indispensable to international exchange across the still perilous Atlantic. Notes written on insured cargoes at sea, which would not be delivered and paid for until months had passed and dangerous oceans had been crossed, were necessary to keep the manufacturer in business in the meantime, to finance new production, and to trade in other goods. Such insured bills of lading and exchange were in fact the prime international currency in the early years of world trade. Similarly, in the domestic economy, mortgages on buildings insured against fire were a crucial stimulus of commerce and construction in housing and a key source of industrial capital. Insurance can cultivate the good faith that is the prerequisite of enterprise.

Even money itself has often been based on insurance. The government promise to redeem paper notes with precious metals—gold or silver— was an insurance policy against a debasement of the currency or a break- down of production and trade. The gold behind the dollar did not consti- tute its worth any more than an insurance policy confers essential value on a cargo, or a house. The worth of the dollar always springs from the productivity of the economy—the goods for which the money could be exchanged; the worth of a house derives from the shelter it affords. But just as maritime insurance was indispensable to trade, life and fire insurance foster commerce in housing by enabling mortgages large enough, extended over a long enough period, to finance a home; and the insurance of gold behind the dollar and pound greatly improved confidence in those currencies and promoted their use in increasingly risky and long-term transactions. The removal of the insurance of gold is an important factor in the loss of trust in the dollar, the decline in savings and investment in the U.S. economy, and the renewed turbulence and distrust in interna- tional commerce.

Enthusiasts of capitalism usually stress the values of risk and initiative and discuss welfare and insurance as if they were alien devices adopted from socialism. But modes of welfare and cooperation have been integral to private enterprise systems at every phase of development, from primi- tive tribal capitalism through the current manifestations of the capitalist welfare state. Charity began at home in the family circle, expanded to the tribe, moved into churches and associated benevolent groups, became routinized in mutual aid societies, paternalistic businesses, unions, and insurance corporations, and finally devolved largely onto the state. Each of these bodies retains an important role in the net of cooperation that upholds the struggles of economic growth.

The health of a capitalist system depends on setting a balance between its insurance features and its risks, between solidarity and competition, savings and investment. Capital can grow no better without cooperation and security than it can without the spurs of risk and rivalry. In striking a balance, moreover, leaders must understand that risk is finally inevitable in a tumultuous world. Government can displace risk—by insuring against its effects on some citizens—but cannot finally escape it. If the insurer state attempts to absorb all risks of individuals and businesses—of unemployment, inflation, foreign competition, waning demand, accident, and disability—it will find itself overloaded with larger perils and responsibilities than it can well manage. The insurer state, like Lloyd's of London, can overreach itself. The fact that, unlike Lloyd's, it can print money to pay its bills can only delay a day of reckoning. The near bankrupt government may even be tempted to consolidate its dangers in war—the one risk that the state can manage far better than business. But the entrepreneurial ventures of a Napoleon ill-behoove the modern ruler.

In the delicate balance between the risk and insurance features of capitalism, the boundaries are defined by what insurance companies term *moral hazard*. Moral hazard is the danger that a policy will encourage the behavior—or promote the disasters—that it insures against. This is the limiting point in insurance schemes and it sets the natural boundary of welfare in a capitalist system. Just as a siege of saving, or hoarding of gold, impelled by a fear of economic trouble, may cause depression by greatly reducing consumer demand, so a siege of insurance can bring about some of the dangers that motivate it.

Even private insurance firms, under the pressure of government to extend their services, are currently suffering from a number of serious moral hazards. Arson has for some years been among America's most popular crimes; most of it is induced by fire insurance. Medical malpractice suits have burdened the entire industry and snarled the services of doctors in red tape, largely because juries rush to award huge settlements on the assumption that insurance will pay. Health insurance has so dramatically raised medical costs—by removing any concern with price from the calculations of doctors and patients—that the residual down payments (the deductibles) often exceed the total payments of the past. Theft insurance is routinely cited by jewelry thieves in defense of their trade. One can presume that life insurance policies have prompted murder—and suicide—beyond the pages of *Double Indemnity*. Retirement pensions everywhere encourage early retirements.

In most of these instances, a pressure is exerted on behalf of the behavior insured against and a penalty is inflicted on the behavior that the insurer desires. People with good health habits pay for the smokers, drinkers, and drug abusers, the neurotic propagators of venereal disease, the reckless drivers, the overeaters, the undersleepers, the slothful and improvident, as well as for the malingerers and the entrepreneurial pursuers of disability claims. People who refrain from suing their doctors over the inevitable disappointments of medical care—or who suffer from exaggerated caution and protective paperwork prompted by the rise in malpractice suits—pay for the excesses of the avidly litigious. People who protect their property and hide their jewelry pay for those who flaunt their baubles.

Policemen who pursue full careers in the service pay for the opportunists who retire after twenty years, just when they are most productive.

Obviously, the problems vary enormously among the different forms of insurance (life insurance, for example, might still be worth the risk of an occasional suicide or murder), but no one can deny that collectively they can have a significant and insidious influence on the behavior of Americans. Even these private insurers, who unlike governments are compelled to base their rates and acceptances on sound actuarial principles, face a serious and growing problem of moral hazard, which regulation is making more difficult to remedy.

The expansion of private insurance also creates externalities—problems that go beyond the immediate effects of the policy. Millions of citizens are coming to believe that their best chance of striking it rich comes not from work and investment, but from suing the successful; not from health, but from opportune disability; not from extended and productive careers, but from timely retirement. Most fundamentally, people experience a steady erosion of the link between conduct and its consequences, effort and reward, merit and remuneration. The moral hazards of private insurance thus may contribute to the declining productivity of the American economy.

Most of these unintended results are less likely under the informal, familial, church, fraternal, and tribal kinds of mutual aid that preceded the emergence of mass insurance. The charities of churches, benevolent associations, extended families, and tribal groups exerted strong moral pressures in favor of preferred behavior. In most cases the providers of aid knew well the recipients of it. In Oriental communities in America these disciplines have worked so well that even in the midst of the Great Depression, only a handful of Chinese and Japanese sought government aid.[4]

Nonetheless, there is enough general truth in the depiction of American society as mobile, urban, individualistic, atomized, secular, and rationalistic that the old modes of private assistance and religious discipline no longer can suffice. The insurance companies drove out the parochial charities, funeral societies, and mutual aid groups by offering much larger benefits at far lower cost, while at the same time extending coverage to citizens of the new international economy and secular rationalist culture who lacked reliable affiliations to church, kin, and community. Where the division of labor was expanded and specialized, new modes of cooperation were formed to accommodate it.

With the New Deal the insurance principle emerged as a commanding theme of federal policy. Government rose to assume collectively for its citizens the risks of joblessness, disability, indigent old age, fatherlessness, and other real hazards of life in industrial society, collecting premiums and redistributing them to the victims of misfortune. But even social security, unemployment compensation, aid for dependent children, federal disability benefits, and many of the other fateful initiatives of the period originated not with the radical Left, but in middle-of-the-road Republican administrations on the state level, and even in the presidency of Herbert Hoover. Dwight D. Eisenhower launched the Department of Health, Education and Welfare in 1953, and Texas Republican Oveta Culp Hobby was its first secretary. These programs achieved their largest expansion not under the Great Society of Lyndon Baines Johnson, but during the administrations of Richard Nixon and Gerald Ford. The insurance principles of the welfare state reflect a strong bipartisan consensus for which the entire American political order, business and labor, Democrats and Republicans, deserve the credit and the blame.

Today the most widely backed extension of the actuarial state—national health insurance—commands the fervent support of the largest U.S. corporations, led by General Motors and U.S. Steel, which currently offer free medical benefits to all their employees including, in some companies, the retired. The president of GM has testified that health insurance costs the company more than two hundred dollars per car, which exceeds its unit profits, and U.S. Steel claims that this burden damages its competitiveness in international trade. If what is good for General Motors were good for the country, Congress should perhaps enact not only national health insurance but also no-fault auto insurance, air-bag mandates, and all the other safety measures that diffuse the costs of automotive risk away from the unlucky victims and the possibly liable companies and onto the only somewhat less unlucky and always reliable taxpayers.

The principle of averaging and equalizing risk informs many policies that do not ostensibly resemble insurance, but which share the effect of spreading the consequences of economic misfortune or change. Antidiscrimination laws, for example, may distribute more fairly and less narrowly the risks of unemployment and low income. Subsidies and tax benefits for the purchase of pollution-control equipment broadly distribute the costs of combating environmental damage inflicted and often suffered by the few. Much of the activity of the Department of Energy comprises an attempt to disperse through the entire country effects of energy scarcity that would otherwise fall most heavily on a small number of vulnerable constituencies. Rent controls attempt to diffuse the effects of urban housing scarcity and rising costs.

The result of all this activity by both the public and private sectors—shifting, diffusing, equalizing, concealing, shuffling, smoothing, evading, relegating, and collectivizing the real risks and costs of economic change—

is to desensitize the economy. It no longer responds so well to the bad news of scarcity and disequilibrium—the high prices that signal new opportunities—and no longer provides so dependably the good news of creativity, invention, and entrepreneurship.

This is the overall moral hazard of the welfare state. But all insurance and welfare programs do not present this problem, and some of them compensate for it by creating an atmosphere of safety more hospitable to long-range ventures and investments. The leaders of capitalism must become more discriminating in appraising the claims and demands, dangers and benefits of the eleemosynary state. It is not an alien presence but the now burly offspring of an essentially capitalist idea.

The moral hazards of current programs are clear. Unemployment compensation promotes unemployment.[5] Aid for Families with Dependent Children (AFDC) makes more families dependent and fatherless. Disability insurance in all its multiple forms encourages the promotion of small ills into temporary disabilities and partial disabilities into total and permanent ones. Social security payments may discourage concern for the aged and dissolve the links between generations. Programs of insurance against low farm prices and high energy costs create a glut of agricultural commodities and a dearth of fuels. Comprehensive Employment and Training Act (CETA) subsidies for government make-work may enhance a feeling of dependence on the state without giving the sometimes bracing experience of genuine work. All means-tested programs (designed exclusively for the poor) promote the value of being "poor" (the credential of poverty), and thus perpetuate poverty. To the degree that the moral hazards exceed the welfare effects, all these programs should be modified, usually by reducing the benefits.

There is abundant reason to believe that the American welfare state long ago passed its points of diminishing and counterproductive returns, that the insurance features of American society now so overbalance the risk features that everyone—rather than just the direct victims of hardship or change—feels anxious and insecure.

During the 1970s the forty-four major welfare programs grew two and a half times as fast as GNP and three times as fast as wages. They annually distributed some 200 billion dollars' worth of grants and services to some 50 million individual recipients. (These totals exclude all social security "insurance" benefits that reflect past payments into the system, plus interest, but include the welfare, or unearned, portion of social security income.) The figures indicate that the average welfare family of four received about $15,000[6] worth of subsidies in 1976 and close to $18,000 worth in 1979. These totals, which are real averages, not extreme cases, compare with an American median income of approximately $14,500 in 1976 and $16,500 in 1979, and annual minimum-wage earnings and benefits of about half the welfare level. Excluding measures focused on the elderly, a resourceful welfare family could get benefits from some seventeen programs, among them AFDC, Medicaid, food stamps and supplemental foods, a variety of social, legal, and child-care services, and an array of housing grants and subsidies.[7] Even overlooking the very important benefits of leisure time and unreported earnings, welfare subsidies in general pose a very grave danger of moral hazards, such as workforce withdrawal, familial breakdown, and other adjustments to the terms of the grants.

Such welfare systems, at levels that heavily influence lower middle-class families as well as the poor, illustrate the famous tendency of "poverty" programs to reach far beyond their mandate. Poor families alone, however, received average benefits that brought them some 30 percent above the official "poverty line," something that could only be achieved by two full-time workers at the minimum wage.[8] Again, the potential for moral hazard emerges clearly. Most of these programs have been expanding steadily through the entire period of economic and employment growth of the late seventies, and they have been creating a sense of dependency in millions of families seemingly capable of self-support. Meanwhile the transfers have imposed a rising burden of taxation on working families, which has provoked a spirit of anger and frustration with American democratic institutions.

The rise of welfare and public-service programs has also displaced other modes of support for the poor and dependent. Before 1935 over half of all welfare came from private charity. Now the figure is less than 1 percent. Before the boom in social security, many children cared for their parents. Now there is evidence that parents are more often induced to care for their needy children on into adult life, as they bear the increasing social security tax. The vast expansion of the state college and university system in the United States has brought only a small increase in the share of GNP invested in higher education, since the rate of private expenditures and their growth dropped commensurately.[9] The defenders of the welfare state at its current level usually seem to assume that without the public systems the sick, the poor, the elderly, and the youth would be left to their own devices; that the welfare state has a massive effect on the condition of the needy, but little impact on their willingness and ability to fend for themselves. Much evidence, however, indicates the opposite: that the programs have surprisingly little beneficial effect, but they do have a dramatic negative impact on motivation and self-reliance.

In recent decades, moreover, the problem of moral hazard has emerged in an even more far-reaching way. The welfare state has been displacing not only private families, charities, and schools, but also private savings and insurance. The diastolic process at the heart of capitalism, whereby the system pulls in the savings that sustain it, has been faltering seriously: savings as a proportion of the GNP dropped to under 4 percent in late 1979, a thirty-year low; and over a five-year period in the late seventies U.S. rates of personal savings stood at about one-fourth the Japanese level of 24.9 percent, only somewhat more than one-third the French rate, and half the rate of even Britain. According to Martin Feldstein, head of the National Bureau of Economic Research, an important cause is social security: low savings are a moral hazard of excessive retirement benefits compared, for example, to those in Japan.[10]

Other analysts question such findings. John Kendrick has developed estimates of *total capital formation,* also for the National Bureau, that indicate a shift of savings from private business to nonprofit and governmental institutions. Including investments in human capital through education, training, basic research, health care, improved mobility, and other "intangibles," Kendrick shows steady real levels of investment ever since 1929, but with a significant shift from tangible to intangible forms.[11] Feldstein's point, though, is that the inadequacy of personal savings manifests itself most compellingly in a continuing high, real rate of returns to savings that is thwarted and obscured by government tax policy. The final test, moreover, comes in economic performance. For all the faults of productivity growth as a statistic, its steady decline—to a point below 1 percent in 1979—confirms a failure at the heart of the American economy.

The larger moral hazard of the attempt to nationalize insurance is to upset the balance between risk and security. Insurance attempts to predetermine outcomes, to assure specific levels of income in retirement, unemployment, family breakdown, sickness—in all the adversities of life. But when too many people know where they are going, the economy doesn't get very far. The particular moral hazards of various policies accumulate into a collective danger of national sclerosis, an economy that is closed to the necessarily risk-fraught and unknown future.

CHAPTER 11

The Coming Welfare Boom

FOR MANY YEARS defenders of welfare have acknowledged that the system was harsh on intact poor families. The answer, it was widely agreed, was to extend benefits to families with unemployed fathers. This was done in twenty-six states and, to the surprise of some observers, had no effect on the rate at which poor families broke down. The reason was clear. As under the guaranteed-income plans tested in Denver and Seattle, the marriages dissolve not because the rules dictate it, but because the benefit levels destroy the father's key role and authority. He can no longer feel manly in his own home. At first he may try to maintain his power by the use of muscle and bluster. But to exert force against a woman is a confession of weakness. Soon after, he turns to the street for his male affirmations.[1]

These facts of life have eluded nearly all the sociologists who have studied the statistics of the welfare family. The studies focus on poverty and unemployment as the prime factors in family breakdown because the scholars fail to comprehend that to a great extent poverty and unemployment, and even the largely psychological conditions of "unemployability," are chiefly reflections of family deterioration. In any multiple-regression analysis, these economic factors will loom largest as causes of family breakdown because they contain and reflect all the other less measurable factors, such as male confidence and authority, which determine sexual potency, respect from the wife and children, and motivation to face the tedium and frustration of daily labor. Nothing is so destructive to all these male values as the growing, imperious recognition that when all is said and done his wife and children can do better without him. The man has the gradually sinking feeling that his role as provider, the definitive male activity from the primal days of the hunt through the industrial revolution and on into modern life, has been largely seized from him; he has been cuckolded by the compassionate state.

His response to this reality is that very combination of resignation and rage, escapism and violence, short horizons and promiscuous sexuality that characterizes everywhere the life of the poor. But in this instance, the pattern is often not so much a necessary reflection of economic conditions as an arbitrary imposition of policy—a policy that by depriving poor families of strong fathers both dooms them to poverty and damages the economic prospects of the children.

In the welfare culture money becomes not something earned by men through hard work, but a right conferred on women by the state. Protest and complaint replace diligence and discipline as the sources of pay. Boys grow up seeking support from women, while they find manhood in the macho circles of the street and the bar or in the irresponsible fathering of random progeny.

The crackdown type of welfare reform attempts to pursue and prosecute these fathers and force them to support their children. But few of these fathers have permanent jobs that they value enough to keep in the face of effective garnishment. Those who do have significant incomes often give money voluntarily to the mothers of their children. But these funds are rarely reported. The effect of child support prosecutions in such cases is usually to reduce the amount of money going to the children by effectively diminishing the welfare allotment and to transform the father's payments from a morally affirmative choice into an embittering legal requirement. He tries to escape this situation as soon as he can. Attempts to force people to work and support their children—when it is clearly against their financial interests and their children's—will always fail.

In the cases of the so-called "love children," born of barely postadolescent fathers or of others passing by, the child-support litigations are equally futile, for the children are really the offspring of the welfare culture of Aid for Families with Dependent Children (AFDC or ADC). In a free society a man cannot long be made to work to pay for children whom he rarely sees, kept by a woman who is living with someone else. Work is not a matter of mere routine but of motivation, X-efficiency as it has been called. The fathers arraigned for child support in the welfare culture typically make a few desultory payments and then leave their jobs or leave town. Some of them enter the world of part-time work for cash, or the more perilous but manifestly manly world of crime. Others eventually get new jobs in the often reliable hope that the computers will not catch up with them again. But the general effect is to add to the perils of employment and marriage.

Work requirements are particularly futile because they focus on women with small children, the official welfare clients, rather than on the unlisted beneficiaries—the men who subsist on the system without joining it, who live off welfare mothers without marrying them. These men are not necessarily fathers of the particular children they happen to be living among. They are just men who live for a while with a welfare mother, before moving on to another one. These men are the key beneficiaries— and victims—of the system. Because the system exists, they are not forced to marry or remain married or learn the disciplines of upward mobility.

There are hundreds of thousands of these men. Their legion is the inevitable counterpart of the mass of welfare mothers who preoccupy all the social workers and reformers. Yet the mothers in general cannot lift their families out of poverty, nor can the social workers. Making the mothers work confers few social benefits of any sort and contributes almost nothing to the fight against poverty. Only the men can usually fight poverty by working, and all the antipoverty programs—to the extent they make the mother's situation better—tend to make the father's situation worse; they tend to reduce his redemptive need to pursue the longer horizons of career.

These unlisted welfare men form a group almost completely distinct from the "able-bodied men" actually listed on the rolls—aging winos, over-the-hill street males, wearied ex-convicts, all the halt-and-lame founderers of the world—who receive money under the general assistance category and are harassed mercilessly during every crackdown. The real able-bodied welfare fathers are almost universally contemptuous of welfare and wouldn't go near a welfare office. In county jails across the land, these men disdain all transitional programs designed to give them aid after release while they get back on their feet. Welfare-based employment programs, like those envisaged in many reform proposals, will tend to miss all the youth on whom the future of poor communities will finally depend.

Even the antifraud efforts, necessary as they are, can have unfortunate results in the context of the welfare culture. The usual way to combat welfare fraud is to compare the welfare rolls—including all listed husbands and fathers—with lists of the holders of jobs, savings accounts, homes, and other assets, in order to find any duplications. This approach can discover several types of fraud. One is the most obvious and reprehensible: the fully employed woman with children who at the same time collects a day-care subsidy and a welfare check, or sometimes several, perhaps even on the basis of false representations of the ages and number of her dependents. This kind of case, though relatively infrequent, always gets lots of publicity and is a great triumph for the welfare investigator. The more usual types of fraud are much more ambiguous. They consist of women on welfare with working husbands. Often these men no longer live with their wives or have anything much to do with them; the wives normally are living with other men. This case of fraud differs from all the legal welfare cases, which also involve absent fathers and new men in the home, chiefly in that the woman made the mistake of once getting married and the man made the error of taking an officially recorded job, buying a house, or acquiring some savings.

The fraud cases, in other words, can often arise among the more honest and ambitious of the welfare recipients, the ones who tell the truth about the whereabouts of their husbands or the fathers of their children, the ones who make an effort to marry or save or accept regular work—the ones, in general, who try to leave the welfare culture and thus come into the reach of welfare department computers. The antifraud techniques necessarily miss the welfare mothers who live and bear children of dubious paternity, with a succession of men working from time to time in the cash economy of the street, or those who dabble in prostitution, sharing apartments with other welfare mothers while leaving the children with a forty-five year old grandmother upstairs, who is receiving payments for "disability" from a sore back.

Indeed, the ideal client according to the computer is a woman with several illegitimate children of unsure paternity who goes deeply into debt and spends all her money as soon as it arrives. This ideal has proved easy enough to achieve for some hundred thousand young mothers in recent years. The efforts to radically reduce the welfare rolls by cracking down on morally unsatisfactory recipients—"shirkers" and "cheaters" and other miscreants whose crimes can bring crowds indignantly to their feet—normally offers a small yield of real offenders but a large number of marginal cases that would take thousands of Solomons to fairly sort out.

No one argues that welfare should not be resourcefully policed. The law must be enforced. But endless injustices and anomalies are absolutely unavoidable in any means-tested system, any system for which one qualifies by showing a low income. There is no such thing as a good method of artificial income maintenance. The crucial goal should be to restrict the system as much as possible, by making it unattractive and even a bit demeaning. The anomalies and perversities become serious chiefly as the benefits rise to the point where they affect the life choices of millions.

As in all insurance policies, it is the level of benefits that determines the moral hazards. Fire insurance, for example, becomes an inducement to arson chiefly when a neighborhood declines to the point where the policy payoff exceeds the value of the housing. Our welfare system creates moral hazards because the benefits have risen to a level higher than the ostensible returns of an unbroken home and a normal job.

Under these circumstances *most* of the cases are fraudulent, in the sense that most of the fathers could presumably marry the mothers of their children and could support them if they had to. But from another point of view, very few cases are fraudulent, since neither the mothers nor their men, in the context and psychology created by the system, could support their children at the levels of "decency" or "adequacy" specified by the U.S. government in its "low-income budget."

For an ill-educated man from the welfare culture to support a family at that level requires delay of marriage and childbearing until after the development of economic skills and then the faithful performance of work over a period of years. These requirements are most essentially moral and familial. The attempt to elicit them by legal pressures while deterring them remorselessly by contrary financial incentives is as hopeless a venture as has ever been undertaken by government.

The most serious fraud is committed not by the members of the welfare culture but by the creators of it, who conceal from the poor, both adults and children, the most fundamental realities of their lives: that to live well and escape poverty they will have to keep their families together at all costs and will have to work harder than the classes above them. In order to succeed, the poor need most of all the spur of their poverty.

By the early seventies, however, a national consensus had been reached favoring a program of "welfare reform" designed to conceal such realities, not only from welfare families but from all American families. A negative income tax was to be established, distributing money to perhaps one-third of all Americans as automatically and comprehensively as the IRS takes it from the rest of us. Poverty was to be abolished by redistribution. Endorsed on various occasions by such diverse voices as Richard Nixon, Milton Friedman, George McGovern, Paul Samuelson, and—above all in eloquent persistence—Daniel Patrick Moynihan, it was an idea whose time had apparently come. But no sooner had the consensus prevailed, so it seemed, than it collapsed.

Senator Moynihan announced, with great courage and simplicity: "I was wrong." Books and articles poured forth, declaring that the present welfare system, for all its manifest faults, was, as it were, "our welfare system, right or wrong," an almost geological feature, one expert described it, with rocks and rills and purpled hills like America itself. "A wonderfully complex array of programs, payment levels, and eligibility rules," wrote Martin Anderson, Ronald Reagan's counselor, "a complex welfare system dealing with the very complex problem of the poor in America."[2] Anderson thought benefit levels could even be raised if work and child-support requirements were stiffly enforced.

Richard Nathan, Nelson Rockefeller's former adviser on the subject and long a high level Republican at HEW and the White House, agreed: no large changes were needed, just marginal reforms. Three liberal professors from the University of California at Berkeley endorsed this view in an intelligent article in *The Public Interest:* "The uniform, efficient welfare system of the economic textbooks is nothing but a mirage. Even the most comprehensive reform will leave a system with many of the current problems, and much of the current public unhappiness."[3] They called for incremental changes only. Senator Russell Long read Anderson's book and distributed it to all members of the Senate Finance Committee, which would have to approve of any reforms; and Senator Moynihan held hearings that finally interred the idea of the kind of guaranteed income which he had often previously acclaimed as "the most important domestic proposal since social security."

Meanwhile, out in Wisconsin at the Institute for Research on Poverty, Irwin Garfinkel, Robert Haveman, and David Beaton of HEW applied their earnings capacity concept to ten different income-transfer proposals, including Nixon's Family Assistance Plan, Wage Subsidies, Child Allowances, and several Negative Income Tax schemes. Running all of them through their computers, the Wisconsin scholars discovered, much to their academically muted surprise, that AFDC was easily the best in its ability to reach efficiently the truly needy poor—that is, the poor who not only lack money but also lack the means to earn it.[4] AFDC had the advantage, it seemed, of excluding most of the college students, trust-fund remitees, semiretired nearly novelists, willingly part-time cabinet-makers, and other potentially self-supporting types who are heavy beneficiaries of any of the purely income-based programs. After all the years of ingenious research and embattled legislation, all the urgent speeches and recriminations, we had ended up very close to where we had begun—with the established welfare system, admittedly much amended, and a resolve better to enforce its provisions.

What had happened was fairly simple and altogether remarkable: two kinds of experiments were conducted and their results were taken to heart. One was a program of reforms applied statewide in California by Governor Reagan. A determined effort to enforce work and child-support rules while increasing benefits to the "truly needy," the Reagan measures were hailed a success by everyone from Nelson Rockefeller to

Jerry Brown. Over a period of two years costs were controlled and the rolls were reduced by four hundred thousand below previous levels and by eight hundred thousand below projected levels.[5] The other experiment—a test by HEW of the impact of guaranteed incomes on work effort and marital stability—took place in several cities and was climaxed by extensive programs in Denver and Seattle.

In this HEW test, income guarantees turned out, in the view of HEW's own contractors, to be a catastrophic failure, reducing work effort by between one-third and one-half and increasing marital breakdown by about 60 percent, compared to a control group largely on AFDC. It was determined that work force withdrawal would constitute between 25 and 55 percent of the real cost of a program maintaining incomes at a level near the poverty line, and that any benefits in reducing poverty would be nullified by the effect of broken marriages in perpetuating it. The conclusion was that a guaranteed income would be far more destructive in every way than the current welfare system.

Because of the amazing capacity of social-science methods to avoid discovering the most obvious facts of work and family, these findings came as a great surprise even to people who had long ago predicted them.[6] Not only had the results of a previous experiment in New Jersey been interpreted in a way that at first failed to show any such effects, but endless analyses of AFDC, made by apparently scrupulous researchers, had also revealed no consistent causal link between welfare and family breakdown and had indicated that a guaranteed income would be beneficial to families. The consensus of social scientists was that unemployment and poverty were the culprits, causing families both to break up and to go on welfare, and that racism and sexism were the chief causes of low incomes.[7]

The findings from Denver and Seattle, though, banished all confidence in the beneficial impact of federal income supports of any sort, whether AFDC or radical reform. Since no one was proposing structural reforms that did not move in the direction of guaranteed incomes, Ronald Reagan's California crackdown loomed as the new hope for a better system.

Most of what Reagan accomplished in California was indeed impressive. By the time he acted in 1971, the rolls had quadrupled in less than a decade, reaching a total of more than five hundred thousand families (2.1 million total recipients) and were still rising by some eight thousand cases a month.[8] Similar upsurges in other states had met with numb indulgence, as in Massachusetts and Michigan, and with feckless appeals for help from Washington, then considering the Family Assistance Plan. Accompanying the bail-out demands, all too often, were foolish posturings. New York attempted to reimpose a six-month residency requirement, though it had already once been ruled unconstitutional and though residency rules have the perverse effect of tying down the poor at the very time they most need to move around in search of jobs.

Reagan instead developed a set of legislative proposals and administrative measures designed to put teeth into the work requirement, remove from the rolls all cheaters or others with adequate income or assets, and search out delinquent fathers and force them to make child-support payments. These actions halted the flood of new applications in their tracks and slowed the growth rate of welfare expenditures from 25 percent a year to 5 percent a year.

Nonetheless, for all its short-run effectiveness, the Reagan program reflected a serious misunderstanding of the welfare problem. After closing the barn door, applying an elaborate system of locks and alarms, after hiring new detachments of police to patrol the premises and bureaucrats to manage the new paperwork, the Reagan reformers, it might be said, set the whole new structure on fire—by agreeing to index the benefits to the rate of inflation. Moreover, they raised the grants for families certified to be truly needy by 43 percent. The result was fine for Reagan, who managed to gain political support to retrench the rolls during the final years of his administration, but the longer-run effects were less appealing.

Governor Brown later asserted that the program was "holding up well." But, in fact, by 1978 California—a sunny state with relatively low living costs and a buoyant economy—was running behind only Massachusetts in the continental United States in the percentage of its budget devoted to welfare, the level of payments to each family, and the amount of welfare spending and number of recipients in proportion to its population. With about 25 percent more cases than economically stagnant New York, California's case load was increasing at a rate that was 40 percent faster, in the face of a far greater welfare bureaucracy, enlarged by Reagan to enforce the new rules. Of course, Massachusetts' rolls, which were expanding at about the California pace when Reagan acted, were growing almost five times as fast toward the end of the decade. The worst approach to welfare is still to do nothing to restrict its growth. But California may well have hit on the second worst approach.[9]

Thus, in the new consensus for "conservative" reforms, is evident the same illusion that was earlier found in the arguments for a guaranteed national income: the mirage of a "good" welfare system, the idea that one can create a "rational" and "compassionate" program that raises truly needy recipients above the poverty line while rigorously excluding the unworthy, forcing fathers to support their children, and requiring all able-bodied recipients to work.

Any welfare system will eventually extend and perpetuate poverty if its benefits exceed prevailing wages and productivity levels in poor communities. A change in the rules can produce immediate cutbacks, as Reagan proved. But in time welfare families will readjust their lives to qualify for what is their best available economic opportunity. As long as welfare is preferable (as a combination of money, leisure, and services) to what can be earned by a male provider, the system will tend to deter work and undermine families. Rigorous enforcement of the rules only means that the families must adjust more and conceal more in order to meet the terms specified by Washington.

This does not mean that welfare families carefully calulate their benefits and deliberately choose to break up, that teenaged girls forgo contraception in the assurance of welfare, or that welfare mothers reject tenders of marriage consciously in order to stay on the dole. All these things may happen; but in the more usual pattern, welfare, by far the largest economic influence in the ghetto, exerts a constant, seductive, erosive pressure on the marriages and work habits of the poor, and over the years, in poor communities, it fosters a durable "welfare culture." Necessity is the mother of invention and upward mobility; welfare continuously mutes and misrepresents the necessities of life that prompted previous generations of poor people to escape poverty through the invariable routes of work, family, and faith.

Above all, by making optional the male provider role, welfare weakens and estranges the prime mover in upward mobility. Unlike the mother's role, which is largely shaped by biology, the father's breadwinner duties must be defined and affirmed by the culture. The welfare culture tells the man he is not a necessary part of the family: he feels dispensable, his wife knows he is dispensable, his children sense it. The combination of welfare and other social services enhance the mother's role and obviate the man's. As a result, the men tend to leave their children, whether before or after marriage. Crises that would be resolved in a normal family may break up a ghetto family. Perhaps not the first time or the fifth, but sooner or later the pressures of the subsidy state dissolve the roles of fatherhood, the disciplines of work, and the rules of marriage.

The fundamental fact in the lives of the poor in most parts of America today is that the wages of common labor are far below the benefits of AFDC, Medicaid, food stamps, public housing, public defenders, leisure time, and all the other goods and services of the welfare state. As long as this situation persists, real family poverty will tend to get worse, particularly in areas congested with the poor.

The battle between the two kinds of "reform," liberal and conservative, then, is largely fake. Neither side is willing to tolerate fraud, both sides advocate largely fraudulent work requirements, and neither side understands the need to permit a gradual lowering of the real worth of benefits—by allowing inflation to diminish their money value and by substituting relatively unpalatable in-kind supports. In fact, both sides are willing in principle to index the benefits to the price level, thus making them yet more reliable and attractive, still more preferable in every way to the taxable, inflatable, losable, drinkable, druggable, and interruptible earnings of a man (not to even consider the female recipient's own potential earnings, which require many hours a month of lost leisure and onerous work). All earnings, moreover, entail the hazards of forgoing Medicaid for the sick, food stamps for the hungry, housing subsidies for the lucky, and public defenders for the unlucky, often needed in the welfare world. The conventional wisdom on welfare has not even begun to acknowledge or come to grips with the implications of this long series of generous and seductive programs.

The Denver and Seattle experiments give what should be shocking testimony to the existing dangers of AFDC. These tests are ordinarily discussed as if their interest was chiefly academic, bearing on the problems of some now utterly unlikely program of guaranteed incomes. But, in fact, AFDC already offers a guaranteed income to any child-raising couple in America that is willing to break up, or to any teenaged girl over sixteen who is willing to bear an illegitimate child. In 1979 there were some 20 million families that could substantially improve their economic lot by leaving work and splitting up. Yet they did not. Three-fifths of eligible two-parent families even resist all the noxious advertising campaigns to apply for food stamps,[10] which they can have merely for the asking. Millions of qualified couples continue to jilt the welfare state. Only in the ghetto, among the most visible, concentrated, and identifiable poor, have the insidious seductions of the war on poverty and its well-paid agents fully prevailed over home and family.

What the HEW experiments showed, however, was that many of the yet uninitiated families are vulnerable to a better marketing effort. They will break down rather readily when fully and clearly informed of the advantages and not effectively threatened with child-support suits. In other words, the test showed that millions of jobs and marriages would be in jeopardy if placed in the midst of a welfare culture where the dole bears little stigma and existing jobs pay amounts close to the welfare level or pay cash untraceable by official investigators.

As serious as existing welfare problems may seem, they are dwarfed by the potential crisis. At present, even among the actual clients of AFDC, only about one-fifth have capitulated to the entire syndrome of the welfare culture. Only 20 percent accept the dole as a more or less permanent way of life. That 20 percent, though, takes some 60 percent of the money.[11] The rest of the beneficiaries dip into the system during a few years of family crisis and then leave it, often never to return. One danger of benefits indexed to inflation is that they will induce increasing numbers of welfare cases to become welfare cultured, with results resembling Denver and Seattle. More recent evidence suggests that this is happening in California, where nearly 30 percent of the recipients appear to be long term.[12]

The more profound threat, however, arises from the current demographic situation. There are three principal trends relevant to welfare: one is a fifteen-year period of declining birth rates; two is the aging of the baby boom generation; and three is the increasing reluctance of the American poor to perform low-wage labor. These trends mean that beginning in the mid-1980s, there will be a long-term decline in the number of workers available to support the increasing numbers of the retired.[13] This development portends a grave crisis for our social-security and pension systems. It is doubtful that work effort will persist if pension taxes rise to double and triple the current levels, even if largely disguised in value added taxes or other concealed imposts.

The solution to this problem, though, is close at hand, looming beyond the shores of the Rio Grande. The current flood of immigration, legal and illegal, will be permitted to join the official economy and replace the unborn workers of the baby dearth, workers who might have paid for the pensions of their elders. It takes no special feat of insight or imagination, or even much scrutiny of Latin American birth rates and economic growth levels, to predict that the current Hispanic minority, which now numbers some 12 million, about half of the black population, will equal it within a decade or so. Whether the Hispanic minority will follow the footsteps of blacks into the welfare culture should be a paramount concern of American domestic policy.

As the seventies drew to a close the portents were dire. Hispanic families, once more stable then black families, retained a small advantage in the proportion of those still intact, but they were breaking down at about twice the black pace. Legalized aliens were moving onto welfare in distressing numbers. Hispanics were increasingly adopting a posture of confrontation with the government, seeking aids and subsidies and minority status, and they were discernibly slowing their movement into business and low-wage jobs.[14]

Even more disturbing was the response of the U.S. government. Rather than learning the clear lessons of the American experience with Indians and blacks—the previous minorities reduced to a state of bitter dependency by government—the Washington bureaucracies were rushing to accommodate the new immigrants within the old formulas of "discrimination" and "poverty". Far worse, HEW adopted, in defiance of the entire glorious history of previous immigrants in America, an utterly indefensible program of bilingual education, which in practice means education in Spanish. At the same time, HEW is issuing requirements that all public documents and forms be translated for Hispanics. These actions simultaneously undermine the group's entry into American life and culture, segregate it in presumably separate but equal classrooms, often run, according to many reports, by anti-American teachers, and open the group chiefly to two influences: Spanish-speaking politicians with an interest in segregation and Spanish translations of bureaucratic social programs.[15]

These approaches together constitute, for Hispanic women, a gilded path into the arms of the welfare state, and for Hispanic leaders, a glittering invitation to a politics of sedition and violence—to a prolonged posture of protest, with a segregated and subsidized captive audience, against the country that seduced their women and left their men without a role.

This is the danger that the welfare culture poses in coming years. It is a danger, however, that can be easily avoided. The necessary steps are clear. Welfare benefits must be allowed to decline steadily in value as inflation proceeds. The Medicaid program, which alone provides a more than adequate reason to remain in poverty, must be amended to require modest payments in all but catastrophic cases. Rents must be paid directly to landlords, who are easier to supervise than hundreds of thousands of welfare clients, most of whom pay their rents only sporadically.

Under the present system, recipients treat their rooms as disposable items, so much residential packaging for their lives of dependency. Moving from apartment to apartment as landlords finally manage to evict them—leaving their quarters in a shambles—the members of the welfare culture tend to consume more housing, in terms of its financial value and depreciation, than does the middle class. This process is as demoralizing for the clients as for the landlords and for the government officials who condone it. It leaves vast stretches of many cities in a state of physical and social ruin. It can be mitigated by paying the money to landlords, a procedure widely used until a federal court vetoed it, or by issuing some kind of rental stamps that are difficult to convert into cash.

A solution to the welfare problem is possible if the essentials are understood. The preoccupation with statistics of income distribution has led to a vision of poverty as the steady state of an inert class of citizens. Social policy is conceived as acting on these persons, but *they* are not believed to act on it—to exploit it in their own interests. For most people, however, poverty is a passing phase, caused by some crisis in their lives.

The goal of welfare should be to help people out of these dire but temporary problems, not to treat temporary problems as if they were permanent
ones, and thus make them so. This goal dictates a system nearly the
opposite of the current one.

The current system, like Harvard in a popular epigram, is very difficult
to get into but relatively easy to stay in. It is of comparatively little
help to people in emergencies. Applicants normally have to wait weeks,
fill out forms by the ream, and submit to prolonged tests and evaluations
before they are finally admitted to the promised land. As a rule, the
more generous the grants, the narrower the gates. The more commodious
the benefits for the qualified recipients, the harder is the regimen for
the unpremeditated poor: the woman newly arrived from afar, the man
who lost his job or lost his wife or suffered a medical catastrophe but
did not choose to sell his home. New York State's welfare program, for
example, is third in the country in the real value of its benefits but,
according to one study, it ranks fiftieth in ease of entry. California is
not much ahead. Both programs create maximum incentives to qualify
for them: maximum rewards for maximum familial strife and disruption.
A sensible program would be relatively easy on applicants in emergencies
but hard on clients who overstay their welcome.

Ideally such a system should be supplemented with child allowances
given to every family, of whatever income, for each child. These payments,
which would be taxable, are designed to relieve the pressure on large
families to become female headed, because welfare is the only income
source that automatically increases as the family grows. Allowances also
reduce the pressure for constant inflationary increases in the minimum-
wage rate, by counteracting the idea that every wage by itself must support
a family. If Moynihan's career in welfare reform yields any clear lesson,
it is that professors in politics should advocate their favored programs
rather than invent compromises supposedly more acceptable to the public.
Moynihan's preferred policy was always child allowances, but he urged
a guaranteed income scheme instead because he thought it would be
more appealing politically to the Nixon administration. The result was
a lost decade of initiatives of little political appeal or objective validity.

Child allowances are currently in effect in most Western industrial
nations, but the system has been most fully developed in France. There
they were enacted as a program to promote large families. The evidence
is that it failed in that goal but succeeded in strengthening all families
and in permitting France to avoid the blight of dependency that afflicts
the United States.[16] Child allowances succeed because they are not means
tested. Because they do not create an incentive to stay poor, they avoid
the moral hazards of the war on poverty while giving support to the

most welfare-prone families. There is no panacea. Overcoming poverty still inexorably depends on work. But in a world where children are little permitted to earn money for the family, payments to those families that nurture and support the next generation represent a social policy with its heart in the right place.

Such approaches to welfare will win their advocates no plaudits from welfare-rights organizations and few perhaps from politicans who enjoy the power of granting excessive benefits to some and cracking down on others. But a disciplined combination of emergency aid, austere in-kind benefits, and child allowances—all at levels well below the returns of hard work—offers some promise of relieving poverty without creating a welfare culture that perpetuates it. That is the best that any welfare system can be expected to achieve.

Welfare now erodes work and family and thus keeps poor people poor. Accompanying welfare is an ideology—sustaining a whole system of federal and state bureaucracies—that also operates to destroy their faith. The ideology takes the form of false theories of discrimination and spurious claims of racism and sexism as the dominant forces in the lives of the poor. The bureaucracies are devoted to "equal opportunity" and "affirmative action." Together they compete with welfare in their pernicious influence on the poor—most especially the poor who happen to be black.

CHAPTER 12

The Myths of Discrimination

ONE OF THE PROBLEMS in dealing with the expanding array of claims of discrimination—reaching far beyond the obvious and paramount victims in American history, the blacks—is that anyone looking for bias can always find it. The persecution complex is a standard psychological ill and its sufferers of every race, creed, and condition have little trouble confirming, to their own satisfaction, their visions of a hostile world.

The last thirty years in America, however, have seen a relentless and thoroughly successful advance against the old prejudices, to the point that it is now virtually impossible to find in a position of power a serious racist. Gaps in income between truly comparable blacks and whites have nearly closed. Problems remain, but it would seem genuinely difficult to sustain the idea that America is still oppressive and discriminatory.

Nonetheless, the liberal imagination has been quite up to the task. Even the very least oppressed citizens—upper-class Jews, millionaire athletes, aristocratic women, wealthy Catholics, patrician WASP scholars, and foreign-service officers—have managed to envision continuous conspiracies against themselves or their generic kith and kin.

When all else fails, aspiring victims resort to vicarious persecution complexes. In recent decades the favored focus of altruistic suffering has been blacks and women. But Hispanics have been making a strong claim for future consideration and arithmetically inclined politicians have noted with interest the ever-expanding numbers of these evident masochists thronging to the shores of oppression.

Vicarious persecution rides high in Washington, where it has occasioned the most lordly feats of enterprise since the age of the "robber barons." The initially tiny Equal Employment Opportunities Commission, once with the relatively small and diminishing purview of offenses against blacks, has diversified with the times and become a mightly conglomerate, combatting discrimination against an array of victims comprising some 70 percent of the population, including the holders of more than three-quarters of the national wealth. In an early confrontation, EEOC brought a major rival in enterprise, the American Telephone and Telegraph Company, humbly to its knees. Not to be outdone, HEW's Office of Civil Rights has contrived a bilingual education program that now assures some seventy minorities their civil right to be taught in tongues, incurring disabilities that will lead to bias suits far into the future. In fact, the politics of persecution is now embodied in a complex of some twenty federal agencies, with tentacles in every state, which, one might say, grow in arrogance and power virtually in proportion to the disappearance of the problem.

But that is not exactly true, for the problem in many instances is not really discrimination at all, but an attitude endemic to the affluent society: that wealth can be taken for granted rather than produced by toil and thrift; that life is supposed to be easy and uncomplex; that its inevitable scarcities, setbacks, and frustrations are the fault of malevolent others; that good intentions should be worth their weight in gold and good credentials should convert instantly into power and glory without sordid interludes of productive competition and struggle; that the world is only superficially awry and can be made smooth and straight and rational by rulings from on high, if only the evil overlords can be removed. This set of attitudes may well arise from visions of abundance everywhere clashing with the reality of human hierarchies that narrow and steepen as they approach their peaks (from which the television images are beamed). But for whatever reason, when the government accepts and propagates the fantasy vision of free goods and teaches people to believe that they are not responsible for their lives and choices, the problem inevitably grows.

Launched to rectify the age old wrongs against blacks, EEOC and the other agencies of equal rights have made some modest but important progress. But now they are rapidly, and in many ways seriously, becoming enemies of black progress. Black men are already a small minority of less than 10 percent in the agency's jurisdiction. It is not nearly as preposterous as it seems to suggest an affirmative-action program in their favor within the precincts of Washington's equal-rights conglomerate, as it turns from its limited minority market of blacks to its teeming majority of women and its inviting growth stock of Hispanics, leaving aside for the moment the handicapped, the ex-addicts and alcoholics, the homosexuals, the aged, the young, and the Indians, all of whom are staking claims in the Klondike of bigotry. Now that courts have upheld mutimillion dollar settlements for victims of bias (more than 67 million dollars, for example, to be divided among a few thousand telephone company employees and millions for unpromoted women at *Newsweek,* NBC, and *The New York Times*), lawyers are crowding forward with statistically tenable victims in tow.

Judges have already overruled the laws of economics in such cases. Salaries are normally determined, to a great degree, by supply and demand. If there is a glut of professors in nursing and a shortage in engineering, the male engineers will be paid more for their "equal" work than the female nursing teachers. In general anyone who accepts a job has agreed to its conditions and pay and in all probability could not find a better combination elsewhere, or he would threaten to depart and the threat would suffice to raise his pay. People who are unwilling or unable to leave will always have to settle for less. If women are less mobile than men because they must live where their husbands are employed, their lower pay for equal work is an effect not of discrimination but of locational preference.

Most of the differences in pay between men and women, though, derive from the fact that women between the ages of twenty-five and fifty-nine are eleven times more likely than men to voluntarily leave work, and the average woman spends only eight months on a job compared to almost three years for a man.[1] Throughout the economy, moreover, men and women alike with college degrees and doctorates, technical fields included, often earn less than plumbers and garbage men and miners and truckdrivers who have high-school credentials at best. Everyone seems to want indoor work with no heavy lifting, but only women nearly always get it, thus driving down their pay. Equal pay for equal work is a principle that applies nowhere, even among men. Even in identical jobs, work effort varies vastly from worker to worker. What EEOC implicitly demands is carte blanche powers over the entire job market and thus the destruction of the vital freedom of workers to choose their own jobs from among the competing offers of employers.[2]

An equal rights effort—even an affirmative action program—was feasible when concentrated on the 10 percent of the American people with real grievances. But affirmative action that potentially involves more than half the work force is necessarily an exercise in futility regardless of whether thousands of women and lawyers are gratified. The victims of this growing mockery are black men who might have benefited from a disciplined program but are now forced to join an undignified queue with such improbable victims as Yale coeds molested by their tutors, ex-addicts denied reemployment, assistant professors at Smith rejected for tenure, and telephone operators who discover, years later, that what they had always wanted was to climb a pole.

Perhaps the most fundamental problem of the equal-rights agencies, though, is the incomparability of persons doing apparently equal work or serving in similar circumstances. Just as the women's basketball coach at the University of Kentucky holds a chair not remotely comparable to the throne established by basketball czar Adolph Rupp, just as any two writers of books may be vastly different in the quality of their product and the market for it, just as Reggie Jackson and Elmore Jackson are both right fielders and Miles Davis and Herman Davis both play the trumpet in jazz bands, just as productivity figures for people doing the same work vary vastly, similar job categories cover a huge range of work performances. Any court proceeding will necessarily miss most of the infinite variety of influences—X-efficiencies, transcendental margins, mundane differences in diligence—that affect the market for jobs and are reflected in a scale of pay. Any government program interfering in personnel decisions will necessarily be arbitrary and unfair.

The offense is serious. It consists in reducing personnel decisions, which normally involve hundreds of considerations reflected in the labor market, to a few key elements—sex, race, and documented credentials—and discriminating massively in favor of these often unimportant factors by excluding all other evidence as hearsay or prejudice. Such bias now distorts the labor market far more than racism and sexism. In fact, it can be shown that bigotry of the traditional kinds no longer plays a significant role in the market for jobs.

In determining a pattern of discrimination, one must begin by setting aside the anecdotes and ethnic jokes often adduced as evidence of American depravity. Although judges have admitted such data in courtroom testimony, even the fact that someone tells an applicant that he has rejected him on racial grounds does not always prove the case. In the current situation it is easier to tell (or hint to) a black or a woman or a white male that he is being categorically excluded than to tell him he doesn't measure up. That was why *The New York Times* and *The New York Post* told Percy Sutton he was rejected for mayor, both by them and by the voters, because the city was not ready for a black, rather than not ready for a lackluster pol. The same is true for the private jokes flaunted as evidence of racism and such. Caricature is a staple of humor, and however crude or unappealing it sometimes is, it reveals little or nothing about the actual behavior of the humorists. Polish Americans were the prime butt of jokes throughout the very period that they exceeded the supposedly discriminating WASPs in per capita incomes. This, of course, is not conclusive proof of an absence of discrimination; it might merely point to its ineffectiveness. But in either case, the government should have no interest in random and ineffectual bias, unless one believes that there are no serious problems more worthy of its concern.

The test of discrimination must come in its effects. To justify the works and powers of the equal-rights conglomerate, one must show a broad pattern of poverty and differential treatment that is best understood as being caused by racism and "sexism." Such discrimination may be defined as a persistent, even if unconscious, preference for white males over blacks and women who seek the job with equal ardor and would do it as well and as faithfully for equal or slightly lower pay. In appraising the arguments, one should begin with blacks, both because of slavery and segregation and because unlike women, blacks do not raise the question of substantial biological differences. There is much evidence that without discrimination, present and past, blacks would achieve earnings comparable to whites. In fact, a case may be made that during the twenty-five years since the massive dismantling of legal barriers against them, blacks have indeed performed far better than other Americans—catching up from far behind and in some categories even excelling the performance of the white majority.

Before appraising the evidence, however, it is crucial to rid oneself of the widespread misconceptions endlessly propagated by public agencies. Much of the difference between black and white incomes simply reflects the fact that the black population is on the average around twenty-two years of age, about seven years younger than the white population, and that half of blacks live in the South,[3] the nation's poorest region in income (though probably not—judging from the winter movements of Northerners—in real standards of living). In any case, families headed by twenty-two-year-olds, white and black, had median incomes approximately five thousand dollars less than families headed by thirty-year-olds.

Blacks in New York earned almost two and one-half times the incomes of blacks in Mississippi, and a third more than blacks in Atlanta. When age and location are held constant, the difference between young black men and white men substantially closes and blacks are found to earn about 80 percent as much as whites of the same age and location.[4]

The remaining gap, the evidence increasingly suggests, relates not chiefly to discrimination against blacks but to earlier discrimination against their parents and to government-induced dependency and female-headed families. These phenomena largely reflect discrimination in favor of blacks by the welfare and poverty programs, which have signed up a twice greater proportion of all poor black families than of poor white ones.[5] This divergence does not arise, however, from conscious discrimination in favor of the black poor (though it may well be that many social workers believe blacks have a right to welfare that would be begrudged to whites). Nor does the difference signify any special white resistance to the dole. Poor blacks are more likely to go on welfare chiefly because many of them are visibly concentrated in inner-city communities, where all the wiles and appeals of the social-service bureaucracies can be focused on them. In nonmetropolitan settings outside of "poverty areas," as the census calls them, black and white poor families have similar proportions on the welfare rolls. The numbers of poor female-headed families of both races began to climb in 1967, with the effective launching of the war on poverty, and it continued to rise through the early 1970s. But because the programs concentrated on the ghetto, female-headed white families among the poor rose by only 20 percent while the black numbers nearly doubled.[6] Since welfare can be shown to intensify and perpetuate the causes and effects of poverty, much of the statistical discrepancy between black and white incomes derives from differential coverage of welfare within the two groups.

All analyses that find high levels of discrimination neglect the fact that creation of female-headed families not only contributes to family poverty, it also tends to explain male poverty. Divorced, separated, and single men of all races work 20 percent fewer hours than married men,[7] and even with the same age and credentials bachelors earn less than 60 percent as much money as husbands and about the same amounts as single women.[8] There are proportionately twice as many black as white single men.[9] If the differences between blacks and whites are corrected for marital status, the gap between the earnings of black and white males of truly comparable family background and credentials completely disappears. Background, of course, reflects past discrimination, and singleness is partly an effect of poverty and unemployment as well as their cause. Discrimination persists to some degree in some parts of the labor market. But it has only a small impact on the relative incomes of blacks and whites.

This thesis is heavily confirmed by the experiences of the offspring of nonwhite immigrants who also faced bias and exclusion into the second half of the twentieth century. Japanese Americans and black West Indians are ethnic groups with harrowing histories of persecution in America and physical features that make them instantly identifiable by the potential discriminator. If discrimination were a key source of poverty, both should be poor. Yet West Indians born and raised in the United States and second- and third-generation Japanese in 1970 exceeded WASPs in median incomes, in years of education, in proportion above the poverty line, and in percentage in the professions. The performance of the second-generation West Indians is particularly relevant since they are presumably indistinguishable from other American blacks. (The chief difference is that the West Indians have darker skins and less white blood.)[10]

There are many examples of American black groups that earn essentially the same incomes as comparable whites. Among doctoral scientists and engineers, blacks earn slightly more than whites; among young two-earner families outside the South, blacks outearn comparable whites; on college and university faculties, blacks with top credentials outearn whites. As the earnings-capacity utilization studies show, such groups tend to work as hard or harder than their white competitors.

The continuing problems of black men do not lie in the upper echelons. Comparisons that fail to differentiate between the high-income scientific doctorates and the lower-income social science Ph.D., between professional engineers and professional school teachers, or between credentials from elite universities and from the valuable but inferior Southern black institutions, will continue to show bias against the most educated blacks. Similarly spurious levels of discrimination will be shown by comparisons that fail to differentiate between the average quality of black and white high-school diplomas, since the Coleman report found blacks to be an average of three years behind whites. Older blacks who attended segregated schools that were open one-third less hours than white schools also earned depreciated credentials. Corrected analysis shows that the black return from truly comparable schooling now exceeds the white return, and that "unexplained" inferior earnings are concentrated among poor black males.[11]

The problem of black male poverty arises at those income levels where AFDC is more than competitive with work. At those levels black men work less hard than white men, although upward mobility is always dependent on exceeding the efforts of the better-credentialed competitors above. This lesser effort, though, is a reflection not of indolence but of singleness. These men lack the motivation conferred by familial demands and the strength imparted by marital support.

It is argued by most observers that female-headed families are a fact of life among the black poor. Since more than half of all black children are raised without fathers (compared to less than 20 percent of whites), it is argued that the best way to help black children is to help their mothers. Whatever the situation of black men, it is maintained black women suffer from double discrimination, both racist and sexist, and require massive aid and affirmative action.

As long as this argument prevails, black poverty will inevitably persist.

Black women already earn 80 percent as much money as black men, while white women earn less than 60 percent as much as white men. Even feminist sociologists now concede that the *independence effect* conferred by high female incomes is an important cause of family breakdown among men and women of all races and educational levels. Any increase in the independence of black women, secured both by welfare and by jobs, will only further expand the appalling percentages of black children raised without fathers.

In addition, there is very little evidence that black women suffer any discrimination at all, let alone in double doses. College-educated and professional black women earn 125 percent as much as their white counterparts, and this is *without* correcting for quality differences in years of education.[12] Across the entire economy, black female workers tend to earn about as much as whites and are more likely to have jobs and work hard in them.[13] With appropriate corrections for background, presence of children, and other factors, it would appear that black women face no net current discrimination. What they face is far worse: an impossible ghetto plague of divorce, separation, and illegitimacy, children living on the streets and beyond their control, and a dearth of loving and supporting husbands. This problem, made ever more acute by well-intentioned officials in Washington, is an ordeal more bitter by far than any affliction of bigotry. Yet every year all the most prestigiously virtuous institutions of America—the liberal editorialists, the leading foundations, the most fashionable publishers and publications, the universities across the land in their social science classrooms, the Protestant churches in their group pronouncements—all urge with rare unanimity policies to make the problem worse. Beyond the ritual demands for more welfare, they call for campaigns to uproot what they call sexism. This effort could not come at a worse moment for black men. The danger is that it will uproot the family as well.

There is no way to reconcile the interests of black men with the cause of feminism. In their present pass, black men need a diminution of the emphasis on credentials and qualifications in the American economy and an increased stress on aggressiveness, competitiveness, and the drive to get ahead. These qualities have always been the chief assets of lower-class men as they contest for advancement with the groups above them and a key source of productivity in the economy. It is the greater aggressiveness of men, biologically determined but statistically incalculable, that accounts for much of their earnings superiority.

The biological factor is particularly important in giving black men their small edge over black women. Unlike the larger advantage of white men over white women, the black male superiority, according to statistical analyses, is almost entirely attributable to sexism. Because of the difficulty female-headed families face in disciplining boys, black women are several times more likely to have high IQs than black men and are substantially superior in academic performance.[14] On credentials alone, black men would not be able to compete with either black or white women in employment or to function as preferable providers.

The biological difference in aggressiveness, though, is sufficiently real and important under most circumstances to sustain the male provider role. Even if it eludes most of the computer models that show high levels of discrimination, the male impulse to compete and the need to dominate affect all relations between the sexes. Feminist scholars Carol Jacklin and Eleanor Maccoby, chairman of the Stanford University department of psychology, sum up the evidence in their voluminous study of *The Psychology of Sex Differences:*

(1) Males are more aggressive than females in all societies for which evidence is available. (2) The sex differences are found early in life, at a time when there is no evidence that differential socialization pressures have been brought to bear by adults to "shape" aggression differently in the two sexes. (3) Similar sex differences are found in man and subhuman primates. (4) Aggression is related to levels of sex hormones, and can be changed by experimental administrations of these hormones.[15]

A related male trait—manifested in every human society but just as hard to capture in a computer study—is aptitude for group leadership. Partly a result of greater aggressiveness and larger physical stature, partly an expression of the male need to dominate (perhaps based on the neurophysiological demands of the sex act itself), males in all societies ever studied by anthropologists overwhelmingly outnumber women in positions of leadership and hold authority in relations with females. Steven Goldberg's rigorously argued book *The Inevitability of Patriarchy,* described by Margaret Mead as "flawless in its presentation of the data,"[16] refutes every anthropological claim that there has ever existed in human affairs either a society where women rule or a society where final authority resides with them in male-female relations.

Just as important as these biological differences are differences in familial roles. Because of the long evolutionary experience of the race in hunting societies, the provider role accords with the deepest instincts of men. When they are providing for women and protecting them, men feel masculine and sexual; when they cannot perform these roles, as in the welfare culture, they often prefer the company of the all-male group at the bar or on the street. Here they find an atmosphere that does not make the larger and deeper claims of familial and sexual love, which are hard for men to meet without a sense of masculine dominance.

These differences between men and women give ample explanation for the greater willingness of men to work hard outside the home, to compete aggressively for advancement in bureaucratic hierarchies, and to make earning money a prime motive in their lives. These differences between the sexes fully explain all gaps in earnings. What is peculiar and worthy of further analysis is not the black males' edge over their women but the reasons it is so inadequate to sustain the male role as provider and the father's place in the home.

One of the reasons, surely, is the activities of the equal-rights organizations. Even when they do not directly favor black women and white women over black men, these agencies encourage employers everywhere to defend their personnel policies in documentary fashion. Citations of biological differences do not go far with Eleanor Holmes Norton, the black woman who became the head of EEOC in 1977 and symbolizes its current role. Even though the Washington agencies have sued in court to reduce emphasis on tests and credentials and even though an important victory was won in the case *Griggs* v. *Duke Power Company,* the overwhelming effect of continuous federal surveillance of employment policies is to encourage companies to protect themselves with paperwork. It leads them to favor the documented qualifications of women over the drive and aggressiveness of men, even though studies of productivity show that its intangible sources in diligence and motivation are most important.

The result is that the antidiscrimination agencies have become an enemy of black progress nearly as deadly as the welfare system. Again, the impact falls not on the successful, who benefit from affirmative action, though they don't need it, but on the poor of all races. Just as the equal-rights campaign discriminates in favor of female credentials over male aggressiveness and drive, it also discriminates in favor of the established classes over the poor and in favor of the credentials that the rich and middle classes can buy over the competitiveness, hard work, and drive to get ahead that are the chief assets of the classes below.

This effect can be measured. When the job market is skewed in favor of women and well-credentialed men, the victims must be the men and women without documented qualifications who get ahead by working longer, harder, and more imaginatively. Again the computer analyses of discrimination show it: the group that supposedly benefits most from sexism is husbands, black or white, with twelve years of education or less and with large families to support.[17] This, in fact, is the only group that seems to achieve income far beyond their education and background. The main impact of feminism is to take jobs and promotions away from these men and give them to educated women. This impact, moreover, does not chiefly derive from the immediate activities of EEOC and the other agencies. It stems from the overall influence of antibias policy on the attitudes and practices of employers.

This is only the beginning, however, of the negative impact of government on blacks. Government agencies make far more diligent efforts to recruit blacks than whites, visiting black campuses some twenty times more often on a proportionate basis.[18] These efforts are bearing fruit, as some 25 percent of all black Ph.D.s work for government bureaucracies. The black leadership is increasingly oriented toward Washington as the source of all progress, toward discrimination as the root of all evil, and toward secure billets in bureaucracy and away from the risk-taking and enterprise that is the source of most wealth.

The last ethnic arrivals to emphasize politics and patronage as the key to success were the slowest rising of all the European immigrant groups: the Irish. The Irish triumphed magnificently in the electoral process, creating political machines that dominated city politics for generations and persist into the 1980s in Chicago, Albany, and other localities. But wealth does not derive from politics or from patronage sinecures; it comes from the competitive honing of skills and enterprises, from mastery of modern machines and technology, from a willingness to venture and create, from a sense of the margins of profit and loss. These assets are rarely cultivated in civil service or city offices. While the Irish dominated urban government, Jews, Poles, and Italians mastered the American economy.

One of the problems of government jobs is that many of them are best suited to women. It is perhaps relevant that the only previous group in America to approach the current number of black big-city mayors was also the only group to record comparable levels of female-headed families and male disorders such as riots and crime. One study of an Irish slum on the West side of Manhattan at the time of the First World War indicated that half the families were headed by women. But, in any case, government jobs do not often lead to a business or professional career. They allow immediate consumption but not investment and savings.

The government probably does blacks no favor by hiring so much of their leadership class. It is even more certain that by cultivating a pervasive expectation of bias and futility, a posture of upward resentment and appeals for rights rather than upward movement and self-reliance, Washington is profoundly damaging the prospects of the black poor. At a time when it is hard to find discrimination anywhere, blacks are being induced to see it everywhere. This attitude would be destructive to success even if it were true most of the time, for it would prevent blacks from exploiting their real opportunities. But in a world of decreasing bias, the anticipation of it creates an air of ambivalent resignation and pugnacity unattractive to any employer. Discrimination is not the problem of the

American poor. To the extent they think it is, they will be unable to read the signals of the real world in which they live.

Nonetheless, throughout the 1970s, many influential Americans of both races seemed determined to perpetuate the idea of racism, the rhetoric of it, even as the reality evaporated. The real Southern sheriff, the strange fruit on Southern trees, the real historic segregation and savagery, North and South, were parodied and trivialized in a series of seventies charades: lame notions like "subliminal racism," UN agitprop like "contraceptive genocide," judicial figments like "de facto segregation," statistical trumpery like "underutilization" of minorities, even the word *ghetto* itself, so common as to be unavoidable, yet charged with an ideology, vague and out of date, of racial grievance and sequestration. It is as if there were some strong current in American thought that cherishes the idea of racism, that cannot, indeed, do without it. Many intellectuals, in particular, seem to feel yaws of emptiness and anxiety at the notion of an America, the real America in which we live, in which for all practical and political purposes—leaving aside the imagery of literature and the phantoms of the couch, James Baldwin's personal demons and Father Hesburgh's dim statistics, and leaving aside the way of all flesh to seek first its like and fear differences—the big threat of racism has become a bad joke by an Earl Butz or a Billy Carter.

The reasons for the strange nostalgia for bigotry are perhaps not unfathomable. But they are all the same false. There is a fear lurking in many a confident liberal heart that blacks cannot prevail in a truly free competition. The fear is itself invidious and wrong. The evidence all suggests that blacks will continue to surpass whites in such fields as athletics long after all barriers are down and that they are potentially equal in any other realm in which they choose to compete. But if racism is dead, blacks and their political patrons will not much longer be allowed to run the bureaucracies—or subsist intellectually on the rationales—of civil rights, affirmative action, busing, Equal Employment Opportunity suits, expanded welfare, and compensatory employment programs. There will be grounds to continue a few of these policies. But the idea that America is a racist society won't wash as a reason.

Past racism explains a good deal, but not enough, about the current condition of blacks in the United States. The demoralizing blandishments of the War on Poverty and the explosion of welfare explain much more. Millions of Americans, liberal and conservative, black and white, are going to have to reach the conclusion boldly asserted by Daniel Patrick Moynihan—"I was wrong"—on the effects of giving people money, and they will have to extend that humbling insight to such matters as denying in policy the sexual realities of people's lives.

CHAPTER 13

The Jobs Perplex

TO SAY that liberalism, not racism, accounts for the enduring poverty of blacks in America will seem beside the point to many economists. In their view neither bigots nor doles have very much to do with poverty. What matters is not the welfare culture but the job market. During the 1970s several young economists, led by Boston University's Peter Doeringer, and by MIT's Michael Piore and Lester Thurow, developed ingenious theories to show how racist effects in employment could persist even after racism disappeared.[1] The nature of the jobs available to the poor, they said, accounts for the nature of the poor avilable for jobs. Called the dual labor-market theory, it serves as a useful complement to John Kenneth Galbraith's popular concept of a two-tier economy: on the upper level the *price makers*, a *planning sector* of large, monopolistic firms that treat their work force well because they can pass on all costs to the *ad-mass* of consumers; on the lower tier, a *market sector* of *price takers*, smaller firms with low profiles and profits, which have to accept whatever the laws of supply and demand, buffetted by big business and government power, will give them.[2] These smaller firms cannot grant high wages and fringes without suffering inroads from the competition. This theory allows professed socialists like Galbraith and others to "come to terms" or "make peace" with large U.S. corporations as protosocialist institutions, while they gaze indulgently at the market sector as it evolves toward a more rational form and is bought out or beaten down by the giants.

In its labor-market version, the upper tier in general becomes the *primary* sector. It contains the better-paid, more established jobs. These are often unionized and in large and stable companies, with privileges of training from the outset, seniority as time passes, and rights in retirement funds that own large portions of American capital. These are jobs that workers come to see as their own vested property and leave only involuntarily when laid off and that they expect to regain when the economy improves. *Secondary* sector jobs, on the other hand, are low paid, unstable, and short term, offering little chance for training or promotions and a large likelihood of layoffs and discharges.

Acquisition of a primary job, the theory suggests, is like buying a house. It creates incentives for mature and responsible behavior and is often associated with the assumption of long-term family commitments. Secondary jobs, erratic and dead-end as they are, foster the erratic and short-term perspectives associated with the lower class and discourage any enduring break from the impulsive behavior of youthful male groups. Even when one or two members of a gang manage to get primary jobs, so the theory goes, they may not perform faithfully because all their peers remain in the secondary market or on the street, where job disciplines are derided and undermined. The influence of peers thus creates a Catch-22 of tokenism: carefully selecting a few extraordinary tokens from ghetto groups may produce less-disciplined workers than hiring a whole bunch. A community moves upward when groups of youths enter good jobs together, and time clocks—then wedding bells—break up the old gang.

Accompanying this concept of a radically bipolar labor market is a theory of inevitable capitalist discrimination. Even with no conscious racism or sexism, it is said, the primary sector will tend to exclude most blacks and women. Because primary jobs may entail long-term commitments by the company to its workers, the company will seek to avoid workers who may not make long-term commitments to their jobs. Because it may be very difficult to fire a primary worker or even to long deny him promotions, a company will choose entry-level employees by higher-level criteria: enlisting only those who are judged suitable for advancement. Since a personnel office cannot exhaustively analyze every case, so the argument runs, it must develop rules of thumb—rough, empirically valid stereotypes, based on demonstrable probabilities—by which to sort out applicants.

One rule of thumb is to exclude women, who may leave to bear children, and blacks who may have the erratic traits associated with the low-level jobs from which they come. Since mistakes in personnel policy can be very expensive in a world of vested pensions, training rights, and seniority systems, the exclusionary rule of thumb may well make sense for an employer, even if it bars many applicants who could do the job for which they apply and some who could excel at higher echelons also. But efficient or not, the rule will crowd the secondary market with blacks and women, lowering still more their average pay, discouraging job discipline, and confirming to many potentially able workers the widespread rumors of a bigoted white male establishment hostile to their success—even though the companies may have merely been following a reasonable business practice based on real experience.

In essence, the theory says that jobs make the man, and bad jobs make for bad work habits, weak families, and low incomes. These conditions tend to keep blacks poor and aggrieved. Discrimination and racial bitterness, though, also may stem from rational company behavior. The competitive quest for profits, long supposed to combat discrimination, actually can foster a racially and sexually segregated work place and leave an underclass with dead-end jobs and disheveled lives. Thus, according to the argument, capitalism creates poverty.

Beyond the familiar appeals for "social change" and the "radical restructuring" of this and that, this concept of the sources of poverty is seen to dictate two lines of policy: for the primary market, it is a renewed emphasis on antidiscrimination suits and pressures, with quotas where necessary to break down entrenched patterns of de facto bias; and for the secondary market, it is full employment—a government-primed expansion of aggregate demand that improves the bargaining power of low-income workers and lifts increasing numbers of jobs into the primary sector.

For observers more jaded about the magic of aggregate demand, Nathan Glazer offers a similar, though more sophisticated, analysis and a more sensible program. He urges measures to "reform work, not welfare"; to make secondary jobs more attractive by surrounding them with government fringes, such as medical care, child allowances, unemployment pay, and other benefits that are now more easily gained through nonwork (welfare) than through secondary jobs.[3] Glazer's approach has the advantage of not expecting small struggling firms themselves to develop big corporate fringes. Any growing capitalist economy, it would appear, must have a secondary sector. But welfare and social-service systems could be more fully integrated with jobs—as in France—rather than separated from them by means tests, as in the United States.

In general the dual-market theories partake of the institutionalist critique of conventional economics. The institutionalists point out that the world differs greatly from the classical models of pure competitive markets. They do not point out that no one much believes otherwise, that a model is a camera, not a photograph—a tool that can be used, well or badly, to capture reality, not to depict it. In any event the institutionalists seem to replace heuristic models of economic men in a free marketplace with an even more dubious image of institutional structures shaping an inert and malleable mass of humanity.

The idea that jobs—or institutions—make the man, that the secondary labor market creates desultory laborers seems unworthy of the support and attention the theory has received, even though it is combined with interesting sociological observations about street society and job experience. At a time when most social scientists are reaffirming home and family as the key influences on character and achievement, the faith in jobs shown by allegedly radical economists seems rather naive. Anyone who has spent any time among black young men knows that their problems begin long before their first rejection from a primary job and often persist long after they receive one.[4] Anyone who has associated with many small businessmen in urban areas knows that the flaky attitudes of the secondary work force are a significant source of instability, not a reflection of it. Because of more personal, informal, and less specialized job patterns, however, small businesses can usually offer a better work experience to motivated youths than can large corporations. Private agencies that work with the hard-core unemployed normally seek financial support from big business but get the jobs from secondary companies. Small businesses are not the problem but part of the solution.

Primary companies in large cities, such as General Motors in Detroit, moreover, have usually been ineffective in changing the dilatory attitudes of ghetto employees. An experiment in the sixties, when a thousand primary jobs were opened, first come first served, to local blacks, failed because of absenteeism and erratic work habits. "Those thousand jobs must have been held by four thousand workers," said the chief of the project.[5] A good job, one should think, is hardly enough to create a good worker. To believe otherwise—that anyone can do construction work, for example—is to show serious signs of the intellectual disdain for the working class that is so dramatically revealed when professors oppose affirmative action for women in universities but advocate it on building sites.

At the same time, high-techology corporations like Control Data, Borg-Warner, and IBM show phenomenal success when they establish ghetto factories and have the time, patience, and federal subsidies to assemble and train a work force. These essentially segregated factories with a wide range of functions, from binding books and magazines to building display terminals and peripheral equipment for computers, have demonstrated that at least parts of the ghetto work force are eminently trainable for key jobs in complex industries. But the effort takes two years of subsidies, blandishments to community leaders, legal assistance for employee emergencies, and intense training before the sloth and suspicion in the welfare culture is overcome. Once established, however, all these plants show levels of productivity and low absenteeism comparable to any other company operation. Crucial to their success is a commitment to run them not as training facilities but as fully profitable factories, and no concessions are made on quality, deadlines, or work attitudes after the first two years.[6]

Such experiences show there is some truth in the theory that group movement into primary work can be effective in breaking down bad work habits. But there is little evidence that the affirmative-action programs favored by the dual marketeers help the process. Under pressure from government, which tends to see a large minority element at low-earning levels as a sign of discrimination, Borg-Warner, AT & T and other corporations are now stressing efforts to promote women, blacks, Hispanics, and other groups within their companies rather than reaching out for new employees at entry levels (an effort which would bring forth the usual charges that "sure they hire blacks, but they're mostly in lower-level jobs"). Government also deters ghetto employment by threatening discrimination suits when ghetto employees are paid lower wages and by imposing quotas in proportion to the racial composition of the work force in the locality. It is usually easier to duck the whole problem by building in the suburbs, as most large companies do.

EEOC pressures have sometimes helped the cause of blacks in the past. But the current concern with numerical patterns would be counterproductive even if women and Hispanics were not increasingly the beneficiaries. EEOC and other equal-rights agencies are conducting a war against big companies in which every spurious victory by the civil-rights lawyers is a precedent for yet more campaigns. The large companies know they cannot win, so they capitulate whenever tolerable terms are offered. But the lesson the companies learn is to avoid at all costs any entanglements with government social programs. This attitude is a major problem for other federal agencies attempting to secure the cooperation of business in On-the-Job Training (OJT) and other work-training operations.

The academic and federal preoccupation with large companies seems to reflect an even greater incomprehension of small business. To Galbraith and the dual-market theorists, small businesses are some quaint "secondary" leftover from an earlier phase in the evolution of the economy. These firms are discussed in somber tones, as sickly and short-lived anomalies in a world of gigantic corporations, as feeble price takers in a world of oligopolies, as flickering testimony to the nostalgic commitment of millions of Americans to a futile dream of independence.

The government sees small businesses chiefly as a problem. They are said to cause trouble because they are too numerous to be effectively supervised. The acts of their "bigoted and tax-evading" owners too often elude the regulation of EEOC, the Occupational Safety and Health Administration (OSHA), the Immigration and Naturalization Service (INS), the Department of Labor, and other federal servants of the poor and unemployed. These firms are said to exploit their workers, particularly "minorities," dupe and gouge their customers, especially the poor, and survive only as a kind of seamy underside to the monopolistic topside of the U.S. economy.

But four-fifths of minority workers hold jobs in small companies, which tend to be far more labor intensive than large ones and also experienced much greater net increases in capital value than the giants since World War II.[7] Smaller companies often give their workers a sense of vital productive activity; absenteeism tends to be highest in big firms. Although smaller businesses do have a faster turnover of employees than large businesses, the difference does not seem worth the stress the theories put on it. In the late seventies businesses with more than one thousand workers averaged a monthly turnover of 1.4 percent; smaller firms averaged 1.8 percent. Estimated turnover for the bulk of very small firms was somewhat, though not radically, higher.[8] In a kinetic economy full of change, in which more than half of the unemployed have voluntarily quit their jobs and less than half stay out of work for more than eight weeks, a turnover rate of 25 percent a year in the smallest businesses— five points higher than in the large ones—does not seem capable of explaining the dramatic sociological disorders of poverty in America.

The theory of de facto racist rules of thumb seems equally simplistic as a description of the U.S. job market. If the false application of negative stereotypes were in fact the problem of blacks, the answer would be credentialism—an enlarged emphasis on tests and academic credentials in hiring. Young blacks now receive almost the same years of schooling as whites, and with comparable test scores, blacks are somewhat more likely than whites to go to college. In some parts of the job market blacks may have slightly better credentials than whites of the same tested ability and therefore might benefit from an emphasis on educational degrees. Indeed, the equal-rights agencies are currently trying to improve black incomes by forcing employers to place more emphasis on objective qualifications and then to hire certain numbers who can roughly be said to qualify.

This approach has a perverse result. An employer who thinks he may be charged with discrimination begins to document his personnel policies much more fully. Because he cannot any longer exclude, on a subjective hunch, a young black who seems unsuitable as he would exclude any other applicant, he decides to upgrade his labor force, excluding everyone without credentials, including stable blacks he might have hired before. He may trust his intuition more than the tests, but he knows intuition will not stand up in court. Partly as a result of government equal-rights activity, credentialism thus is expanding everywhere in the American job market.

The consequences are becoming clear. Young blacks of both sexes holding university degrees or doctorates have benefited significantly and now earn substantially more than comparable whites. These groups, however, are perfectly able to fend for themselves. The equal-rights efforts merely accelerated their advance and cast shadows of favoritism over successes that would have occurred anyway.

The favorable results, however, end abruptly at lower levels of black society. Here credentialism is a wholly negative influence, balking the upward progress of many blacks who are attempting sometimes halfheartedly to escape the welfare culture. Blacks are not Jews, briefly frustrated by prejudice, who could rush forward as soon as barriers and quotas were lifted. Nor does the black problem even vaguely resemble the problem of women, amply tested and credentialed, but in need of federal lawyers to make up for a wholly commendable lack of careerist drive and aggressiveness. The problem of impoverished blacks is not at all new, subtle, or insidious. It is essentially the problem of most previous generations of American poor: how to make up by dint of effort and ambition for a lack of family background and educational qualifications. In this predicament the welfare state is obviously a hulking obstacle since it manifestly deters work. But hardly less demoralizing is the system of credentialism so dear to most American liberals, teachers, and government workers, among whom it plays a role obstructing new ideas, much resembling the role that experience in the "last war" is said to play in the minds of generals.

In place of the bigotry of race has arisen a new bigotry of schooling, based on a series of half-truths about the link between education and work. Characterized by a worship of degrees, diplomas, tests, credentials, and qualifications, this system has created a schoolmarm meritocracy that steadily extends the reach of its primary rule: you cannot pass if you cannot parse; if you cannot put the numbers in the right boxes at the requisite speed; and if you cannot perform in the accustomed academic mode.

This system reaches its extreme in government civil service, where it has become a kind of religion of numbers in which faith in testing devices can completely eclipse works. No matter how well you do on the job you can not move up if your test score is too low; conversely, no matter how badly you do—nearly—you cannot be moved out if your score is OK. In general only the numbers count.

In interviews with unemployed youths conducted for Vocational Foundation in New York as well as in other ghetto surveys in my experience, the credentials problem arises repeatedly:

—"After they give me all the tests and I fill out all these papers, they tell me I couldn't do it because I don't have my diploma."

—"I wasn't qualified for nothin' but selling reefer."
—"I was doin' the job good, but to get anywhere you have to pass all these tests."[9]

Impelled by government, and by corporate personnel policy responding largely to government, the system year by year stretches its tentacles ever further into the American working place. Year by year, the ante is raised: first a high-school diploma, then a special test, then a further degree, finally a grant of virtual tenure for the "qualified," all with the effect of downplaying performance on the job and exalting effort on the test, all with the effect of protecting any schooled but shiftless members of the middle class from the competition of unschooled but aggressively hardworking poor people.

In short, this system depreciates the assets of diligence, determination, and drive to get ahead, which have launched other groups into the middle class and above, and that every close study has shown to be most important to productivity; and it exalts the assets of the advantaged classes—schooling, testing, computing—that are often irrelevant to productivity in most jobs.

One result, as Herbert Beinstock of the Department of Labor has said, is that "we are in the process of creating a first-job barrier in this country."[10] This barrier ensures that ever larger portions of any unemployment in the American economy will be concentrated on the unacademic: chiefly high-school dropouts and especially black high-school dropouts. The victims are both the new dropouts of the fatherless welfare culture and the old dropouts of the age of segregation.

Even those who hurdle the first-job barrier often run into the problem later in the form of a promotion barrier: the same worship of credentials is applied now to decisions about whom to move ahead—a credentialed woman, for example, or an aggressive and ambitious young man. This second obstacle means that ever larger numbers of jobs are seen as dead-end work and ever larger numbers of academic dropouts of all ages withdraw in discouragement from the work force. Few experiences, after all, are more demoralizing to a devoted worker than to see indifferent competitors leap ahead on the basis of credentials.

At times of need or crisis, the "unqualified" often perform above expected levels. Untrained blacks and women surged into the labor force during World War II and made key contributions to the war effort. Unschooled aliens and colonials who do not know the language of their host countries have performed high-level work in the economy of many European nations, including functions normally reserved for high-school or even college graduates in the United States. Unschooled peasants in Taiwan, Singapore, South Korea, and Japan build television sets, automobiles, electronic devices, semiconductor chips, and musical instruments that compete successfully in American markets. Contrary to widespread belief, academic attainments are of little real importance in performing most jobs. What education is required can be given selectively to motivated workers, who learn rapidly for some clear purpose. As Doeringer, Piore, Thurow, and others often point out themselves, most skills in the U.S. economy are learned on the job and well under half require the knowledge entailed in a high-school diploma.

Technological progress does not change this reality. It makes some jobs simpler by incorporating the skills in the machines; other jobs become more refined and specialized and must be learned on the work site with the equipment involved. But the employment value of academic learning—beyond the three Rs—has increased very little.

Some analysts deny that credentialism itself is a serious problem because it can be overcome merely by a diligent effort to acquire the credentials and because the requirements are often suspended for attractive black workers. But the effects of the problem are being greatly enhanced by new licensing and other regulatory devices (affecting everything from forklifts to taxis), by increases in the size and coverage of the minimum wage, and by the impact of other labor-market restrictions (like the Davis-Bacon Act in the construction business) that artifically raise wages.

When employers are forced to pay high wages for low-productivity jobs, they attract a glut of applicants who can best be sorted out by credentials. Bricklayers, toll-booth personnel, building workers, and truck drivers have all often been required to have high-school diplomas. Because government jobs are mostly overpaid, the credentialism problem becomes especially serious in federal bureaucracies, even when they are politically opposed to credentialism. The best example is HEW, which has been shown to have an employment pattern, combined with irrelevant testing requirements, that would subject it to antidiscrimination suits from its civil-rights officers if it were a university or a hospital rather than a branch of government.[11]

The influence of credentialism, like the influence of the racism myth, reaches beyond its actual application in the job. To tell black dropouts, who are reading and computing at the fifth-grade level, that you can't get a job without a high-school diploma is as destructive as telling them that they cannot get ahead because of the racist white establishment. Both claims are essentially false, but both, too, are effective in reinforcing the blandishments of the welfare culture and the seductions of the street. HEW spends millions to propagate these myths. Especially noxious is the antidropout campaign—TV ads artfully aimed toward blacks—that

graphically communicate the hopelessness of life without school credentials.

There is no question that credentialism can be overrated as an obstacle.
Experienced bureaucrats can recite scores of strategies for circumventing
civil-service rules, particularly for promoting blacks. But the ideology
of schooling, like the culture of welfare and the ideology of discrimination,
demonstrably haunts the ghetto mind and discourages the efforts and
ambitions that are indispensable to progress.

There is no point in denying that the job market has failed to work
well for some groups of blacks. Inner-city teenagers are now famous
victims and offenders, with soaring rates of unemployment, illegitimacy,
and crime. But it is perhaps more revealing to consider the fate of a
previous generation of successful black family men who were in their
early thirties in 1957. This group of blacks had already acquired good
jobs in the primary sector and were ranked among the top third of all
American earners. Since the 1950s they have not committed crimes or
otherwise attracted sociologists, but they comprise a group of men, presumably victims of segregation, who had shown great ability in their
work and thus could be expected to respond well to the elimination of
racial barriers.

Longitudinal studies of the economic mobility of particular groups over
time show striking gains for most Americans since 1957, with the average
worker who was in his early thirties in 1957 moving up an entire quintile,
or at least one-fifth of the way up the ladder of incomes. The successful
young black workers of the 1950s had everything going for them that
liberalism could give. One might have expected them to move up more
rapidly than whites. But no such thing happened.

Instead, well employed in primary jobs twenty years ago, by the 1970s
they had plummeted one-third of the way down the income scale. In
the top 30 percent in 1957, they were in the bottom third, on the average,
by 1971.[12] Several hundred thousands of black men who had overcome
all obstacles to win primary jobs in a bad time—and who were thoroughly
beyond the welfare culture—failed entirely to keep pace as the barriers
fell. As racism declined, so did their relative incomes.

One reason is clear. As rapidly as the old obstacles were removed,
new ones were erected. Credentialism moved through the American work
place and entrenched itself ever more deeply in the government bureaucracies where many blacks were employed. This fifties generation had been
educated mostly in Southern schools, which were often closed as much
as one-third more days than white schools. Most blacks of that generation
left high school to work. As teenagers in the late forties, their labor-
force participation levels were higher and their unemployment rates were

lower than those of their white contemporaries. Their long years in the work force were paying off for some of them by the mid-fifties. But the blacks had received far fewer and less intensive years of education. When the mystique of civil rights lured many into government work, they were trapped by civil service in much the way the Irish before them had been trapped by the seductions of patronage.

By 1960, for example, 17 percent of all the postal *clerks* were black, and the number was to more than double by 1970. But even in 1970 black post*masters* numbered well under 1 percent.[13] Even at HEW itself in 1978, white men earned 35 percent more than black men, despite the massive recent movement of black Ph.D.s into federal jobs.[14] In government, credentialism always overcomes affirmative action.

As credentialism moved into the private sector as well the earlier generations of black men also tended to stall there. The aggressiveness and ambition that these men exhibited in a heavily segregated world could not prevail against the categorical rules and exclusions of a credentialist system.

Nonetheless, credentialism alone cannot account for the catastrophe that occurred. Many men from other ethnic groups have overcome similar barriers by entering business, studying at night, working at two jobs, finding employers—and there are many—who value leadership and productivity more than years at school. But the leading young blacks of 1957 did not choose these arduous routes. There was some problem of motivation or psychology, and like most such problems it originates not at the job but in the family, specifically with their wives, a group that suffered far less from credentialism.

Black women in 1957 had substantially higher IQs, more years in school, more college degrees, and much lower labor-force participation than black men. During the next twenty years, they increased their labor force participation by 40 percent. At the same time, they improved their median incomes, occupational status, and penetration of high-level positions at a rate more than three times as fast as black men did. Beginning with incomes around 50 percent of the incomes of black men and 57 percent of the incomes of white women, black women ended the period by earning more than 80 percent of black male incomes and 99 percent of the white female level.[15]

In the class of blacks represented by the leading male earners of 1957, black women increased their number of college faculty positions by a factor of four, to a level just 15 percent below the number of male faculty, and they moved massively into nursing, teaching, and government work. As Moynihan reported in 1965, some 70 percent of the blacks in the Department of Labor were women, compared to 40 percent of the whites, and black women outnumbered men by four to one in the nonprofessional positions open to modestly credentialed civil servants.[16] By 1969 there were 16 percent more black women than men in professional and managerial positions in the U.S. economy and these women were earning three-quarters as much as black men.[17] The crucial change here was in the family, not the society. The earnings of black men and women are often compared to white earnings, but what matters is how they compare to each other.

The problem of the fifties generation of successful black men was neither racism and discrimination, nor secondary labor markets, nor a static and discriminatory American distribution of income and wealth. The problem was similar to the problem of poor black men: namely, American liberalism and credentialism—with its fetish for government jobs and its obsession with equality—had led them to work less hard than comparable whites and withdraw from the work force in larger numbers, while their wives, with better credentials, worked much harder. By 1978, 30 percent of all black male heads of families were unemployed or out of the work force.

Male earnings cannot be considered without regard to female earnings. Most men make the sacrifices necessary to reach the higher reaches of the American economy chiefly to support their wives and families. When the wives earn more, the men feel a decline of urgency in their work and a loss of male nerve and drive. When the wives earn less, the men tend to work more and are far more likely to reach the pinnacles of achievement.[18] This idea—essentially that obstacles and problems elicit motivation and creativity and impel progress—defies all the canons of current sociology. But the opposite idea—that the stresses of poverty and the provider role, the obstacles and challenges of life, thwart effort and achievement—defies all the experience of history, most especially the history of ethnic groups in America.

The 1960s attack on the motives of black men continued apace through the 1970s, although it was counteracted to a large degree by their rapidly improving educational status. Nonetheless, the analysts of "discrimination" maintain, with nearly fabulous incomprehension of human nature, that even the current 20 percent advantage black males hold over their women is 94 percent attributable to sex discrimination. Meanwhile only 64 percent of the white male advantage over women, and only between 20 and 30 percent of the white male advantage over black men, is said to be a result of bias.[19] In other words, the elimination of what the equal-rights agencies call bias would nearly close the already small lead in earnings that black men hold over black women. But white men would keep most of their advantage over black men. Therefore, black men have little to gain from a continuation of current activity by the equal-rights agencies, which base their policy on the same credentialist criteria used by the academic analysts and ignore all the black male virtues of diligence and drive, which produced the gains of the 1950s. Even if disguised by regular litigation in favor of black men, the antidiscrimination drive can only reap a harvest of demoralization, work-force withdrawal, and family breakdown, and a decay in the spirit of work, family, and faith on which enduring upward mobility depends. The crucial goal of all antipoverty policy must be to lift the incomes of males providing for families and to release the current poor from the honeyed snares of government jobs and subsidies. These policies, unfortunately, are the opposite of the ones now favored by both government and the academy, which is one reason why poverty amid American riches is unlikely to end soon.

CHAPTER 14

The Make-Work Illusion

WHENEVER the American economy approaches recession, there is always a boom in the business of saving or creating jobs. Unlike most enterprises, this business tends to be run by politicans, and it thrives not on savings and investment but on taxation and talk. John Connally, for example, repeatedly brought crowds to their feet during his 1980 presidential race by promises to protect the jobs of U.S. workers by reducing foreign trade and competition: "Let the Japanese sit on their docks in their Datsuns and watch their Sony TVs themselves." The Carter administration proposed to create jobs by expanding the Comprehensive Employment and Training Act (CETA), already spending some 12 billion dollars annually, into a national program of guaranteed employment for all.

As the economic and political portents of the new decade darkened our horizons in late 1979, politicians on all sides rushed to save jobs by subsidizing Chrysler, the embattled automotive firm that managed to lose nearly a billion dollars in 1979. Connally even proposed a federal come-and-get-it fund for all large and failing companies. Even such a staunch conservative as columnist Patrick Buchanan, a former Nixon speech writer, demanded government action on behalf of the afflicted automotive firm. "This is a time for Republicans to rise above principle," he wrote, and "leave Ralph Nader to mouth the moth-eaten clichés from Republican conventions of generations ago." Buchanan went so far as to quote the dubious findings of the Congressional Budget Office, which predicted "the permanent loss of a quarter of a million jobs" if Chrysler melted down.[1]

The country was moving toward a system like Great Britain's in the seventies. Business was flogged mercilessly by government officials and regulators until it proved itself innocent—and perhaps worthy of subsidies—by reason of failure and incompetence. Steel firms that could show only a modest level of ineptitude were compensated by import protections and exemptions from antitrust laws (which never should have been applied in the first place). A catastrophic series of blunders, such as Chrysler's, already causing massive layoffs of workers, might win for the company an award from Washington as a precious provider of jobs.

Meanwhile the prevailing research on employment depicted most unsubsidized jobs as bad for health and family. According to the litany, farm workers are woefully exploited; industrial workers are poisoned; secretaries are sent for coffee and Danish; assembly-line laborers are made to perform repetitive tasks; telephone operators are denied the opportunity to climb poles. Technicians in high-technology companies destroy the jobs of others. Workers in energy companies cause cancer and traffic jams.

In fact, the only employment generally acceptable in scholarly circles is work which does not produce anything. The identifying mark of these functions, apart from being well-paid, is that they allow the jobholder to pretend he isn't in it for the money. As David B. Wilson of *The Boston Globe* writes:

Never mind that manufacturers of bologna, unleaded gasoline, and screwdrivers, grain farmers and real estate salespeople actually do more for their fellow human beings than any number of bureaucrats and teachers of sociology. . . . The new class members, their status fixed and enriched by tax exemptions, their tenures and civil-service protections firmly emplaced, manage still to perpetuate the fiction that they are somehow more devoted to the public interest than the drivers of eighteen-wheel tractor trailers.[2]

Yet there is a sense in which people not in it for the money—people whose work does not yield a profit—do not have jobs at all. A more common term for what people do when they are spending money earned by others is *consumption,* and the usual word for what people do when they are not in it for the pay is *leisure.* Turning the consumption and leisure of subsidized or "created" jobs into activity lauded as idealistic and sacrificial public service—while at the same time disparaging the activities of the private sector as a grubby rat race—takes ingenuity and resourcefulness. But such ideology has come forth in tomes.

A cottage industry has emerged, trafficking in reports, studies, conferences, seminars, lectures, brochures, videotapes, monographs, colloquia, documentary films, symposia, and photographic essays. The conclusions, as reported by the media, grimly denounce productive labor and predict the end of a job-based economy.

Many public-sector and nonprofit jobs are well worth subsidizing. Even though they do not technically earn profits, they produce a tremendous yield for the society. But all such jobs subsist on the productive labor of others. The proliferation of public work depends entirely on the enlargement of profit from marketed goods. Yet in recent decades, marketed output as a proportion of GNP has steadily declined in the United States.

This shift means that the subsidized workers of government are consuming an increasing proportion of the nation's output, leaving less for workers in business and for exports abroad. Since the 1950s the share of marketed goods and services taken by government has been rising in the United States nearly twice as fast as in England, which has long had a much higher level of public employment. By 1975 the United States almost closed the gap, with 34 percent of marketed GNP going to the government, compared to 37 percent in Great Britain.[3]

The remaining difference, moreover, was entirely attributable to the British system of National Health. Although the United States, in its public and private sectors, spends almost twice as much money per capita on health care as Britain, and although most of this U.S. spending is heavily supervised by government, the bulk of it is assigned to the private totals. Yet there is little difference in the economic character of the medical transactions going on among doctors and patients in the two countries. The combination of regulated private insurance with Medicare and Medicaid operates in more or less the same way as the British National Health. American health care is merely more elaborate and advanced. In any case, according to the Organization for Economic Cooperation and Development (OECD), the U.S. marginally exceeded Great Britian in the share of GNP spent by government on private-sector goods and services—that is, government spending exclusive of transfer payments such as social security and Medicaid.[4] Since transfers merely shift private-sector output from one citizen to another, they do not reduce the total of goods and services available outside government. Britain might have lead in transfer payments, but the United States exceeded almost all capitalist countries in proportion of GNP devoted to direct government appropriations of private-sector resources, for all purposes from housing to defense. This is probably the most important index of government impact on an economy.

Without the energy crisis, such government growth might have been manageable. But unlike Britain with its North Sea oil, the United States, in order to pay a $60 billion tax to OPEC, was forced to expand its exports massively. Government, unfortunately, despite its many uses, is not usually an exportable item. As the United States increased its exports, therefore, unsubsidized workers had to make do with less in order that civil servants and OPEC might have more. Many private citizens and companies began to suffer.

Apparently to conceal the real sources of this distress, the governing class launched a series of charades. These were designed to persuade the people that in fact, because of excess profits and other derelictions by business, they would henceforth have to depend on the public sector for employment. Politicians could suffer silently while uncountable small-business jobs were destroyed by new taxes, regulations, and minimum wages. But the failure of a large firm—or its exposure to superior foreign competition—would arouse too much media attention and union protest to ignore. Government soon would step in under the guise of "saving" American jobs. The result was a further decline in the total of marketed output available for private-sector workers, because a portion of this output was diverted to support the favored unions and corporations. But the public was given to believe that jobs were being saved and the state was doing it. Politicians could preen themselves on playing the role of savior of employment, even when solutions to other problems eluded them.

Under the Carter administration, however, government decided to go beyond the mere "saving" of jobs to a national program, unprecedented in size and scope, of "creating" jobs. A total of some 12 billion dollars was appropriated in 1979 and more was budgeted for 1980 and beyond. This process diminished still further the amount of national output available for the people who produce goods and services for sale at home and abroad. But politicians again could step forward as defenders of the family income.

This process reduces total employment in the economy. But no one should underestimate the plausibility and seductiveness of the arguments adduced at every step of the way. Conservatives and liberals alike succumb to them when the pressures mount in the make-work economy.

Who can oppose CETA job programs if they do anything at all to prevent the costly increases in dependency, crime, and family breakdowns that are inevitable with unemployment? Who could object to government support for a firm such as Chrysler when the alternative might have been its purchase by foreign companies, themselves partly owned or heavily subsidized by government? Who could resist loan guarantees that obviate outlays of welfare and unemployment compensation estimated at 16 billion dollars in the Chrysler case? Because the costs of letting a large firm fail are essentially measurable and obvious, while the costs of saving it are initially small—and because federal job-creation programs always seem preferable to the tortures of joblessness—in every instance an analysis of evident costs and benefits will tend to favor action by government, whether for CETA or for Chrysler. But as productivity in U.S. industry declines, there arises the danger that all this job creation and development will result in an uncreative and undeveloping economy.

The basic approach of the U.S. government to unemployment—like its approach to so many of life's misfortunes—is insurance. But like most government insurance the system of unemployment compensation is full of moral hazards, and the average family receiving it now has an annual income well above the national median.[5] Workers who lose their jobs are currently given payments at a level some 70 percent as high as their after tax earnings from work—a level much higher in real value, particularly for a family's second earners, since it affords time for leisure and unreported earnings. To the average American the word *unemployment* came to mean not joblessness, but a nice weekly check. Some unions now grant priority in layoffs to the most senior workers. Being fired became a fringe benefit or a perk of seniority.

Economists and sociologists who have no idea how the system works will tell you that unemployment benefits, which grow steadily as inflation pushes workers into higher tax brackets, are not a major cause of unemployment. But any worker knows better. For this middle-class welfare system, moreover, you don't have to break up your family. The worker gets the money. It is better in every way than AFDC. The problem is that the program does not apply to most of the jobs that are held by the poor—the relatively short-term clerical, agricultural, and manual realm associated with much of America's hard-core unemployment. An intelligent social policy would substantially reduce the unemployment-compensation benefit level and extend the system to all jobs, thus restricting the blight of welfare. But American politicians imagine that it is "generous" to destroy poor people's families and middle-class work habits.

Eventually, however, after six months or a year or so, depending on the state of the economy—which is rendered more sluggish and inflexible by such subsidies—the payments run out. Hardships ensue for the particularly improvident among the unemployed. In addition there are many workers with uncovered jobs and many who are entering the work force, or reentering it, and thus lack access to any but the less dignified forms of welfare. For these groups there is the Humphrey-Hawkins approach, under which the government, through such vehicles as CETA, guarantees work to the otherwise uninsured. The federal government is to become, in some way or other, the employer of last resort: to ensure a job of some kind to everyone who needs one.

Alas, as many a rich man knows, and the richest government in the world should learn, generosity is fraught with pitfalls. The trouble in this case is that most government jobs, because of their special nature—

which Senator Bob Dole characterized in 1976, in his pursuit of a prominent sinecure, as "indoor work with no heavy lifting"—are already becoming a first resort for all who wish to avoid the stresses of real productive
labor. Guaranteeing work turns out to be even more complicated—and
more expensive—than guaranteeing incomes. It may indeed be impossible.
As José Ortega y Gasset has written: "All life is the struggle, the effort
to be itself. The difficulties which I meet with in order to realize my
existence are precisely what awaken and mobilize my activities, my
capacities."[6] A guaranteed job denies the crucial fact that all jobs are to
some extent created by the worker; it is only he who can guarantee the
job, by the act of supplying labor, undergoing hardship, achieving distinction, and thus becoming part of the struggle by which human life improves
itself.

The test of real work is usually the market: is the job of sufficient
difficulty, unpleasantness, or need for people to pay to have it done? Is
the product sufficiently desirable or rare to command a profitable price
as shown by the willingness of others to exchange their own work for
it? These constraints, which are palpable in the very texture of the job,
are what distinguish work from play or from make-work.

Because work is initially unpleasant, it is done chiefly under the spur
of a psychological or material necessity. One of the hardest jobs is forcing
or inducing others to work. Businessmen under the pressure of the market
can do it; Marine Corps drill instructors, with total power over their
recruits, can do it. But the average bureaucrat or CETA supervisor—who
is no Marine drill instructor to begin with, and who knows that it makes
no difference whether the jobs are done or not—cannot find it in his
heart to be hard-nosed.

Most CETA jobs, therefore, are not work, even though they are sometimes unpleasant. At present one title of the bill provides so-called summer
work experience for some three hundred thousand impoverished youths.
But the youths themselves can sense the emptiness of it. The ones inter-
viewed by Vocational Foundation, Inc. (VFI) unanimously called their
time in the Neighborhood Youth Corps a shuffle and a farce. "Mostly
the kids just go to the park or the beach and mess around for their
money," one VFI counselor said. "They get the idea that's a job."[7]

City governments always manage to announce this program and restrict
the period of applications to it in a way that each year ensures long
telegenic queues outside their offices. The media collaborate, and the willingness of the youths to line up is widely seen as evidence of a craving
for employment as, in an obscure way, it is. But the more immediate
reason for the queue is that at present these summer shuffles are the
best sources of welfare for youths without children. The "hassle" of the

jobs themselves is resented because it deceives neither the recipients nor the administrators about what is going on—welfare in disguise. Cynical supervisors teach impoverished youth their own contempt for the world of work, while public-service unions keep most of the genuine public employment for themselves, sometimes at wages that contain an implicit welfare component as large as CETA's.

In any event the bulk of CETA jobs in the late 1970s did not go to poor youths, but to the premeditated poor of the middle class, who also wished to avoid work, in the name of self-expression, without the excuse of a prevailing welfare culture in their communities. In 1978, 8 billion dollars of the money went to pay the salaries of white-collar and blue-collar municipal workers. In some cities, such as Detroit and New York, many of the jobs were legitimate. The program allowed certain big city mayors to avoid facing the hard choices necessitated by their exorbitant settlements and pension agreements with public-service unions.

Increasingly, however, as the CETA program matured, the premeditated poor began to twist it to their own ends. CETA money began to crop up in the most peculiar places, financing the efforts of radical filmmakers in Chicago, artists' collectives in Cambridge, and a modern-dance troupe in the Berkshires. Frazzled "community organizers" clambered aboard, along with gay-movement militants, protest mobilizers against nuclear plants, long tails of entourage for petty officials, actors in deserted community theaters, tired chroniclers of already chronicled historic sites, pot-farming "foresters" in state parks, laid-back paralegals and rape-crisis emergency aides, spaced-out makers of little-needed maps, courtroom attendants dallying with the public defender, haze-headed workers in youth drug clinics—all very vaguely supervised by a large complement of employment counselors and "coordinators" with earnest expressions of concern and "job developers" with heads full of reasons why none could find jobs.

These youths are only partly to blame for their plight. Like welfare recipients, they often work hard and sacrifice much (more than they know) to acquire their sinecures. Far more at fault is the political order that fosters this self-destructive and socially erosive behavior—the adults who create these insidious systems of dependency and self-indulgence.

These programs are anything but generous to their recipients. Like welfare, CETA often has the effect of shielding people from the realities of their lives and thus prevents them from growing up and finding or creating useful tasks. In a strange etymological turn the word *meaningful* as applied to work has come to signify *meaningless*—employment that in fact consists of the consumption of valuable resources and the debauchery of human capital.

Although job creation is something government can only rarely do well, distributing money it can do with great efficiency. When the public grows resentful of "welfare," Washington may continue it in the guise of distributing "work," which can be more acceptable to the public, as well as more appealing to potential recipients. The welfare state expands by offering more attractive packaging for its products. But beneath the surface it may still be the same old trap of dependency and demoralization.

Real public jobs are often extremely productive—sometimes more valuable than private jobs. Though the "profit" is often elusive to measure, it may well be very important. Three-quarters of all the productivity growth in America this century is similarly hard to pin down, not coming directly from investments in land or labor or capital but from intangible accumulations of knowledge and X-efficiency, the invisible profits of the system. Although much of the gains came from the competitive efforts of private firms, a large and necessary contribution derived from government, and not only from the immense and obvious benefits of research, education, and science.

Incalculable gains to the nation accrued from the civil-rights effort that brought the energies of blacks more fully into the economy and transformed the South, with cities such as Atlanta that welcomed the change, growing twice as fast as cities such as Birmingham that resisted it. Similar gains arose from the system of land-grant agricultural colleges and extension services that fostered the modernization of American farms. The early phases of the environmental movement may later be seen as comparably valuable. The yield of a teacher or a road builder, a tree pruner or a veterans' counselor, a youth-services worker or a historic preservationist, a garbage collector or a tax collector, a prison warden or a zookeeper is often difficult to compute. That is why government— for all its apparatus of "political science" and cost-effectiveness studies— is still mostly an intuitive art.

A private business knows that creating jobs is difficult, for failures readily reveal themselves in the accounts. Losses quickly add up, force new efficiencies, or compel early bankruptcy. Because of the power of taxation, however, government sometimes can imagine that the process is easier in the public sector, that it is "creating" jobs or producing goods and services when, in fact, it may be merely wasting or consuming wealth, with a net effect of destroying jobs in the economy. Though the difference between useful and wasteful public activities may be difficult to measure directly, it is nonetheless just as real as the difference between private-sector jobs that bring returns and those that bring insolvency.

In government, waste only becomes clear over time, but its consequences can become even more serious—a gradual sinking of productivity in the entire economy, a prolonged downturn in employment, a steady alienation of voters, increasing avoidance and evasion of taxes, a decline in patriotism and public spirit, and a decay in the real standard of living.

Because many of the indices of failure may also reflect private and cultural change, however, the situation is rarely as clear as in a private firm. Even New York City on the edge of bankruptcy could posture as a heroic contributor of intangible benefits to the public weal, giving externalities of culture and liberalism well worth the patronage of inferior communities (which lacked comptrollers and labor statesmen who could see through the bottom line and appreciate the elegant Greek revival facade of the federal treasury beyond).

To create real jobs in the public sector—jobs which produce more than they consume, and which earn a profit in the mystical and multifarious ledger of the public interest—is altogether as difficult as creating private-sector work. If it seems easy, the result is probably consumption. As a general principle all public-sector work that is created to "develop jobs" rather than to accomplish a needed end may be assumed to represent waste.

The waste reaches well beyond the immediately unprofitable activity and imposes far wider costs. Public-sector make-work necessarily deters the creation of real jobs. A person, like a nation, who is forced to experience the economic foundation of his life, gains valuable knowledge, which renders him to a greater degree an economic man. He becomes a person better able to find his most useful role and more likely to invent a profitable job or business. The risks and exigencies of life define its bounds and possibilities. One of the key moral hazards entailed in government job programs and other insurance schemes is the loss of knowledge—a real capital loss—that they inflict on citizens who never learn their own best abilities and opportunities. Such invisible debits on the productivity account are the counterpart of the intangible credits that engendered three-quarters of our growth. As the debits accumulate, the economy declines.

Such intangibles compound the immediate burdens of government-created jobs. It may now well be that each CETA job destroys more than one private-sector job for the poor. According to a General Accounting Office report, CETA jobs cost a total of more than twenty thousand dollars each, including overhead expense. This amount is somewhat less than the costs of creating major manufacturing jobs in the private sector. But it may be nearly twice as much as the cost of employment in the labor intensive small businesses that would otherwise be most likely to hire CETA's assigned clientele.

If we assume, for the sake of argument, that CETA jobs do not make any net contribution to the economy, the twenty thousand dollars that they cost to maintain can be registered as a loss. Where does this money come from? It comes from the output of productive jobs elsewhere, either through increased taxes, expanded federal borrowing, or directly inflationary creation of money. All three possible sources diminish the wealth available to the private sector for purchasing capital equipment that sustains jobs, for spending on goods and services produced by jobs, and for savings that go into job-creating home construction and renovation.

Meanwhile the federal government will be raising the tax level on private-sector profits and wages, thus deterring creation of marginal firms and jobs. To finance a deficit the treasury will be borrowing in the capital markets, where it will offer tens of billions of dollars' worth of safe securities at high interest rates with which only the largest corporations, usually capital intensive, can compete in the market of bonds and commercial paper.

The result is that whether the federal government borrows or taxes or inflates to finance its job-creation programs, the victims are likely to be the very small- and moderate-sized firms that can more cheaply and efficiently and productively employ the poor. Since CETA was spending over 10 billion dollars annually in the late seventies and much of the money was going to unionized municipal workers and middle-class social servants, the simultaneous rises in unemployment, labor-force withdrawal, and small-business failure in the inner city are not as surprising as they may seem. Indeed, in view of welfare, unemployment compensation, and minimum-wage policies that further harden the core of ghetto unemployment, the uselessness of CETA seems obvious and inevitable.

A key effect of such programs, however, is not financial, since, particularly in the ghetto, few businesses resort to bank loans. Here the main effect is to deprive ghetto businesses of potential low-cost labor. By paying the minimum wage and more for work far less stressful than the petty manufacturing, retailing, and other menial jobs available in the lower reaches of the private sector, the CETA jobs raise still further the labor costs of small businesses and decrease their number and profitability. Potential permanent jobs involving real work are replaced by artificial jobs that offer a deceptive and demoralizing "work" experience and that once again deprive the poor of an understanding of their real predicament: the need to work harder than the classes above them in order to gain upward mobility. This insult is compounded by the injury of a net creation of many fewer jobs and the shift of new jobs from petty enterprise to credentialed bureaucracy and countercultural self-expression.

Although New York has claimed more attention, the Commonwealth of Massachusetts is perhaps the exemplary state in which to see the systems at work. Not only did it have the highest welfare levels and some of the highest unemployment rates in the country, but for several years during the mid-seventies, 57 percent of the state's net job growth came from CETA[8] Here the federal government certainly appeared to be creating jobs, and the state government fully collaborated. During the ten years after 1967 the commonwealth's budget grew from 700 million to 4.3 billion dollars, nearly tripling in real terms, while the population rose only 5 percent.

Contrary to the widespread impression of a sun-belt bias in the distribution of federal moneys, federal aid for the region rose steadily during this period. After several years of posturing by Northeastern officials, the General Accounting Office finally made a careful analysis in 1977 that confirmed the previous findings of Warren Brookes and others that the Northeast as a whole got back one dollar and six cents for every tax dollar it sent to the feds, and Massachusetts—as might have been expected from the eminence of its representatives in Washington—received one dollar and eight cents.[9]

Throughout this decade of booming government in the region, Massachusetts remained one of the wealthiest states in the nation per capita, heavily middle class, highly educated, only 3 percent black, and relatively exempt from the huge migrations from the South that allegedly account for the high welfare and CETA activities in other states. Massachusetts, in fact, gives a nearly conclusive answer to those who believe that the crisis of the American welfare state is a racial problem. Moreover, as the home of the country's most prestigious private educational institutions and as a center of advanced technology—with 2.8 percent of the nation's population and 3.5 percent of the jobs in 1960—the state seemed well situated to thrive even without this massive infusion of moneys from other parts of the land.

Yet Massachusetts did not thrive. Including all the government jobs, employment growth in the state was less than half as rapid as in the rest of the country, only 60 percent as fast as the rest of New England, and through the late seventies only one-fourth as fast as neighboring New Hampshire. The prospects for the future seemed worse, at least for private employment. According to the First National Bank of Boston, the state suffered an acute decline in capital investment; and according to a 1977 study by *Fortune,* the commonwealth ranked dead last among all the fifty states in its share of new corporate plants within its borders.

Massachusetts ended the decade, however, ranked either number one or near it in welfare payments, welfare growth, welfare percentage of the state budget, and welfare percentage of the state population; it ranked high both in unemployment and unemployment compensation, with youth joblessness at close to 40 percent. Lest anyone worry, however, about these hapless souls without work, the average family income of the long-term unemployed (those unemployed for fifteen weeks or longer) was $15,311 excluding the payments,[10] and the state ranked high in the nation in unanswered advertisements for workers. Companies all over the state list manufacturing jobs, at 40 to 70 percent above the minimum wage, with the Department of Employment Security, only to be informed repeatedly that "there is no one suitable for your type of employment.

When commonwealth officials lament the loss of jobs to other states and call for renewed federal aid, they do not often mention that companies are literally driven away, if not by the lack of workers, then by government or community harassment as firms are accused of hiring aliens, exploiting fundamentalist religious sects (who are willing to work), or even emitting unsavory smells, as a maker of large-screen television sets was said to be doing in Cambridge, despite full conformance with all Environmental Protection Agency (EPA) regulations. The television manufacturer's real offense, one suspects, was creating a public nuisance—conspicuous capitalism. He and his plant were shortly seen off to New Hampshire with an apopemptic front page spread in *The Boston Globe*, stressing the callous withdrawal of jobs from the poor, when the real danger was that all too soon the jobs would withdraw to Japan.

Writing about New York, Senator Moynihan, in a remarkable passage of prose, suggests that the plight of the Northeast, in the grips of adverse economic trends and government policies favorable to the sun belt, is a profound crisis of liberalism. He wrote:

What if it comes to be believed that the policies of the New Deal brought about the downfall of the region that nurtured them and gave them to the nation? I will tell you what will happen. There will be a response of bitterness and reaction that will approach in duration if not in intensity the response of the South to its defeat in what we now call the War Between the States. It would be one thing to lose, as it were, the Northeast. It would be a very different and vastly greater blow to lose the tradition of national liberalism that the Northeast did so much to give the nation.[11]

States, however, no less than individuals, are responsible for their fate in normal times. New Hampshire, no less Northeastern if rather less liberal, has been the nation's leading job creator. Those states with the smallest return flow of federal tax dollars, such as Ohio, Illinois, Indiana, and Iowa, have all performed far better than New York or Massachusetts. Illinois, the land of Abraham Lincoln, Adlai Stevenson, and Senator Paul Douglas, with a liberal tradition near the equal of New York's, and with a proportion of blacks 25 percent greater than New York and five times greater than Massachusetts, received back just 70 cents per tax dollar for the entire decade. Yet its unemployment rates were lower and its personal income—in the late seventies 15 percent above the national average and 11 percent above Massachusetts—grew 12 percent faster. It also spent about 25 percent less on welfare.[12]

The GAO analysis indicates, as cogently as any such statistics can, that there is no correlation between federal aid and economic growth. As Brookes concluded,

Just as welfare does little to help individuals grow, and can even make them more and more helpless, the GAO study shows that the same holds true of states like Massachusetts and New York. Massachusetts has become a federal 'dependent child,' and it isn't doing us a bit of good.[13]

What happened in Massachusetts was not the New Deal on trial. Nor was it, as some have suggested, a collapse of will and the work ethic. Rather, Massachusetts represents a kind of derangement of entrepreneurship. The energies of job creation that fuel the growth of capitalism instead found their outlet in the enterprise of expanding government.

Job creation is performed chiefly by individuals. Their supplies of work and human capital can engender their own demand. In Massachusetts there emerged a generation of youth jaded by Vietnam and by a cultural scorn of business much like the upper-class English disdain for "trade." This generation was educated to profess a politics of "social change," a concern for the poor, and a psychology of liberation and individual fulfillment. These attitudes fused in a demand for "meaningful jobs" uncontaminated by capitalism and devoted to working with people.

It was not a slack or silent generation; there was fire in their eyes and enterprise in their secret hearts. But, disdaining business, there were few places for their energies to go but to the government. Their great triumph came in 1972 when they managed, alone among the nation's liberals, to carry a state for McGovern. They further managed, in a commonwealth dominated by Catholics, to elect first a Republican Yankee liberal and then a Greek Protestant reformer to the governorship, to lead a legislature dominated by liberals. They had their way.

And did they "create" jobs! It was a display of enterprise and resourcefulness worthy of the great epochs of business growth. It was not easy, for example, in a time of steadily declining school-age population, to secure a 60 percent gain in educational spending, but they did, mostly through a bloated bureaucracy.[14] Their more important contribution, though, was to transform the very concept and structure of government service. In a great syncretism of the varying strands of social work, the state created an interdisciplinary mass of social healers and provocateurs.

State mental-health services devolved to the communities and cropped up sometimes as "crime prevention" programs, with law-and-order subsidies from Nixon's Law Enforcement Assistance Administration; or they merged with special education, aid to the growing ranks of certified retarded children, and state youth services, which combined with halfway houses and environmental-outreach groups. There were also programs in encounter training, and consumers' advocacy, with offshoots in alternative energy, nuclear protest, and solar worship, in a parlay with urban revitalization, yoga training, T-group organizing, and community action and equal rights—all elided somehow with preteen sex education, birth-control marketing, abortion counseling, and child developing, with satellite agencies for rape crises, battered wives, and food co-ops. All were part of a Massachusetts social-service conglomerate in which the various units were nearly indistinguishable, led by the same polymorphous activists with amorphous duties and lawyers everywhere on hand, and with no effective oversight or administration by the government or the legislature. Exploiting the general disarray for all it was worth were the public-service unions, which managed to negotiate contracts and pension plans as generous as New York City's.

The crucial event, however, was the display of aggressive entrepreneurship in a setting of liberal government with no sense of fiscal limits. The jobs that were created with such ingenuity and abandon, cajolery and lobbying, protest and pettifoggery, legal acumen and bureaucratic invention—all sufficient to launch a thousand businesses—turned out not to be jobs at all but rather seats at the trough, where the workers consumed their own human capital and the income of the state with every righteous assurance, at least some of the time, that they were serving the sacred cause of "social change" and progress.

Alfred Marshall, the teacher and precursor of Keynes at Cambridge, once wrote:

Government is the most precious of human possessions; and no care can be too great to be spent on enabling it to do its work in the best way: A chief condition to that end is that it should not be set to work for which it is not specially qualified, under the conditions of time and place.[15]

The precious resource of government was squandered woefully. Although tax cuts and high technology have since fostered economic revival in the state, Massachusetts in the seventies was a microcosm of Washington. The national government doggled its boons far off the budget and out of the organizational charts into thousands of consultancies, commissions, and contract units, ponzied into great satellite bureaucracies, lucratively whirling in federal space and animated by the barest wisps and figments of legislative intention or executive will. Here again is the impulse of job creation and enterprise, so positive a force in the private economy, now on the loose and overriding the market test and fiscal constraint. It is the capitalist gift of giving, in the mere expectation of return, transformed into the public gift of giving the money of others, in the virtual assurance of eventual profit from the taxpayer. The activity is the same: a vision of opportunity to serve, a mobilization of capital and support, an organization of labor, and a marketing of product, but without, most of the time, any real sense of a bottom line or public demand.

The ironic result is to destroy jobs and capital. The government boom in the name of full employment, in the vision of job entitlement and insurance, will end by reducing the availability of real work at inviting levels of pay. No matter how secure each bemused and pensioned government worker may feel, his future remains in the hands of the creators of wealth and the absorbers of risk. Production is the source of all demand, and as supplies of marketable products decline, so does the worth of the specious job contracts and blue-sky pensions of the public sector.

The intoxication of the power to tax unleashed a new cultural force in America, devoted to "meaningful work" and "social change," without a sense of real costs. That force, toward the end of the 1970s, met a counterforce of tax revolt, inspired by an ideology of enterprise that can redeem the American economy. That movement may in the end do more for the ideals espoused by Senator Moynihan than any siege of welfare reform or federal flows toward his beleaguered Northeast. Economies, like individuals, need bounds of scarcity and motives of struggle to fulfill their higher role: "The difficulties [they] meet . . . are precisely what mobilize and awaken [their] energies."[16]

Redemption through struggle, as the senator knows so well, has been the history of America. There is no alternative. In the 1980s as before, the greatest economic gains will go to the groups who sweat and save and create their own work. During the seventies, this very period of welfare glut and CETA expansion in response to a supposed crisis of joblessness, America underwent one of its prime epochs of immigration, comparable to the great floods of Irish, Italians, and Jews in the nineteenth and early twentieth centuries. Four hundred thousand legal immigrants a year entered the country along with some eight hundred thousand undocumented aliens, and everywhere they went they found and created jobs.

In this strange era it sometimes seems helpful in America *not* to know the language, and thus to be exempt from the blandishments of the welfare culture as it reaches out hungrily toward the new arrivals on our shores.

On Ferry Street in the middle of Newark, where unemployment was at 20 percent, Cubans and Portuguese with no government aid or bank loans have created a bustling retail district of bakeries and furniture stores, liquor and millinery shops, groceries and restaurants.[17] In Florida some three hundred thousand Cubans found work at a 93 percent rate in the middle of Miami, where 16 percent of inner-city American citizens were unemployed. Similarly in and around Los Angeles, where 20 percent of Americans were jobless, aliens poured into the city from Mexico and found work on farms and in factories, in hotels and restaurants, in the garment industry and as domestics—all jobs that they now dominate in many American cities.[18] Most of the aliens, like earlier immigrants, work for low pay at menial jobs, disdaining the dole. In San Diego County, a center of Mexican flows, officials could discover only 10 illegal aliens among 9,132 welfare cases surveyed in 1975.[19]

These newcomers are a great American capital asset. Senator Chafee of Rhode Island has said that "Our best urban renewal program is Portuguese immigrants."[20] Of the thousands of Vietnamese who arrived in the United States wide-eyed and battered from harrowing ordeals on land and sea, only 10 percent ended on welfare, and hundreds have opened shops, laundries, and restaurants. In San Diego thousands work in the city's electrical-component assembly shops, which operate under contract to larger manufacturers of ordnance and communications equipment.[21] They receive low pay, but it is far higher than that of their competitors in Taiwan, Hong Kong, and Singapore.

A job guarantee gives what cannot be given. It implies that everyone could diminish effort and slackly accept pay without causing the entire system to decay. If, under guarantees such as those that pertain to civil service, all workers merely performed at the minimal level, the U.S. standard of living would collapse. Crucial to a real job is the risk of being fired if the work is not performed. A guaranteed job implies that the work is mostly optional, and thus, like the average CETA slot, no real job at all.

More important, the essence of productive work under capitalism is that it is altruistic. As Richard Posner has written: "Because the individual cannot prosper in a market economy without understanding and appealing to the needs and wants of others, and because the cultivation of altruism promotes the effective operation of markets, the market economy . . . also fosters empathy and benevolence, yet without destroying individuality."[22] Make-work, despite the claims of altruism by its advocates, is more often selfish. It is done to satisfy the donor rather than the donee. The irony is that the holders of such jobs frequently resent their sinecures and shuffles of paperwork. Meanwhile, performers of hard,

productive labor can attain deep gratification from their jobs. By expanding the realm of subsidized work, the country undermines the morale
of the entire work force and stifles the spirit of charity that infuses the
most creative effort.

The effect of subsidizing giant companies to save jobs is no better
than creating or guaranteeing them through CETA. It was said that to
save a firm like Chrysler was to rise above principle. That assertion was
false. To save Chrysler was merely to establish a different principle—
namely, that major U.S. corporations, even if they serve no crucial public-
interest or national security role, will not be allowed to fail.

That principle dictates an accelerating decline in American productivity
and the surrender of U.S. leadership in the world economy. The possibility
of failure is as important to capitalist enterprise as the opportunity to
succeed. As the experience of the U.S. railroad industry, the Post Office
Department, and the New York City public services all attest, access to
the U.S. Treasury cripples management in negotiating with unions. The
resulting contracts consistently exceed productivity gains and thus erode
the assets of any company until, at last, it fails, and it must seek the
support of government. A federal fund to subsidize failing companies
is a self-fulfilling prophecy of company failure.

Extensive experience in Europe, moreover, demonstrates that once a
company becomes a ward of the state, it only rarely again becomes reliably
profitable. Of the fourteen largest state-owned manufacturers in Western
Europe, all of which benefit from numerous special advantages from government, only one, DSM, a chemical firm in the Netherlands, has earned
a consistent return, and a modest one at that. Even Renault, the most
celebrated example of nationalized success, has been hardly more profitable than Chrysler. Indeed, as the *Harvard Business Review* has pointed out,
the French auto firm's private-sector rival, Peugeot-Citroën, has paid as
much in taxes to the government (1.8 billion francs over the past five
years) as Renault has received in subsidies (1.7 billion francs).[23] Renault
has essentially been sustained by Peugeot. In Italy and Great Britain,
nationalized firms, afflicted with voracious unions, have caused grave
budgetary crises.

The U.S. bail-out of Chrysler will be a disaster if it is used as a precedent
for further government intervention. A policy of subsidizing failures will
end in an economy strewn with capital-guzzling industries long past their
time of profitability—old companies that cannot create new jobs themselves but can stand in the way of job creation.

CHAPTER 15

Laffer and Liberal Economics

ROBERT L. HEILBRONER, one of the nation's most eloquent and prestigious economists, late in 1978 arrived at a solution to the enigmas of the American economy. For maximum impact and visibility, he divulged his findings on December 22 on the op-ed page of *The New York Times*. Some three weeks later, early in 1979, John Kenneth Galbraith, an even more famous and voluble authority, appeared in the same spot with nearly the same revelation. The two experts agreed that the problem of the U.S. economy was an insufficiency of taxation and controls.

As usual Galbraith was crisp and quotable. After offering his familiar analysis of the pricing power of big corporations, he said that price controls would be practical and effective: "It was learned in World War II and often then remarked that it was not hard to fix prices that were already fixed." Controls alone would not suffice, however. Taxes would also be needed. He urged "a very modest increase . . . on incomes above $30,000. . . . It would affect fewer than 5 million taxpayers (4.8 million in 1976) while bringing a measure of restraint to bear on recipients of between one-quarter and one-fifth of all taxable income. The effect would be to moderate expenditure on more expensive automobiles, more costly real estate, fancier dress, more imaginative furniture, more memorable social observances, and other outlays of less than life-supporting urgency. . . .

"The incentive effect of upper income taxation," Galbraith assures us suavely, "is not adverse. In times past, when the taxes on higher incomes were far higher than now, economic growth was much greater. A modest restraint on upper income expenditure (and the resulting outcry) should make it easier to ask blue collar workers to accept limits on their wage increases."[1]

And again as usual, Heilbroner was more portentous and less complacent, but his prescriptions were essentially the same: a combination of "drastic taxes" and wage-and-price controls.[2] Such measures, together with increased economic planning, could "give a new measure of life, albeit a limited one, to the capitalist system." But it will remain "crisis-prone," and as Heilbroner had said in an essay published a few months earlier, "even a relatively mild crisis . . . brings spectres of collapse, revolution, the end of the world."[3]

The United States did indeed seem to be reaching the end of an era. But it was a final phase not of capitalism but of the fashionable economics of the Left. Together the two articles represent a confession of irrelevance on the part of America's two leading writers of liberal economics. Although it is conceivable that a combination of wage-and-price controls with higher and more progressive tax rates would bring a "solution" of some unneeded sort to the American economy, "for advice like that," as Irving Kristol has remarked, "we don't need economists." It appears that after decades at the forefront of their profession, after numerous best-selling books and innumerable self-confident articles, after earnings in the millions from texts and consultancies, these two luminous scholars end up resorting to, as an answer to inflation, the kind of dull reflex that most readily occurs to respondents of public-opinion polls.

The enjoyment of such ironies is one of the many rewards open to the observer of the still free markets of modern America. But more important than the sales of Galbraith's and Heilbroner's works, more revealing than the elitist poses of their socialism, is the increasing inanition of their ideas. It is hard to summon breath to respond to a recommendation of higher taxes as an antidote for inflation at a time when taxes have been rising for a decade at a rate 80 percent faster than prices.

The economists, it is true, did wish to focus the tax increases on the highest brackets. But the top 1 percent of America's income earners already pay nearly 20 percent of the federal income taxes and the top 25 percent pay 72 percent. Neither Galbraith nor Heilbroner signified the slightest awareness that further increases in marginal tax rates are likely to bring reductions in revenues, particularly from high-bracket earners who can move their incomes to the least productive and least taxable uses.

The eagerness of the two economists for wage-and-price controls is equally stupefying after what Robert Schuettinger has described as "forty centuries" of dismal experience with such measures.[4] Galbraith & Heilbroner cited the "success" of wartime restrictions, which both failed to halt inflation and were followed by an inflationary explosion after they were removed. Galbraith lauds the controls of the Korean War period, though price limits were irrelevant at a time when many prices were actually declining as a result of restrictive fiscal and monetary policy.

Neither of our economists faced the profoundly perverse impact of controls, particularly on the crucial group of fast-growing technological enterprises afflicted by job-hopping technicians and engineers, or considered the other destructive effects of price limits on investment and productivity. The controls, in fact, would be likely in the end to enhance inflationary pressures rather than relieve them, because productivity, but not the money supply, would decline.

It is not merely the futility of the programs, however, that signifies the end of an era. Galbraith and Heilbroner could plausibly maintain that as socialists they favor more sweeping measures, but that under current political circumstances stopgaps are all that are possible. More significant is the obsolescence of their entire vision of America: their incomprehension of its class relationships and economic structures and their blindness to the rise of new economic modes of thought.

Galbraith suggests their view of the world in his roguish list of the marginal expenditures of the rich, to be tempered by modest rises in the tax level. Essentially he believes that more progressive taxation would reduce spending on luxuries. He urges the closing of "loopholes" and ending the differential treatment of capital gains in order to impose a new austerity on the lives of the well-to-do. As a result, so he supposes, programs for the poor could be more generously sustained.

Here again we encounter the old fallacy of partial equilibrium. If Galbraith should give up his winters in Gstaad in order to make donations to an indigent professor in Cambridge, Galbraith's own income and style of living would decline, and the poor man's would rise, at least for a while. Galbraith would have taxed himself more progressively and redistributed to the poor. But as Keynes has taught us, what applies to one does not necessarily apply to all. There is a paradox of redistribution. Beyond a certain point already reached in most modern democracies, raising the taxes on high incomes leads to more, not less, luxurious living by the rich, and to less, not more, support and opportunity for the poor. This illumination, slowly dawning on the overcast horizons of the Western welfare state and beginning to transform the landscape of political economy, is not thoroughly appreciated even by conservatives. But understanding it is necessary to comprehend what is happening in the world.

The crucial question in a capitalist country is the quality and quantity of investment by the rich. A tax increase will not greatly affect their consumption, which represents a relatively modest and steady portion of the wealth of the upper class. What is affected is the calculation by which a rich man decides to save and invest and by which he chooses what kind of investments to make.

Visitors to London in the 1970s—at a time when tax rates on earnings rose steeply to 90 percent and income from investments was taxed at an incredible 98 percent—were often given to remark on the displays of luxury and affluence. Mercedes and Aston Lagondas maneuvered for parking space among chauffeured Austin Princesses near the glittering jewelry stores and art galleries on Bond Street. On any inclement day a fifth of the nation's managers and professionals might have been found, redistributed by taxes, among the French restaurants in midtown New York, along the beaches of Ibiza and the Algarve, and in winter perhaps even on the slopes of Gstaad. Galbraith might have imagined that he could get them out of his way and back to London by closing the two-point gap on "unearned income" to 100 percent, or further confiscating salaries. But, alas, the English accents would only have proliferated on the slopes.

The chief effect of steeply progressive tax rates is to lower the price of luxury and leisure in relation to investment and work. Paul Craig Roberts has elucidated the point:

Take the case of a person facing the 70 percent tax rate on investment income. He can choose to invest $50,000 at a 10 percent rate of return, which would bring him $5,000 per year of additional income before taxes. Or he can choose to spend $50,000 on a Rolls Royce. Since the after-tax value of $5,000 is only $1,500, he can enjoy a fine motor car by giving up only that amount. Britain's 98 percent tax rate on 'unearned' (investment) income has reduced the cost of the Rolls in terms of forgone income to only $100 a year. The profusion of Rolls Royces seen in England today is mistaken as a sign of prosperity.[5]

As Scott Burns has put it with reference to the United States, "we will see more Cadillacs and Mercedes on the roads and more yachts in the water until the very day the economy falls apart."[6]

High taxes, together with inflation, cause the economy to fall apart in the same way as the high interest rates that preoccupied Keynes. High tax rates, though, are worse because high taxes choke off enterprise— and thus can reduce government revenues—while high interest rates can have the self-correcting effect of eliciting a higher amount of savings. Both wreak their destruction by inducing, or forcing, potential investors to eschew investment, thus impoverishing the economy—by pushing the rich out of it and onto their yachts.

Let us assume, for example, that Professor Galbraith becomes disgusted with the antics of wealth in Europe and affronted by the conglomerate movement in American publishing. He decides to return to New York City and publish his own works.

He has recently received an object lesson in neophyte finance from his skiing companion, William F. Buckley, Jr. Buckley had tried to run several companies while writing two novels and two hundred columns, editing a biweekly magazine and newsletter, giving innumerable lectures, conducting a television interview program, mastering Bach on the harpsi-chord, sailing across the Atlantic on a small sloop, and visiting China and Gstaad. During a moment of free time Buckley had signed some reports that led to a bankruptcy, opened him to charges of stock fraud, and brought still more vividly home to him the perils of wealth and paperwork in regulated American commerce.

In any case, Galbraith decides to run his company in detail himself, without absenteeism or remote reliance on lawyers. He invests 1 million dollars, arranges additional financing, rents a suitable headquarters, hires editors and artists and secretaries, contracts with compositors, printers, and binders, and in general endures the diurnal trials of business in New York City.

After a year of struggles, the company survives. In the second year it publishes a Galbraith best-seller and earns him a 10 percent profit on his capital—after his workers have paid federal, state, and local income taxes and the company has paid property taxes, licenses, and all other fixed fees to government.

The Wall Street Journal describes what happens next in a similar case:

Of the hundred thousand dollars in profit, the city clears away roughly $5,700, leaving $94,300. The state clears away about 10 percent of that, leaving $84,870. The IRS, levying at progressive rates, snatches $38,000, leaving $46,870. Our good rich person then pays this to himself as a dividend.

Being rich, our man is of course in the highest personal income-tax brackets, and after paying 4.3 percent to the city ($2,015) has $44,855 left. The state clips him for 15 percent of that ($6,728) and leaves him $38,127. Uncle Sam "nicks" him for 70 percent of that, which is $26,689, leaving him with $11,438.

Thus, on the investment of 1 million dollars in capital and two years of hard work in assembling an enterprise that is risky to begin with, this lucky fellow who turned a profit of $100,000 has $11,438 to spend. He has given up two years on his yacht to gain $5,719 in annual income.[7]

A brilliant professor would never do anything as foolish as that. But let us imagine instead a man who invested in the stock market and sold his shares in 1973 (a year for which detailed figures are available). In that year investors had nominal capital gains of 4.63 billion dollars. Many of the stocks, however, had been purchased years before, in uninflated dollars. After correcting for inflation the 4.63 billion dollars became a net loss of 910 million dollars. Nonetheless, because they showed a capital gain in nominal dollars, they had to pay taxes of 1.13 billion dollars, for a total real loss of more than 2 billion dollars, none of it reportable as anything but a gain. The year 1973 was not unusual. Between 1968 and 1977 most major stock and bond indices, including even ninety-day treasury bills, ran behind inflation by at least 20 percent, and individual savings accounts did far worse.

The Steiger Amendment breakthrough of 1978—lowering the maximum tax on capital gains from 49 to 28 percent—has not fundamentally altered the situation. Martin Feldstein, president of the National Bureau of Economic Research, has estimated that even if corporate profits and share prices manage to keep pace with inflation and show the traditional rates of real growth, a 20 percent tax on nominal capital gains would mean an 80 percent tax on real gains if the inflation rate is 7 percent. Eight percent inflation would lift the effective tax rate to over 100 percent, where it stood during the 1970s before the reforms.[8] The capital-gains tax, through inflation, has become quite simply a tax of wealth confiscation.

Inflation has similarly raised the tax on unearned income from investments (dividends and interest). Galbraith writes that "in times past, when taxes on higher incomes were far higher than now, economic growth was far greater."[9] He is presumably referring to the early 1960s, when the top tax rate was 91 percent on investment income and he was urging President Kennedy to "get America moving again" by expanding spending in the public sector. Kennedy instead urged reduction of the highest bracket to 70 percent and eventual reduction of the highest rate on "earned" income to 50 percent. The economy surged forward after President Johnson signed the bill.

In the decade of the 1970s, however, contrary to Galbraith's contention, the real tax rate on investment income—even excluding state and local taxes—was far higher, not lower, than it had been in the days of Kennedy's Camelot. The real tax was not 70 percent, but 70 percent of a nominal amount of earnings that was mostly inflation, combined with a decline in the value of principal equal to the rate of inflation.[10] (On a $10,000 certificate of deposit earning 10 percent interest, for example, pretax earnings would be $1,000, taxation would be $700, exclusive of state levies, and the loss in principal due to an inflation rate of 7 percent would be $700. The *real* tax, therefore, would be $1,400 on earnings of $1,000, or 140 percent.)

As the 1980s began, the combined impact of taxes and a declining currency was approaching 200 percent of unearned income as inflation destroyed a portion of principal nearly double the usual interest payment, which itself was taxed at the highest rates by both state and federal authorities. Between 1973 and 1978, according to an estimate by Warren Brookes, the *taxflation* rate was 132 percent, one-third higher than it was when the nominal rate was 91 percent in the sixties.[11] Incredibly enough, however, liberal economists like Galbraith and Heilbroner, and the counselors of President Carter and Senator Kennedy, were urging still higher taxes throughout this period. There are only two possible explanations: these men are totally out of touch with the economy or they really are determined to nationalize American wealth, regardless of the consequences.

In any event, the result was the withdrawal of 6 million investors from the stock market, the withering of opportunities for successful new issues by smaller companies from several hundred to a few handfuls yearly, and the collapse of the share value of corporations below the book value of their underlying assets. If investors could not buy the stock, other companies would. They had no reason to endure the risk and expense of building and equiping new facilities if they could buy existing plants more cheaply. So while populist politicians railed against corporate size and proposed new laws and policing powers against bigness, the government's very own policies caused some twenty-one hundred corporate merger and acquisition announcements in 1978 alone.

By actions that spoke far louder than its feckless and deceptive words, the U.S. government was massively and persuasively telling its citizens and corporations to disinvest in the productive capital of America. But this federal message did not mean that the rich had nothing to do with their money but to buy yachts, Rolls Royces, and luxurious leisure. When it is impossible to earn reasonable returns from durable capital, the only thing to do is to grope for the much larger though perilous yields of speculation. Between 1968 and 1977, while all indices of investment values in productive capital were averaging real losses—compounded by high tax rates on illusory gains—many thousands of speculators soared and tumbled among the breakers of the commodity market or rode the surf of Atlantic City gambling stocks. Several thousand shrewd or timely purchasers of Swiss francs, diamonds, rare coins, objets d'art, and, most of all, gold, made a killing. Nonetheless, these speculations were relatively insignificant in total amounts. Most Americans, even wealthy ones, wisely eschewed the treacherous markets for rare items of connoisseurial value or the game of outguessing the gambling business.

What happened instead was that citizens speculated on their homes. While 24 million investors in the stock market were being buffeted by inflation and taxes, 46 million homeowners were leveraging their houses with mortgages, deducting the interest payments on their taxes, and earning higher real returns on their down payment equity than speculators in gold or foreign currencies. Then they parlayed their gains into second mortgages to be spent on durable goods—the washers and storm windows, color televisions and automobiles—that they would use for their retreat from the perils of money in inflationary America.

Not only did their houses tend to rise in value about 20 percent faster than the price index, but with their small equity exposure they could gain higher percentage returns than all but the most phenomenally lucky shareholders. America's middle class was doing better in the housing market than all of the shrewdest investors in the capital and financial markets of the world. By 1979 the value of individually owned dwellings had reached 1.3 trillion dollars, twice the worth of individually owned corporate stock.

American citizens had found a way to invest even if the nation's capitalists could not. Americans found an inflation shelter, one in which they could also live. They had invented a way of saving with no levies on interest. They had found a capital asset with low and declining taxes, deductible for the purposes of the IRS. Though the exceptions were more famous, the property tax dropped in most states and localities throughout the 1970s. Even in California before Proposition 13, the statewide burden had declined in five years from $71.50 per $1,000 of personal income to $65.14.[12]

Behind the housing bonanza, as behind the decline of capital, stood the power of government. The National Mortgage Association and the Federal Home Loan Bank—agencies not even on the federal budget— were channeling close to 30 billion dollars into shelters by the end of the decade, selling mortgage-backed securities to private investors, using the proceeds to finance new mortgages, either directly or through savings and loan associations, and then later purchasing the new mortgages to finance the issue of yet new securities to back a further expansion of mortgage debt, all in a spiral that relies finally on the authority of Treasury guarantees.

New credit laws that require counting thirty years of income not only from the husband but also from the wife further stimulated the expansion. It was not chiefly an expression of demand or population growth. The intensification of government support for housing in the seventies came after two decades when the United States was already spending eight times more of its capital on housing than countries in Western Europe and three times more than Japan, which had undergone far faster population growth. New or marginal corporations that lacked guarantees, exemptions, and subsidies simply could not compete with the hydra-headed mortgage machine.

Most of the housing would continue yielding shelter through the 1980s, and the equity gains made people feel rich enough to plunge into unprecedented levels of consumer debt. People no longer saved more than they borrowed to buy houses; the home industry became a net dissaver. Consumer debt rose 50 percent faster than consumer incomes.

Nonetheless, most value in an economy ultimately derives from the production of goods and services. Speculation in housing—essentially a commodity—carried the American economy through a tax-inflicted depression in the value of its corporate assets. But very soon, if payments of mortgage principal and interest near double digits are to be met; if property taxes are to be paid, roofs and furnaces repaired, exposed surfaces painted, pipes, wiring, gutters, and insulation maintained; if the foundations are to be shored up, appliances kept working, heating and electric bills defrayed—if, indeed, the current equity value of housing is not to suffer a sudden collapse, leaving debts unsecured and banks exposed, with reverberations incalculable—American business will have to renew its capital. Housing values ultimately depend on jobs and business; we cannot much longer sustain business with our homes.

In the absence of investment income America has leveraged its commerce on consumer speculation. While population, production, real profits, and currency values stagnated or declined, the housing boom gave shelter to American wealth. In the early 1970s Great Britain had seen a similar housing boom, also heavily promoted by government. After holding its value while stocks crashed in 1968 and 1969, the real worth of houses soared for three years, at first rising with the market and then exceeding it, with a total real gain of more than 20 percent. Then, between 1973 and 1975, housing values plummeted by almost one-third, to a level nearly 10 percent below 1956, and did not rise again until investment had recovered.[13] There are key differences between the two countries, but in both the same feeling prevailed that housing values could be made immune to collapse. They cannot.

In the 1980s the U.S. economy will be exposed to the weather and opened to compete in a world where its rivals have been investing far more heavily. The United States has been consuming its future in much the same way as the more prodigal economies of Europe. Our investment and productivity growth have trailed all Western rivals. During the 1970s U.S. investment as a percentage of GNP was half the level of Japan and two percentage points behind Great Britain, which was force-feeding its economy with favored capital projects. Our average growth in output per man hour was one-third below Great Britain's, although our growth in real GNP exceeded Great Britain's (and *only* Great Britain's).

Even the investment that did occur was excessively devoted to responding to government regulations or circumventing them, expanding the legal
and accounting departments rather than the production lines. David Ranson of Wainwright and Company has estimated that

in 1976, no more than five cents out of every dollar invested in plant and equipment actually reflected a net increase in the capital stock. Some ninty cents went
to replace preexisting capital used up by depreciation; and at least five cents
consisted of mandatory outlays for pollution abatement and occupational safety.[14]

Roger Brinner of Harvard and Data Resources and Douglas Greenwald
of McGraw Hill's economics division have made similar estimates. Government was simultaneously hobbling business and ruthlessly competing
with it. The result was that only the capital of government and its vast
constituency of homeowners really grew.

Behind all that growth—much of dubious value and negligible yields—
was a deepening maw of debt, largely based on inflationary expectations
that would have to be fulfilled if the debt was to be repaid in a stagnant
economy. Yet this expected inflation would radically erode the capital
prospects of American business unless taxes on wealth were drastically
reduced.

In this predicament the liberal economists found it possible to sing
all their same old songs. They cited Denison's law to show that savings
rates over the centuries had maintained an even level, regardless of interest
rates, although Nobel winner Simon Kuznets had widely different estimates; and the idea that interest rates do not affect savings is self-evidently
false. As economists have done for centuries, the liberals speculated that
the vital energy and innovative genius of capitalism was near exhaustion
and that government would now have to take the lead. They spoke of
loopholes and martini lunches and hunger in America. They cried of
unemployment and monopoly profits and unequal distributions of wealth
and income. But when it came down to it, they had nothing to propose
but still higher taxes and more controls.

It could be said in response that all the opposition offered was lower
taxes and less controls. But that would be deceptive. These conventional
recommendations of the Right sprang from an increasingly articulate consensus, which accorded far better with emerging world conditions and
met more clearly and directly the converging crises of inflation, innovation,
and growth.

First, and most important, despite all its mostly irrelevant flaws, was
the politically galvanic Laffer curve. The Laffer curve indicates that there
are normally two different tax rates that will bring in a particular amount
of revenue. For example, a zero rate will bring in no revenue, and a

100 percent rate will also bring in nothing because it would halt taxable activity. Arthur Laffer's contribution, though, as his ebullient Boswell, Jude Wanniski made clear in *The Way the World Works,* was not chiefly a mathematical formula, but a vision of how to cut the Gordian knot of government growth and private-sector stagnation. He showed that lower tax rates can so stimulate business and so shift income from shelters to taxable activity that lower rates bring in higher tax revenues. The private sector can be relieved of its onerous tax rates without requiring cuts in public-sector services. The idea was simple and demonstrably true. But liberal economists derided it and conservative ones were coolly skeptical.

The critics used an idiom of rejection that is becoming familiar in all the social sciences, as they eschew original reasoning and adopt the role of programming and interpreting their computers. The problem of this approach arises from the need to aggregate varied and somewhat erroneous data in ways that omit crucial dimensions of quality and dynamics. The evidence tends to cancel itself out whenever many variables are included and to be vulnerable to charges of bias and oversimplification when a significant few are chosen. In all cases novelty, creativity, imagination, and surprise—the elusive variables of all our lives—are left out.

Nonetheless, the computers provide an all-purpose mode of refutation for any theory the experts dislike or did not think of first. The technique is to run regression equations with ever-larger numbers of variables and ever more refined and therefore dubious statistics until all meaning washes out. Then they announce that "more recent analysis and breakdown of the data indicates there is no evidence . . . absolutely no evidence . . . not a shred of evidence . . ." or especially "only anecdotal evidence . . . not a bit of data"—in this case—no persuasive testimony to indicate that the United States has reached the upper portions of the Laffer curve; that American tax rates are at a point where tax reductions can enlarge revenues. With real tax rates on gains from wealth rising well above 100 percent, the evidence loomed so overwhelmingly, towered so massively, that it seemed invisible to most of the experts in the field.

Chesterton, though, explained the problem half a century ago:

One of the four or five paradoxes which should be taught to every infant prattling at his mother's knee is the following: that the more a man looks at a thing the less he can see it, and the more a man learns a thing the less he knows it. The Fabian argument of the expert, that the man who is trained should be the man who is trusted would be absolutely unanswerable if it were really true that the man who studied a thing and practiced it every day went on seeing more and more of its significance. But he does not. He goes on seeing less and less of its significance.[15]

For whatever reason, America's normally most sophisticated and inter-esting economists were incapable of comprehending an economic reality—the greatly excessive marginal tax burden on American income and invest-ment—that was manifest to a former football player trained in physical education, Congressman Jack Kemp; a *Wall Street Journal* editorial writer with little economic training, Jude Wanniski; and an economist, Arthur Laffer, who was widely seen as most "unsound" by all his more prestigious colleagues.

Part of the problem was a confusion between tax rates and tax revenues. All economists, liberal and conservative, learn that what matters most, for good or ill, is not the way money is raised by government, but how much is spent. This is a vitally important but partial truth. Between two tax programs raising roughly similar amounts of revenue, the marginal rates—the rates on each successive increment of earnings—will make all the difference. It is the marginal rates that determine the impact of a tax on motives and expectations, on ambitions and drives, on the willing-ness to go out and work to earn—or invest to gain—one more dollar.

A crucial question will be how much of that dollar will go to govern-ment, how much reward will there be for those who endure risk or expend effort, and forgo consumption or deny themselves leisure. The impact of marginal taxation is great on those, such as welfare clients and wealthy men, who already have assurance of support. The impact may be greatest, though, on the willingness to initiate risky or time-consuming projects. For these, at least a faint possibility of fabulous windfalls may be needed to call forth the high energies and heroic innovations of pioneering enter-prise.

It is psychological forces that above all else shape the performance of an economy with given resources and technology. It is ambition and resolve that foster the impulses of growth, enterprise, and progress. A particular high tax rate or tariff may so deflate the hopes of businessmen that it brings certain kinds of effort to a halt. Thus that tax will bring in no revenue at all. It can choke off commerce without leaving tracks.

Rates and revenues at the higher portions of the Laffer curve are in-versely proportional. The higher the rates the less the revenue. Under these circumstances it is irrelevant to allege that the United States bears low tax burdens because the proportion of GNP taken in taxes is relatively low.

This distinction was repeatedly missed by administration critics of the Steiger Amendment, which advocated cutting the tax rate on capital gains. Treasury Department lobbyists argued that the existing 49 percent top bracket could not be important because it accounted for little revenue. In fact, the very lack of revenue revealed its destructive impact on the incentive to achieve capital gains among the rich people who have most of them at the top rates. By measuring revenue effects alone, liberal economists also persistently missed the effects of rising progressivity in the income tax caused by reductions in lower brackets and inflation in higher ones.

In the same way, economists miss the distinction between rates and revenues when comparing tax burdens in different countries. But just as important in appraising the effect of government, they miss the difference, in economic impact, between transfer payments, which shift demand within the private sector, and direct government spending on goods and services. In percentage of GNP devoted to government taxes and spending, the United States in the 1970s ranked well behind most major European countries, including the buoyant economies of Germany and France. Economists have usually concluded that the U.S. tax burden is therefore substantially lower. More than the entire difference, however, comes from European transfer programs—medical insurance, child allowances, and pensions—chiefly financed by relatively regressive social-security and sales or value-added taxes, which are far higher in Europe than in the United States. Medical payments and disbursals, for example, are managed by the government in Britain and Germany and are accounted as public taxes and spending.

In the United States such payments and disbursals are processed by quasi-private entities such as Blue Cross and Blue Shield, and the entire system is heavily regulated by government and subsidized by Medicare and Medicaid. But there is, as has been observed, little difference between the two modes of medical management in their impact on a nation's economy, except that the American mixture of public and private systems consumes a much higher proportion of the GNP.

In any case, excluding transfer payments substantially provided by private insurance and pension systems in the United States, only two countries in Western Europe—Sweden and Denmark—exceed the United States in government spending. OECD statistics indicate that as a proportion of GNP, U.S. government appropriations in the 1970s marginally exceeded Britain's, were 6.8 percent higher than Germany's, and were more than twice as high as Japan's.[16] In mobilizing the resources, goods, and services of the private sector for public purposes, from energy development to "child development" and defense, the United States stood near the lead among the major capitalist countries.

Because of loopholes, exemptions, and extremely lax enforcement, which are the rule rather than the exception in most of Europe, there are serious analytical problems in comparing income tax rates among different countries. Therefore, many observers fail to understand that the United States compounds its high direct appropriation of goods and services with what is probably the most progressive, complex, and commercially destructive tax system in the free world. In general it imposes a larger relative burden on the rich and a smaller one on the poor and middle classes than, for example, the systems of Japan, Germany, France, Sweden, Great Britain, or Italy.

Most European countries raise some two-thirds of all their revenues by social-security levies and sales and excise, or value-added, taxes. The United States raises less than 40 percent of its funds by these relatively regressive means. The United States gets 11 percent of its revenues, a far greater measure than most other countries, through business profits and capital-gains taxes, which tend to have the heaviest impact on the rich who hold the bulk of stock.[17] From these sources the United States gets substantially more than twice as high a proportion of its revenues as do either Sweden or Germany, while it taxes capital gains and assets at rates eight times higher than Sweden and about four times higher than Germany or Japan.[18] Germany, Sweden, France, and other European countries, moreover, have a wide range of loopholes that exempt many large and profitable businesses from any profits taxes at all, and they have long permitted much faster depreciation of new technology.

Except for Great Britain, the United States is the only country to raise substantial revenues through property taxes, a high measure of which is paid by business. Although the exact incidence of the property tax, like the corporate income tax, remains obscure, analysts are developing considerable evidence that both levies fall heavily on the wealthier classes. Liberals are increasingly hostile to the revolt against property taxes. It turns out that in recent years landlords have been notably unable to pass these taxes on to low-income renters.[19]

Combining levies on property with those on personal income and business profits, United States taxation from relatively progressive sources amounted to 17.6 percent of GNP in 1977, a 16 percent higher share than Germany, 57 percent higher than Italy, 70 percent higher than Japan, and 90 percent higher than France.[20]

As a result, in the United States average and lower-income workers pay less taxes than in major European countries, and high earners pay more. Persons earning less than half the average income pay 14 percent of the taxes in the United States, 18 percent in Britain, 19 percent in Germany, and 31 percent in Sweden. Only in France do low-income workers pay a smaller percentage than in the United States. The middle group of taxpayers also pays less in the United States than in other countries. This group provides 31 percent of the taxes in the United States, 36 percent in France, 45 percent in Germany, and some 60 percent in

Sweden.[21] The upper ranks of American taxpayers provide a far greater proportion of tax revenues than do the wealthy in Europe or Japan. The top 30 percent of American taxpayers pay 74 percent of the income taxes and the top 1 percent pay 20 percent.[22]

The top marginal tax rates on earned income are not higher in the United States than in most other major industrial nations, but the U.S. top rates, federal and state combined, hit much lower incomes. In Germany, for example, the highest rate is 56 percent, the same as the top U.S. rate, but the German rate does not take effect until income rises to $140,000, more than twice the U.S. top bracket of $60,000. In France, the top rate is 60 percent, but it does not strike until income reaches $92,000. Both Japan and Italy have top marginal rates over 70 percent, but they apply to incomes more than six times as large as the highest American rate. Switzerland has a top marginal rate of 41 percent, and the booming Asian economies in Hong Kong, Singapore, Korea, and Taiwan also have much lower rates than the United States on high, upper-middle, and average income earners. Hong Kong's top rate is 15 percent.[23]

Unlike Western leaders, the Asian capitalists understand the role of tax cuts in releasing enterprise. In Taiwan a series of deliberate tax reductions launched its economic surge in the mid-1950s[24] and cuts continued through the 1970s. In 1980 Singapore reduced its already low tax rates by 16 percent and Trade Minister Goh Chok Tong explained to a receptive parliament: "Several advanced countries, like Britain, have been hypnotized by a 'soak the rich' slogan, only to discover that by heavy taxes on personal incomes they have stifled the drive to excel and succeed."[25]

What all these figures suggest is that despite a deceptively smaller total burden of taxes, the United States may well have a real rate structure that is more steeply progressive and more comprehensive in taxing the rich than any other country. Because Britain and Sweden have very high top income-tax rates that yield little revenue, they have been even further up the Laffer curve in some parts of their tax system than is the United States. But both European countries impose higher rates on the middle classes and lower rates on business than the United States, and thus the rate of progression to the highest levels has been less steep than in America, even before Britain's substantial tax reforms of 1979 and 1980.

There is no doubt that by any measure the U.S. tax rates are more progressive than those of our major competitors—Germany, France, Japan, and the booming Asian capitalist countries. Steeply progressive rates may have an idealistic ring, but their effect is to reduce incentives for economic success, work, and risk, and to favor the search for unproductive sinecures that make small encroachments on leisure time or household comforts. If the economy cannot offer large rewards to enterprise, the ambitious man will seek the advantages of insurance and security, political power and bureaucratic pelf. In short, high marginal rates continuously under-mine the very diligence and determination that are necessary to accomplish any useful work in the world. They diminish the motive to move up and promote the impulse to pull out and return to the household econ-omy.

Since the United States has one of the most steeply graduated tax systems in the world—the rates most punitive to wealth—and since the United States demonstrably has lower rates of private savings and invest-ment than any of its rivals, there is no doubt whatsoever that our capital and investment taxes should be drastically lowered in the upper brackets. Such measures would not only improve the diversity and quality of our capital stock, particularly through the formation of new companies, but the cuts would increase revenues, as Laffer maintains.

France and Italy, on the other hand, could move decisively down the Laffer curve by lowering their phenomenally onerous social-security taxes. These taxes, three-quarters of which are nominally paid by the employer in France, and nine-tenths by the employer in Italy, have driven large portions of the work force underground in both countries. In Italy an estimated one-third of all workers operate in a _lavoro nero,_ a black market for labor that consists of some four million citizens often performing manufacturing work in basements and abandoned lofts.[26]

Britain, Sweden, and the United States could also move decisively down the curve by cutting their income-tax rates. Particularly in Britain and Sweden there is ample evidence that tax avoidance reached epidemic levels in the late 1970s. In Sweden worker absenteeism rose to an annual average of 16 days (compared to 3.5 days in the United States)[27] and work-force withdrawal became such a problem that the government pro-posed to tax hobbies and other leisure activities. Famed economist Gunnar Myrdal, a lifetime socialist, was led to denounce income taxes. Myrdal wrote:

My main conclusion is that income taxes are bad taxes from several points of view . . . . For the majority of people . . . a high and progressively increasing marginal tax rate must decrease the willingness to work more than necessary. . . . Through the lowering of the income tax, the irrational diversion of invest-ments from production to durable consumer goods would not be so severe. . . . The fact that the consumption tax [he was urging the adoption of value-added sales taxes] is a tax on living standards instead of income, and therefore puts a premium on saving and capital accumulation, should be liked by almost everyone especially in these times. . . . Of all the deficiencies in our income tax system, for me the most serious is that the laws directly invite us to commit tax evasion and tax cheating. The honesty of Swedes has been a source of pride to me and my generation. Now I have a feeling that we are becoming a nation of hustlers because of bad laws.[28]

Gunnar Myrdal, meet Arthur Laffer.

In the late 1970s Governor Carlos Romero Barcelo of Puerto Rico was so fortunate as to meet Laffer; and Jude Wanniski, who had also conferred with Barcelo, was bold enough to end his book with a prediction that retrenchment of Puerto Rico's upper-bracket tax rates would bring higher growth and revenues. Barcelo took the advice, cutting territorial income-tax rates and removing two 5 percent surtaxes in 1978. By the next year, according to official statistics, tax revenues increased by $15 million over the previous year, the unemployment rate dropped by 1.2 percent, and inflation slowed down. Further reductions were enacted in 1979, with a 13.5 percent increase in revenues and 100,000 more taxpayers coming onto the rolls in 1980.[29]

Governor Romero Barcelo took his inspiration from the so-called Kennedy tax cut of 1964, signed by Lyndon Johnson after John Kennedy's death but well on its way to passage in 1963. The United States should have taken a similar inspiration in the 1970s. The Kennedy measure, which reduced the top rate from 91 to 70 percent and dropped other rates proportionately, brought almost surgically beneficial effects to the economy. Perhaps the most striking result of the announcement of the Kennedy cuts was a dramatic expansion of private investment and its shift from land and property into business. In the four-year period before the cuts 27.4 percent of investment went to business and 38.5 percent to real estate. In the four years after the cuts 58.6 percent went to business and only 11.2 percent to real estate.[30] Such a shift in investment priorities was also needed in the late 1970s, after more than a decade of tax increases—a 10 percent surcharge in 1968, a near doubling of the rate on capital gains in 1969, and the effects of inflation every year—had completely nullified the Kennedy achievement and stultified the American economy.

With the guidance of Paul Craig Roberts, then a key senatorial aide, Congressman Jack Kemp of New York and Senator William Roth of Delaware introduced a tax-cut bill in 1976 patterned on the Kennedy program of 1964. As vitally needed as it was, however, the bill affronted many influential American economists, liberal and conservative. Many of them acknowledged the destructive effects of progressive taxes in higher brackets but believed that most U.S. taxpayers faced marginal rates that were too low to deter effort or to prompt a widespread search for legal ways to avoid taxation.

This belief that most Americans were free of serious tax disincentives is totally erroneous. During the late 1970s citizens everywhere, from Harlem to Hollywood, from Wall Street to Walla Walla—from taxi drivers and shopkeepers to screenwriters and business financial officers—were heavily preoccupied with sheltering or concealing income and profits from the government. Financial finagling became a major growth industry.

The reason why becomes evident from a perusal of *The Distribution of the Tax Burden* by Edgar K. Browning and William R. Johnson, a comprehensive study of the distributive impact of the entire U.S. tax system. Published by the American Enterprise Institute in 1979, this analysis differs from most previous studies in that it includes in its computations of marginal tax rates not only the increase in tax payments resulting from a gain in earnings, but also the loss of transfer payments (such as Medicaid, welfare, and food stamps) that occurs when a transfer recipient enlarges his income by working. Browning and Johnson conclude that the effective combined marginal tax rate on the incomes of American households begins at over 60 percent for the bottom third (chiefly because of lost transfer payments), averages over 40 percent for the middle group, and moves up toward 50 percent for the top fifth of earners.[31] But the study leaves out all tax increases after 1976. Including the hikes in social security and other levies in the late seventies and those proposed for the early eighties, the Browning-Johnson analysis would indicate that the vast majority of American households faced marginal tax rates of 50 percent or more.

This means that most Americans could expect to keep less than half of any additional earnings they might choose to seek. There is no question that such marginal tax rates, hitting middle- and low-income recipients, have a substantial negative impact on taxable economic activity, work effort, and productivity. But though such effects were everywhere visible to the casual observer, economists often failed to see them because of the large expansion of the work force during the late seventies. Aggregate analysis seemed to show an increase rather than a decrease of work effort.

Indeed, higher marginal rates do tend to bring more women into the work force, often holding part-time jobs.[32] But the quantitative increase in workers conceals a deterioration and fragmentation of work effort, a decline of career commitments, a breakdown of families, and a vast movement into the underground economy.[33] Altogether these trends indicate that the U.S. economy is high on the Laffer curve and that cuts in tax rates would cause dramatic shifts from sheltered to taxable activity while also improving productivity and growth.

In 1978, as it happened, the state of California put some of these ideas to the test in Proposition 13, a drastic cut in property taxes. This bill reduced the effective tax burden on personal income in the state by approximately 30 percent over the following two years. Most expert observers were appalled. Economists everywhere anticipated a disaster for employment. The California Business Round Table foresaw "explosive inflation." The Congressional Budget Office (CBO) consulted its econometric model and predicted a "slowdown in economic activity," but envisaged a drop in the state's Consumer Price Index because of the impact of reduced property taxes on housing costs.[34] According to the CBO report, Proposition 13 would depress the California economy, reduce employment, and cut tax revenues in the state.

The Congressional Budget Office was right about inflation, but for the wrong reasons, and was wrong about everything else. The state's CPI was a full percentage point below the nation's despite the fact that housing costs continued to soar. But personal income in the state grew 40 percent faster than in the nation, employment grew by some 400,000 jobs, and tax revenues continued to rise, creating a 1 billion dollar surplus in the state's accounts. The only economist who predicted such results was Arthur Laffer.

For liberals concerned with the distribution of income, moreover, the Laffer curve offers a promise as seductive as any of the Keynesian strictures against austerity and thrift. Regressive taxes help the poor! It has become increasingly obvious that a less progressive tax structure is necessary to reduce the tax burden on the lower and middle classes. When rates are lowered in the top brackets, the rich consume less and invest more. Their earnings rise and they pay more taxes in absolute amounts. Thus the lower and middle classes need pay less to sustain a given level of government services.

In recent years steeply progressive rates, exacerbated by inflation, seem to have steadily reduced productive investment among the upper economic classes in many Western countries and thus have forced a steady enlargement of the tax burden on the middle class. This situation, if one is lucky, ends in middle-class tax revolts, but it is caused by upper-class rates and, ironically, will be worsened by reducing taxes on the middle class alone. Cuts in middle-class rates will merely make the system more progressive and reduce still further the productivity of the rich. The middle class will have to support the government one way or another. This is the dead end of egalitarianism: to help the poor and middle classes, one must cut the tax rates of the rich.[35]

These realities have been dramatized most spectacularly in England and Sweden, where the highest nominal rates brought in negligible amounts of revenue, and anyone who struck it rich immediately fled to Malta or Nassau to shelter his winnings, leaving the immobile middle class to pay the taxes. But Wanniski demonstrates that the effects of progressive taxation as taught in the West are most devastating in the Third World, even in once thriving countries being reduced to that condition by a vicious interplay of inflation and taxes. The once solid economy of Turkey, for example, by 1980 was struggling under a 55 percent rate applying at incomes of $1,600 and a 68 percent rate incurred at just $14,000, while the International Monetary Fund (IMF) urged new "austerity" programs of devaluation and taxes as a condition for further loans.[36] This problem is also widespread in Latin America where economic emigration, brain drain, and capital flight have been stifling the impulses of growth.

In the United States the drastic decline in receipts from capital gains taxes after the rates were raised in 1973 shows that economic emigration can occur internally as well; potential investors simply withdraw their money from its most productive and taxable uses. Speculation abounds in existing commodities, in land and gold and art, or in gambling stocks, while the durable capital of the nation—necessary for all its further wealth—wastes away.

CHAPTER 16

The Inflationary State

THE ESTABLISHED THEORY had a powerful answer to all the flood of Republican arguments for the Kemp-Roth bill and Lafferite economics. Solid citizens, from Galbraith to President Carter, agreed that to cut tax rates by 30 percent as the bill proposed would be wildly inflationary— and inflation, as they suddenly recalled from three decades of conservative speeches, is surely "the cruelest tax of all."

The liberal economists did not mince words or convictions. Their arguments were heard with great uneasiness by many conservatives as their own party seemed to turn cavalierly away from the canons of fiscal responsibility. When the tax cutters answered vigorously, the debate raised in a decisive way some of the most crucial issues of economics.

It is true that as the argument unfolded, many of the combatants looked to the red glare of the fracas and the occasional flashes of light only for proof that their favored flags of partisan economics were still firmly in place, fluttering in the breezes of their own rhetoric. But for those who followed the debate closely, there dawned some new illuminations. It was becoming clear, for example, that the usual Keynesian remedies for inflation—raising taxes to sop up excess demand, restricting the supply of credit, reducing government spending—were all either extraordinarily difficult to invoke or ineffective when they were applied. This situation caused great perplexity on every side. Then, however, there arose a new dissent. What had begun as a timid hypothesis—could it be?—grew into a widely uttered heresy, not modifying the Keynesian analysis, but turning it inside out: *inflation is caused by taxes.*

Anyone unsure that the idea was revolutionary had only to observe the offhand way it was announced. Truly revolutionary ideas do not prevail by overwhelming their foes. More often they win by the "of course" effect, as in "Of course, *some* taxes are inflationary." At first liberals mentioned *sales* taxes when they argued against a value-added levy. Next they cited payroll taxes in urging retrenchment of the social-security hikes of 1978. Then there was widespread notice of property taxes after Proposition 13 cut them back in California, and the Congressional Budget Office predicted a resulting drop in the housing component of the Consumer Price Index. Finally, the inflationary inpact of the 100 billion-dollar burden of regulations, a form of taxes, became a staple of every presidential speech on the subject. Many experts tried to hold out on the matter of income taxes. But once they had given in—"of course"— on sales, payroll, and property levies, income taxes seemed to be just a matter of time.

The meaning of this development, though, remained obscure, and many economists, such as Galbraith and Heilbroner, refused to acknowledge it at all. If a decade of taxes rising 80 percent faster than the pace of inflation would not bring that inflation to a halt, the answer was still more taxes. Other disagreed. But there were nearly as many explanations offered as there were economists who considered the matter.

As usual the simplest and most lucid case came from Milton Friedman. Friedman endorsed the Kemp-Roth bill only because it would exert pressures for cuts in spending. "The total tax burden," he said, "is what the government spends, not those receipts called 'taxes.' And any deficit is borne by the public in the form of hidden taxes":[1] chiefly, through a decline in the value of their dollars and through interest on the federal debt. Without cuts in spending, therefore, nominal tax cuts merely conceal rather than reduce the burden.

This was indeed the beginning of wisdom on the issue. But it was not the end of the argument, for it neglected the potential impact on business of changes in the structure of tax rates. Although he has written as eloquently as anyone on the importance of incentives to businessmen and workers, on the Kemp-Roth bill Friedman returned to sterile computations of dubious aggregates—spending and demand—rather than stressing the dynamic effects on business creativity and investment. Ironically, he was far more sensitive to the dynamic political effects: how lower taxes would lead politicians to cut spending, although this result was likely only if the Lafferites were wrong.

Addressing the inflation issue more directly was Paul Craig Roberts, one of the framers of Kemp-Roth and by all odds its most economically sophisticated advocate. He maintained, in essence, that high taxes were a brake on production, and that this *tax brake* caused inflation by reducing the supply of goods without limiting the supply of money. The result was the classic inflationary situation of "too much money chasing too few goods," but this time as an effect of less goods rather than more money. Roberts was following the footsteps of Dennis Robertson, one of the first of modern supply-side economists, who rebuked Keynes in 1927 for denying that an income tax hike could create inflation. Robertson said the tax hike would have supply-side effects, reducing the quantity supplied and raising its price.[2]

The tax-brake argument, however, left unanswered the contentions of monetarist economists, such as Friedman and Herbert Stein, that even if some Laffer effect eventually occurred, Kemp-Roth would at first cause inflationary federal deficits because of necessary lags in its impact on production. Roberts responded, in simple monetarist terms, that deficits are only inflationary if they are financed by printing money. Kemp-Roth would expand savings sufficiently to finance the deficit.[3] No one seemed to have thought of that, and no one could deny the possibility. As the decade ended with taxes on income from savings at well over 100 percent when adjusted for inflation—and with the U.S. savings rate dipping below 4 percent of GNP—there was ample room for increases in savings as a response to cuts in taxes on interest income. Income taxes doubly inhibit savings, by taxing both the initial income from which the savings will be taken and the later earnings which the savings will generate. The potential saver is deterred both from earning the additional funds in the first place and then from saving them. Cuts in marginal rates, therefore, are likely to elicit a larger relative increase in savings than in consumption.

Rounding out the supply-side case, Michael Evans, then president of Chase Econometric Associates, extended the tax-brake argument in macroeconomic terms. Historically, he maintained, inflation has tended to increase whenever production rose to the point that it pressed against the physical capacity of the system—whenever the gap narrowed between actual and potential GNP. One way of meeting this problem is to lower production by raising taxes. A better way, however, is to raise productive capacity by lowering taxes. Tax cuts will be counterinflationary whenever they enlarge plant and equipment more than GNP.[4]

To realize the benefits of tax cuts in combatting inflation, therefore, government should reduce taxes on investments and capital gains by somewhat more than it reduces taxes on incomes. The most inflationary combination is to lower taxes on income while raising them on investment, as occurred in the late 1960s and early 1970s, when the highest rate on earned income was reduced from 70 to 50 percent, while the nominal capital-gains rate was lifted to nearly 50 percent and the real or inflation-adjusted rates on "unearned" income rose to more than 100 percent. Meanwhile state and local taxes soared, rising at twice the rate of federal levies. Not only did these changes fail to expand the quantity of investment, they diminished its quality by discouraging entrepreneurship. When taxes on incomes are significantly higher than taxes on capital gains, aggressive young managers in large companies can be more easily lured out into the perilous world of new business.

David T. Morgenthaler, head of the National Venture Capital Association, explained:

The kind of achievers who will build a successful new enterprise are exactly the people that large companies pay well—much better cash incomes and benefits programs than small, often not-yet-profitable firms can possibly afford. Our tax policy in recent years has operated to make it much less attractive for such achievers to leave the well-paid comfort of large corporations for the low incomes in early years and hoped for capital gains of new businesses.[5]

And new businesses tend to increase productive capacity much faster than the old.

The tax-brake theory for fighting inflation with tax cuts was persuasive even if the short-run savings and investment effects remained unclear. The arguments of Roberts and Evans were clearly true in the long run and sufficed to justify the policy. Nonetheless, they failed to mention a more direct way that taxes cause inflation. Even before taxes inflict their brakes on productivity, they have the inflationary tendency to raise immediate costs. A large portion of the current inflation in capitalist countries is best characterized neither as *demand-pull* inflation nor even exactly as *cost-push*. The best term is *tax-push,* in which taxes are seen to have an immediately inflationary impact on wages and prices.

This idea has long had currency on the fringes of economics. A brilliantly cantankerous former *Time* correspondent in Latin America named William Krehm has presented it in several books published by himself in Toronto. John Hotson of Waterloo University, also in Canada, has developed the idea. Walter Eltis of Oxford University has broached it in his important book, written with Robert Bacon, *Britain's Economic Problem: Too Few Producers.* It first surfaced in the United States, perhaps, at a conference on inflation and income tax at the Brookings Institution in Washington in 1975. Arnold Lovell of the British Treasury, Vito Tanzi of the International Monetary Fund, and Robert Gordon of Northwestern University all suggested that rising income taxes may be inflationary because workers attempt to keep their aftertax earnings constant. Gordon cited studies in the United States indicating that wages rise by one-fifth of any income-tax hike. Lovell referred to the English experience that the rise in wages is much greater with higher levels of inflation and inflationary consciousness among workers.[6]

Orthodox Brookings economist George Perry then stepped in to keep matters under control. He sternly dismissed all such speculations because they implied that tax increases are inflationary and decreases deflationary, an "extremely remote" possibility. But the possibility was being seriously discussed at Brookings, and in it were the seeds of more radical theories on the role of government in modern economies.

The orthodox theory of how taxes can cause inflation comes essentially through the law of costs. Taxes are costs and when costs rise, profits fall, marginal suppliers fail, output declines, demand continues, and prices rise for the remaining supplies. This circuitous process operates fully within the bounds of conventional economics. The tax-push concept is both simpler and ultimately more far-reaching. From it has been developed a new general theory of inflation.

Like the Laffer curve, the new theory found its fullest expression outside of the circles of academic economics. Also like the Laffer curve—at least in Wanniski's hands—the new theory referred as much to the long historic record as to recent experience. Appearing first in a major article in *Forbes* magazine by then Associate Editor David Warsh, assisted by Lawrence Minard, the theory produced a flood of mail and won its authors the Loeb Award for the best financial writing of 1976. Warsh developed the theme further in an even longer piece, winding through some seventy pages of *Forbes's* sixtieth anniversary issue of September 1977.[7] By the end of it, few of its readers could again think of inflation in the same way.

Warsh's analysis will not seem convincing to anyone who seeks in economics the sure laws that can be found in some of the physical sciences and that monetarist schemes seem to offer. For one thing the kind of historic record on which he relies could have been devised only for England, which maintained an essential gold standard for a millennium. A comparable French or German graph would have seen the price level often fly off the page, as currency values were totally destroyed in political debauches such as the French Revolution and the Weimar Republic.

Historic and structural arguments do not refute the Quantity Theory of Money. No one denies that an increase in the supply of money, without new flows of goods, reduces the value of money. The theory is a mathematical truth. As long as goods and money can be satisfactorily defined, along with various velocities and such, the relations among them can be reliably computed.

The monetarists also specify some crucial real constraints on policy. The historic record compiled by them shows that any growth in the money supply exceeding the rise in productivity will eventually cause prices to rise and currency values to decline, and that a flood of new money can create a hyperinflation and entirely destroy the fabric of an economy. The general warnings, together with numerous conceptual refinements and insights, represent a crucial contribution both to economic science and to the public weal.

Nonetheless, the monetarists cannot conclusively answer the question of whether monetary discipline is always possible, or even desirable; or whether the price level can be easily measured by the conventional tools; or whether the money supply can be easily defined or controlled during periods of rapid economic change. A perfectly valid theory may be irrelevant if the real world fails to offer the clear signals and instruments needed to apply it, or if the factors which it treats are not the controlling ones.

The quantity theory may explain every inflation and deflation, and prove the disastrous effects of erroneous policy, without demonstrating that the history of the price level is best considered as a saga of central banking rather than a narrative of art and industry, science and hysteria, technocrats and technophobes, potatoes and computer chips, sheiks and mullahs, antibiotics and bombs—all of which, from time to time, can distract or discombobulate and shake down or shake out a central banker and his money supplies. Today money supply categories M_1 and M_2 multiply like guns, from M's $_3$ through $_{14}$, and finally to M_x; they swirl from gold to oil to multinational grease; pop up as embossed plastic; drop briskly underground for a rare irregular run in cash, a monetary limbo; are bet and embosomed, baptized by tellers and statistically reborn in Eurodollars; are semiconducted through silicon to be stored in million-bit bubbles; and then are bounced off a satellite onto a tax-free Caribbean beach, to be glitched by a cosmic ray before leaping to London for an overnight binge in commercial paper. Eventually they may even land in a New York bank seeming perfectly cool and collected and available for discipline by Paul Volcker.

Like aggregate demand, the money supply is an essentially mathematical concept that means less than it seems; and like a high siege of savings, inflation is not necessarily a portent of decline and fall. Under some social, entrepreneurial, or technological conditions, it variously appears as a positive phenomenon or a negative one best combated by nonmonetary means or a neutral development of little concern. Like many other things, inflation is a catastrophe in its extreme forms, and an occasion for vigilance even at low levels, but it is not necessarily or always a pathological affliction. If an eceonomy is an organism evolving over long historic periods, inflation might be regarded on occasion as a healthy adaptation to new conditions rather than as a disease of the body politic. Warsh indeed brought such a perspective to bear.

His analysis was inspired by the elaborate historical research of two professors at the London School of Economics, Sir Henry Phelps-Brown (president of the Royal Economic Society) and Sheila V. Hopkins.[8] Perhaps inspired by the wage-price researches of a school of French economic historians, including François Simiand and Fernand Braudel, the two Britons had invented a single new standard by which to measure changes in the price level over long historic periods. For indices of the "general level of prices," they substituted a particular basket of goods, containing food, fuel, and cloth, designed to show the essential costs of living in any era. As a measure of the movement of prices, apples would no longer be compared to interest rates, dishwashers to fur rugs, television sets to donkey carts, and airplane tickets to walking boots, as tends to happen over extended periods in the Consumer Price Index and GNP deflators.

Phelps-Brown reasoned that the changes in the contents of the basket necessarily overshadowed in importance the price changes between the baskets of different eras. Prices, it was implied, could not be interpreted as the ratio between the quantity of money and the quantity of goods, because "goods" in a society are continually and multifariously changing in quality and context, and they elude all simple measurement. Over time, even identical products can shift radically in usefulness. A car, for example, is more or less valuable not only through its own qualities, but through the quality of roads and places to drive, the availability of fuel and alternative modes of transportation, the level of real incomes, the opportunity costs of such a large purchase, and the existence of suburbs and shopping centers. These and endless other considerations affect price and value but defy quantification or comparison to the prices in previous eras, whether of automobiles or horse-drawn carriages. In a footnote to his famous essay on inflation, Robert Solow airily observes that all who raise such concerns "can sign up for the course on index theory, but they will find it dull."[9] Dull or not, such matters constitute the essence of the problem of defining, measuring, and treating inflation.

These problems render the usual indices nearly useless in scientific terms in the long run and of doubtful worth even in the short run. Since what we see as inflation is the product of these problematical basket trends, the London study called into question the very statistical foundation of price-level theory and thus impugned the most enduring images of the history of inflation, which economists hold in their minds as they interpret current events.

The chief of these images is a graph that appears in so many basic texts and journalistic studies that it is etched, one might suppose by now, in the cerebrum of every economist. In the American version, the graph conveys the impression that the price level rises and falls through time in a jagged alpine range of peaks and valleys, with roughly equal wartime summits in 1866, 1918, and 1945. Crucial to current perceptions is the fact that every high point was quickly followed by a brisk descent, with one exception. That was the bizarre climax of the story after World War II when a major break occurs: *the price level does not go back down.*

As Heilbroner and Thurow write in their text, *The Economic Problem*, "in a vital way, contemporary experience differs from that of the past . . . inflation seems to have become a chronic element in the economic situation."[10] In a contribution to *The Political Economy of Inflation*, a British symposium published by Harvard in 1978, C. Panic calls this amazing unsinkable price level "the worst peacetime inflation in history."[11] After presenting the usual graph, Solow calls this presumed change "certainly something worth talking about."[12]

In analyzing inflations of the long past, however, the standard of a changing basket of goods almost necessarily dictated an essentially unchanging historic cycle of rises and falls, since the fundamental or secular shifts occurred within the basket; they were embodied in the changes in the nature and quality of the goods that the different baskets contained. Phelps-Brown and Hopkins instead followed their single basket of human necessities over no less than seven centuries of English history and compared it with the changing purchasing power of a carpenter and a laborer over that period. They published their findings in two articles in the mid-1950s in the prestigious British journal, *Economica.* Their conclusions shattered the conventional view of historic inflation as a cyclical phenomenon gyrating up from a steady base in times of war or in response to discoveries of new gold and silver or other incidental cataracts of money. They refuted the idea that the current period is historically exceptional and that the problem is "integrally linked with the stability conditions of twentieth century capitalism," as historian Charles S. Maier put it in *The Political Economy of Inflation.*[13] In fact, they impugned many of the usual clichés of inflation.

Warsh took the new findings and, with the help of researchers at *Forbes,* extended the analysis back another three hundred years, to 950. The result was a consistent graph depicting one thousand years of the price level of subsistence goods in England.

Rather than the usual alpine range, familiar in the single-century graphs, there emerges a millennium of long plateaus, each lasting hundreds of years and each ending in a prolonged inflationary surge to a new level. The most iconoclastic finding was the complete absence, anywhere, of prolonged or profound drops. Economists now look with perplexity at the failure of the price level to go back down to an earlier level after World War II. But the London study showed that never throughout measurable history has inflation gone back down. Several times, though, it has moved massively and persistently up.

Phelps-Brown and Hopkins conclude, describing the critical upsurges:

For a century or more, it seems, prices will obey one all-powerful law; it changes, and a new law prevails; a war that would have cast the trend up to new heights in one dispensation is powerless to deflect it in another. Do we yet know what are the factors that set this stamp on an age; and why, after they have held on so long through such shakings, they give way quickly and completely to others?[14]

These were the questions that Warsh set out to answer.

A clue was the record of the British carpenter's purchasing power over seven centuries, for in this graph there actually occur the phenomenal peaks and precipices, the range of mountains and valleys, that are usual in the graphs of inflation. Each of the long upsurges of inflation in the price-level graph is punctuated in the carpenter's graph by an occasional catastrophic fall in his purchasing power. The fall comes not from a drop in money wages (nominal wages scarcely fell in seven centuries), but from the collapse in the value of the money unit in relation to the subsistence basket.

What are these ghastly periods of inflation that last up to a century, increasing the cost of human necessities by four and five times and often putting the average worker through a wringer? They are, as Warsh shows, none other than the most glorious stages of human economic history, precisely the periods long identified by historians, depending on their semantic tastes, as "seminal," "transitional," or "revolutionary." These are the times when new classes emerge, organized in new ways, applying new technologies, when new tides of energy and invention surge through a society, casting forth new roles and specializations, structures and hierarchies, attitudes and ideologies, as men collectively slough off the institutional coils of a previous age and launch a new era, with a different and far more complex division of labor arising among the ruins of the old. Including the present epoch, there have been four of these inflationary metamorphoses in the last one thousand years.

The first surge marked the emergence of the feudal and commercial era in the thirteenth century from the protracted plateau of the Dark Ages. From a tribal England ruled by warring thanes arose the intricate structures of feudalism, with new canons of social behavior, new manorial hierarchies of lords and knights and vassals, new shops and crafts, and new systems of landholding, exchange, and distribution. "At the beginning," Warsh writes, "there were towns and churches and warrior chieftains; at the end, there were cities and cathedrals and mighty kings with a penchant for crusading in the Middle East."[15]

Once this great transformation of the structure of the economy was achieved, by about 1325, a new plateau of relatively steady prices took hold for some two hundred years. Then under the Tudor regimes England again underwent a siege of change and growing complexity in its division of labor and its organization of society. Prices again leapt upward for a century, and government grew in size to one-third of the national income.

This second convulsion was the revolution of mercantilism, when international capitalism and the nation-state emerged from a realm of feudal baronies. Britain dispatched her war and trading ships around the world; the Spanish Armada was vanquished in 1588; the merchant fleet doubled its tonnage in seven years; sugar and tobacco poured in from the colonies; the East India Company was formed; and global business, with its complex panoply of bankers, merchants, guilds, tax collectors, shipbuilders, and traders arose from the congeries of local crafts, shops, small moneylenders, and fragmented nations of previous centuries.

As Warsh observes:

Ask an economist why prices rose in England during the sixteenth century, and he'll tell you there was an influx of precious metals from the New World. Even John Kenneth Galbraith gives that reason in his book *Money*.

But was it really that simple? Did the presence of more gold "cause" the "inflation"? Or did the increasing complexity—and the need for more money to pay those rising prices—"cause" the gold to be found?[16]

In any case, the inflation hit countries such as Sweden on the fringes of Europe nearly as hard as it hit Spain, the recipient of the gold, and England, which made the best use of it. And despite a rapidly increasing output of precious metals from South America, prices steadied in about 1620 and remained on a plateau that persisted until the industrial revolution.

Beginning in the mid-eighteenth century the industrial revolution produced a new period covering some six decades of rapidly mechanizing complexity and "roaring" inflation. When it ended in the early nineteenth century, there followed the price plateau of the industrial age, from which we are emerging now, amid a surge of inflation that has lasted some thirty-five years and probably has decades to go.

Warsh's thesis, put simply, is that inflationary periods mark the capital-intensive gestation of new and more complex social and economic systems. Once the new order is established, economies of scale and specialization halt the rise of costs and prices, consumers shift their demand to the new patterns of supply, and new savings balance the flow of investment. But first there is a long, dynamically inefficient siege when new infrastructures are put laboriously into place, new attitudes arise and are bitterly resisted, new divisions of labor, new specialties, crafts and services, businesses and bureaucracies, institutions and systems emerge at great expense and without comparably swift returns.

Each of the great metamorphoses creates a new governmental form and extrudes a characteristic new sector of enterprise. The feudal era gave birth to a commercial sector of small traders; mercantilism produced strong national regimes and a sector of national and international trading companies; the industrial revolution established the rationalized democratic state and the sector of great manufacturing corporations. The modern era, among many global exfoliations, has given us the bureaucratic welfare and regulatory state and a booming, but still massively inefficient and unproductive, sector of services, in government, business, nonprofit, and international forms.

These periods of gestation of vast new divisions of labor are costly and convulsive. They resemble the initial stages of corporate formation and expansion, when large capital purchases are made, large numbers of workers are hired and trained, great debts pile up, bottlenecks and inefficiencies abound, and huge sums of money are disbursed, all into an economy with as yet, from all the new investment, no new finished products to buy. In the most recent period much of the investment has occurred outside the capital accounts of business. But as John Kendrick has shown, inclusion of investments by the government and nonprofit sectors and in human and intangible capital such as training, research, and mobility, reveals an expansion of total investment spending in recent decades.[17]

Such intensifications of capital are characteristic of the initial inflationary phases of the business cycle. What Warsh, in essence, has done, with the help of the pioneering researches of Phelps-Brown and Hopkins, is to project these now familiar phases of the business cycle onto the vast historic panorama of social and institutional change.

Where does that leave us today, in "Tudor" America, launching our ships of multinational enterprise around the world and into space and mobilizing through government a similar one-third of the gross national income? Where does that leave us, as we fitfully and often unsuccessfully attempt to achieve an industrial revolution in the pullulating sector of services? If past inflationary ages lasted as long as a century, what can we expect from an increasingly integrated world economy—flooded with anarchic new supplies of money and credit—that is simultaneously and tempestuously undergoing all four of the great inflationary metamorphoses at once, as some of the Third World grapples out of the Dark Ages, some of it forges mercantilist nation-states, and some of it rapidly industrializes, while the West moves into the postindustrial age and projects its industrial and financial power around the globe. What we can expect, it is obvious, is rising prices.

Since World War II rising prices are what we have gotten, not only in America but around the world. Although Warsh's analysis does not apply everywhere, it offers a useful view on this panoramic process. Many current national inflations reflect earlier phases in capitalist development, when government and services were normally a smaller part of the economy. Moreover, even most advanced countries, free of the heavy U.S. burdens of defense and of the morbid U.S. suspicion of wealth, have managed to avoid the huge U.S. enlargement of real government spending relative to GNP. Nonetheless, the surge of change, both positive and negative, has everywhere been associated with rising prices. In particular, global financial developments—the massive and multiplying expansion of banking services far and wide, the creation of the immense Eurodollar markets, the launching of huge multinational corporations, and even the rise of OPEC—have all enlarged and internationalized the world's supplies of liquidity.

Japan worked its postwar miracle of growth with a steady siege of inflation, which allowed its capital-hungry corporations in effect to tax its heavily saving citizens. Japan's monetary indices—whether currency and demand deposits (M_1) or currency, demand deposits, and savings deposits (M_2)—grew far faster than its GNP. During the economically halcyon years between 1960 and 1965, Japan's basic monetary supply (M_1) more than doubled, its M_2 rose two and one-half times, its consumer price index jumped forty points, its real GNP rose by two-thirds, and its industry emerged as a commanding force in the world economy. By 1966 Japan's ratio of M_2 to GNP had reached 99 percent, compared to the U.S. level, then and now, near 70 percent. After 1966 Japan's M_2 began rising at about the pace of its nominal GNP, with little perceptible impact on either real growth or inflation until the shock of the OPEC impost in 1973.[18]

In sum, through the sixties and seventies, Japan has led the industrial world both in inflation and in growth. Part of the reason is a stress on exports. But countries with balance of payments deficits usually have suffered more. The crucial reason for Japanese inflation has been a vast and heavily leveraged expansion of its productive facilities, building for the future and adapting readily to volatile patterns of opportunity.

Taiwan, Korea, and the other thriving Asian economies that have changed the course of world history in favor of capitalism have also undergone long sieges of inflation while growing at a world-leading pace and replacing Maoism as the Asian paradigm. In fact, of all the major industrial countries that exceeded the United States in productivity growth over recent decades, only Germany had a slower rate of inflation. France, Sweden, and Italy, as well as the Asians, all raised both their productivity and their price levels faster than the United States.

Examining the monetary systems of different economies, one finds certain rough relationships that accord retrospectively with the monetarist view. When M_1 grows more rapidly than productivity, inflation usually results as predicted. But one also discovers a crazy variety of successful monetary systems. In some countries, such as Japan, demand deposits and currency (M_1) seem to be about one-third of GNP while M_2 is almost equal to it. By contrast, in Germany M_1 is usually about one-sixth of GNP and M_2, by various measures, between 50 and 65 percent of it.[19] In the United States M_2 remained near 70 percent of GNP for most of the booming 1960s, and at times it declined as a proportion of GNP during the stagflationary 1970s. Meanwhile less developed countries with rampant inflation have tiny money supplies in relation to nominal GNP because of restrictions on interest rates and lack of effective banking systems.

Such an array of historic relationships between money, inflation, and growth does not support the thesis that inflation is the prime problem of economies, or that any particular level of money supply is uniquely favorable to economic health. The best way to fight inflation and to contain its effects is private-sector growth. Monetary restrictions chiefly dampen private-sector growth and promote the very expansion of the public sector, which caused the problem in the first place.

The only lesson for the U.S. economy that is evident from the German and Asian examples is the need to enhance investment and productivity by lowering the now confiscatory tax rates on high incomes from investment. We have reached the end of the line for demand-side economics, whether Keynesian or monetarist in character. Rather than attempting to rigidly control unruly aggregates, we should focus on the impact of specific policies on the incentive to work and invest, on the ultimate sources of the pressure for cash and credit and for the goods and services for which they are created. This is the message of the new economics, from both the Lafferites and from the theory of diffusion.

It is also important to come to terms with the structural dimension of the most advanced and perplexing inflation: the one in the United States. Before the interplay of supply and demand, the basic price of each marketable good is the tip of a pyramid of production, consisting of all the intermediate contributors or claimants to its value. It is the sum of its own intermediate costs plus a share of other costs passed on in its price. When the pyramid grows and productive processes become more complex and specialized; when new groups of workers and managers participate in the productive structure; when the state extends its services and raises its taxes; when foreign gangs or governments extort an additional take; when simple tasks are broken down and industrialized; and when the universe of economic activity enlarges and unifies, the price at the tip necessarily tends to rise in proportion to the growth of the intermediate claims on it. Then, as the whole system gains experience and efficiency, the price of any particular pyramid will stop rising, and it may even fall. During a period when many new price pyramids are being launched and enlarged, when the proportion of intermediate costs to final prices is expanding, the general price level will rise.

I write in early April, surrounded by tropical greenery and large mirrors and handsome blond wood, in a restaurant perched expensively on the side of a steep hill in the market district of Seattle, overlooking Elliott Bay with a clear view to the Olympic Mountains on the horizon through panoramic picture windows. I pay three dollars and twenty-five cents for a "French" cheeseburger and a dollar and a quarter for a Cappucino (coffee with a little hot milk and cinnamon). Elsewhere in Seattle I could get the same coffee, and a much larger cheeseburger, for less than half the price. I am paying for architects and carpenters and sellers of tropical plants, for advertisements in *The Seattle Times*, for printers of the menu, for the black ties and brisk service of the waiters, for cooks and dishwashers and entrepreneurs, for ranchers and truckers and Brazilian generals, for metalworkers and glaziers, and accountants and lawyers. But most of all, as Warsh shows, in the late seventies in America all final prices embody the pyramid of public services, paid for by taxes at every point in the productive system.

This latest inflation, according to Warsh, most essentially reflects the *diffusion* through the price structure of the rising costs of government around the world, from OPEC to Health and Human Services (HHS, once HEW). It is government, with its ever-proliferating goods and bads, services and inefficiencies, with its costs rising in the United States since 1965 at a pace 68 percent faster than GNP, 80 percent faster than the price level, and 70 percent faster than personal income;[20] it is booming and boondoggling, enterprising and diffusing public power that chiefly caused the seventies' inflation. Tax hikes began the spiral and tax push continued it. The reaction of other sectors, though real and sometimes excessive, was essentially defensive. Between 1940 and June 1979, for example, the price of government rose four times faster than the price of food and six times faster than the price of oil.[21]

The case is quite clear and simple. No group in society, including organized labor, did remotely as well as government—federal, state, and particularly local—during the inflationary siege. The spiral began with necessary spending to accommodate the baby boom as it moved into schools and colleges. But then the surge acquired a momentum of its own, impelled as much by political enterprise as by social needs. Perhaps the single key fact in the behavior of the economy between 1970 and 1975 was a quadrupling of spending by state and local governments after 1965.

Government, as Warsh argues, has become for better or worse, like land, labor, and capital, a factor of production. It is compensated not by rents, wages, interest, or profits but by *taxes,* which are the rents of bureaucracy. Much government activity is useless or worse. So it would seem are the multibillion dollar private markets in narcotics and smut, not to mention cigarettes. But even conservative congressmen celebrate every item of public spending in their own districts and wave through multibillion-dollar boondoggles on the floor of the House once the programs are established. Big government is obviously here to stay.

Under these circumstances it is self-destructive for conservatives to pretend that the inflationary impact of taxes on costs is chiefly a problem of the money supply. Sooner or later the American liberals, like the British Labourites, are going to discover that monetary restrictions are a wonderful way to destroy the private sector while leaving government intact and offering pretexts for nationalizing industry. Since government has become a factor of production, the only way to diminish its impact on prices is to economize on it—just as one would economize on the use of land, labor, or capital—by reducing its size or increasing its productivity.

Government costs are only partly absorbed or shifted around in the private sector; mostly they are passed on. They are diffused into all the charges, wages, salaries, and fees of strategically situated business and labor—added on to every union contract and commercial price in the system as every citizen bargains in *real* terms to keep his place—until in the end all the serially multiplied spending of Washington and the states is accommodated by the monetary system, by the Treasury, and by the Federal Reserve.

Many American conservatives believe that the Federal Reserve should not permit this enlargement of spending, that it should restrict currency and credit and attempt to force a halt to the spiral of costs. But it is already too late. Once the debts have been incurred and the new division of labor is in place, once the pyramids have been extended, the central bank has little further choice. The prices will continue to rise until the change is consummated and made efficient and until consumers adjust their demand to the new pattern of supply.

To say that the Federal Reserve should not accommodate government spending is, in practice, to say that business should pay. Not the broad range of middle-class wealth in housing and consumer goods or the wages, pensions, and fringes of organized bureaucracy or unionized labor. Not, chiefly, even the largest corporations with their ability to float their own commercial paper or borrow from banks at the lowest rates. These groups are too powerful politically to be made to bear the brunt of contraction. The victim will be the future: the vital investments of the private-enterprise system, the creative energies of real prospective growth, and the necessary sources of marketable new production—all the private forces that must ultimately support government and uphold the future American position in the world economy and in the military balance of power.

Although the Federal Reserve should expand credit only in a prudent way, in proportion to the growth of government and business, any attempt to fight inflation by monetary contraction alone at a time of repeated shocks to supply will cause new, yet more destructive, and more permanent inflation. If the chief problem is a disproportion between the size of government and the size of the private sector—the number of public-sector workers stacked up behind each private-sector price—this imbalance will be worsened by efforts to contract private borrowing. Even if the restrictions are disguised by a trumpery of government cutbacks (which will last only until a new recession comes), inhibitions on private growth will just intensify the original inflationary disproportion between private and public power.

At this juncture there is no practicable antiinflationary program except Lafferite economics and supply-side stimuli, no alternative to new productivity in both the public and private sectors. It is not principally the federal deficit that causes inflation. If the deficit were closed by higher tax rates—and the money supply were held constant—the price level would likely rise in the orthodox way of the law of costs. There would be less investment and production and fewer new products, but the prices of the narrowing circle of old products would have to increase to reflect the additional burden of direct government costs. The expanding money supply merely makes it possible for private activity to continue despite the massive diffusion of taxes, throughout the world economy, by every government body, from OPEC to City Hall. The only way to relieve the world economy of this burden is to increase productivity, in particular the productivity of government and services—the now expanding sectors in the new epoch in the history of capitalism.

CHAPTER 17

The Productivity of Services

THE INFLATIONARY new sectors of the modern economy are government and services—all the nonmanufacturing, nongoods-producing, often nonprofit and tax-dependent parts of the society—from lawyers and social workers to teachers and travel agents, from nurses and computer programmers to rock singers and management consultants. Here, in the merging world of government and services, many of the characteristic new roles of the era have been invented. Into the services of the "postindustrial" age hundreds of thousands of people are channeling their energy, ambition, and spirit of enterprise. They will not be easily rolled back into the industrial age. For all the talk of a return to the farms or a revival of small crafts and cottage industries, this social change is an imperious fact of life. The nature and potential of the service sector will largely determine, in the Warsh model, the future of the current inflation, for good or for grave ill to the country.

The services comprise a wide spectrum of activities and professions, many of them very old and familiar—from the world's oldest to the corner store—that do not build or manufacture a final product. Any definition must be somewhat arbitrary. In a sense all goods are services. When one buys a car or a television set, one could be said to acquire transportation or entertainment services, the rents for which are capitalized in the price. Nonetheless, when the term is used in the social sciences, as in an explanation of declining national rates of productivity or in a prediction of the shape of "postindustrial society," phrases like "the revolution in services," "the emerging service economy," and "the low-productivity, people intensive services" refer to two groups of activities that minister to people's needs without making anything themselves.

Schools, hospitals, museums, retail shops, merchandising chains, restaurants, employment agencies, professions, and the like and unlike, comprise the smaller group. The larger group embraces the whole economy outside of mining, manufacturing, construction, and agriculture, and thus includes finance, insurance, real estate, transport, communications, and utilities as well as all the retailing and ministering activities in the smaller group.

The large group of concerns made a big stir in the early sixties, when, excluding government, they exceeded America's manufacturing sector in employment and total sales, thus giving rise to some grandiose theorizing that the United States was a "service society" entering a "postindustrial age." Although by a similar measure Great Britain became a service economy in 1850,[1] we can agree that something important has been going on and that the idea of a postindustrial age is useful.

Such notions converged with a congeries of concepts suggesting the emergence of a "new class": a knowledge sector of computer programmers, laboratory technicians, media experts, lawyers, paralegals, doctors, paramedics, architects, draftsmen, special librarians, social workers, professors, social administrators, and a cornucopia of varied consultants. Conflating all these service functions into some kind of bloated generality and then distilling it into a crystal ball, sociologists could depict a society in which goods-producing industries had declined to one-third of the work force and now comprised a group that was subordinate to a "new class," a "knowledge technocracy" of service personnel.

All these analyses conveyed some valid perceptions of the changes going on in America. The theory, however, went on to predict a number of dubious outcomes. The goods-producing realm was fated to grow still smaller as automation and other new technology outmoded its work force and lowered its prices. Meanwhile the service sector, with its irreducible needs for labor and its generally low productivity, would continue to absorb new workers, achieve political and economic strength, raise its relative wages and prices, and gain an ever greater proportion of the GNP. As some scholars saw it, this would perpetuate structural inflation and declining productivity.[2]

The shift from manufacturing to services thus was seen as reversing the great productivity gains that arose from the previous shift from agriculture to manufacturing. The more lyrical of the prophets could predict a new pastoral age, as the grimy business of production was automated and people were left, in a service society, to go around stroking one another in interesting ways, many, no doubt, requiring advanced degrees in sociology.

In various refined and sophisticated forms, this vision has been entertained by such scholars as Daniel Bell, Peter Drucker, and Scott Burns among others. If the theory were true, it would bear a dire portent. If the services are inherently unproductive, inflation in the service society could be combated only by monetary means. Including government—also seen to be immune to the normal means of productivity improvement—fully two-thirds of the labor force were depicted as bogged down in intrinsically expensive tasks beyond the reach of technical enhancement.

This theory, prevailing in the social sciences, would cast the current inflation largely outside of the Warsh model. What is being gestated is not a new division of labor that will soon work out its bugs and attain steadily increasing gains in scale and specialization, thus reducing costs and halting rises in the price level. Rather, the advanced nations are preparing for a stagnant economy to be ruled by a leviathan government. The current capital costs and national debts will never be redeemed by future yields. Instead, the nation will go on new binges of inflation merely to fulfill its existing commitments. "Debauching the currency" is still a sure road to poverty and decline.

Indeed, history offers many more examples of sclerotic bureaucracies stifling the sources of creativity and growth or destroying most private wealth in runs of inflation than it offers examples of Warshian ascent from debt. The vision of services and government as leading sectors of growth in a movement toward postindustrial prosperity may strain credulity. It is always easier to envisage continuation of existing trends into decline and catastrophe than it is to imagine the creative surprises and innovations that can lead to a new era of noninflationary peace and progress.

There is much evidence for the gloomy scenario. The service and government sectors achieved their current dominance only partly in response to real public needs. Together they were unique among American industries in benefiting heavily from inflation itself. In 1978, for example, government gained some 50 billion dollars in additional tax revenues from bracket creep, spurious capital gains, dubious corporate profits, and social-security increases required by inflation, and it received a 58 billion dollar reduction in the value of its debt, for a total inflationary dividend of 108 billion dollars, all coming ultimately from the wages and savings of the private sector.[3] Whenever one hears that debtors gain from a declining dollar, one should keep foremost in one's mind the identity of the leading borrower, government, and its trillion dollar total debt.

Services are less well known as beneficiaries of inflation, but as is shown by several studies reported in the Brookings text, *Inflation and the Income Tax*, services, narrowly defined, were the only sector that gained from the impact of the rising price level on depreciation schedules and other tax-accounting rules.[4] Profits in services are less likely to be nullified by the increasing replacement cost of capital equipment and inadequate allowances for depreciation. The capital of services tends to be human beings, and the development costs are often defrayed by the taxes that support public schools and colleges. Moreover, such service industries as law, health, education, accounting, and nursing homes benefited heavily from government programs and regulations such as Medicare, Medicaid, aid to education, and the multiplication of administrative rules covering everything from the environment to product liability, and all tending to impose new burdens on the manufacturing sector.

When it becomes clear that services have grown in part through subsidies and that government has boomed from its own inflation, the likelihood of great future benefits from this decade of debt seems somewhat remote, and the other great historic pattern of bureaucratic growth and national decay seems most probable.

Despite all the contrary portents though, government and services fit the Warsh model very well. Closer analysis shows that most service industries have undergone efficiency gains comparable to the rest of the economy, and services in general seem on the verge of vast new gains from technology and management. Even the government, despite all its extraneous operations, dubious programs, and waste of resources, is open to major advances in productivity that over time can reduce its burden on the economy, even if large retrenchments in spending cannot be achieved soon. Although there is no doubt that government could be substantially cut back, to the great benefit of the country, there is no sign, even in the Republican party, of a willingness to slash existing programs, even such entirely bootless ones as Aid to Education in Impacted Areas. Arms spending is being increased. Defense is perhaps the most "inflationary" of all activities since it pumps money into the economy; and it competes for scarce and valuable resources of both technical manpower and matériel, but it produces no domestically consumable goods. We are left with the imperative of expanding the private economy and increasing the productivity of services in both the public and private sectors. Fortunately this can be done.

The central arena of services is the office. What the factory floor is to manufacturing industry, office space is to service industry. Office technology is the fixed capital of most service companies. During the seventies manufacturing productivity increased by a total of nearly 90 percent while office productivity rose by just 4 percent, less than one-half of 1 percent a year. Yet, in a paradoxical turn, the manufacturers that expanded fastest were very often the companies providing equipment designed to enhance the productivity of offices. From IBM to 3M, from Control Data to Wang Labs, from Texas Instruments to Hewlett-Packard, from Olivetti to Motorola, the makers of mainframe computers, semiconductors, microprocessors, telecommunications, and data-processing systems—the entire panoply of the modern electronic office—have been growing at an annual rate of some 20 percent.

Early in 1979, the year of the Iranian oil crisis, leading market analysts ranked office equipment behind only energy among their five favored industry groups, and IBM still ranked first and Xerox fourth among the individual stocks favored by the experts. Offices of all sorts were purchasing new apparatus at a steadily rising pace: complex and costly devices difficult to master quickly, but promising great gains in the future.

The new office equipment was increasingly linked to management systems. Rather than selling particular devices, most of the computer and data-processing companies had begun to sell "information networks," "distributed data-processing capabilities," "planning analysis and control partnerships," "integrated functional performance teams," and "shared-logic linkages"—all jargon that points to the need and ability to reorganize and rechannel office activity to exploit the new technologies. As these methods are perfected, office productivity rises in the same sort of quantum leaps that Adam Smith described in his famous analysis of the economies of scale and specialization in the manufacture of pins.

The new office technology is already having a dramatic impact on many service companies. Indeed, on the list of favored industry stocks for 1979, three service groups came after energy and office equipment: they were banks, health care, and airlines, all heavily dependent for growth on the use of the new computing, data-processing, and telecommunications systems. Other services that have benefited from the semiconductor and microprocessor revolution include fast foods, discount retailing, communications, insurance, real estate, and the media, both print and broadcasting. In terms of the Warsh paradigm, all these industries have been investing in expensive equipment that begins by raising costs and ends by expanding productivity and value. The services are becoming more complex in preparation for imparting a major impulse of growth to the entire economy.

Services are now entering their industrial age. As Theodore Levitt of the Harvard Business School has written:

Only recently have some of the traditional service industries and service occupations begun to think industrially. Only recently have they begun to look at "service" with the cognitive style of the industrialist instead of the humanist, much as people began, in the latter eighteenth century, to look at work in the style of the manufacturer rather than the craftsman. . . . The so-called post-industrial society is not industrially "post." Industrialization is as possible in the service as in the goods producing industries, in the service occupations as in the craft occupations.[5]

Perhaps the epitome of the service sector as an inflationary problem is the hospital. In 1950 the average cost per patient per day was sixteen dollars; by 1979 it had exceeded two hundred dollars. But here, too, the phenomenon of the changing basket of goods arises in acute form. As Martin Feldstein testified to the subcommittee on health in the U.S. Senate,

The most obvious thing about hospital care today is that it is very different from what it was twenty-five years ago or even a decade ago. Today's care is more complex, more sophisticated and more effective. The cost of health care rises more rapidly than the price level in general because patients and their doctors are no longer choosing the same old product but are buying a different and much more expensive product. The rapid rise of hospital costs is therefore not a form of price inflation but represents an increase in the quantity of hospital services that are packed into a day of hospital care.[6]

What pure inflation did occur in health care, moreover, is mostly the result of steadily expanding first-dollar insurance coverage, both publicly through Medicaid and Medicare and privately through Blue Cross/Blue Shield. Feldstein points out that the average real additional cost to an insured private patient of a two-hundred-fifty-dollar room is just eight dollars. As long as these new services are deceptively rendered at old prices, the demand for them will soar.

Nonetheless, the new technologies are offering the promise of substantial new efficiencies that are often balked by attempts to impose price controls. Medicine well exemplifies the snags and inefficiencies, as well as the promise and opportunity, of management and technology in the revolution of services.

Because federal control and oversight requirements have been imposing large new burdens of medical paperwork, the automation of this aspect of health care tends to free nurses and doctors to concentrate on their real duties with patients. The average intern today, for example, spends perhaps 90 percent of his time on paperwork. It is the growth of human bureaucracy, with its necessary rules and reporting requirements, that creates alienating and impersonal jobs. Automation tends to enhance the administrators' span of control and reduce the need for middle managers and clerks doing machinelike tasks.

All such improvements do not depend on full automation. An example of the kind of small advances in management that can yield large gains in efficiency is the hot line for diabetics, which was pushed by Dr. Reese Alsop and by Dr. Peter Bourne before his departure from the White House. Diabetic comas now cost America's hospitals several billion dollars a year. When a diabetic goes into a coma, he must be hospitalized for long periods and undergo intensive and expensive treatment. In 1970 in Los Angeles a hospital experimented with a twenty-four-hour telephone line always open for diabetic crises, and it discovered that this device alone reduced the need for hospitalization by two-thirds and saved many lives and more than 2.5 million dollars at that one institution. The national application of such systems would save many billions.[7]

Industrialization has always relied as much on innovations in management as on technological advance. The possible gains from better management in health services are immense, as the booming but still embryonic hospital-management industry shows. Other promising innovations in management include the new ambulatory surgicare centers, which provide simple operations to essentially healthy patients for as little as one-quarter the hospital price, and central laboratory and diagnostic clinics, which allow patients to undergo, in one place, a broad range of tests and examinations that would cost far more time and money in conventional facilities. These profit-making medical and surgical units, which are multiplying rapidly in the United States, benefit chiefly from advances in specialization and management. Their increasing successes indicate huge room for productivity improvement in American health care, even without new technology or medicines.

But hospitals are also experiencing great productivity gains from medical science. An example is the use of surgical staplers that simultaneously cut and close "bleeders" during operations, achieving in minutes a result that formerly required more than an hour of careful stitching and tying off of arteries. Electrocardiograms that far outperform the stethoscope, cardiological units concentrating a wide range of advanced services on heart patients, CAT scanners (computerized axial tomographers) that identify tumors in the brain, and a whole new generation of antiviral drugs are among the gains from science that are now increasingly available in medicine.

Hospitals are becoming more expensive, more complex, and more capital intensive. They are far more costly to build and maintain. In the late 1970s many of the gains were far less evident that the costs. But it is likely that in future decades the 1970s will be seen as the period of gestation of more humane and more productive techniques of health care delivery—developments that might be greatly inhibited by federal cost controls.

Similar gains are likely in mass retailing—the initial breakthrough in the industrialization of services—oppressive to many, but a magnet for their dollars. The 1970s saw the evolution of the supermarket into the shopping center and the refinement and elaboration of the shopping center from great gray rectangular lumps surrounded by asphalt into secular cathedrals of commerce, aggregating hundreds of small shops and large chains, in glittering arcades with great spiral staircases and openings to the sky, with restaurants made from railroad cars and abandoned boats and remnants of gas stations, with trees and sculptures and fountained plazas.

James Rouse has extended and enriched this concept in the center of cities in such bustling cornucopias as Quincy Market in Boston and the Gallery at Market East in Philadelphia. Comparably dazzling developments have been launched in San Francisco's Ghirardelli Square and in many other cities, while Rouse is creating dramatic new commercial arrays at Harborplace in Baltimore and the South Street Seaport in New York. His Boston venture transformed six acres of abandoned buildings behind Faneuil Hall into a coruscating complex of stores and restaurants that have drawn larger crowds than Disneyland and brought in sales of 60 million dollars during its first year.

Of course, most shopping centers are less a feast for the eye. But the initial supermarket has evolved in many surprising ways—back to more luxurious and diverse old-fashioned markets in the open air, with the savor of fish and cinnamon on the breezes, and forward into gigantic plazas and discount stores everywhere. But all this development has entailed huge capital outlays, by both government and the private sector, to be amortized far in the future and to be diffused through all the current prices in the system.

The process of industrialization is under way in every branch of service activity, as plastic cards revolutionize the extension of credit, television transforms the productivity of the entertainer, word processors exalt the efficiency of secretaries, and beepers make firemen and doctors more immediately available. The system becomes initially more expensive and later more productive, just as it has in the previous epochs of transition.

The productivity of government poses problems that are very difficult but not insuperable. Many government services—from tax assessment in Ohio to financial accounting in Orange County, California, from fire fighting and ambulances in Arizona to garbage collection in many cities—have been devolved to the private sector and thus remitted to the disciplines of profit.[8] The result is almost invariably a dramatic lowering of costs and a lifting of productivity. Other public services have gained from a plethora of new technologies and management techniques similar to those employed by business.

The Commerce Department, for example, chose fourteen employees for a special productivity team and trained them to develop and apply efficiency standards throughout the Census Bureau. The result was a full 52 percent increase in productivity, saving the taxpayer 117,000 payroll hours. It was found that like personnel in every other industry, government employees work at about 60 percent of a reasonably high level of production when there are no standards or measurements of performance. When the census bureau applied its productivity program, the effort rose to 91 percent. When wage incentives are combined with measurements, all groups tend to lift their productivity to 125 or 135 percent of the standard. A consultant analyzing the census program concluded that

Improvement in government productivity whether it be federal, state or local . . . can equal or exceed that of industry when the principles of scientific management are applied effectively. . . . Congress, state assemblies and city councils would do well to spend less time making and remaking laws and devote more attention to determining . . . that the effectiveness of every unit and employee be measured. . . . Current budget . . . gyrations are totally inadequate and tend to result in grossly excessive expenditures. Congress has created a working environment for government operations where the "name of the game" is to obtain a generous budget and then make sure it is all used by the end of the fiscal year. This climate must be changed.[9]

As in all the services, productivity in government is largely a management problem. In the diversity of its roles and enterprises, government resembles a giant conglomerate. In business, conglomeration sometimes affords efficiencies of scale, typically in finance, publicity, and personnel policy. It works because each part of the enterprise will survive only if its unit costs are low enough to allow profitable operation. Business is fundamentally a productivity system.

Government, however, is a rule-and-consent system. The larger the budget granted to a government bureau by the citizens, the greater the "consent" expressed by them. In addition, one way to gain the consent of the governed is to give them money and jobs. Government can thus assimilate its own constituency. But the assimilation can work both ways. Elected officials, particularly in states and localities, find themselves deeply constrained by their government workers, who are not only a powerful voting bloc but also have monopoly power over necessary government services for which the officials are responsible. As government extends its functions of operational management, it may assimilate its own consent. But public employees also assimilate the powers of government. This is a counterproductivity system. When it is working best on its own terms, when government budgets and payrolls grow most rapidly, productivity usually declines, and its decline, engorging ever greater resources, drags down the entire economy.

Public-sector productivity is a relatively novel concern. In the past only the private sector produced. Public virtues, like charisma, wisdom, majesty, and martial spirit, could no more be tested for productivity than could the numbers of angels that might dance in the head of an idealistic mayor.

Those days are gone forever. We now elect people not only to make policy decisions but also to run things, to be managers as well as leaders. As the public sector—federal, state, and local—absorbs an ever-increasing portion of the nation's available resources, this role of running things productively becomes a vital economic problem, crucial to the fight against inflation.

This is why, regardless of the sometimes crude instruments chosen by the movement, the tax revolt that began with Proposition 13 is the most important part of the struggle to control inflation. But this effort will fail if it is not combined with a consciousness that cutbacks must be combined with efficiency improvement. Very often the first thing cut by a threatened bureaucracy is public service; the last thing cut is excess employees. If an agency reacts to tax cuts in this manner, it will become yet a larger burden on the economy, because the public will feel poorer from those taxes that they still pay but they will be receiving virtually no return on them at all. The wedge effect of taxes—the extent to which they deter productive effort in the private sector—depends not on their amount alone but on the attitude of the public toward them.

If, as in wartime, the public feels that it is being adequately served for its money, work will continue despite tax rates approaching 100 percent, or even, Wanniski points out, exceeding 100 percent, as during the siege of Stalingrad, when people willingly went without food to hold off the enemy. But if government fails to provide services that the people feel to be valuable—if it is palpably unproductive—the public will sense it soon enough and will regard their taxes as an absolute loss, to be compensated for by increases in pay.

The surest sign that taxes are too high is the increasing tendency, quite novel in our history, for citizens at all levels of income to speak exclusively of *real earnings* or *take-home pay*. This preoccupation is more significant than the usual measures of inflation because it suggests that the public believes it is not getting anything more for its money, any valuable services in exchange for the added taxes that government diffuses through the economy. Public officials try to deflect resentment onto private institutions— doctors, hospitals, and medical insurance, for example—but the people still do not regard their payments for these services as the nearly dead loss they see in every tax increase.

Liberal politicians and their client economists must come to terms with the Warshian reality of taxes not as an external claim on the private sector, but as an integral cost of profitable operation; they must recognize government not as an external necessity, but as a factor of production. If the American government could make itself more productive than the private sector throughout the spectrum of needed economic activity, the public would gladly surrender its earnings to the state. At present, however, government is disastrously unproductive even in its most limited roles of keeping order, national defense, and public education. Far more than private services, government must be made to become productive.

The poet Randall Jarrell entitled one of his most poignant protests against the modern age "A Sad Heart in the Supermarket." Later he wandered out onto a turnpike near his home and was run over by a truck. Although the poetic sensibility has now largely come to terms with the factory, the frontiers of industrialization are now moving toward public and private service, and life in a world of supermarkets and superhighways, supreme symbols of modernized service, still seems ugly and alienating. Yet if one looks beyond the early stages of the process, one can glimpse a better world beyond. Not a world that resolves any of the deeper human tragedies that afflicted Jarrell, but a world in which many of the most barren and trivial of human activities can be relegated ever more to the fringes of our lives.

What we do with our liberated time and energy is a problem of imagination and worship, not of economics. But to obstruct useful, if merely technological and instrumental, progress in the name of spiritual values is to ascribe to the superficial trappings of our lives an importance far beyond their deserts. It is also to risk ultimate economic failures that imperil the future of free societies.

CHAPTER 18

The Imperatives of Growth

THE GREAT DEBATE between monetarists and Keynesians is largely over. Even Keynesians now acknowledge the importance of money. Money demonstrably matters, and monetary errors can cause drastic damage to the real economy. Excessive expansion of the money supply in the late seventies and abrupt contraction of it during the Great Depression both vitally affected the well-being of the world.

The widespread recognition of the facts of money represented a major triumph for monetarism. Following the example of the classical economists, the Keynesians had often treated money as a veil—a translucent medium through which could be seen, in the light of economic analysis, the more meaningful contours beyond. But it turned out that the medium was diaphanous only when it was immobile. Erratic monetary changes would turn the veil into a fluttering and distracting screen—a bullfighter's cape that induced entrepreneurs and economists alike to waste their energies charging off after spurious signals of opportunity and value, profit and loss.

In their preoccupation with inflation and deflation, the monetarists and Keynesians joined forces even as they fought. Pulling at the two ends of the quantity theory equation, $MV = PT$ (money × velocity = prices × transactions), they imagined that they were in an intellectual tug of minds in the central arena of economic thought. The monetarists clung to the money supply side (MV), while the Keynesians cleaved to aggregate demand (PT), but both schools were leaning on the same rope for analytic support, the same key formula of aggregates. For all the heat of their conflict, they were inexorably linked within the equation itself, and few noticed that the equation was peripheral to the most crucial matters of economics.

The supply-side movement, on the other hand, by focusing on the processes of production and innovation, turns the equation inside out. Rather than stressing aggregate demand for goods and services, they stress the dynamic supply of new ones. Rather than emphasizing control over the supply of money, they emphasize the generation of demand for money through the production of goods: the supplies that create the need for a store of value and a medium of exchange. Rather than dwelling on the quantity of money, they stress the quality of it: its anticipated worth in goods and services, or in gold.

The desirability of holding money, after all, depends most fundamentally on acts of savings and investment that will provide new objects for purchase in the future. No monetary policy can stop people from bidding up the real prices of a declining store of goods in an economy that is running down or that has lost its faith in the future.

The long-run answer to the Keynesian concern with aggregate demand is not a concern with the money supply, which is merely another facet of aggregate demand. The answer is an unremitting cultivation of the supply of new goods—the sources of creativity and expectation that create the demand for money. The key equation of economics is between long-run innovation and growth and long-run monetary quality.

The fundamental problem of the U.S. economy is not inflation. It is collapsing productivity caused by declines in innovation and research, by a diversion of resources to real estate and collectibles, by steady expansion of the burden of government on every productive worker, by stagnant and misdirected business investment, by a booming tax-free underground economy of little long-run ability to generate technical progress, by the increasing age and obsolescence of plant and equipment, and by a 40 percent slowdown since 1973 in the rate of growth of capital stock per unit of labor. All these problems are either caused or made much worse by a perverse and destructive pattern of taxation.

Inflation at current levels is significant chiefly as it reflects and intensifies the burden of government spending on productivity. It is only when productivity is flat—when new wealth is not being created—that taxes cut ever more deeply into the incomes of the people. It is only then that the normal struggles of citizens for advancement result in an inflationary spiral of claims on a stagnant pool of goods and services. What matters, once again, is the supply side—expanding and improving the pool of products by promoting new opportunities, rather than propping up old auto companies and hyping the market for existing land and housing.

The recognition that monetary and fiscal prodigality—deficit spending and money creation—is only the proximate cause of inflation in America, and that it is not altogether regrettable at a time of steadily rising taxes, will come hard to many conservatives. But it is a necessary recognition if appropriate policies are to be adopted. Most of the monetarist analyses, for all their insights on what inflation is, tend to lose track of what inflation does. Chiefly it redistributes resources from the private sector to the government. Inflation is a tax. As such, it reduces the real federal deficit below its official levels. The tax is mostly paid by the holders of money and bonds as their value declines.[1]

If inflation is chiefly a tax, it is necessary to decide whether inflation, plus existing taxes, is more or less damaging to the economy than the likely alternative ways of financing the government. People who call inflation the cruelest tax should at least consider the effects of the other ones on the prospects of our citizens, especially widows, orphans, and the poor, when economic growth declines. In other words, one must determine whether the depletion of cash balances and government bonds—together with the other costs and risks of inflation—is more or less destructive to wealth and production than measures that directly increase tax rates on business and income.

An easy answer is that the holders of government securities (that is, lazy or risk-averse investors) and hoarders of cash (largely members of the underground economy) make very desirable targets for any tax increases entailed by new government spending. Inflation might be seen as a wind that blows ill chiefly on those who try to hide from it. People who keep on investing in the economy and producing marketable goods will do well.

But if inflation were merely a way of meeting fiscal crises by bilking hyper-cautious financiers, foreigners, fiduciaries, insurance companies, and pension funds, or a way of closing deficits by filching from the wallets of pimps, pushers, bookies, and other bankshy sorts, no one would have ever called economics a "dismal science." If inflation were merely a way of rewarding the alert and risk-bearing investor, the active manager of business, and the resourceful scout of opportunity at the expense of the complacent clipper of coupons and keeper of inert funds, the world would be a far richer place.

Unfortunately, the situation is less benign, in both correctible and uncorrectible ways. By raising taxes on real income to confiscatory levels, inflation now heavily promotes the growth of all tax-exempt or sheltered parts of the economy at the expense of the taxable parts. The earners of taxable income must support an ever-growing mass of low-taxed and unproductive spending. There are four leading groups of beneficiaries: legitimate, illegal, real-estate, and nonprofit concerns—what might be termed the above-ground, underground, ground, and ungrounded economies.

Some of the above-ground effects arise within particular businesses, as management diverts its cash flow away from profitable investment and into martini lunches, fees for celebrity consultants, vast and monumental corporate headquarters, objets d'art for the president's office, prestige advertising and charity, season's tickets to sports events, country club memberships, and trips in the company jet to management conferences in Hawaii in January. Labor gets pensions and fringes, medical plans and stock plans, and executives get perks, and awards for statesmanship rather than denunciations for excess profits.

Somewhat lower in prestige but still above ground is the balmy culture of tax shelters and avoidance devices and the sudden mushrooming of money market funds, which waste much of our most valuable financial talent in a superfluous intermediation of money. The canny legions of lawyers, accountants, and other financial finaglers are of considerable value to their clients, but in this field they contribute little to the long-run growth of the economy. A tumescence within the corporate structure, these ancillary departments grow in direct proportion not only to rising taxes, but also to the rise of regulation and bureaucracy in Washington.

In competition among enterprises, taxflation also increasingly favors the least taxed rather than the most productive. Among the leading shelters is shelter itself and the land it sits on: the ground economy. The construction business gains directly from the deduction of inflated interest payments and from increasingly generous depreciation rules applying to properties that do not actually depreciate at all. Homeowners similarly benefit both from the tax exemption for "imputed rent" and from the mortgage-interest deduction. Although this benefit may be seen as the way homeowners get back what they lost to the government on their savings, the penalty to small savers has been diminished by Congress while the deduction of mortgage interest goes on forever.

Most homeowners understandably scoff at the idea that just living in their own house and getting a break on their mortgage bill makes them major beneficiaries of government largesse. In a laissez-faire world they would be right to scoff. But in a highly taxed and inflated economy, any access to untaxed income is a real advantage. The shelter services that the homeowner receives represent "income" gained from the ownership of housing. A renter must pay for these services as well as for some of the landlord's capital costs, all from taxable income. Meanwhile, the homeowner is also mostly exempt from capital gains taxes on his property, and through the exemption of mortgage interest he is free of taxation not only on the true interest on this debt, but also on the inflation premium which, in fact, helps him pay off the real principal. Moreover, he can borrow on his enlarged housing equity and buy land, gold, or consumer durables, again with no taxes either on his true interest charges or the inflation premium. It is no surprise that half the new multimillionaires hailed in a 1978 *Fortune* study were in real estate.

Nonetheless, the huge general subsidies for shelter have not previously prevented this sector from collapsing during times of tight money. In fact, the vulnerability of housing in recessions has been a major stabilizer of the U.S. economy, shielding less seasonal and adjustable businesses from the effects of monetary policy. The construction trade is always episodic and project-oriented, using unemployment compensation to cushion its work force. Most businesses have less flexibility; they must be able to borrow or they often go bankrupt. To announce an antiinflationary drive and then heavily stimulate the housing market is a national policy of industrial suicide. Yet at the very height of the dollar crisis of 1978, Stuart McKinney, head of the Federal Home Loan Bank Board, expanded the mortgage supply by lowering the reserve rquirements for savings and loan associations, and the president promised the housing industry that he would not fight inflation with their jobs. Meanwhile the panoply of federal mortgage insurance agencies poured new funds into the mortgage market. Upward leapt all housing prices, half in response to the rise in price of the unchanging real factor, land. Thus the ground economy is both a beneficiary of inflation and a major cause of its tenacity.

Increasingly noticeable among the other taxflation effects, despite all efforts at concealment, is the underground economy, from gypsy cabs and cash-paid domestics to drug dealers and prostitutes, from double bookkeepers and inventory skimmers to moonlighters and teenage laborers, from alien labor brokers to household pieceworkers. Small businesses in many large cities are virtually forced to avoid taxes to make ends meet while also paying "protection" and other unreportable bribes to city officials, from housing inspectors to the police. The taxi commission in New York in 1980 concluded that cabs legally operating in the city lost money every mile they drove. Yet the medallions signifying a taxi franchise were rapidly increasing in real value.[2] Throughout the society, people were adjusting to high taxes and transfers, usually protecting themselves in ways inefficient for the economy as a whole.

Perhaps the most numerous group of unreported workers is fake retirees on social security, who account for an estimated 10 percent of all the hours worked in America (compared to 20 percent in Sweden).[3] All these earners evade the tabulations of census and IRS and falsify most American statistics relating to poverty, unemployment, and profits.

This thriving underground realm, which comprises perhaps 20 percent—some say 25 percent—of GNP, grows more attractive in direct proportion to the increase in tax rates. One index of its growth is the dramatic expansion of currency holdings. Although proliferating credit cards would seem to have relieved many Americans of the need for cash, holdings of paper money have far outrun increases in demand deposits (checking accounts, NOW accounts, and other traceable ways of keeping money for transactions). From a nearly even growth of currency relative to deposits in 1973, holdings of cash outside banks have swept upward far more rapidly than deposits,[4] to a level of almost 100 billion dollars at the end of the decade, or almost five hundred dollars for every man, woman, and child in the land. The fastest growing units, moreover, were hundred-dollar bills. However one interprets this development (and one can only speculate on the size and character of the transactions involved), it is largely a result of the tax increases entailed by inflation.

Like the real estate boom and so many other effects of inflation, however, the underground economy is also a cause of it and an obstacle to combating it. With cash comprising the greatest increases in the monetary base, the money supply becomes more difficult to control by restrictions on demand deposits. To achieve a specified result, the Federal Reserve is forced to cut credit more drastically for legitimate business, perhaps even driving some of it into the arms of loan sharks and others in the underground.

Last, and perhaps more benign, among the inflation winners is the ungrounded or ethereal economy—the nonprofit world of churches, charities, and foundations, all of which tend to gain resources as rising taxes increase the relative value of exemptions and diminish the appeal of material investments. These beneficiaries, however, are living on borrowed time, because no matter how flush they may feel, they ultimately depend on the ability of the economy to produce wealth and maintain their endowments.

By contrast, the taxable and more productive parts of the economy tend to lose. While the real-estate industry gets to charge rapid and false depreciation on buildings that in fact are increasing in value, high technology manufacturers have not even been allowed real depreciation of equipment that grows obsolete overnight. The government, moreover, has long permitted depreciation only on the historic or original cost of capital equipment, though it will be vastly more expensive to replace. Many businesses thus are taxed on profits that in truth may be capital consumption: the wearing out or obsolescence of facilities without setting aside enough money to repair or replace them.

IRS also taxed spurious inventory profits derived from price hikes that were required by the growing costs of new inventory. Any company that priced on the historic rather than the replacement costs of its product would soon go out of business. Most of the so-called windfall profits of oil companies are simply attributable to the ever-growing costs of replacing old inventory in a hostile world, with continuing threats of nationalization and war and with necessary resort to ever more expensive modes of production using inferior stocks of crude and shale.[5]

Finally, if new equipment was purchased by debt, the inflation premium in the interest charges was tax-deductible and the debt steadily declined in value. This gain has been so great in recent years that some companies with easy access to loans may well have been tempted into unwise capital projects. Although this problem is less serious in the United States than in England, which now grants 100 percent one-year depreciation of new capital projects, and offers a raft of benefits and subsidies to large firms, the United States will risk a deterioration of the quality of capital whenever tax policies greatly favor debt over equity and internal riches for corporations over the invested wealth of individuals.

The sum of inflationary costs and benefits varies greatly among different corporations and capital structures. But apart from cyclical changes in booms and recessions—particularly the earnings binge of the late sixties— the potential profitability of corporations probably has not declined in recent years. Instead they have lost equity value because of the excessive taxation of their potential investors. They have lost because of the uncertainty that inflation adds to all long-term planning, because of the estimated 100 billion-dollar burden of new and proliferating regulations, and because of the normal deterioration of all established business in a world of peril and change.

Those smaller corporations with less access to loans, no access to the equity markets, and less control over their prices suffered more obviously. But again it is not clear that their problems were attributable to inflation itself rather than to the related distortions of the tax code. What is clear is that a rigorously antiinflationary monetary policy would hurt small but rising companies more, since they stand toward the end of the credit queue. It is new business that suffers most when lendable funds decline.

The most fundamental damage inflicted by the seventies inflation, then, comes from a disorientation of the economy away from productive activities and toward diversionary or tax-evasive ones. Part of the problem is an increase in risk and uncertainty as contracts made under one set of conditions might have to be fulfilled under radically different ones. High taxes raise the rate of return that an investment must promise before it is undertaken. Long-term commitments are eschewed in favor of projects with an immediate payoff. Research and development and other farseeing activities are stinted despite their crucial role in the creation of new wealth and efficiency throughout the economy.

Much of the damage of taxflation can be mitigated or overcome by tax cuts. For example, the bulk of essentially legal underground activity— cash work, barter, and profit suppression and avoidance—will likely disappear nearly as fast as it arose if taxes, minimum wages, and paperwork are reduced and other policies deterring the legal employment of youths, aliens, and old people are reformed. But a monetarist attack on inflation that leaves current tax rates in place will scarcely touch the underground economy and therefore will likely not affect inflation as much as it will hurt legitimate business.

Even easier to combat is the problem of declining research and development. R & D benefits not only the company pursuing it but also competitive firms, and indeed the entire economy, since most discoveries can be imitated and lead to other inventions and applications. Roger Brinner of Data Resources reports that the total private and social rate of return on investment in R & D is, according to different assumptions, between 17 and 25 percent.[6] Most productivity studies attribute at least half of all U.S. productivity growth to technological advance. Between 1950 and 1974 high-technology companies grew about twice as fast as the rest of the economy, while showing a rate of price increase only one-sixth as great.[7] The correlation between rapid growth of earnings and low growth of prices is so high as to be a virtual law of economics.

The combination of research and enterprise is the supreme source of productivity and wealth. Without this catalyst, stable prices will mean poverty and decline. With it, rising prices will be a manageable problem. A prime measure in any serious effort to retard inflation must be a drive radically to expand our now declining levels of private investment in this seminal area. Heavy investment credits and other subsidies for R & D merely compensate for the necessary market failure to measure broad social returns.

The abolition of capital-gains taxes on stocks would further enhance the climate for creativity and correct the current bias in favor of housing, largely exempt from these and other levies. Many of the favored programs to promote capital formation, such as accelerated depreciation, do little for the struggling business with a new product and little profits. The deductability of inflated interest only helps companies heavily in debt, and loans are least available for risky ventures. Bankers must always exaggerate the possible risk factor, since they can suffer from it, but only the equity owner benefits heavily from success. Tax relief for non-real-estate capital gains—together with benefits for R & D—will prove strongly antiinflationary in the long run.

The impact of inflation on productivity can be reduced if inflation is seen as a tax and its most perverse effects are counteracted by tax cuts. When productivity growth is restored and innovation renewed, the problem will no longer seem so grave, and indeed it will likely disappear. If the problem is seen first as deficit spending and excessive monetary growth, however, policies may be pursued that have the effect of eroding productivity and wealth, and exacerbating the fundamental disorders of the economy.

Most Western countries face a period of rising pressures for public spending. The United States is committed to an expansion of the defense budget. We will need growing outlays for health and pensions as the population ages, and growing outlays for the maintenance of public capital facilities as *they* age. Wealth may be required for environmental protection, for restoration of the decaying infrastructures of aging cities (from crumbling water mains to mass transit), for schools, roads, bridges, dams, and other public works. Politicians will probably manage to continue subsidies for the usual variety of strategically placed pressure groups, from farmers to maritime unions. The Department of Energy will presumably continue to scatter its largesse across the land and try to claim credit for any private-sector breakthroughs. Public spending may well go up even if the gargantuan waste and perversity of leftist giveaways decline.

Under these circumstances we should continue to resist every unnecessary new program. But even if Congress manages to pass the usual boondoggles, we should not abandon the drive to retrench taxes. The purpose of the cuts, it must be continually stressed, is to expand the tax base— to make the rich pay more taxes by inducing them to consume less and to work and invest more. If deficits arise as an initial result, no one should panic. In an economy with an overweening public sector, deficit spending, even in substantial amounts, is decidedly preferable to tax increases.

The case against government deficits is extremely plausible and telling. Because government spending must necessarily come from current output, so it is said, the government's use of goods and services is the real tax. Why, it is asked, should we compound this tax by distorting the price level and imposing interest payments on future generations? To imagine that issuing a bond is better than levying a tax is to suffer from "bond illusion"—the idea that we can get something for nothing by manipulating financial instruments. There is no such thing, we are told, as a free lunch; all lunches must come out of the real production of the economy.

This is a hard-earned and valuable truth. But it is a half-truth, for it implies that "the economy" and other such concepts, like "the money supply" or "industrial capacity" or "the supply of labor" or "the reserves of natural resources" are definite and measurable things, subject to mathematical laws. If the government resolves to spend an additional billion dollars to build a submarine, it will be said, the private sector will inexorably have to relinquish a billion dollars worth of technical and manual labor, natural resources, industrial capacity, and other goods. Private consumption and investment will have to fall by that amount, whether the government chooses to raise taxes, sell bonds to private citizens, or sell bonds to the Federal Reserve (thus expanding the money supply and creating inflation). But these computations, for all their apparent rigor, are spurious. There is indeed such a thing as a free lunch. But there is no such thing as a measurable "economy" or an absolute "supply" of money, labor, or resources.

Labor and resources, for example, are enormously elastic. The average worker exerts himself at about half of capacity and the average executive is vastly less productive than the best ones. Modern economies are filled with fat, grease, and underused or much abused manpower and industry, above ground and below. In an overtaxed system, the statistics of economic limits and capacity are mostly mush.

Any resource depends largely on ideas and technologies, which change rapidly. In recent years they have transformed supposedly exhausted oil wells and useless heavy crude, as well as the slag heaps of old copper mines and the silicon in beach sand, into industrial treasures. The money supply is similarly elusive. New forms of money and credit proliferate in the United States, and an 850 billion-dollar Eurocurrency market, which sprang forth without any government guidance and little comprehension, plays a key role in world trade and exchange.

When the government chooses to spend a billion dollars more, what chiefly matters is not the extraction of resources or use of capacity that the spending entails, but the impact on the incentives and creativity of businesses and workers. To say that bonds and inflation impose less of a burden than direct taxation suggests not a "bond illusion" but the reality of the economic noosphere, governed by emotions, visions, and ideas, which can expand or diminish the nation's resources and capacity far more rapidly than any government plan. At present all our tax laws join to narrow the horizons of the noosphere—to belittle the true returns on investment at the creative frontiers of business.

Deficit spending can be a way of protecting the private sector and its most catalytic investments from the effects of direct taxes. A particular business may not welcome inflation or the future taxes that debt implies. But if it is a growing firm, it can deal with inflation by raising its prices (inflation will strike its competitors too), and under some circumstances the company may even benefit from inventory profits. Taxes, though, are an immediate and direct burden, with effects that are magnified by the high return on investment of rapidly growing firms. Even start-up businesses without profits and labor-intensive, high-technology companies will bear a heavy load of social-security taxes and will probably have to defray part of every increase in income taxes as well, since their employees will demand more money. Higher marginal tax rates on capital gains will further damage small and growing firms by depriving them of equity financing.

It is always best to cut government spending wherever its yield or benefit is less than private spending. But in the absence of this best policy, governments should not, as nowadays they so often do, resort to the worst policy: increasing marginal tax rates or rejecting their retrenchment in order to achieve a "balanced budget" and fight inflation. It will not work. Under the right circumstances, as in Japan, huge deficits can be entirely absorbed by new public saving, while tax cuts continue annually and private capital expands.

Where does this leave the canons of fiscal integrity that have so long been preached by most responsible economists? It turns fiscal integrity from a numerical exercise into the vital art of preserving and expanding the real and seminal wealth of the nation. This means not merely balancing income and outgo but balancing the prospective yields of government and private activity and financing profitable long-term projects in either sector by appropriate issues of debt. Under current circumstances reversion to the conventional kind of fiscal integrity of accounting balances will always result in an irresponsible and destructive resistance to tax cuts. As long as capacity is considered to be an inelastic number—as long as the economy is treated as a sum of measurable quantities—increases in government spending will inevitably require rises in tax rates and the closing of the horizons of growth. Conservatives will always and irrefutably be able to point out that deficits merely compound the real impact of government spending, by adding a rising price level and a burden of interest payments in the future. Thus taxes will be raised and the growth of government will invariably be financed at the expense of business.

This is no abstract or hypothetical danger. Conservatives around the world, elected to office on promises of tax cuts—from Herbert Hoover through Dwight Eisenhower and Richard Nixon in the United States to Joe Clark in Canada, Malcolm Fraser in Australia, and Edward Heath in England, and even Margaret Thatcher, who initially raised value-added taxes more than she cut income levies—end up increasing the tax burden on grounds of "fiscal responsibility" when confronted by the apparently rigid calculus of monetary economics. But within that calculus of pay-as-you-go lunches there is no room for creativity and inspiration, no

room for the incalculable and unprovable supply-side responses that are
the mustard seeds of the capitalist miracles of growth. As Warren Brookes
has said, it is only the physical part of our wealth that is finite. Its metaphysical sources (imagination and creativity) are infinite. There are free
lunches under capitalism because there are free minds and free men—
because of the limitless returns on metaphysical capital, because of the
manifold rewards of giving, and because of the magic of the golden rule.
But these benefits always elude the computations of aggregate economics.

If American conservatism can come to terms with the meaning of debt,
it will represent a nearly unprecedented intellectual triumph. Thomas
Macaulay's *History of England*, written in the mid-nineteenth century in
some of the most elegant prose ever applied to economic affairs, recounts
the saga of the great debt of England. It is worth quoting from it here.

> When the great contest with Lewis the Fourteenth was finally termi-
> nated by the Peace of Utrecht the nation owed about fifty million;
> and that debt was considered, not merely by the rude multitude, not
> merely by fox hunting squires and coffee-house orators, but by acute
> and profound thinkers, as an incumbrance which would permanently
> cripple the body politic. . . .
>
> Soon war again broke forth; and under the energetic and prodigal
> administration of the first William Pitt, the debt rapidly swelled to a
> hundred and forty million. As soon as the first intoxication of victory
> was over, men of theory and men of business almost unanimously
> pronounced that the fatal day had now really arrived. The only states-
> man, indeed, active or speculative, who was too wise to share in the
> general delusion was Edmund Burke. David Hume, undoubtedly one
> of the most profound political economists of this time, declared that
> our madness had exceeded the madness of the Crusaders. [For] it was
> impossible to prove by figures that the road to Paradise did not lie
> through the Holy Land; but it was possible to prove by figures that
> the road to national ruin was through the national debt. . . .
>
> Adam Smith saw a little, and but a little further. He admitted that,
> immense as the pressure was, the nation did actually sustain it and
> thrive. . . . But he warned his countrymen [that] even a small increase
> might be fatal. Not less gloomy was the view which George Grenville,
> a minister eminently diligent and practical, took of our financial situa-
> tion. The nation must, he conceived, sink under a debt of a hundred
> and forty million, unless a portion of the load were borne by the Ameri-
> can colonies. The attempt to lay a portion of the load on the American
> colonies produced another war. That war left us with an additional
> hundred million of debt, and without the colonies whose help had
> been represented as indispensable. . . .

Again England was given over; and again the strange patient persisted in becoming stronger and more blooming in spite of all the diagnostics and prognostics of state physicians. . . . Soon however the wars which sprang from the French Revolution, and which far exceeded in cost any that the world had ever seen, tasked the powers of public credit to the utmost. When the world was again at rest, the funded debt of England amounted to eight hundred million. . . . It was in truth a gigantic, a fabulous debt; and we can hardly wonder that the cry of despair should have been louder than ever. . . . Yet like Addison's valetudinarian, who continued to whimper that he was dying of consumption till he became so fat that he was shamed into silence, [England] went on complaining that she was sunk in poverty till her wealth showed itself by tokens which made her complaints ridiculous. . . .

The beggared, the bankrupt society not only proved able to meet all its obligations, but while meeting these obligations, grew richer and richer so fast that the growth could almost be discerned by the eye. . . . While shallow politicians were repeating that the energies of the people were borne down by the weight of public burdens, the first journey was performed by steam on a railway. Soon the island was intersected by railways. A sum exceeding the whole amount of the national debt at the end of the American war was, in a few years, voluntarily expended by this ruined people on viaducts, tunnels, embankments, bridges, stations, engines. Meanwhile, taxation was almost constantly becoming lighter and lighter, yet still the Exchequer was full. . . .

Those who uttered and those who believed that long succession of despairing predictions erroneously imagined that there was an exact analogy between the case of an individual who is in debt to another individual and the case of a society which is in debt to part of itself; and this analogy led them into endless mistakes. . . . They were under an error not less serious touching the resources of the country. They made no allowance for the effect produced by the incessant progress of every experimental science, and by the incessant effort of every man to get on in life. They saw that the debt grew and they forgot that other things grew as well as the debt.[8]

Most of the greatest episodes of economic history—from the commercial revolution to the industrial revolution—occurred in the midst of rising prices and rising debts. The great triumph of capitalism in Asia over the past decades hung on debt and inflation. The most awful deficit disasters have befallen the Japanese. Even in 1979 Japan had a shortfall approaching 70 billion dollars. In an economy half the size of America's, it had an official deficit more that twice as great. Yet it financed its deficit with no explosion in the money supply or in the inflation rate. This achievement merely required tax policies heavily favoring savings and investment.

Between 1963 and 1978 the Japanese savings rate rose from 16 to 23 percent and the tax burden fell at the same pace, while the U.S. savings rate dropped and taxes soared. Productivity growth increased in Japan and declined here. For all the obvious differences between the two economies—in cultural attitudes, export orientations, and spending on police and defense—there are lessons to be learned from the Japanese experience. The Japanese have accepted debt and inflation, but for the entire quarter century of growth, they have enacted a tax cut every year but two. In 1980 the average rate on individuals was under 20 percent.

Debt that is wantonly monetized or accompanied by chaos, as during the French revolutionary era, or debt that is prodigally incurred in order to destroy the unit of account of other debt, as in Weimar Germany, can bring ruin. Debt such as that in America, which is piled up to finance programs paying people not to work, combined with penalties on business for being profitable, can destroy an economy. But debt that is incurred for capital projects of benefit to citizens and their productivity, or debt that is incurred to avoid inflicting destructive taxes on growing firms—such liabilities can become vital assets of growth and progress. The worst economic disaster is to blight the future by suppressing the catalytic ventures on the economic frontier.

In an expanding economy money available now for investment is many times more valuable than money paid later in interest or payments diffused through the economy in higher prices. To the enterprising capitalist the future always promises more abundance than today. Only in a static, uncreative economy does it pay to pay as you go. Only within the cramped horizons of zero-sum budgeting (where every gain for one man must mean a loss for another) and linear or homogeneous time (where money does not grow in value as it moves toward the present), only in an abstract mathematical world can the burdens of debt seem crushing.

Budgeting in a growing capitalist economy is not zero-sum, and time is not linear. Money to be paid beyond a certain future point dissolves almost entirely; even in accounting, an annual payment of a hundred dollars forever has nearly the same value as a payment of a hundred dollars for twenty years. Time is capital in a growing system and dwarfs all debt.

The U.S. debt has long been declining. The United States emerged from the Second World War with a debt accumulation larger than its GNP, and Britain had liabilities two and one-half times as large. In three decades the U.S. debt was reduced to less than one-quarter of GNP and

Britain's to less than half. Even including private debt, there is virtually no evidence that the burden is now greater than it was ten or twenty years ago. The statistics of growing private debt chiefly reflect not an increase in final claims on income and wealth, but an expansion in the number of intermediary institutions lending to one another, diversifying portfolios, and probably making the system more stable. The problem in the United States and Britain is not debt but waste, not deficit spending but a redistributionist war against wealth that makes everyone poorer— and ironically even promotes inequality.

These countries now face a series of dire challenges that will require massive mobilization of resources and creative energies. Both have recently been undergoing a period of stagnation, largely inflicted by excesses of taxation and wasteful or counterproductive government spending and regulation. In the midst of the Great Depression of the thirties, the response of both governments to a very different but similarly exigent crisis was to protect, control, and subsidize the private sector and balance the federal budget. It did not work. In the 1980s the United States must remove the tax burdens and paralyzing protections and subsidies from the private sector, and release its energies, even in the face of conclusive mathematical demonstrations by the most eminent conservative economists that the result will put us on "the road to national ruin." The fact is that tax cuts provide the only desirable way of either balancing the budget or supporting new spending for defense.

The crucial question on the inflation tax is what is it used for. As Nobel-winning economist W. Arthur Lewis has written:

Some naive investigators have professed to show that inflation does not increase capital formation, by showing that in a number of places where inflation has occurred (notably in Latin America), capital formation has not increased. It is not sensible to generalize about the effects of inflation in this way. Inflation used for destructive purposes has destructive effects, whereas in [many countries] or in the upward phase of every trade cycle, inflation which is due to the creation of money for the purpose of accelerating capital formation results in accelerated capital formation.[9]

If the United States diverts the proceeds of its inflation tax into the creative core of capitalist growth—the new research and industry of the future—both the problem of inflation and the problem of growth will disappear. If we continue to subsidize the dying parts of the economy and the deadening growth of bureaucracy, inflation and torpor will persist, regardless of all the heroic discipline of debt and money. We will continue to contemplate, in claustrophobic pain, the illusory limits of growth. We will still glumly measure the spurious statistics of capacity and resources, income and outgo, of our false budgetary confinement, and therefore keep in very real and crippling shackles the energies and incentives of free men and businesses.

The United States must overcome the materialist fallacy: the illusion that resources and capital are essentially things, which can run out, rather than products of human will and imagination which in freedom are inexhaustible. This fallacy is one of the oldest of economic delusions, from the period of empire when men believed that wealth was land, to the period of mercantilism when they fantasized that it was gold, to the contemporary period when they suppose it is oil; and our citizens clutch at real estate and gold as well. But economists make an only slightly lesser error when they add up capital in quantities and assume that wealth consists mainly in machines and factories. Throughout history, from Venice to Hong Kong, the fastest growing countries have been the lands best endowed not with things but with free minds and private rights to property. Two of the most thriving of the world's economies lost nearly all their material capital during World War II and surged back by emancipating entrepreneurs. The materialist vision, by contrast, leads merely to newer versions of the fate of Midas.

PART III

The Economy
of Faith

CHAPTER 19

The Kinetic Economy

IN EVERY ECONOMY, as Jane Jacobs has said, there is one crucial and definitive conflict.[1] This is not the split between capitalists and workers, technocrats and humanists, government and business, liberals and conservatives, or rich and poor. All these divisions are partial and distorted reflections of the deeper conflict: the struggle between past and future, between the existing configuration of industries and the industries that will someday replace them. It is a conflict between established factories, technologies, formations of capital, and the ventures that may soon make them worthless—ventures that today may not even exist; that today may flicker only as ideas, or tiny companies, or obscure research projects, or fierce but penniless ambitions; that today are unidentifiable and incalculable from above, but which, in time, in a progressing economy, must rise up if growth is to occur.

Except in the very short run, growth does not consist of the kind of booming demand and rising productivity—the sale of more soap and Chevrolets—that the president discusses with the Business Roundtable when they gather to consider how to stimulate the American economy. Growth may not even spring from what most of the business establishment calls investment: the repair, duplication, and expansion of existing capital plant and equipment. Existing systems become more expensive and less appropriate as time passes and conditions change. Their reproduction is often a burden on growth, a diversion from always necessary investment in new technology. Long-term growth can be virtually defined as the replacement of existing plants, equipment, and products with new and better ones.

Sir Henry Bessemer, the creator of the Bessemer method of large-scale steel production, vividly described such a nineteenth-century moment of discovery and displacement. In 1854, after his first breakthrough in tests for making steel, he wrote:

I could now see in my mind's eye, at a glance, the great iron industry of the world crumbling away under the irresistible force of the facts so recently elicited. In that one result the sentence had gone forth, and not all the talent accumulated in the last 150 years . . . no, nor all the millions that had been invested in carrying out the existing system of manufacture, with all its accompanying great resistance, could reverse that one great fact.[2]

Bessemer was right. Although the adaptation and diffusion of his method took far longer than he expected, Bessemer's invention indeed ended by wreaking ghost towns and bleak motionless factories from the British Midlands to eastern Pennsylvania. By the last decades of the nineteenth century the Bessemer system was producing some 85 percent of America's steel output, replacing wrought iron everywhere in the vast extension of railroads. But the Bessemer technique also was to succumb to change. By 1910 the open hearth process, with its radically different capital plant, had usurped Bessemer and had taken over some two-thirds of the steel market in the United States.

As Schumpeter so memorably wrote, "Creative destruction is the essential fact about capitalism . . . it is by nature a form or method of economic change, and not only never is, but never can be stationary. . . . The fundamental impulse that sets and keeps the capitalist engine in motion comes from the new consumer goods, the new methods of production or transportation, the new markets, the new forms of industrial organization that capitalist enterprise creates."[3]

In the struggles of creative destruction neither large nor small companies have a decisive advantage. In general large companies are most valuable in making incremental (though cumulatively very large) productivity improvements and in extending their markets into the world economy, where political and financial clout are often more important than innovation. Small companies are collectively far less efficient. But they are also more likely to create totally new items. Large firms can sometimes succeed in buying or forming subsidiaries, such as Exxon's Zilog and Vydec, that display much resourcefulness in imitating and improving the innovations of others. What large firms lack is the fertility of numbers and the flexibility of uncommitment. Although any particular small firm may be less creative than a large corporation, the millions of small businesses together are the prime source of creative destruction—the chief initiators of valuable change.

The very virtues of size—the economies of scale they offer—are the corollary of their vices: their huge and settled investments in particular capital and management practices. Without expressing any hostility toward the large corporations, one can maintain that the struggle between past and future is in part a struggle between David and Goliath, and this struggle will never end. Although Schumpeter himself came to underestimate the changeless implications of the imperative of change—and many contemporary economists astonishingly imagine that we are now entering a stationary or stagnant technological age—creative destruction is always the essence of growth.

From this fact arises the central question about any system of political economy, any platform of a political party, any inspiring scheme of leadership: will it allow the future to prevail? Will it favor the promise of the unknown against the comforts and passions of the threatened past? Little else matters. As at every other point in the harrowing course of human history, current technologies and productivities are inadequate to a rapidly growing and, above all, increasingly demanding world population. As at every other historical epoch, faithless and shortsighted men attempt to halt the increase of knowledge and the advance of technology; they dream of "stationary states," "economic equilibria," "alternative lifestyles," "diminishing technological returns," "ecological stasis," and "a return to nature," all the while mumbling of "the threat of scientific progress." Such fantasies, endlessly refuted and endlessly recurrent, are the prime obstacle to the survival of civilization.

The problem emerges with ever more insistent urgency in every modern state. Governments everywhere are torn between the clamor of troubled obsolescence and the claims of unmet opportunity; between the sufferers of aging pains and the sufferers of growing pains; between enterprises shrinking from competition or asking subsidies for their errors and companies seeking human and capital resources to create new products and new markets for them.

Socialist and totalitarian governments are doomed to support the past. Because creativity is unpredictable, it is also uncontrollable. If the politicians want to have central planning and command, they cannot have dynamism and life. A managed economy is almost by definition a barren one, which can progress only by borrowing or stealing from abroad.

After a trip to the Soviet Union Luigi Barzini described the results of "progressive" leadership in that vastly endowed land. Many operating Russian factories, Barzini said, resemble nothing so much as beautifully maintained and managed industrial museums for nineteenth-century machinery, all oiled, buffed, and polished like an old Packard ready for presentation at a rally of antique cars. Except in the vital realm of national defense, where Soviet businesses must compete with the United States, communism in general is a purely reactionary system, a kind of dream come true at a conference of industrial archaeologists. This creative sterility can in theory be overcome by socialist countries that "plan" for freedom and change (that is, become partly capitalist). But as a practical matter it is on capitalism we must rely to unleash the forces of creative destruction that can save the world in its perpetual crisis of population and scarcity.

Nonetheless, as capitalist governments weave themselves ever more deeply into the economic fabric, capitalist and democratic political systems enlist themselves more and more on the side of the established order—on the side of stagnation and against creative growth. A democratic legislator normally supports the most powerful businesses and cultural influences in his constituency. Labor unions, deeply important in the politics of all non-Communist countries, normally back the interests of the large companies they have already organized. Bureaucracies often are closely allied with the industries they regulate, particularly when the regulations—together with excessive taxation—so damage the industry that, like the American railroad and utility corporations, they finally fall helplessly into the arms of the state.

Detailed systems of regulation understandably tend to favor the products and patterns of behavior that have been adjusted to the rules—the "good" companies that can be easily understood and supervised by the existing expertise of the incumbent regulators. Innovation always has unpredictable and possibly dangerous results. In early stages, it is always uncertain, inefficient, and if it is based on new scientific findings, even inscrutable. Any fail-safe system of regulation to prevent environmental damage, work-place hazards, and every possible peril to consumers would never have permitted the launching of an airplane, let alone an industrial revolution. Regulators must always rely on existing knowledge, commanded by existing scientific disciplines and their leading proponents.

Yet scientific expertise is nearly always as narrow as it is deep, and established scientists resist change as doggedly as any other establishment. William Shockley was one of the inventors of the transistor, one of the heroic innovators of the modern age. But in the early 1960s he was as blind to the potentialities of the semiconductor as he is now to the genetics of intelligence. Most scientific breakthroughs are made by men in their twenties or early thirties. The National Laboratories, the Food and Drug Administration (FDA), the Environmental Protection Agency (EPA)—all used by government to appraise the products of civilian science—are full of men who are past their prime, emotionally and intellectually committed to earlier technologies, and deeply resistant to progress. Asking them to judge the implications of new breakthroughs in fusion energy or microbiology is like using railroad technicians in the nineteenth century to appraise the plans of the Wright brothers.

These realities do not preclude regulation. But they suggest its inevitable pitfalls and grave unaccountable costs. The more comprehensive the regulatory systems, the more surely they will be dominated by mediocrities, and the more surely mediocre will be the growth of the U.S. economy. Excessive regulation to save us from risks will create the greatest danger of all: a stagnant society in a changing world. The choice is not between comfortable equilibrium and reckless progress. It is between random deterioration by time and change and creative destruction by human genius. Our current regulatory apparatus is in danger of becoming an enemy of creative destruction.

Thus the EPA has for nearly a decade relentlessly obstructed the use of new biological insecticides—pheromones, pesticidal bacteria, and other organic pest controllers of the sort celebrated by Rachel Carson as potential replacements for DDT. This stance has led to continued use of chemicals such as parathion, which is far more poisonous and destructive than DDT, although most of the new biological substances pose no environmental threat at all. The cause of the paralysis, William Tucker of *Harper's* concluded in a prize-winning analysis of the situation,[4] is not any deliberate or conspiratorial opposition to the new devices, but a characteristic ineptitude in the face of novelty.

As the manufacturers saw it, the chief technical problem of the new pesticides was how to keep them in the environment long enough to affect insects, not to mention humans. And the chief commercial problem has been that their narrow effectiveness, usually against just one pest, restricts their market and thus the amount of money that can be profitably invested in testing them.

Yet EPA applies to these exotic microbial substances, designed to confuse the mating patterns or otherwise disrupt the lives of specific species of bugs, exactly the same testing requirements developed for toxic chemicals that kill a wide range of insects, are used in large quantities, and persist tenaciously in the earth. EPA did not anticipate the organic pest controllers and thus was bureaucratically maladapted to approve them. Businesses arose and went bankrupt year after year, scientists achieved spectacular breakthroughs and then turned in frustration to other fields, while EPA ruminated endlessly over what to do with the new inventions, prescribed testing programs costing hundreds of millions of dollars, and shifted personnel so often that the companies could never determine the locus of responsibility for their plight. The result was to block progress in its tracks, and to promote regression to pesticides far worse than the DDT that prompted the initial regulations.

Similarly, the Food and Drug Administration is dominated by doctors who cannot really understand the new developments in pharmacology but who cling to a Frances Kelsey complex, obstinately obstructing anything new on the grounds that it might turn out to be thalidomide. The fact is that a system that prevented testing of any drug with possible side effects as bad as thalidomide would preclude almost all progress in pharmacology and cost far more lives than it saved. Today the FDA is the chief obstacle to U.S. medical progress, foolishly blocking and deterring innovation in drugs, including a whole new generation of antiviral agents, which cannot be proven safe and effective without the very decades of use by humans that the FDA forbids.

In 1974, through the Toxic Substances Control Act, Congress threatened to extend this kind of snarl to the entire compass of American industry, involving thousands of chemicals in myriad combinations, most of them toxic in varying degrees and applications. This assignment is essentially impossible, entailing a recall demand for the entire economy. Like the Occupational Safety and Health Administration, this law constitutes a license to the government to harass any company that offends it, for whatever reason. The most likely reason, however, is that a company persists in creating new products. The best way to avoid trouble is to avoid innovation. Under this law the more conscientious EPA becomes, the more destructive the effect will be. In this instance, the only hope is incompetence.

The frequent perversity of such interventions in the marketplace has been often shown. But despite all problems, regulation is sometimes needed, and should be adopted, as all agree, "whenever the benefits exceed the costs." But the calculation is by no means simple. Many of the costs are impossible to measure, for they consist of the benefits of a more open and competitive economy that allows the ready exploitation of new technologies. The most serious damage inflicted by excessive controls is the discouragement of innovation and entrepreneurship and the perpetuation of slightly laundered and government-approved obsolescence. Government, for all its seductive uses and virtues, is almost always an obstacle to change. Since, throughout the world, people live longest in the most industrialized, dynamic, and polluted countries—and longevity continues to rise in industrial societies—the burden of proof should normally fall on those who wish to halt progress in the name of saving lives.

One reason for government resistance to change is that the process of creative destruction can attack not only an existing industry, but also the regulatory apparatus that subsists on it; and it is much more difficult to retrench a bureaucracy than it is to bankrupt a company. A regulatory apparatus is a parasite that can grow larger than its host industry and become in turn a host itself, with the industry reduced to parasitism, dependent on the subsidies and protections of the very government body that initially sapped its strength. Such industries exist all over Europe today, firms feeding on the societies they once amply fed. Not one of the nationalized manufacturing companies in Europe has made a consistent profit; all are burdens on the economies they seemingly dominate but actually subvert.

In Great Britain the discovery of North Sea oil is sometimes called a "curse in disguise" because it allowed that country to continue financing its parasite leviathans throughout the 1970s and even to endow new nationalized firms such as Inmos, a hopeless laggard in the computer industry, as well as virtual government creatures like DeLorean Autos. This firm will probably never pay back the immense subsidies by which Britain outbid lucky Puerto Rico for the right to deplete the national economy in order to "create" a few jobs and destroy many more.

Even when governments give more modest help to independent business, they often act in ways that favor established firms against potential rivals. Tariffs, import quotas, accelerated depreciation, and other tax and trade policies all are most useful to settled firms with long established product lines to protect, equipment to depreciate, and profits to offset. These policies, often hailed for being targeted to achieve specific social benefits, generally promote the enlargement and reproduction of the existing capital stock: the factories and machines used to build and sell more automobiles, color televisions, dishwashers, hairdryers, chemical fertilizers, and insecticides—all estimable products but all also items of declining relevance to the rising problems of a changing national predicament. As our circumstances change, our capital stock must be transformed, and this will inevitably mean the decline in the fortunes of all the least foresighted owners of existing capital, all the unions that depend on them, and the localities and bureaucracies that the businesses support.

These government tendencies toward regression are reinforced by the media. Every report of a defective new product, a possibly poisonous industrial waste, a vaguely carcinogenic chemical, produces headlines in the newspapers and somber commentary on television news. But the valuable products and services that are never created or marketed because of regulatory excess have no voice. When a corporate leviathan suffers a setback or retrenches its payroll—whether because of import competition or simple obsolescence or even government policy—cameras and microphones are wheeled forward to record every whimper and complaint. But hundreds of thousands of small businesses involving millions of jobs expire annually without notice. Again the image of the economy as a conglomeration of big businesses and governmental bureaucracies is propagated for the public and the true sources of long-term growth are obscured. Imports are seen as a threat, progress is depicted as a peril, and governmental leaching of the economy to finance mismanagement and failure is presented as a way of "saving jobs," although in fact many more jobs are eventually lost when the disciplines of competition are allowed to decay.

Labor unions and politicians join the press in pretending that the bankruptcy of a Penn Central, a Chrysler, or a Lockheed would be a dead loss for the economy rather than a means of reorganizing the companies' assets in a more profitable way. Indeed, the greatest problem of the railroads is the idea that the present pattern of train service is indispensable in all its parts and must ultimately be supported by government if the private sector fails. This notion, demonstrable nonsense, becomes a self-fulfilling prophecy because no industry (or city) can successfully negotiate with its unions if workers believe that the firm has ultimate access to the federal treasury.

Similarly, the field of energy is full of self-fulfilling prophecies as the media spread technophobic propaganda about nearly all forms of fuel production and transport. Power plants, oil and gas refineries, and all new energy development is invariably obstructed and delayed in the name of saving lives or protecting the environment. Yet the blackouts, power shortages, increased energy costs, and industrial stagnation of coming decades will cause far more death and destruction later, when the society resorts to desperate measures: nationalizes utilities, returns to coal, and heightens the risk of environmentally pollutant wars. In celebrating decay and cringing before technology, the media promote the emergence of truly dangerous crises in the future.

The phenomenon of government support for mismanagement, inefficiency, and reaction reaches far beyond business. Comfortable failure will always and inevitably turn to politics to protect it from change. Just as declining businesses turn to the state, people and groups that shun the burdens of productive work and family life will proclaim themselves a social crisis and a national responsibility—and sure enough, they become one. The more federal aid that is rendered to the unemployed, the divorced, the deviant, and the prodigal, the more common will their ills become, the more alarming will be the graphs of social breakdown. A government preoccupied with the statistics of crisis will often find itself subsidizing problems, shoring up essentially morbid forms of economic and social activity, creating incentives for unemployment, inflation, family disorder, housing decay, and municipal deficits, making problems worse by making them profitable. As government grows, there all too quickly comes a time when solutions are less profitable than problems.

Throughout the Washington of the seventies, behind the inevitable rhetoric of innovation and progress, the facades of futurity, the forces of obstruction gathered: an energy department imposing counterproductive new taxes and price controls; a department of housing promoting rent controls; even a National Center for Productivity forced to celebrate the least productive of all unions per man hour—the American Federation of State, County, and Municipal Employees.

Despite his best intentions, the government planner will tend to live in the past, for only the past is sure and calculable. In response to the inevitable crises of scarcity, he will prescribe, as progress, a series of faintly disguised anachronisms: a revival of bicycles, a renaissance of consumer cooperatives, a new federal scheme of price controls, a massive return to coal, or a recrudescence of small-lot farming and windmills.

The entire range of current government programs can be seen as a far-reaching and resourceful defense of the status quo against all emerging competitors. Economic policy focuses on stimulating aggregate demand for existing products rather than on fostering the supply of new ones. Investment credits and rapid depreciation allowances—although better than no tax cuts at all—tend to favor the recreation of current capital stock rather than the creation of new forms of capital and modes of production. Antitrust suits are directed chiefly against successful competitors (such as IBM) and ignore the government policies at the root of most American monopoly. The system of floating exchange rates deals with lapses in international trade by depreciating the dollar rather than by forcing a competitive response of greater productivity and new products. Our taxation and subsidy systems excessively cushion failure (of businesses, individuals, and local governments), reward the creativity and resourcefulness chiefly of corporate lawyers and accountants, and wait hungrily in ambush for all unexpected, and thus unsheltered, business success.

There is a similar bias in our social and employment programs. Under current affirmative-action rules and perennial threats of litigation, civil service now passes out jobs and promotions on the basis of nearly immutable credentials such as test scores, diplomas, race, and sex rather than on a competitive performance of work. The nation's employment policies are increasingly based on new forms of tenure and entitlement rather than on expanding opportunities and new kinds of jobs.

Most of these policies are ostensibly designed to shield the poor and vulnerable from the costs of change, but regardless of the cosmetics of egalitarian policy, the chief effect is to deny to the lower classes the benefits of a progressing economy. Risk and competition, death and change are the very essence of the human condition. The effort to escape inflation by indexing the incomes of favored groups and to fight unemployment by subsidizing outmoded jobs merely makes these problems worse and foists them onto the unorganized majority: onto small businesses, onto nonunion workers, and onto the public at large in a stagnant economy.

Even voluntary wage-and-price controls mostly penalize the rapidly growing and changing companies in competitive industries, which need to pay their personnel highly to prevent them from moving to other companies or which need to charge heavily for rare services and products in which the company commands a brief monopoly. In addition, the controls shift the largest burdens to the uncontrollable sectors. To the extent the government can artificially repress the prices of automobiles and television sets, it will increase the pressure on prices for food, fuel, and housing. Since government will usually be able to influence the prices of luxuries more than of necessities, with a given money supply controls will always tend to raise the prices of necessities dominant in the budgets of the poor. This effect was evident under both the Nixon and Carter efforts for price stabilization.

In general the most important effect of the government attempt to shield itself and its clients from uncertainty and risk is to place the entire system in peril. It becomes at once too rigid and too soft to react resourcefully to the new shocks and sudden challenges that are inevitable in a dangerous world.

Supporting the future, though theoretically simple, provides plenty of challenges for human governance. Government can bring forth miracles of creativity and growth merely by enforcing the laws equally; protecting patents and property rights; promoting educational excellence—above all, in science and technology; restricting public powers to create and sustain monopoly; removing barriers to trade; lifting wherever possible the dumb hand of bureaucracy; imposing sensible penalties and incentives on industries that endanger the environment; fostering an atmosphere of stability and security both in domestic and international affairs.

Such assignments offer ample responsibilities for the Washington bureaucracy. To fulfill them will require heroic efforts. The more ambitious agenda of contemporary liberalism simply ensures that government will do nothing well, except to expand itself as an obstacle to growth and innovation. Government best supports the future by refraining as much as possible from trying unduly to shape it, for the impact of government policy nearly always conforms with the current incidence of political power, which derives from the configuration of existing capital and labor.

Perhaps the supreme symbol of the struggle between past and future is the continuing battle over tax policy, particularly on capital gains. The stakes are relatively simple. Although large companies naturally will benefit most in absolute terms, cuts in the tax on capital gains are a redemptive boon to companies that expect to grow fast, that is, new and innovating companies. Capital gains are the chief source of new wealth in a capitalist economy. It is the way people get rich. With a rate of inflation over 8 percent, a 20 percent tax on capital gains quickly rises above 100 percent in its average impact on assets held more than a few years.[5] One still can make money, if one is wise or lucky, by speculating in stocks and bonds, commodities and collectibles, and trying to outguess the market or the Fed. But an early purchase of shares in a pioneering firm—if held through the span required to launch a new product—will often be taxed at confiscatory levels when sold.

This tax constitutes a big business protection act—a defense of large companies against small, old wealth against new, the past against the future. But so called progressive politicians bitterly resist its removal from stocks. Although most liberals now acknowledge the need to promote investment, they all favor, in the words of Senator Kennedy, Treasury Secretary Blumenthal, and President Carter, a "targeted approach" of bonuses and subsidies for the kinds of investment they prefer, rather than the general cuts that will create new wealth and multiply the numbers of rich entrepreneurs.

Liberals seem to want wealth without the rich. Yet most real wealth originates in individual minds in unpredictable and uncontrollable ways. A successful economy depends on the proliferation of the rich, on creating a large class of risk-taking men who are willing to shun the easy channels of a comfortable life in order to create new enterprise, win huge profits, and invest them again. It will be said that their earnings are "unearned" and "undeserved." But, in fact, most successful entrepreneurs contribute far more to society than they ever recover, and most of them win no riches at all. They are the heroes of economic life, and those who begrudge them their rewards demonstrate a failure to understand their role and their promise.

The attitudes of politicians—at least about wealth—are quite understandable. To a great degree politicians are American aristocrats. They attained their eminence by submitting to competition as intense, taking risks as great, and making sacrifices as large as any entrepreneur. Winning politicians are at the very pinnacle of their profession. Yet they are paid less than a professional such as a doctor or a lawyer, who is assured a lifetime of risk-free income and prestige, and they have incomes vastly smaller than the fortunes of comparably successful and risk-taking entrepreneurs. It is understandable that politicians resent the mode of distribution of American wealth. Senators, governors, mayors, and congressmen should be paid at least four or five times their current salaries. The only reason they are not is their irrepressible populist demogoguery, for which they are themselves to blame, and the inherited wealth that many of them hold, cherish, and resent, which relieved them of the usual economic risks of political contest.

Understandable or not, however, the hostility of politicians toward the chief sources of wealth in America makes most of them—regardless of their professed beliefs in progress and equality—reactionary defenders of the old plutocracy against the forces of innovation and progress. Politicians who have prevailed in ruthless rivalries of wit and risk become natural allies of bureaucracy and privilege and diehard opponents of economic growth and vitality. Yet politicians, through their lives of ambition and adventure, are spiritual kin of entrepreneurs. Politicians, if they consider their own careers, and their final attainment of a fortune in prestige, should be able to comprehend the dynamics of capitalism and the necessity of great rewards for triumph against great odds.

The future of American capitalism depends of this shift of the political order from a reactionary defense of the past to a progressive embrace of the future. In the anomalous world of American politics, this change almost necessarily entails overcoming the "progressive" trends in the society.

CHAPTER 20

The Bullheaded Brewer

TO THE MIND that doubts the decisive role of genius, courage, and chance in the past, the future usually seems impossible: the Western world appears doomed to decay and coercion as its growing populations press against a closing frontier and science and technology meet the law of diminishing returns. A sociology of despair is emerging, based on spurious science, incomprehension of the hardships of all human history, and blindness to the perennial sources of human triumph. While physicists begin to concede freedom for microscopic particles, social scientists still begrudge it to human beings. Atomic structure is allowed room for the random and incalculable; but social structure is supposedly under siege by mechanistic forces of entropy and exhaustion, playing out their logic in a "closing circle" of ecological decline.

These attitudes lead to systematic distortions of vision and policy. The mind set that prompts a man to see the future blighted by coercion and scarcity also inclines him to believe that the present can be made as free of risk and uncertainty as the past, receding unchangeably in the lenses of hindsight. Because an intelligible logic is seen to have determined the past and is predicted to shape the future, the modern political thinker wants to impose a similar pat rationality on current events. He calls on government to create an orderly and predictable economy, with known energy reserves always equaling prospective needs; with jobs always assured in appropriate geographic and demographic patterns; with monetary demand always expanding to absorb expected output of current corporate goods; with disorderly foreign intruders banished from the marketplace or burdened by tariffs and quotas; with factories controlled by workers and prohibited from rapid movement or change; with invention and creativity summoned by bureaucrats for forced marches of research and development; with inflation insurance in every contract, unemployment insurance in every job, and bankruptcy insurance for every corporation; with all windfall wealth briskly taxed away and unseemly poverty removed by income guarantees. In this view, held in varying but essentially discernible forms by every "humanist" intellectual, risk and uncertainty are seen to be the problem and government the solution in a fail-safe quest for a managed economy and a quiet and predictable world.

These notions deeply affront the most essential conditions of economic growth and human progress. The quest for calculable rationality in human affairs defies the incalculable subjectivity of human beings and the danger and indeterminacy of all human life. In economics the problem surfaces most clearly in the failures of planning, which in turn are perhaps most vividly on display in the small and struggling economies of the Third World. Here contemporary ideas are applied with an abstract directness that is not feasible in the dense and multifarious societies of the industrialized northern hemisphere. With a passionate devotion to the ideals of welfare and central control, and an undeniable need for public works and investments, the developing countries provide continuing lessons in the perplexities of rational management.

Albert O. Hirschman, an economics professor at Harvard and Princeton who has long specialized in the study of retarded economies, launched, some fifteen years ago, an analysis of the development schemes and achievements in some fifty less-developed countries. He discovered, as might have been expected, a morass. He met "comprehensive programs" that parlay a medley of vain hopes, expert jargon, and jaded pieties into a "multipronged" agenda of "development"; he found spuriously "imitative" ventures, envisioning any random river valley as a site for "another TVA"; he saw grandiose steel mills and automobile plants looming over insulated little national markets. There was usually an elegant plan and a sophisticated rationale, followed by a dismal or unexpected result.

In other words, Hirschman found all the usual pretensions and fatuities of economic uplift in the Third World. It would have been perfectly possible for him to issue the usual report, applauding the ambitious schemes and aspirations, while criticizing the faulty execution, the lack of technical skill, the absence of adequate capital, the inhibitions of primitive culture, and the parsimony of the industrial world that prevent the carrying out of the Western prescriptions for growth. But instead he discovered in the trials and errors—and occasional successes—of these countries, a crucial principle of economic progress.

His key finding was that it is not only the failed projects that do not fulfill expectations. Most of the *successful* projects also drastically diverge from the plans and intentions that give them birth. A factory will be built in the midst of a bamboo forest to exploit this source of pulp. The bamboo will all go bad and the factory will thrive instead on scrap pulpwood shipped by water to the plant. A hydroelectric station is built to stimulate industrial development in a rural area. No industrial development occurs and the station seems a complete fiasco, until transmission lines are provided to deliver the power to a neighboring country. Demand grows so much that the station must be twice enlarged.

Recounting scores of examples, Hirshman proposed as a theory "the principle of the hiding hand."[1] Economic plans and projects rarely come to their intended fruition. But leaders in Third World countries need them nonetheless. They can muster in themselves and their followers the confidence and willpower to commence a major undertaking only if its dangers and difficulties are obscured. This "hiding hand" takes the form of a plan, a show of expertise, often vastly overestimating the benefits and underestimating the difficulties. The authoritative scheme and agenda serve to persuade a timid leadership that all problems have been anticipated and the solutions are known.

Such a "hiding hand" seems to have been active in the industrial development of the United States during the first half of the nineteenth century. Economic historian John Sawyer has observed that "miscalculation or sheer ignorance" of costs and difficulties was the key to launching a number of great and successful enterprises, from canals and railroads to mining and manufacture.[2]

Again folly seems to bear fruit. What is happening here? Do these experiences mean that economic advance is essentially accidental, the statistically predictable outcome of innumerable trials and errors, a random accretion of chances, building on one another like a Darwinian process of natural selection among probabilistic mutations? There are better explanations, and Hirschman gives us a key to them.

Success in any difficult undertaking is always a product of human creativity. But

creativity always comes as a surprise to us; therefore we can never count on it and we dare not believe in it until it has happened. . . . Since we necessarily underestimate our creativity, it is desirable that we underestimate to a roughly similar extent the difficulties.

[Then we will undertake tasks] which we can, but otherwise would not dare tackle. . . . The Hiding Hand is essentially a mechanism *which makes a risk averter take risks* and turns him into less of a risk averter in the process.[3]

Of course, the entrepreneurs themselves will not see it this way. They will not imagine that they may have stumbled into their greatest achievements. As Hirschman puts it, in a linguistic *aperçu:* "We fall into error, but do not usually speak of falling into truth."[4]

Hirschman has fallen into some of the most vital truths of human society, but he does not quite dare to extend them beyond the less developed world or seek to explain their deeper meaning. Things are different, he seems to assume, in modern economies.

He implies (though he surely knows better) that in modern societies planning is successful: costs are correctly estimated and benefits clearly foreseen. Yet it is apparent that if he had directed his attentions to the advanced industrial world, he would have discovered the same pattern that he found in nineteenth-century America and in the Third World: growth is an effect not of detailed plans and predictable processes but of individual leadership, initiative, and creativity. Planning is always necessary, often useful, but rarely adequate. The essential unpredictability that Hirschman took to be a malady of underdevelopment is, in fact, the incalculable condition of all economic progress. Progress and creativity cannot be forced or prescribed except for short periods and at costs far beyond the reach of any Third World country or any competitive firm anywhere. There is no way to escape for long the necessity of openness and risk.

This truth is anathema to those who seek a risk-free scheme of development and growth, whether they be unlettered leftist generals assuming control of small nations or smooth-talking corporate leaders in the United States. The rule of risk applies alike to national planning and private business, to advanced technical industries like lasers and microprocessors, and even to the movies.

John Gregory Dunne's extraordinary book *The Studio* tells of the foibles of planning during a year of high expectations under new leadership at Twentieth-Century Fox. In preparation—and preoccupying the executives—were several "sure things," including *Doctor Doolittle* with Rex Harrison, *Star!* with Julie Andrews (coming off her *Sound of Music* bonanza), and *Hello Dolly* with Barbra Streisand. The "sure-thing" superhits, however, would nearly have bankrupted the company, if it had not been for an afterthought cheapie (several times nearly cancelled in the interests of economy) named *Planet of the Apes. Star Wars* was later to perform a similar miracle for the studio. This experience is not untypical of business success. As clothing executive Richard Salomon told *The Wall Street Journal,* "Everybody praises carefully tested methods and long-range planning. Yet the most successful moves are often on-the-spot responses to completely unexpected situations, taking a company to places it never before imagined."[5]

In this respect, microeconomics converges with macroeconomics, the economics of the firm with the economics of the nation. Unpredictability dictates openness as a prime prerequisite of growth, and it requires flexibility as a key to successful planning. Closed systems of enterprise can sometimes succeed in manipulating markets or governments, in making incremental advances of productivity, or in initiating the innovations of others. But these systems rarely generate new enterprises or substantial growth.

Aaron Wildavsky in a celebrated study of national plans could not find a sure success anywhere.[6] From France to the Philippines, plans are propounded, given lip service, and flouted. Countries such as Taiwan and the Ivory Coast, which leave room for uncontrolled private ventures, grow faster than their centralized neighbors. In the late 1970s, while many centrally managed and financed European economies were stagnating, Italy, with its chaotic government and haphazard system of taxation, accommodated a huge and thriving black market making textiles, shoes, and even automotive parts in abandoned basements and attics—raising the national product by as much as one-third. With this *lavoro nero* as a leading sector of growth, Italy's economy outperformed those of Britain and Sweden with their unionized work forces, "social contracts," and armies of dutiful bureaucrats.

The center of Italy's underground prosperity, ironically enough, was the Communist province Emiglia Romana. As *Forbes* magazine observed: "Beneath a public veneer of collectivism, there is a bubbling free-enterprise sector, probably as productive and healthy as its counterparts in right wing havens like Hong Kong or Singapore. And . . . even Communist politicians acknowledge it as an engine of national economic recovery."[7]

It takes more, however, than a system of openness and low taxes to launch economic growth. Through most of human history, taxes have been low and governments incompetent without evoking enterprise. Enterprise, in fact, seems most improbable where it is most needed: in a depressed or undeveloped economy, with low "demand" and little evidence of opportunity. How ventures emerge under these conditions is a key question of economics. In an attempt to answer it, David McCord Wright has speculated on the reasons why "a brewer, say, might build a new brewery even though the volume of total beer sales, or the price of beer, or both, were falling. There are three causes: the better beer, the cheaper beer, and . . . the 'bullheaded brewer' " who "may simply feel he is smarter than the market. . . ." His supplies can create demand in accordance with Say's Law. "It is undeniable that his courage and the stimulus of the construction he is carrying through may start the economy once more expanding."[8]

The bullheaded brewer is essentially responsible for *the entrepreneurial accelerator* that Hirschman and Sawyer found in nineteenth-century American economic development. During this crucial period "collective overestimations" of returns "operated to accelerate the processes of growth and often, in varying measure, produced the result"[9] that in retrospect made their initial overestimates valid. This phenomenon goes to the heart of economic development.

David McClelland sums up the point with reference to the building of railroads across the American continent:

When they were built they could hardly be justified in economic terms, as the subsequent ruin of many stockholders demonstrated. Furthermore, they would never have been economically justified if the country had not been "swarming" with thousands of small entrepreneurs who repeatedly overestimated their chances of success, but who collectively managed to settle and develop the West while many of them individually were failing.

. . . it is hard to explain in rational economic terms why men settled in the Middle West in the 1860s and 1870s. Trollope (1862), in his travels down the Mississippi River could never stop marvelling at why people who knew better would voluntarily choose to live under such primitive conditions in caves or sod huts. He found them laboring from dawn to dark just to keep alive and with no immediate prospect of improvement in their lot. Yet they were cheerful about the future and did not want to return to "civilization," even though they were under no compelling reasons to leave it in the first place. Their behavior is the more impressive by contrast with peoples in South America and Java who have refused to leave crowded urban centers for fertile, unsettled lands not far away.[10]

In the United States today, a similar defiance of the odds impels economic creativity. The Internal Revenue Service estimates that some 4,700 small manufacturers are spawned in this country each week, while 4,500 others fail. More than two-thirds of all ventures collapse within five years, and the median small businessman earns less than a New York City garbage collector.[11] Of the thousands of plausible inventions, only scores are tested by business, and only a handful of these are an economic success. By some estimates, 90 percent of trade hardcover books lose money for the publisher, and a still higher proportion represent a net loss for the author; an even greater number, comprising untold months or years of labor, are never published at all. But such waste and irrationality is the secret of economic growth. Because no one knows which venture will succeed, which number will win the lottery, a society ruled by risk and freedom rather than by rational calculus, a society open to the future rather than planning it, can call forth an endless stream of invention, enterprise, and art.

In order to have growth, openness must be joined by a certain "bullheadedness," some Keynesian "animal spirits," and an essential optimism and willingness to risk. In order to take the hill, someone must dare first to charge the enemy bunker. Heroism, willingness to plunge into the unknown, in the hope that others will follow, is indispensable to all great human achievement. Indeed, such human qualities have been evident during most periods of progress, under most governmental and social systems. But they are supremely the human qualities of capitalism.

The attempt of the welfare state to deny, suppress, and plan away the dangers and uncertainties of our lives—to domesticate the inevitable unknown—violates not only the spirit of capitalism but also the nature of man. Even the most primitive societies invent forms of gambling (dice in many places preceded the wheel). The government devoted to suppressing uncertainty finds itself forever having to channel or repress the human will to risk. The effect is often to drive it from positive and creative avenues into negative or destructive ones.

In this country the impulse to gamble and risk is often diverted from the economy, from serious life, into fantasy and frivolity—games and wagers—or deflected from productive activity into courtroom assaults against the productive. One of the best remaining ways to strike it rich— the best remaining scene for gambling, with the odds against the productive stacked ever higher by government—is the civil suit: malpractice, product liability, discrimination, antitrust, libel, pollution—whatever. The government has created a vast new sweepstakes open to the man willing to play for high stakes and to the law firms that join in the new champerty.

Among the most mischievous of these opportunities for profit is the product-liability suit. Under the worker's compensation law an employee can sue the original manufacturer of machinery, regardless of how old, how much altered, or how often resold it is. Small companies are particularly damaged, with annual insurance rates rising a hundred fold or more to cover this threat and driving many firms out of business. In a good many cases the victims of such suits and insurance rates are men of ingenuity and courage who dare to risk their own money to bring a new product or service to the public. *Caveat productor* is the new rule.

For citizens without the means or litigious bent to sue for a living, the state is widely setting up simpler lotteries of its own, opening in every neighborhood a storefront for the gambling impulse, advertising on billboards the government games. And everywhere it tells the insidious lie that its lottery affords a better deal ("where no one has a better chance than you"), a fairer opportunity than the real and continuing lotteries of lower-class life; that it is more promising to place your wagers on "The New York Bets" than in the U.S. economy. This effect is to trivialize and stultify the will to risk and work that is the only real hope of the poor.

Similarly with the rich, the government makes the dubious claim that it can use wealth more productively than a free capitalist; so its tax policy raises the always adverse odds of enterprise to the point where they may no longer invite the investor. While the poor man swings between welfare and the state lottery, the rich man alternates between personal gambling and municipal bonds. The stochastic margin of progress—the frontier of the economy—can be closed off by obtuse taxation and bureaucracy.

Most redistributive activity is based on serious misunderstandings of the nature and sources of wealth and innovation. Seeing the high levels of evident chance involved in each particular business success, many officials and intellectuals conclude that most large capital gains are in a sense both unearned and unanticipated, and are not a factor in either personal motivation or efficient allocation of resources. Two of the nation's leading thinkers on the Left, Lester C. Thurow and Christopher Jencks, ended their ambitious studies of inequality with the conclusion that crucial in most fortunes, great and small, is luck. The beneficiary, like a raffle winner, was at the right place at the right time, and in a rational system he should not be permitted to convert his luck into real economic power, any more than the myriad losers should suffer more than limited liability for their losses.

There are several problems with this approach. The first is that these economists use luck as a kind of residual category, containing any factors that they do not understand. Since there is much that they do not comprehend in the economy, they naturally exaggerate the importance of chance.

A more serious error, however, is a misunderstanding of the nature of chance itself. Critics of capitalism often imagine that they have discovered some great scandal of the system when they reveal its crucial reliance on luck: its distribution of benefits and attainment of riches by unpredictable and irrational processes—its resemblance at some level to a lottery. Chance, to many economists, is something bad, arbitrary, haphazard—a descent to aimlessness or chaos and a domain for the remedies of government. At best, by a strained Darwinian analogy, the chance happenings so frequent in successful enterprise are assigned the role of "mutations," randomly produced, that are "selected" when particularly fit for their environment. This theory explains the complex and dynamic structures of capitalism no better than it comprehends the prodigally various plenitude of the natural world.

Chance, however, is not the realm of the anarchic and haphazard but the area of freedom and the condition of creativity. It taps the underlying and transcendant order of the universe. We call it chance because it is beyond the ken of ordered rational processes, part of "the mysterious" realm that Einstein called "the cradle of true art and true science."[12] When

Hirschman writes that "creativity always comes as a surprise to us,"[13] he is acknowledging this essential quality of invention. Any attempt to reduce the world to the dimensions of our own understanding will exclude novelty and progress. The domain of chance is our access to futurity and to providence.

Capitalism succeeds because it accommodates chance and thus accords with the reality of the human situation in a fundamentally incomprehensible, but nonetheless providential, universe. Economists who attempt to banish chance through methods of rational management also banish the only sources of human triumph. It is no coincidence that the most deeply pessimistic of economic and social analysts are the advocates of radical and comprehensive systems of planning.

John Kenneth Galbraith in 1979 as much as gave up on the economic development of much of the Third World. According to Galbraith, the prime obstacle to progress is what he calls the "accommodation" of the poor to their plight. He does not object to this attitude. He finds in it a reasonable "refusal to struggle against the impossible. . . . They accept [their poverty]. Nor is such acceptance a sign of weakness of character. Rather it is a profoundly rational response."[14] Galbraith is exactly right. As long as men are "profoundly rational," economic development will seem "impossible" and it will not occur. Instead, as Galbraith shows, there will persist "an equilibrium of poverty"[15] and the best way to escape it is to emigrate to the industrial world, which fortunately has not yet fully accepted the rationality of resignation.

Nonetheless, there is a movement of economists and sociologists who urge "accommodation" by the West as well. Essentially neo-Malthusian or Doomsday Adventist, they recite, in tones of portentous revelation, the long familiar asymptotes of rational despair. Economist Robert Heilbroner predicts despotism and war as the almost certain outcomes. Marvin Harris, making a bid for anthropology as the truly dismal science, proposes a prospect of cannibalism and infanticide (a vista brightened, though, by the possible end of sexism).

In two books Barry Commoner has popularized a biological doom theory, *the closing circle* of ecological limits to growth, that requires the adoption of socialist planning in the United States to prevent the familiar catastrophies. All in all, *The Limits to Growth* may have been revised and amended by its authors in the wealthy and prestigious precincts of the Club of Rome, but it remains the crucial book of our time. While its graphs and computations have been discredited, its emotional symbolism and trajectory were uncannily on target, and it has reverberated throughout our culture and politics ever since its publication.

These attitudes, for all their appeal to secular America, are nothing less than fatuous. Economic and technological breakthroughs always seem impossible in the calculus of closed rationality. Anyone having the slightest familiarity with the history of either science or capitalism knows that leading analysts, generation after generation after generation, have always predicted the exhaustion of capitalist dynamism and the end of technological progress.

In the fifteenth century the longbow—with its unlimited supplies of ammunition, its rapid-firing capacity (twelve shots per minute), and its long range of some two hundred yards—was regarded as the ultimate weapon. Leading seventeenth-century intellectuals imagined that all the available inventions were already behind us.[16] In the eighteenth century even Adam Smith himself envisaged the eventual decline of capitalism into a stationary state. Sismondi thought economic development was all over in 1815[17] and John Stuart Mill supposed that we had reached the end of the line in 1830.[18] In 1843 the U.S. Commissioner of Patents thought that the onrush of inventions might "presage [a time] when human improvement must end."[19] Alvin Hansen and scores of other economists predicted socialist stagnation as the likely human prospect after World War II. Even Thomas Edison believed that the major inventions had all been accomplished during his own lifetime.[20]

Decade after decade experts have predicted exhaustion, first of wood fuel, then of coal, and now of oil and gas. Today, when there is a wider variety of new energy sources available or in view than ever before in our history, and when most of the world has yet to be explored for fossil fuels to one-tenth the degree the United States has been explored, there is a prevailing idea that we are running out of energy and must revert to a preindustrial reliance on wind and sun. At a time when radically important new technologies are being spawned on every hand, leading experts imagine that we are entering a technological climacteric, a period of diminishing scientific returns. Such views are suitable for analysis not in the universities (where they often prevail) but on the couch.

The most obvious source of such beliefs is the individual life cycle. Because human beings become exhausted and decline as they grow older, they are inclined to believe that societies do as well. It is a kind of pathetic fallacy: the ascription of individual human characteristics to large group phenomena. Many intellectuals, moreover, like to suppose that human evolution reached some climactic pinnacle with their own publications and that nothing very important will follow them. As they grow older, they lose track of new developments and find it easier to dismiss them than attempt to master their implications.

The chief problem, however, is a profound incomprehension of the human situation. Human life itself, from any rational and scientific perspective, is wildly unlikely—in fact, impossible. Modern civilization is hopelessly contingent and problematical, subject to destruction any day by possible climatic reversals, astrophysical mishaps, genetic plagues, nuclear explosions, geological convulsions, and atmospheric transformations—all conceivable catastrophes originating beyond the ken of plausible remedy or control.

People like to speak of the "delicate balance" of nature, as if the present natural order represented some static consummation rather than an ongoing struggle of survival. Natural history is a saga not of balance but of convulsive changes, wiping out whole species left and right, transforming continents, evulsing mountains, and flooding vast plains and valleys. There is no such thing as equilibrium, in ecology any more than in economics. Any static state is doomed to disaster. Our supposed current crises of energy and protein pale before the perpetual crisis of human existence itself.

At any time in human history, a rational calculus of our possibilities would lead to a prediction of doom. But over the millennia, the race has flourished. It has thrived, however, chiefly on one condition, one cluster of conditions, combining faith and freedom with risk and work. It is chiefly when we give up on chance and providence, when we attempt to calculate and control our own destinies through ever greater regulation by a demiurgic state, that disaster occurs.

Marvin Harris's grim catalog of the rise and fall of previous societies dramatizes this reality.[21] He describes a recurrently vicious cycle of population growth and resource depletion. The climax always begins with an intensification of productive activity, followed by a still faster rise in population and by industrial, agricultural, or hunting pursuits taken beyond the point of diminishing returns. The usual result is a dearth of protein and other sustenance and the emergence of ever more brutal social arrangements, marked by war and infanticide, and leading at last to cannibalism and other bestiality.

The worst of all the societies he describes were the *hydraulic dictatorships*, which arose in narrow river valleys or other enclosed regions and created huge bureaucracies and mass mobilizations to build and manage great waterworks and irrigation projects. Although Harris does not emphasize this point, the result is the commitment of the entire social order to rigid bureaucratic and administrative systems, which respond to the worsening crunch by raising taxes and increasing controls. Every new measure of desperation by the prevailing powers raises still higher the obstacles to innovation and progress and makes the final disaster still more ineluctable.

Amazingly, though, Harris ends his book by calling for expanded regulation and controls to meet the new crises of scarcity in America. He sees little possibility of solving the problems as free men. What he fails to comprehend is that the visibly possible breakthroughs, the clearly available resources, have always been measured and discounted. At any time in the history of the race, the extended future has usually appeared to be hopelessly grim, uninhabitable by free humans. All plans based on the calculable present, on the existing statistics, necessarily presume a declining field of choice, a contraction of possibilities, an exhaustion of resources, a diminishing of returns—entropy and decay.

To combat these exigencies, the planner will always see a need for regulation of ever more intimate and intrusive kinds, invading the family and the home. In the end, as reserves expire, the planner becomes a tyrant and a killer—the Moloch of the closing circle.

Like the anthropophagus dictatorships of the Aztec kingdom and the other monstrous hydraulic despotisms described by Harris, a state that responds by confiscation and coercion to the inevitable crises of closure, the inexorable pressures of population against the land, ends by consuming its own people. The rates of taxation climb and the levels of capital decline, until the only remaining wealth beyond the reach of the regime is the very protein of human flesh, and that too is finally taxed, bound, and gagged, and brought to the colossal temple of the state—a final sacrifice of carnal revenue to feed the declining elite. This is the destination of all dictatorship, unless it is saved by the unanticipated boon, the serendipitous cavalry of providence that awaits only the bugle of freedom and faith.

Leszek Kolakowski, the expatriate Polish philosopher, in another context has well depicted the essential human predicament. We are in a convoy, lightly but adequately equipped to cross a stretch of desert if all goes well. But it doesn't. We misread our maps and go astray. Sandstorms erupt. The camels balk. Water runs out. But we have hope, a belief in providence, a "myth." Our faith calls forth a kind of

Fata Morgana which makes beautiful lands rise before the eyes of the members of the caravan and thus increases their efforts to the point where, in spite of all their sufferings, they reach the next tiny water hole. Had such tempting mirages not appeared, the exhausted caravan would inevitably have perished in the sandstorm, bereft of hope.[22]

It is a powerful image and richly suggestive, but I do not believe that the point is exactly right. We do not need "myths" so much as we need religious beliefs, which, for all their dubious "irrationality," bear in their symbolic depths the greatest of pragmatic and historical truths. They tell us that free humans with faith in the future and a commitment to it will prevail.

CHAPTER 21

The Necessity for Faith

OUR CENTRAL PROBLEM arises from a deep conflict between the processes of material progress and the ideals of "progressive" government and culture. Equality, bureaucratic rationality, predictability, sexual liberation, political "populism," and the pursuit of pleasure—all the values of advanced culture—are quite simply inconsistent with the disciplines and investments of economic and technical advance. The result is that all modern governments pretend to promote economic growth but in practice doggedly obstruct it.

Material progress is ineluctably elitist: it makes the rich richer and increases their numbers, exalting the few extraordinary men who can produce wealth over the democratic masses who consume it. Material progress depends on the expansion of opportunity: geniuses identify themselves chiefly through their works rather than by their inheritance or test scores. Material progress is difficult: it requires from its protagonists long years of diligence and sacrifice, devotion and risk that can be elicited only with high rewards, not the "average return on capital." Material progress, although democratically demanded, is procedurally undemocratic: it means the expensive support of activities thoroughly beyond the ken of the people, and often even of their leaders. Material progress is radically unpredictable (to foresee an innovation is in essence to make it): the most important developments happen on a frontier where things are forever slipping slightly out of control. Material progress is inimical to scientific economics: it cannot be explained or foreseen in mechanistic or mathematical terms.

All those who seek a rational and predictable world—a system of scien-

tific management and control—can prevail only by thwarting material
and scientific progress. A world without innovation succumbs to the sure
laws of deterioration and decay. As resources predictably dwindle, governments will extend their controls. Distribution becomes paramount. Planning works. Even such a somber certitude seems better to many than
the notion of a continuing and incalculable struggle to extend the mastery
of man over nature and to increase the fund of material wealth.

It is the idea of economic futility—not capitalist growth—that gives
license to the culture of hedonism and sensuality. In an imperfect and
suffering world, the possibility of progress implies a responsibility to
attempt it. Only in a world of socialistically managed "limits to growth,"
where human effort, enterprise, and creativity can never long prevail over
needless poverty and suffering, can the progressive dream of sexual liberation, leisure, redistribution, and sensual pleasure lose its onus of decadence
and injustice.

The dream of stagnation exalts the politician as well as the hedonist.
Only in a stationary economy can government no longer defer to scientists,
technologists, and businessmen as the heroes of the age. In the stationary
state all that matters are the works of power and bureaucracy: mass behavior and its regulation. Conservation, distribution, and control become
crucial values. Economists, too, come into their own. Without the surprises
of creativity, their models can actually predict the future.

In a world without material growth, poverty will increase nearly everywhere. But experts will come forth with new rationales for ignoring, in
all but rhetoric, the plight of the global poor. Just as the alleged laws
of classical economics doomed the workers to subsistence wages, the new
laws of contemporary ecology doom them to a stagnant world economy.
No Ricardian law of rents, no Malthusian cycle of population, was ever
more coldly remorseless in its rejection of the dreams of the poor than
Commoner's *Closing Circle*.

The new dismal science of permanent poverty—propagated in fashionable salons and foundation offices across the land—relies heavily on the
concept of a deteriorating world, governed by the concept of entropy.
Entropy theory purports to be progressive, since it is offered as a way
of refuting the mechanistic classical theory of perfect competition. Allegedly the mainstay of capitalism, this concept appeals to the abstract and
timeless universe of the first law of thermodynamics, where nothing fundamentally changes or deteriorates. The real world, say the entropy theorists, is a world of irreversible time, governed by the second law of thermodynamics: the entropy law—the tendency of energy *(negentropy)* to dissipate
irretrievably into entropy as it is used. Because heat only moves one
way, toward cooler bodies, and once it has been lost can never be retrieved,

the universe is ultimately doomed to entropic death. As Clausius put it: "The entropy of the Universe tends toward a maximum state."

More simply put, everything is running down and running out. Energy, soil, protein, iron—you name it—is deteriorating into lukewarm gases. This means that fuel becomes steadily more costly to get, both in money and in the BTUs (British thermal units) expended in extracting it. Hence inflation, as a rebellion of the biosphere against the increasing claims made upon it, is essentially seen as an ecological problem. Capitalism, with its imperative of growth, can be depicted as violating the very law of nature.

In its own simple scientific terms, this theory suffers from a rather extended time frame. We still have hundreds of years of fossil fuels, probably even of oil and gas, and billions of years of negentropic sunlight. But we should chiefly listen not to the words but to the music and acknowledge that despite the pretense of science, entropy theory is essentially a metaphor. It lends the usual critique of capitalism a tragic poetry appealing to the conservationist upper classes, wearied at once by the struggle to keep their wealth in an inflationary time and by the Marxist prophecies of class war.

Metaphor or not, entropy theory is the latest of a long series of attempts to outfit economics in the official livery of the physical sciences. For centuries, from the quantity theory of money, which for all its uses David Warsh has shown to be a dubious corollary of Boyle's law of gasses, to classical value theory as a Newtonian interplay of mathematical equations, economists have tried to lend their findings the ostensible order and certitude of physics and chemistry. For very good reasons these efforts always fail.

Because economies are governed by thoughts, they reflect not the laws of matter but the laws of mind. One crucial law of mind is that belief precedes knowledge. New knowledge does not come without a leap of hypothesis, a projection by the intuitive sense. The logic of creativity is "leap before you look." You cannot fully see anything new from an old place. The old saw of "look before you leap" provides only for the continual elaborations and refinements of old ideas that comprise the bulk of scholarship (and the bulk of "industrial progress" in large and static companies).

The concept of information theory in economics similarly misses the necessary bound of surprise in all radical innovation. The idea that businesses buy knowledge like any other factor of production, until its cost exceeds its yield, that businesses can safely and systematicaly assemble facts until the ground ahead stretches firmly before them, misses the radical difference between knowledge and everything else. It is the leap, not the look, that generates the crucial information; the leap through time and space, beyond the swarm of observable fact, that opens up the vista of discovery.

Galileo broached the modern age of science not by observing thousands of factual trajectories and deriving from them the law of gravity; rather "I conceived as the work of my own mind a moving object launched above a horizontal plane and freed of all impediment."[1] Freed, that is, of the facts; freed, by a leap of imagination, of the conditions of all real moving bodies as they are buffeted through the resisting air. Imagination precedes knowledge. Creative thought is not an inductive process in which a scientist accumulates evidence in a neutral and "objective" way until a theory becomes visible in it. Rather the theory comes first and determines what evidence can be seen.[2]

Imagination, intuition, and hypothesis are merely the first steps of learning. Since the human mind is capable of endless ideation, the thinker must select particular concepts to believe. As in choosing a woman, a man must trust his intuition, and act before he can really know. The idea will not fully reveal itself and its possibilities until the man trusts it and commits himself to it, engages emotion in it—in a sense loves it. Creative thought requires an act of faith. The believer must trust his intuition, the spontaneous creations of his mind, enough to pursue them laboriously to the point of experiment and knowledge.

Love appears blind to outside observers, but lovers know that it is guided by a more exalted vision and it opens new realms of knowledge and creativity. Commitment can create its own confirmation. To the man who dares not love, the entire world seems barren and dull, the future pregnant with doom. It is love and faith that infuse ideas with life and fire.

All creative thought is thus in a sense religious, initially a product of faith and belief. But not all ideas (or women) are true. Commitment is necessary but not sufficient. The fanatic is the man who seizes an idea and imposes his will on it regardless of the response of the world and the facts. Crucial to creative thinking is a sensitivity to responses, another aspect of love. Creative thought must be open to change and surprise. Another way of putting it is to say, without any notion of Popperian dogma, that ideas should be falsifiable (that is, expressed in a form in which they can be proven either true or false). There must be a process of divorce and rejection. Unless wrong ideas could be abandoned, no one could risk commitment to them in an uncertain world, and progress would be halted.

But what is the source of the ideas by which intellectual progress occurs? The answer, we may agree, is chance. Theories arise spontaneously and mysteriously, by intuition or happenstance. This mystery constitutes the crucial problem of intellectual history. A secular rationalist will distrust a mystery and will wish to develop more automatic and rationalized modes of progress. Throughout the history of thought, but especially in the modern era, men have tried to develop systems of ratiocination that are self-contained; that move from step to step by hermetically sealed links of logic; that look before they leap, gathering "data" or evidence "objectively" and 'deriving theory inductively. Rationalist men have always wished to reduce the process of thought to the compass of the individual human brain, with its demonstrable experience and structure, rendering ideas in the terms of matter, governed by coherent, even physical, laws. Logical positivism, behavioral psychology, Freudianism, Marxism, classical economics, neo-Keynesianism, Bayesian probability analysis, information theory, socialist planning—all represent ways, asserted with varying degrees of conviction and flexibility, of excluding chance and novelty from human behavior, either in fact or in theory.

All these movements reject the idea that the crux of change and creativity is chance. All assume that chance notions are random and undependable because, so they believe, beyond the compass of human rationality is an intellectually blank and responseless universe. Like the fashionable theorists of entropy, the modern thinker assumes the universe is essentially dead. The human mind is seen as a solitary consciousness reaching out to grasp the objects beyond it and is ultimately governed by the things it reflects and recollects and by its own substance and structure: it is alleged to be part of a system ruled by physical laws.

This approach involves a fundamental fallacy. As America's greatest philosopher Charles Peirce has written, matter consists of inert or "fallen" mind. It is governed by predictable and calculable laws only because it is dead and its future is foreordained. But the essence of the universe is creative consciousness, continually generating new energy and thought.

The human mind is not necessarily autonomous or limited to the individual brain. The mind has access to a higher consciousness, sometimes anomalously, after Jung, called a *collective unconscious*, sometimes defined as God. As a person's mind merges with the living consciousness that is the ulterior stuff of the cosmos, he reaches new truths, glimpses the new ideas—the projections of light into the unknown future—by which intellectual progress occurs.

All men, however, shrink from this awesome contact with cosmic mystery and power. It is frightening to leave the compass of the individual brain, its small fund of experience, its comfortable tools of reason, and to plunge into the realm of dark transcendence where can be found all true light and creativity. If the idea is truly new and important, moreover, it will entail rejection of many other conflicting ideas, or it will force a further effort of paradoxical synthesis. Again the brain rebels.

Even relatively simple creative processes require a plunge into darkness—a dependence on incalculable providence—that discomfits many. Much of modern culture bespeaks the vainglorious postures, narrow preoccupations, and morbid anxieties of human minds frozen by fear on the thresholds of higher consciousness. Because no one can write anything worthwhile from his own immediate funds of knowledge, writer's block is most essentially a failure of faith, an unwillingness to give oneself up to a higher power. Similarly, the endless tomes of mathematical economics and sociology owe their sterile obsessions and banal outcomes to a refusal to acknowledge that all creativity requires a leap of imagination and faith. The investor who never acts until the statistics affirm his choice, the athlete or politician who fails to make his move until too late, the businessman who waits until the market is proven—all are doomed to mediocrity by their trust in a spurious rationality and their failures of faith.

Perhaps the most characteristic strategem of threshold anxiety is the detailed plan. To a great extent plans are the mythology of a secular rationalist world, the superstitious rites by which a government, a business, or a thinker acquires the confidence for a redemptive act: the forging of supplies that create demand, the adoption of a new idea that casts a saving light, a plunging into the unknown that produces knowledge.

The process of intuition and faith is the initial phase in the career of ideas. New ideas can easily become old. Once apprehended in the intensity of fresh revelation, they tend to spread and diffuse their light, gathering more and more knowledge and facts, until they settle into an immobile generalization resembling matter. As they are elaborated, ideas become increasingly rigid and complex, covering ever wider expanses of knowledge in an ever less satisfactory way.

It is said that when one produces an unduly complicated solution to a problem, one has not a solution but a new problem. One can see, in many fields of modern life, from the Department of Energy to the theory of economic development, the elaboration of the multifarious answers, piling up in greater and greater complexity, which collectively constitute the essential problem of the secular rationalist age.

But a final facet of the law of mind—perhaps the most crucial of all in our current impasse—is the role of problems. Problems, dilemmas, and paradoxes are not sources of discouragement and frustration but the necessary spurs of new knowledge and creativity. The secular rationalist mentality sees problems, hardships, and paradoxes as obstacles to achievement and truth. If a new idea seems to contradict an old verity, one dismisses the new idea. This is the mode of conventional thought, which yields only refinements and elaborations of previous ideas and prohibits the attainment of new illuminations—ways of seeing both sides of a paradox in a different and reconciling light.

The law of mind exalts conflict and trouble as the invariable condition of knowledge in a world that passes through time. The hardships do not repress thought; they elicit creativity and impel resort to a saving transcendence. Trouble may even strengthen faith and liberate new energy and truth. A thinker who shrinks from paradox and conflict is nearly prohibited from innovation.

The crucial rules of creative thought can be summed up as faith, love, openness, conflict, and falsifiability. The crucial rules of economic innovation and progress are faith, altruism, investment, competition, and bankruptcy, which are also the rules of capitalism. The reason capitalism succeeds is that its laws accord with the laws of mind. It is capable of fulfilling human needs because it is founded on giving, which depends on sensitivity to the needs of others. It is open to faith and experiment because it is also open to competition and bankruptcy. Capitalism accumulates the capital gains not only of its successes but also of its failures, capitalized in new knowledge. It is the only appropriate system for a world in which all certitude is a sham.

The dynamics of economic growth thus consist of the fundamental process of all growth and development in nature and thought: a largely spontaneous and mostly unpredictable flow of increasing diversity and differentiation and new products and modes of production. Business begins with a new idea, a better mousetrap, and expands into a differentiated industry of mousetrap marketing, maintenance, and hygiene, leading to a proliferation of mousetrap-related activities, from weasel traps to bear traps, from rat poison to door-to-door household goods, perhaps climaxing with a breakaway mouse meat short-order empire, selling Big Mickeys to teenagers. The pattern of development is usually the same (ideas have an inherent tendency to split up and specialize as they are applied). But the process is nonetheless unpredictable, full of the mystery of all living and growing things (like ideas and businesses).

In order for this process to fructify through the system, there must be activity beyond the system's control. The new production must usually be done by individuals whose work and ideas are not subsumed by a larger institution (the builders and sellers of mousetraps will not look with favor on the diversion of their earnings into a fast-food chain). There must be room for individuals to find their own unexpected way of dividing and specializing labor, originating and adapting new goods and services. These individuals and their new ideas are the way an economic system grows and changes; they lead to the small businesses and new activities that are finally joined with others in new systems, which often become rigid and unresponsive, unless they can continue to assimilate or shoot off new products and processes. It is this very conventional but absolutely crucial interplay of chance, change, and growth that economists so often ignore.

The key thing to notice about this process is that most of its motive activities take place beyond the view of the statistician. It is a personal and psychological drama that decides whether a man dares to borrow and take risks to carry out an innovative idea that all the statistics show will probably—like two-thirds of all new businesses in America—fail within five years. This decision will be affected by government; it will be much deterred by high taxes and interest rates; but it will most essentially express an impulse of faith, a belief in the future, and a sensitivity to the needs of others, even if unstated. Economists who themselves do not believe in the future of capitalism will tend to ignore the dynamics of chance and faith that largely will determine that future. Economists who distrust religion will always fail to comprehend the modes of worship by which progress is achieved. Chance is the foundation of change and the vessel of the divine.

Lottery is a paramount fact of life from the moment of biological conception among millions of sperm. We all begin—in the very DNA (deoxyribonucleic acid) of our individual existences—as winners of a sweepstakes against astronomical odds. Even biology, seemingly the most deterministic of sciences, is thus at its deepest and most decisive levels, stochastic, aleatory, in its view of man.

And yet, there is more to it than that. Peirce has shown that chance not only is at the very center of human reality but also is the deepest source of reason and morality. In his posthumous volume, *Chance, Love, and Logic,* he wrote: "The first step in evolution is putting sundry thoughts into situations in which they are free to play. . . . The idea that chance begets order is the cornerstone of modern physics,"[3] and, he might have added, biology as well. But the movement of chance toward order and truth is not assured in any one lifetime. The odds are against each individual in the serial lotteries of his own life. Chance cannot be shown to work except in the long run of the human adventure. In fact, a rational calculation of personal gain would impel an individual above all to avoid risk and seek security. In our world of fortuity, committed to a secular vision, the invisible hand of self-interest acclaimed by Adam Smith would lead to an ever-enlarging welfare state—to stasis and sterility. This is the root of our crisis and the crisis of classical economics today.

Peirce argues, therefore, that both evolution and progress, whether in science or in society, are dependent on "a conceived identification of one's interests with those of an unlimited community: recognition of the possibility of this interest being made supreme, and hope in the unlimited continuance of intellectual activity. . . . Logic is rooted in the social principle. . . ."[4] Peirce's mathematical *doctrine of chances* leads him to see that all human creativity and discovery require the transcendence of narrow rationality and an embrace of religious values.

"It interests me to notice" wrote this great logical philosopher, "that these sentiments seem to be pretty much the same as that famous trio of Charity, Faith and Hope, which in the estimation of St. Paul, are the finest and greatest of spiritual gifts."[5] They are gifts that work together to free mankind from the bondage of power and the dead hand of the past and open us to the possibilities of the divine.

It is the paradox of fortuity that our lives, to the extent they are free and open to chance, are also fated and determined. *Stochastic* means "by random chance," but it comes from the Greek for "skillful in aiming." In every society the lucky man is seen as somehow blessed. His good chance—and society's redemption—is providence.

The most dire and fatal hubris for any leader is to cut off his people from providence, from the miraculous prodigality of chance, by substituting a closed system of human planning. Success is always unpredictable and thus an effect of faith and freedom.

All human pioneers, from poets and composers in their many epiphanies to scientists on the mystical frontiers of matter where life again begins, are essentially engaged in forms of devotion. All knowledge of living and growing things (concepts and economies) is partly subjective and intuitive and thus mystically dependent on the ideas of others and on the worship, however unconscious, of God. God is the foundation of all living knowledge; and the human mind, to the extent it can know anything beyond its own meager reach, partakes of the mind of God.

In the United States today we are facing the usual calculus of impossibility, recited by the familiar aspirants to a master plan. It is said we must abandon economic freedom because our frontier is closed; because our biosphere is strained; because our resources are running out; because our technology is perverse; because our population rises; because our horizons are closing in. We walk, it is said, in a shadow of death, with depleted air, poisoned earth and water, and a fallout of explosive growth showering from the clouds of our future in a quiet carcinogenic rain. In this extremity, we cannot afford the luxuries of competition and waste and freedom. We have reached the end of the open road; we are beating against the gates of an occluded frontier. We must tax and regulate and plan, redistribute our wealth and ration our consumption, because we have reached the end of openness.

But quite to the contrary, these problems and crises are in themselves the new frontier; are themselves the mandate for individual and corporate competition and creativity; are themselves the reason why we cannot afford the consolations of planning and stasis. The old frontier of the American West also appeared closed at first. It became an open reservoir of wealth only in retrospect, because the pioneers dared to risk their lives and families in the quest for riches, looking for gold (of which there was relatively little in the United States) and finding oil (then of little use). Only in retrospect were the barrens of Texas and Oklahoma an energy cornucopia, the flat prairies a breadbasket for the world, or Thomas Edison a catalytic genius and Henry Ford the salvation of capitalism in the grips of an earlier closing circle. The future is forever incalculable; only in freedom can its challenges be mastered.

The economists, who make the case for stasis and planning in these terms, formulate point by point the case against themselves. The closing circle, the resource crisis, the thermal threat, the nuclear peril, the "graying" of technology, the population advance, the famine factor, and whatever else is new in the perennial jeremiad of the rational budgeteer and actuary of our fate—all these conditions are themselves the mandate for capitalism. To overcome it is necessary to have faith, to recover the belief in chance and providence, in the ingenuity of free and God-fearing men.

This belief will allow us to see the best way of helping the poor, the way to understand the truths of equality before God that can only come from freedom and diversity on earth. It will lead us to abandon, above all, the idea that the human race can become self-sufficient, can separate itself from chance and fortune in a hubristic siege of rational resource management, income distribution, and futuristic planning. Our greatest and only resource is the miracle of human creativity in a relation of openness to the divine. It is a resource that above all we should deny neither to the poor, who can be the most open of all to the future, nor to the rich or excellent of individuals, who can lend leadership, imagination, and wealth to the cause of beneficent change.

The tale of human life is less the pageant of unfolding rationality and purpose envisaged by the Enlightenment than a saga of desert wanderings and brief bounty, the endless dialogue between man and God, between alienation and providence, as we search for the ever-rising and receding promised land, which we can see most clearly, with the most luminous logic, when we have the faith and courage to leave ourselves open to chance and fate.

Reinhold Niebuhr summed up our predicament:

> Nothing worth doing is completed
> in one lifetime.

Therefore we must be saved by hope.
Nothing true or beautiful makes
complete sense
in any context of history.
Therefore we must be saved by faith.
Nothing we do, no matter how virtuous,
can be accomplished alone.
Therefore we are saved by love.[6]

These are the fundamental laws of economics, business, technology, and life. In them are the secret sources of wealth, and poverty.

NOTES

Chapter 1 / The Dirge of Triumph

1. Daniel Bell, "The New Class: A Muddled Concept," *Transaction/Society*, Vol. 16, No. 2 (Jan./Feb. 1979), p. 17; reprinted in Barry Bruce-Briggs, ed., *The New Class?* (New Brunswick, N.J.: Transaction Books, 1979).

2. Thomas Sowell, "Economics and Economic Man," in *The Americans, 1976: Critical Choices for Americans*, Vol. 2, Irving Kristol and Paul Weaver, eds. (Lexington, Mass.: D.C. Heath & Co., 1976), pp. 191–209.

3. The Bible, "Revelations," passim.

4. Irving Kristol, *Two Cheers for Capitalism* (New York: Basic Books, 1978), p. 262.

5. Walter Lippmann, *The Good Society* (Boston, Mass.: Little, Brown & Company, 1943); quoted from the paperback, (New York: Grosset & Dunlap), pp. 193–194.

Chapter 2 / The Economy of Frustration

1. David Hume, *Essays Moral, Political, and Literary*, Vol. 1, Part II, No. VI.

2. Robert L. Heilbroner and Lester C. Thurow, *The Economic Problem*, 5th ed. (Englewood Cliffs, N.J.: Prentice-Hall, 1979), pp. 21–23. See also Kenneth Kenniston and The Carnegie Council on Children, *All Our Children: The American Family Under Pressure* (New York: Harcourt Brace Jovanovich, 1977), p. 44.

3. Thomas Sowell, *Markets and Minorities* (London: Basil Blackwell, 1980), forthcoming; Thomas Sowell, ed., *American Ethnic Groups* (Washington, D.C.: The Urban Institute, 1978), pp. 40–48 and passim. See also Stanley Lebergott, *The American Economy* (Princeton, N.J.: Princeton University Press, 1976), pp. 44–50.

4. Unpublished interview for Vocational Foundation, Inc., 44 East 24th Street, New York, N.Y., 1978, in the research files for *Our Turn to Listen* (New York: VFI, 1978).

5. Kenniston & Carnegie Council, *All Our Children*, pp. 36–37. See also Richard H. de Lone and The Carnegie Council on Children, *Small Futures: Inequality, Children, and the Failure of Liberal Reform* (New York: Harcourt Brace Jovanovich, 1979), passim. These Carnegie studies, ostensibly on children, are in fact chiefly concerned with reducing their number and burden on adults and with propagating a group of adolescent arguments for a massive restructuring of the U.S. economy by redistributing wealth.

6. Herbert J. Gans, *More Equality* (New York: Pantheon Books, 1973), quoted from the paperback (New York: Vintage Books, 1974), p. 19.

7. Martin Anderson, *Welfare: The Political Economy of Welfare Reform in the United States* (Stanford, California: Hoover Institution Press, 1978), p. 15. See also Morton Paglin, "Poverty in the United States: A Reevaluation," *Policy Review*, No. 8 (Spring 1979), pp. 7–24.

8. U.S. Bureau of Census, *Current Population Reports*, Series P-20, No. 311, Household and Family Characteristics: March 1976 (Washington, D.C.: U.S. Government Printing Office, 1977), pp. 11–21, Table 1. (It consists of characteristics of families by type, race, and Spanish origin of head and by farm and nonfarm residence. It is updated in subsequent reports in Series P-20 in preparation).

The best compilation of earlier data on the black family is found in Heather L. Ross and Isabel V. Sawhill, *Time of Transition: The Growth of Families Headed by Women* (Washington, D.C.: The Urban Institute, 1975), pp. 67–88 and passim.

9. A good summary of the evidence, as compiled by The Urban League, is found in Robert B. Hill, "The Illusion of Black Progress," Social Policy, Vol. 9, No. 3 (Nov./Dec. 1978), pp. 14–25. The progress of intact black families outside of the welfare culture remains impressive, however.

10. All of these observations are elaborated in Lester C. Thurow, *The Zero-Sum Society: Distribution and the Possibilities for Economic Change* (New York: Basic Books, 1980), pp. 47–54 and passim.

11. Ibid., p. 49.

12. George Gilder, *Naked Nomads: Unmarried Men in America* (New York: Quadrangle/The New York Times Book Co., 1974), pp. 38–40. Detailed sources can be found in the notes on pp. 169–170. See also Hugh Carter and Paul C. Glick, *Marriage and Divorce: A Social and Economic Study*, rev. ed. (Cambridge, Mass.: Harvard University Press, 1976), pp. 324–357 and passim.

13. Marriage, divorce, and remarriage figures since 1965 appear in *Monthly Vital Statistics Reports* of the National Center for Health Statistics, Rockville, Md., and in Carter and Glick, *Marriage and Divorce.*

14. Edgar K. Browning and William R. Johnson, *The Distribution of the Tax Burden* (Washington, D.C.: American Enterprise Institute for Public Policy Research, 1979), pp. 67–70.

15. Scott Burns, *Home, Inc.: The Hidden Wealth and Power of the American Household* (Garden City, N.Y.: Doubleday & Company, 1975), pp. 16–28. I have adjusted Burns's estimate of the value of domestic services for inflation. The statistics on divorce and separation are summed up in Ross and Sawhill, *Time of Transition.*

16. Scott Burns, "Irresistible Force Meets an Immovable Object," *The Boston Herald American,* 17 September 1978, p. A-26. See also "Why Wage Controls Weigh Heavily on Young Families," *The Boston Herald American,* 26 August 1979 and "Struggling Up Mount Money," *The Boston Herald American,* 6 March 1977.

17. Irwin Garfinkel and Robert Haveman, with the assistance of David Betson, U.S. Department of Health, Education and Welfare, *Earnings Capacity, Poverty, and Inequality,* Institute for Research on Poverty Monograph Series (New York: Academic Press, 1977), pp. 32 and 33.

18. Kim B. Clark and Lawrence H. Summers, "Labor Market Dynamics and Unemployment: A Reconsideration," *Brookings Papers on Economic Activity* No. 1. (Washington, D.C.: The Brookings Institution, 1979), p. 52.

19. Garfinkel and Haveman, *Earnings Capacity,* pp. 32 and 33.

20. Edgar L. Feige, "How Big Is the Irregular Economy?" *Challenge* Vol. 22, No. 5 (Nov./Dec. 1979), pp. 5–13. See also Peter M. Gutmann, "Statistical Illusions, Mistaken Policies," pp. 14–17.

21. Ibid.

22. Laurie Prothro, "Making a Living in Subterranea—Notes From The Underground," *Taxing and Spending,* Vol. 2, No. 2 (April 1979), pp. 8–11.

23. Jacqueline Kasun, "More on the New Sex Education," *The Public Interest,* No. 58 (Winter 1980), p. 136.

24. Quoted in Melvyn B. Krauss, "The Swedish Tax Revolt," *The Wall Street Journal,* 1 February 1979, p. 16.

25. Thurow, *The Zero-Sum Society,* p. 53.

26. David Stockman, private communication.

27. Joseph J. Minareck, "Who Wins, Who Loses from Inflation?" *Challenge,* Vol. 21, No. 6 (Jan./Feb. 1979), pp. 26–31.

28. Ibid. See also Christopher Jencks, "Why Worry About Inflation?" *Working Papers* Vol.

6, No. 5 (Sept./Oct. 1978), pp. 8–11, 75–78 and Vol. 7, No. 1 (May/June 1979), pp. 62–64.

Chapter 3 / The Returns of Giving

1. Marvin Harris, *Cannibals and Kings: The Origins of Cultures* (New York: Randon House, 1977), pp. 71–72.

2. Helen Codere, "Fighting with Property, a Study of Kwakiutl Potlaching and Warfare, 1792–1930," *Monographs of the American Ethnological Society*, Vol. 18, 1950, pp. 90–91.

3. Melville J. Herskovits, *Economic Anthropology: The Economic Life of Primitive Peoples* (New York: W. W. Norton, 1965), p. 178.

4. For an inspired essay in legal philosophy reaching this conclusion, see Richard J. Posner, "Utilitarianism, Economics, and Legal Theory," *The Journal of Legal Studies,* The University of Chicago Law School, Vol. 8, No. 1 (January 1979), pp. 108–144.

5. Ivan H. Light, *Ethnic Enterprise in America* (Berkeley: University of California Press, 1972), p. 30–36.

6. Harvey Leibenstein, *Beyond Economic Man: A New Foundation for Microeconomics,* (Cambridge, Mass.: Harvard University Press, 1976), pp. 34–44.

7. Leo Tolstoy, *War and Peace,* translated by Constance Garnett, Modern Library ed. (New York: Random House, n.d.), p. 963.

Chapter 4 / The Supply Side

1. John Maynard Keynes, *The General Theory of Employment, Interest, and Money,* Harbinger ed., (New York: Harcourt, Brace & World, 1964), pp. 18–22 and passim.

2. Ibid., pp. 161–162.

3. Among the reasons for low investment levels stressed by Keynes were: (1) artificially high interest rates caused by speculation and profit taking in bonds whenever their prices rose very high (that is, interest rates dropped); (2) low profits caused by excessive saving by consumers; (3) low demand caused by wage levels that drop as population grows; (4) financial markets that discourage risk taking by compounding it. (In a particual venture both lender—the bank—and borrower—the business—may lose the entire amount invested, but only the business has the possibility of huge gains; thus bankers are afflicted with undue caution and may not be willing to lend despite the existence of opportunities attractive to entrepreneurs.) Except for this last item, these arguments are among Keynes's weakest and have been little confirmed by subsequent events. Even his observations on the natural caution of lenders seem somewhat overblown in view of the banking trends of the 1970s. However, the bleak Keynesian vision of bond and other loan markets would seem to enhance the importance of stock markets and of private wealth in supporting risky but potentially lucrative projects. Yet Keynes denounced the stock market in fiery language.

4. See Alan Reynolds, "50 Years Later: What Do We Know About the Great Crash?" *National Review,* Vol. 31, No. 45 (November 9, 1979), pp. 1416–1421; Milton Friedman and Anna Schwartz, *A Monetary History of the United States, 1867–1960* (Princeton, N.J.: Princeton University Press, 1963), pp. 299–419; and for a detailed rendition of the case that in 1929 the market simply anticipated the passage of Smoot-Hawley, see Jude Wanniski, *The Way the World Works* (New York: Basic Books, 1978), pp. 116–148.

5. Keynes, *General Theory,* p. 29 and passim. See also ibid., chapter 5 (pp. 46–51) and chapter 11 (pp. 135–146, especially p. 141).

6. Keynes, *General Theory,* p. 155.

7. G. L. S. Shackle, *Epistemics and Economics: A Critique of Economic Doctrines* (London: Cambridge University Press, 1972), p. 429. This view of the central meaning of Keynes's thought is shared by Lord Richard Kahn, perhaps Keynes's closest friend and associate at Cambridge.

In an essay responding to an attack on Keynesianism by Walter Eltis of Oxford ("Mr. Eltis and the Keynesians," *Lloyds Bank Review*, no. 124. [April 1977], pp. 1–13), Kahn wrote that Keynes was much less concerned with hiking government spending to increase employment than with lowering interest rates to stimulate private investment. Kahn derided as "vulgar Keynesianism" the conventional formula that consumption, investment, and government spending together can be managed to achieve full employment. "There is no such thing as a definite level of full employment," he wrote.

8. Keynes, *General Theory*, p. 155.

9. Keynes (in *General Theory*, pp. 297–298) writes, with explicit reference to *his own* mathematical models included in *The General Theory:* "It is a great fault of symbolic pseudo-mathematical methods . . . that they expressly assume strict independence between the factors involved and lose all their cogency and authority if this hypothesis is disallowed; whereas in ordinary discourse, where we are not blindly manipulating but know all the time what we are doing and what the words mean, we can keep 'at the back of our heads' the necessary reserves and qualifications and the adjustments we shall have to make later on, in a way in which we cannot keep complicated partial differentials 'at the back' of several pages of algebra which assume that they all vanish. Too large a portion of recent 'mathematical' economics are mere concoctions, as imprecise as the initial assumptions they rest on, which allow the author to lose sight of the complexities and interdependencies of the real world in a maze of pretentions and unhelpful symbols." Most of Keynes's present-day followers lack the master's modesty, but their mathematical models make the even greater error of assuming that all the variables and interdependencies can themselves be plotted. The most intricate and prestigious models have consistently predicted national output losses as a result of tax cuts.

10. Keynes, *General Theory*, pp. 148–150.

11. John Kenneth Galbraith, "The American Economy: Its Substance and Myth," in *Years of the Modern: An American Appraisal*, John W. Chase, ed. (New York: Longman, Green & Co., 1949), pp. 151–174. Reprinted in *The Galbraith Reader* (Ipswich, Mass.: Gambit, 1977), p. 86.

12. John Kenneth Galbraith, *The Affluent Society* (Boston: Houghton Mifflin Company, 1958), p. 158. *The Revised Sequence*, which is merely *The Dependence Effect* in new packaging, was introduced in John Kenneth Galbraith, *The New Industrial State* (Boston: Houghton Mifflin Company, 1967), p. 212. I owe this insight to Simon Lazarus.

13. Adam Smith, *The Wealth of Nations*, Edwin Cannan, ed. (New York: G. P. Putnam's Sons, 1904). Quoted from Pelican Classics, rev. ed., 1974.

14. Galbraith, *The Affluent Society*, p. 160.

15. Paul Craig Roberts, "The Breakdown of the Keynesian Model," *The Public Interest*, No. 52 (Summer 1978), pp. 20–33.

16. Roberts did not say that the target income theory was necessarily untrue in all circumstances. People with free will can clearly respond to tax cuts any way they like. Roberts showed, however, that the target-income approach would soon tend to nullify the demand-side effects of tax cuts as well as the supply-side effects, thus leaving no explanation for the repeated history of revenue gains in the aftermath of reductions in tax rates.

17. Keynes, *General Theory*, pp. 347–348.

18. Lacy H. Hunt, chief economist for the Fidelity Bank of Philadelphia, quoted by Alfred L. Malabre Jr., in "As Salaries Climb with Prices, People Pay More of Income Despite Rate Cuts," *The Wall Street Journal*, 28 November 1979, p. 48. The Hunt estimate compares with a U.S. Treasury Department figure of 1.67 as the increase in federal revenues resulting from a 1 percent growth in nominal GNP.

19. Keynes, *General Theory*, p. 155.

20. W. H. Hutt, *A Rehabilitation of Say's Law* (Athens, Ohio: Ohio University Press, 1974), pp. 34, 35, and passim. Hutt's interesting argument defines away the problem of possible gluts by classifying them as "unintentional consumption." To supply, in his glossary, is "to offer inputs or outputs at prices or values which induce their sale." The key point, however, is not the definitions, but the appropriate policies. In case of widespread unintentional consumption, such as government often causes in the name of investment, the solution is to relieve the supply side of government inhibitions to commerce.

Chapter 5 / The Nature of Wealth

1. Quoted in Walter J. Levy, "Oil Policy and OPEC Development Prospects," *Foreign Affairs*, Vol. 57, No. 2 (Winter 1978/79), p. 300.

2. Stanley Lebergott, *The American Economy* (Princeton, N.J.: Princeton University Press, 1976), p. 246 and passim.

3. Martin Rein and Lee Rainwater, "How Large Is the Welfare Class?" *Challenge*, Vol. 20, No. 4 (Sept./Oct. 1977), p. 22. Rein and Rainwater rely on the longitudinal data of the Panel Study of Income Dynamics conducted by the University of Michigan Survey Research Center.

4. Robert Eisner, "No Tax Relief for Capital Gains," *Challenge*, Vol. 21, No. 6 (Jan./Feb. 1979), p. 63.

5. Lester C. Thurow, *Generating Inequality* (New York: Basic Books, 1975), pp. 129 and 130.

6. Arthur M. Louis, "In Search of the Elusive Big Rich," *Fortune*, Vol. 99, No. 3 (Feb. 12, 1979), pp. 93 and 98. (Cf. *Fortune*, November 1957, May 1968, and September 1973). "Today's Poor Millionaires," *U.S. News & World Report*, Vol. 85, No. 6 (August 14, 1978), pp. 38–42.

All such journalistic surveys permit only impressionistic estimates of the proportions partly dependent on inheritance. Many self-made rich men elude the surveys, while family wealth is more likely to attract attention over time. Recent fortunes in high-technology firms, for example, are almost entirely absent from the magazine lists. The striking fact is the apparent difficulty of finding the very rich. Studies of mobility below this exalted stratum, however, are increasingly sophisticated. Most show rising mobility in the United States. In particular see David L. Featherman and Robert M. Hauser, *Opportunity and Change* (New York: Academic Press, 1978).

7. Thurow, *Generating Inequality*, p. 129.

8. Lebergott, *The American Economy*, p. 174.

9. Eisner, "No Tax Relief," p. 63.

10. Martin Feldstein, testimony before the Joint Economic Committee, July 1978, published in *Challenge*, Vol. 21, No. 4 (Sept./Oct. 1978), pp. 60–61.

11. Richard E. Wagner, *Inheritance and the State: Tax Principles for a Free and Prosperous Commonweath* (Washington, D.C.: American Enterprise Institute for Public Policy Research, 1977), pp. 35–38. This excellent book elaborates on the "gambler's ruin" analogy.

12. Ibid. Wagner writes: "Whereas an individual might be willing to make an investment with a probability of success of only, say, 0.40 under proportional taxation, he might require a probability of success of 0.45 under progressive taxation. And the higher the rate of tax on winnings, the more favorable the odds must be before an entrepreneur will make the investment. And the more favorable the odds, the slower the expected disintegration of the entrepreneur's fortune. The use of progressive rates of tax to penalize those with high income and large wealth will tend to promote a conservatism that reduces the rate of personal mobility within the distributions of income and wealth. . . . By reducing the rate of mobility among the wealth positions, high rates of tax also reduce the ability of newcomers to enter the high wealth brackets."

13. "Today's Poor Millionaires," p. 38; see also "America's Invisible Millionaires," *U.S. News & World Report*, Vol. 88, No. 10 (March 17, 1980), pp. 34–39.

Chapter 6 / The Nature of Poverty

1. Thomas Sowell, "Race and I. Q. Reconsidered," in Thomas Sowell, ed., *American Ethnic Groups* (Washington, D.C.: The Urban Institute, 1977), p. 208.

2. Richard B. Freeman, "Discrimination in the Academic Marketplace," in Sowell, ed., *American Ethnic Groups*, pp. 167–200.

3. Andrew Greeley, "The Ethnic Miracle," *The Public Interest*, No. 45, (Fall 1976), pp. 20–36.

4. Irwin Garfinkel and Robert Haveman, with the assistance of David Betson, U.S. Depart-

ment of Health, Education and Welfare, *Earnings Capacity, Poverty, and Inequality,* Institute for Research on Poverty Monograph Series (New York: Academic Press, 1977), pp. 32 and passim.

5. Ibid.

6. George Gilder, *Visible Man: A True Story of Post-Racist America* (New York: Basic Books, 1978), p. 188.

7. George Gilder, *Sexual Suicide* (New York: Quadrangle/The New York Times Book Co., 1973); rev. ed. (New York: Bantam Books, 1974), p. 90.

8. E. A. Wrigley, *Population and History* (New York: McGraw-Hill, 1969), pp. 76–77.

9. Ibid., p. 13.

10. Ibid., p. 116.

11. Edward Banfield, *The Moral Basis of a Backward Society* (New York: The Free Press, 1958; paperback ed., 1967).

12. Adolph Berle, *American Economic Republic* (New York: Harcourt, Brace & World, 1963), chapter 7.

13. Christopher Jencks et al., *Inequality: A Reassessment of the Effect of Family and Schooling in America.* (New York: Basic Books, 1972).

14. Lionel Tiger, *Optimism, the Biology of Hope* (New York: Simon & Schuster, 1979).

15. Ivan H. Light: *Ethnic Enterprise in America* (Berkeley: University of California Press, 1972), pp. 170–172.

16. Irving Kristol, *Two Cheers for Capitalism* (New York: Basic Books, 1978), p. 262.

17. Light, *Ethnic Enterprise,* pp. 141–142 and 149.

Chapter 7 / The Entrepreneurial Future

1. A. F. Ehrbar, " 'Bigness' Becomes the Target of the Trustbusters," *Fortune,* Vol. 99, No. 6 (March 26, 1979), p. 37.

2. David E. Gumpert, "Future of Small Business May be Brighter Than Portrayed," *Harvard Business Review,* Vol. 57, No. 4 (July/August 1979), p. 176.

3. Burton Klein, *Dynamic Economics* (Cambridge, Mass.: Harvard University Press, 1977), p. 17.

4. "Information Processing," *Forbes,* Vol. 119, No. 1 (Jan. 1, 1977), p. 143.

5. Barry Commoner, *The Politics of Energy,* Borzoi ed. (New York: A. A. Knopf, 1979), p. 35.

6. Gumpert, "Future of Small Business," p. 174.

7. Roger E. Brinner, "The Anti-inflation Leverage of Investment," in Clarence C. Walton, ed., *Inflation and National Survival,* Proceedings of the Academy of Political Science, Vol. 33, No. 3 (New York: The Academy of Political Science, 1979), pp. 149–154.

8. *Our Turn to Listen: A White Paper on Unemployment, Education and Crime Based on Extensive Interviews with New York City Teenage Dropouts* (New York: Vocational Foundation Incorporated, 1978), pp. 32 and 36. See also David A. Robison, *Six Business Employment Programs, Emphasis: Disadvantaged Youth* (New York: Center for Public Resources, Inc., 1978), pp. 6 and 42.

Chapter 8 / The Clashes of Class

1. G. K. Chesterton, *Orthodoxy* (New York: Image Books, 1959), p. 48.

2. Norman Podhoretz, *Making It* (New York: Random House, 1969).

3. Steven Goldberg, *The Inevitability of Patriarchy,* rev. ed. (London: Temple Smith, 1977); U.S. ed. (New York: William Morrow, 1974).

4. Lester Thurow, *The Zero-Sum Society* (New York: Basic Books, 1980), p. 169.

5. Orlando Patterson, *Ethnic Chauvinism: The Reactionary Impulse* (New York: Stein & Day, 1978), pp. 149–150.

Chapter 9 / The War Against Wealth

1. Edward Banfield, *The Moral Basis of a Backward Society* (New York: The Free Press, 1958; paperback ed., 1967).
2. Orde Coombs, "The Trashing of Lemans: The New Civil War Begins," *New York* (Aug. 8, 1977).
3. Quoted in Peter Collier and David Horowitz, *The Rockefellers, An American Dynasty* (New York: Holt, Rinehart & Winston, 1976), p. 597.
4. Robert Eisner, "No Tax Relief for Capital Gains," *Challenge* Vol. 21, No. 6 (Jan./Feb. 1979), p. 63.

Chapter 10 / The Moral Hazards of Liberalism

1. Thomas Sowell in Thomas Sowell, ed., *American Ethnic Groups* (Washington, D.C.: The Urban Institute, 1977).
2. Ivan H. Light, *Ethnic Enterprise in America* (Berkeley: University of California Press, 1972), pp. 152–160.
3. Stuart Bruchey, *The Roots of American Economic Growth, 1607–1861*, Torchbook ed. (New York: Harper & Row, 1968), pp. 129–130.
4. Light, *Ethnic Enterprise*, pp. 191–192.
5. Martin Feldstein, "The Economics of the New Unemployment," *The Public Interest*, no. 33, (Fall 1973) pp. 3–42.
6. Charles D. Hobbs, *The Welfare Industry* (Washington, D.C.: The Heritage Foundation, 1978) pp. 83 and 84.
7. Ibid., p. 20 and passim.
8. "Studies Indicate New York Welfare Far Exceeds Federal Poverty Line," *The New York Times*, 25 January 1979, p. B6. These analyses, however, exclude many available means-tested benefits. See also Hobbs, *Welfare Industry*, pp. 83 and 84.
9. Gary Becker, "The Effect of the State on the Family," Monograph prepared for the Mont Pelerin Society Meetings, September 1978.
10. For a lucid exposition of the Feldstein position, plus critiques and comments from James M. Buchanan, Nancy Teeters, Arthur M. Okun, and others, see Martin S. Feldstein, "Social Insurance," in Colin D. Campbell, ed., *Income Distribution* (Washington, D.C.: American Enterprise Institute for Public Policy Research, 1977), pp. 71–124. See also Martin S. Feldstein, "Facing the Social Security Crisis," *The Public Interest*, No. 47, (Spring 1977), pp. 88–100; Martin S. Feldstein, "Social Security Hobbles Our Capital Formation," *Harvard Business Review*, Vol. 57, No. 4 (July/August 1979), pp. 6–8; and Martin S. Feldstein, "National Saving in the U.S.," in Eli Shapiro and William L. White, eds., *Capital for Productivity and Jobs* (Englewood Cliffs, N.J.: Prentice-Hall, 1977), pp. 124–154.
11. John W. Kendrick, *The Formation and Stocks of Total Capital*, National Bureau of Economic Research, No. 100, General Series (New York: Columbia University Press, 1976), p. 130 and passim.

Chapter 11 / The Coming Welfare Boom

1. Most of the observations in this chapter are based on two years of empirical investigation and analysis of welfare communities in New York and South Carolina in George Gilder, *Visible Man: A True Story of Post-Racist America* (New York: Basic Books, 1978).
2. Martin Anderson, *Welfare: The Political Economy of Welfare Reform in the United States* (Stanford, California: Hoover Institution Press, 1978), p. 134.
3. Frederick Doolittle, Frank Levy, and Michael Wiseman, "The Mirage of Welfare Reform," *The Public Interest*, No. 47 (Spring 1977), pp. 62–87.
4. Irwin Garfinkel and Robert Haveman, with the assistance of David Betson, U.S. Department of Health, Education and Welfare, *Earnings Capacity, Poverty, and Inequality*, Institute for

Research on Poverty Monograph Series (New York: Academic Press, 1977), pp. 61–69.

5. Charles D. Hobbs, *The Welfare Industry* (Washington, D.C.: The Heritage Foundation, 1978), pp. 74–75.

6. George Gilder, *Sexual Suicide* (New York: Quadrangle/The New York Times Book Company, 1973); rev. ed. (New York: Bantam Books, 1974), pp. 175–183.

7. Many researchers denied any significant causal connection between welfare and family breakdown. The best presentation of such an analysis appeared in Heather L. Ross and Isabel V. Sawhill, *Time of Transition: The Growth of Families Headed by Women* (Washington, D.C.: The Urban Institute, 1975). The authors appraised, updated, and recomputed nearly all the available data on female-headed families and laboriously put to rest every remaining rumor—of an academically respectable sort—that welfare caused such families to form. Ross and Sawhill conceded that AFDC may play some minor role in deterring remarriage by black recipients, but it did not measurably upset their marriages or cause illegitimacy.

Apparently as an afterthought, however, the two scholars did a computer study of the likely impact of a guaranteed income of the sort that was later to be tested by HEW in Denver and Seattle. They brought together in their model some twenty-four variables that they had found to affect marital stability, including church attendance, the husband's role performance (essentially his earnings-capacity utilization rate), the woman's earnings or AFDC income (to judge what they call the *independence effect*), as well as various general demographic and economic factors. Then they added a series of findings derived from their analysis of AFDC. The results of the test confirmed the prevailing belief—long maintained by Moynihan—that a guaranteed income plan or negative income tax would tend to stabilize families. Under the assumptions of the plan, Ross and Sawhill predicted "a modest reduction in the proportion of women who head families among both whites and nonwhites, even when the tax plan involved provides greater than existing benefits to women and children." All such analyses fail to come to terms with masculine psychology: the profound male need to perform the provider role.

8. Hobbs, *The Welfare Industry*, pp. 74–75.

9. Despite a booming economy, California ended the decade with about 13 percent of its children on welfare, among the highest rates in the nation and more than twice as high as most states with low welfare payments. Neither Reagan himself, nor his apologists, such as Martin Anderson, seem to understand the problem. At least both of them express pride at the increase in benefits to the "truly needy." Like most welfare analysts, they fail to comprehend the dynamics of the system and the reactions of the poor to changes in it: chiefly, in California, to benefits increasing at the pace of inflation while potential take-home pay from jobs often diminishes in real terms. Furthermore, they have created a new constituency of welfare workers, with the same kind of interest as the old in the continuation of high benefits and levels of dependency: a "conservative" bureaucracy devoted to administering requirements for work and child support and defending welfare in conservative terms. As one administrator wrote in 1979 in a letter to *National Review*, "By enforcing support, the 'profit' from family breakup is eliminated. By adequately reviewing family composition and income information . . . the expansion of welfare rolls would be eliminated." The writer defended the high benefit levels and urged "the provision of legal services necessary to promote parental responsibility." That is, to enforce by legal means what is massively deterred by financial supports.

10. John Bishop, "The Welfare Brief," *The Public Interest*, No. 53 (Fall 1978), pp. 173 and 174.

11. Martin Rein and Lee Rainwater, "How Large in the Welfare Class?" *Challenge*, Vol. 20, No. 4 (Sept./Oct. 1977), p. 22.

12. Ralph Segalman, "The Welfare Way of Life," a letter to *The American Spectator*, Vol. 11, No. 9 (August/September 1978), p. 40. Segalman, a professor of sociology at California State University, Northridge, points out that transgenerational welfare poverty, which twenty years ago was only 5 percent of welfare recipients, now comprises 20 percent, and on the basis of statistics in Los Angeles, he predicts that this element of permanent dependency will reach 40 percent in ten years.

13. Alan Sweezy, "The Challenge of Social Security Financing," *ZPG National Reporter* (June/July 1978). Sweezy quotes Census Bureau projections that show the porportion of the population 65 and over rising by nearly 80 percent between 1976 and 2030, while the working-age population proportion declines slightly.

14. "Hispanics Fastest Growing Minority in U.S.," *The New York Times,* 18 February 1979, p. 16.

15. Tom Bethell, "Against Bilingual Education," *Harper's,* Vol. 258, No. 1545 (February 1979), p. 30.

16. Vincent H. Whitney, "Fertility Trends and Child Allowances" in Eveline M. Burns, ed., *Children's Allowances and the Economic Welfare of Children,* the Report of a Conference (New York: Citizens Committee for Children of New York, 1978), pp. 123–139 and Nicole Questiaux, "Family Allowances in France," ibid., pp. 76–89.

Chapter 12 / The Myths of Discrimination

1. Kim B. Clark and Lawrence H. Summers, "Labor Market Dynamics and Unemployment: A Reconsideration," *Brookings Papers on Economic Activity,* No. 1 (Washington, D.C.: The Brookings Institution, 1979), p. 52.

2. Cotton Mather Lindsay, "Equal Pay for Comparable Work: An Economic Analysis of a New Anti-Discrimination Doctrine," An LEC Occasional Paper, (Coral Gables, Fla.: Law and Economics Center, University of Miami School of Law, 1980).

3. Thomas Sowell, *Markets and Minorities* (London: Basil Blackwell, 1980), forthcoming. See also Thomas Sowell, ed., *American Ethnic Groups* (Washington, D.C.: The Urban Institute, 1978), and Thomas Sowell, "Ethnicity in a Changing America," *Daedalus,* Vol. 107, No. 1 (Winter 1978), pp. 213–238.

4. Ibid. all of previous footnote. See also Richard Freeman, "Black Economic Progress Since 1964," *The Public Interest,* No. 52 (Summer 1978) and Edward Banfield, *The Unheavenly City Revisited* (Boston: Little Brown & Co., 1974), p. 81. For a contrary view of the data, see Irwin Garfinkel and Robert Haveman, with the assistance of David Betson, U.S. Department of Health, Education and Welfare, *Earnings Capacity, Poverty, and Inequality,* Institute for Research on Poverty Monograph Series (New York: Academic Press, 1977), pp. 70–90. All these analyses, however, ignore the impact of family breakup on the motivation and earnings of men.

5. Computed from statistics in U.S. Bureau of the Census, *Current Population Reports,* Series P-60, No. 106, "Characteristics of the Population Below the Poverty Level: 1975" (Washington, D.C.: U.S. Government Printing Office, 1977), Table 37, p. 141. For figures outside of poverty areas, see Table 41, pp. 172–176.

6. Heather L. Ross and Isabel V. Sawhill, *Time of Transition: The Growth of Families Headed by Women* (Washington, D.C.: The Urban Institute, 1975), pp. 67–88 and the appendix. Statistics updated with data from U.S. Bureau of the Census, *Current Population Reports.*

7. Garfinkel and Haveman, *Earnings Capacity,* pp. 32 and 33.

8. Computed from U.S. Department of Labor, "Median Income in 1972 of Persons by Years of School Completed and by Sex," unpublished data, and U.S. Bureau of the Census, "Census of Population: 1970. MARITAL STATUS," Final Report PC (2)-4C (Washington, D.C.: U.S. Government Printing Office, 1972), Table 1, p. 1. See also an analysis by Jacob Mincer and Solomon Polachek of the National Longitudinal Survey: U.S. Department of Labor, *Economic Problems of Women,* Hearings before the Joint Economic Committee, 93rd Cong. 1st sess., Part 1, July 10, 11, 12 (Washington, D.C.: U.S. Government Printing Office, 1973), pp. 20, 34–35, and 47–48. The survey showed that in 1966 single women earned 86 percent as much as comparable married men and approximately the same as or more than comparable single men.

9. U.S. Bureau of the Census, *Current Population Reports,* Series P-20, No. 255, "Marital Status and Living Arrangements: March 1973," (Washington, D.C.: U.S. Government Printing Office, 1973), pp. 11–12.

10. Thomas Sowell, ed., *American Ethnic Groups,* p. 208 and passim. See also Thomas Sowell, *Markets and Minorities.*

11. Eric Hanushek, "Ethnic Income Variations: Magnitudes and Explanations," in Thomas Sowell, ed., *American Ethnic Groups.* See also David L. Featherman and Robert M. Hauser, *Opportunity and Change* (New York: Academic Press, 1978), pp. 238–252.

12. Richard B. Freeman, "Discrimination in the Academic Marketplace," in Thomas Sowell,

ed., *American Ethnic Groups,* pp. 167–202, and Statistical Data in ibid., pp. 257, 278–291, and passim.

13. Garfinkel and Haveman, *Earnings Capacity,* p. 32 and passim.

14. Thomas Sowell, "The Controversy over Black I.Q.s," *The New York Times Magazine,* 27 March 1977, pp. 57–58.

15. Eleanor Emmons Maccoby and Carol Nagy Jacklin, *The Psychology of Sex Differences* (Stanford, Calif.: Stanford University Press, 1974), pp. 242–243.

16. Steven Goldberg, *The Inevitability of Patriarchy,* rev. ed. (London: Temple Smith, 1977); U.S. edition (New York: William Morrow, 1974). The Margaret Mead review appeared in *Redbook* (February 1974).

17. Computed from U.S. Bureau of the Census, "Census of Population: 1970. MARITAL STATUS," Table 9, pp. 227–252.

18. Nathan Glazer, *Affirmative Discrimination: Ethnic Inequality and Public Policy,* with a new introduction by the author (New York: Basic Books, 1978), p. 63.

Chapter 13 / The Jobs Perplex

1. Peter B. Doeringer and Michael J. Piore, "Unemployment and the 'Dual Labor Market,'" *The Public Interest,* No. 38 (Winter 1975), pp. 67–79; Lester Thurow, *Generating Inequality* (New York: Basic Books, 1975); and Glen G. Cain, "The Challenge of Segmented Labor Market Theories to Orthodox Theory," *Journal of Economic Literature* (December 1976).

2. John Kenneth Galbraith, *The Galbraith Reader* (Ipswich, Mass.: Gambit, 1977), passim.

3. Nathan Glazer, "Reform Work, Not Welfare," *The Public Interest,* No. 40 (Summer 1975), pp. 3–10.

4. George Gilder, *Visible Man: A True Story of Post-Racist America* (New York: Basic Books, 1978).

5. Andrew Billingsley, *Black Families in White America* (Englewood Cliffs, N.J.: Prentice-Hall, 1968), p. 171.

6. David Robison, personal communication. See also *You and Youth,* a monthly publication of Vocational Foundation Incorporated, 44 East 24th Street, New York City, N.Y., for case studies of employment-training successes in the private sector.

7. J. Peter Grace, "The Assault on Economic Incentive," Chart 23, Net New Jobs Created, by Size of Firms, presented at the Symposium on American Capitalism. Grace's paper, available from W. R. Grace, Inc., New York City, stands as the best single compendium of statistics on the decline of the U.S. economy and the confiscatory tax rates that are suffocating its growth.

8. U.S. Department of Labor, *Monthly Review,* 1977.

9. *Our Turn to Listen,* (New York: Vocational Foundation Incorporated, 1978).

10. Ibid.

11. Lindley H. Clark, Jr., "Discrimination at HEW," *The Wall Street Journal,* 5 July 1978, p. 8. Clark summarizes "Discrimination in HEW: Is the Doctor Sick or Is the Patient Healthy?" a paper distributed by the Center for the Study of the Economy and the State at the University of Chicago and later published by *The Journal of Law and Economics,* also at the University of Chicago. The study is based on statistics collected by the U.S. Civil Service Commission. Clark's article elicited a response from Joseph A. Califano, Jr., then Secretary of HEW (*The Wall Street Journal,* 12 July 1978). Displaying utter incomprehension of the nature of the problem, Califano wrote: "HEW has never deemed statistics to be the sole or necessarily the best indicator of employment discrimination." Nonetheless, he went on, "Last August, I appointed a study group to review HEW's Equal Employment Opportunity Program." As a result of the study he created a new *Deputy Assistant Secretary of Personnel Administration for EEO* to enforce an affirmative-action program at HEW. Califano did not say whether HEW would forgo any federal funds if the program does not succeed. Of course, HEW is no more or less guilty of discrimination by any valid measure than most of the institutions the department mercilessly harasses.

12. Bradley R. Schiller, "Equality, Opportunity, and the 'Good Job,'" *The Public Interest,* No. 43 (Spring 1976), pp. 111–120. This important article was scarcely noticed, even by

one of the editors of the magazine that published it. But it issues a difficult challenge to the conventional wisdom of both the Left and the Right on the issues of race and opportunity.

13. Sar A. Levitan, William B. Johnson, and Robert Taggart, *Still a Dream: The Changing Status of Blacks Since 1960* (Cambridge, Mass.: Harvard University Press, 1975), p. 53.

14. Clark, "Discrimination at HEW."

15. Thomas Sowell, ed., *American Ethnic Groups*, Part Two, Statistical Data on American Ethnic Groups, Black Americans (Washington, D.C.: The Urban Institute, 1977), Tables 8–13, pp. 278–295.

16. Lee Rainwater and William L. Yancy, *The Moynihan Report and the Politics of Controversy*, including the text of Daniel Patrick Moynihan's *The Negro Family: The Case for National Action*, Trans-action Social Science and Public Policy Report (Cambridge, Mass.: The M.I.T. Press, 1967), *Appendix*, Table 17, Department of Labor Employment as of December 31, 1964, p. 73.

17. Sowell, ed., *American Ethnic Groups*, pp. 278–295.

18. Irwin Garfinkel and Robert Haveman, with the assistance of David Betson, U.S. Department of Health, Education and Welfare, *Earnings Capacity, Poverty, and Inequality*, Institute for Research on Poverty Monograph Series (New York: Academic Press, 1977), p. 32.

19. Ronald L. Oaxaca, "Male-Female Wage Differentials in Urban Labor Markets," Working Paper No. 23 (Princeton, N.J.: Industrial Relations Section, Princeton University, 1971).

Chapter 14 / The Make-Work Illusion

1. Patrick Buchanan, quoted in *Harper's*, Vol. 259, No. 1554 (November 1979), p. 39.

2. David B. Wilson, "There's a New Class in Our Society," *The Boston Globe*, 16 July 1979, p. 11.

3. Frances Cairncross, " 'Deindustrialization'—Odd Phenomenon," *The Financier*, Vol. 2, No. 4 (April 1978), pp. 11–14. See also Walter Eltis and David Bacon, *The British Problem: Too Few Producers*, rev. American ed. (New York: St. Martin's Press, 1978).

4. Computed from *OECD National Accounts Statistics, 1972* and *OECD Revenue Statistics, 1965–1972*, as tabulated by Alan T. Peacock and Martin Ricketts, "The Growth of the Public Sector and Inflation," in Fred Hirsch and John H. Goldthorpe, eds., *The Political Economy of Inflation* (Cambridge, Mass.: Harvard University Press, 1978), pp. 122–123.

5. Andrew Sum and Maryann Bouba, paper on unemployment compensation, prepared for the Massachusetts Division of Employment Security, February 1979. Among the findings were that 24 percent of nonparticipants in the Massachusetts work force say they want jobs but do not seek them because of the attractions of welfare and other government support. Nearly 84 percent of those out of the labor market "do not want a job now."

6. José Ortega y Gasset, *The Revolt of the Masses* (New York: W. W. Norton, 1932), p. 99.

7. *Our Turn to Listen*, (New York: Vocational Foundation Incorporated, 1978).

8. Warren T. Brookes, "Beware of State's Employment Statistics," *The Boston Herald American*, 21 March 1978, p. 11.

9. Warren T. Brookes, "Is Massachusetts a Federal Dependent?" *The Boston Herald American*, 22 February 1978.

10. Sum and Bouba, paper on unemployment compensation.

11. Daniel Patrick Moynihan, "The Politics and Economics of Regional Growth," *The Public Interest*, No. 51 (Spring 1978), p. 10.

12. Brookes, "Is Massachusetts a Federal Dependent?"

13. Ibid.

14. Warren T. Brookes, "Tax Revolt: Isn't It Time to Slow Down the Education Bureaucracy," *The Boston Herald American*, 27 June 1978, p. 9.

15. Moynihan, "Politics and Economics of Regional Growth," p. 14.

16. Ortega y Gasset, *Revolt*, p. 99.

17. "Newark Is Building for a Hopeful Future," *The New York Times*, 12 July 1977, p. 25.

18. Warren T. Brookes, "Unemployment and the Illegal Alien," *The Boston Herald American,* 3 September 1976, p. 14.

19. Ibid.

20. Senator John Chafee (Republican, Rhode Island), personal communication.

21. "Boat People Find Hardship in U.S., but Also Hope," *The New York Times,* 28 January 1979, p. 47.

22. Richard A. Posner, "Utilitarianism, Economics, and Legal Theory," *The Journal of Legal Studies,* The University of Chicago Law School, Vol. 8, No. 1 (January 1979), p. 136.

23. Kenneth D. Walters and R. Joseph Monsen, "State-Owned Business Abroad: New Competitive Threat," *Harvard Business Review,* Vol. 57, No. 2 (March/April 1979), pp. 160–170.

Chapter 15 / Laffer and Liberal Economics

1. John Kenneth Galbraith, *The New York Times,* 12 January 1980, Op-Ed page.

2. Robert L. Heilbroner, *The New York Times,* 22 December 1979, Op-Ed page.

3. Robert L. Heilbroner, *Beyond Boom and Crash* (New York: W. W. Norton, 1979), p. 89 and passim. This work first appeared in *The New Yorker.*

4. Robert L. Schuettinger and Eamonn F. Butler, *Forty Centuries of Wage and Price Controls* (Washington, D.C.: The Heritage Foundation, 1978).

5. Paul Craig Roberts, "The Economic Case for Kemp-Roth," *The Wall Street Journal,* 1 August 1978, p. 16, reprinted in Arthur B. Laffer and Jan Seymour, eds., *The Economics of the Tax Revolt* (New York: Harcourt Brace Jovanovich, 1979), pp. 57–61. For econometric estimates from three Keynsian models on the savings effect, see Donald W. Kiefer, "An Economic Analysis of the Kemp/Roth Tax Cut Bill, H.R. 8333," in ibid., pp. 13–27; and comment by Jack Kemp, "Vanik's Study Makes Convincing Case for Enactment of the Kemp-Roth Act," in ibid., pp. 28–34.

6. Scott Burns, "Financially It's Better to Hoard than Invest," *The Boston Herald American,* 10 July 1978, p. 15.

7. "Tax the Rich!" *Wall Street Journal* editorial quoted in Jack Kemp, *An American Renaissance* (New York: Harper & Row, 1979), pp. 72–73.

8. Martin Feldstein, "End Capital Gains Tax on Stocks," *Financier,* Vol. 4, No. 1 (January 1980), p. 23; Martin J. Bailey, "Inflationary Distortions and Taxes," in Henry J. Aaron, ed., *Inflation and the Income Tax* (Washington, D.C.: The Brookings Institution, 1976), p. 302. Bailey writes: "As a rough guide, a 7 percent inflation triples the capital gains rates" and in 1975 resulted in a rate of 137 percent tax on real gains on assets held for one year, and a 97 percent tax on gains held for ten years. He made no estimates for the higher rates of inflation experienced in the late 1970s.

9. Galbraith, *New York Times,* Op-Ed page.

10. For a detailed exposition of these effects, see Roger E. Brinner, "Inflation and the Definition of Taxable Personal Income," in Aaron, ed., *Inflation and the Income Tax,* pp. 121–151 and Roger Brinner, "The Impact of Inflation on Investment," in *The Americans, 1976: Critical Choices for Americans,* Vol. 2, Irving Kristol and Paul Weaver, eds. (Lexington, Mass.: Lexington Books, 1976).

11. Warren T. Brookes, "Getting the Rich to Pay More Taxes," *The Boston Herald American,* 22 August 1978, p. 11.

12. For a lucid explanation see C. Lowell Harriss, "Property Taxation After the California Vote," *Tax Review,* Tax Foundation, Inc., Washington, D.C., Vol. 39, No. 8 (August 1978).

13. David Diachaud, "Inflation and Income Distribution," in Fred Hirsch and John H. Goldthorpe, eds., *The Political Economy of Inflation* (Cambridge, Mass.: Harvard University Press, 1979), p. 110.

14. Quoted in Irving Kristol, "The Myth of 'Business Confidence,' " *The Wall Street Journal,* 14 November 1977, p. 22.

15. G. K. Chesterton, "The Twelve Men," in *Tremendous Trifles* (Beaconsfield, Britain: Darwen Finlayson, 1968), p. 55.

16. Computed from *OECD National Accounts Statistics, 1972* and *Revenue Statistics, 1965–72,* as tabulated by Alan T. Peacock and Martin Ricketts, "The Growth of the Public Sector

and Inflation," in Hirsch and Goldthorpe, eds., *The Political Economy of Inflation*, pp. 122–123.

17. Richard Rose and Guy Peters, *Can Government Go Bankrupt?* (New York: Basic Books, 1978), Table A 4.4, The Sources of Tax Revenue, computed from 1974 data compiled in *Revenue Statistics of OECD Member Countries, 1965–1974* (Paris: OECD, 1976).

18. *The Taxation of Net Wealth, Capital Transfers and Capital Gains of Individuals* (Paris: OECD, 1979).

19. Henry J. Aaron, *Who Pays the Property Tax?* (Washington, D.C.: The Brookings Institution, 1975). See also Christopher Jencks, "A New Look at an Old Tax," *Working Papers*, Vol. 5, No. 2 (Summer 1977).

20. Computed from *Revenue Statistics of OECD Member Countries* (Paris: OECD, 1979), pp. 82–94.

21. Rose and Peters, *Can Government Go Bankrupt?*, pp. 86–105.

22. Edgar K. Browning and William R. Johnson, *The Distribution of the Tax Burden* (Washington, D.C.: American Enterprise Institute for Public Policy Research, 1979), p. 58; and J. Peter Grace, "The Assault on Economic Incentive," Chart 30, U.S. Economic and Political Power, presented at the Symposium on American Capitalism. Available from W. R. Grace, Inc., New York City.

23. *Individual Taxes in 80 Countries* (New York: Price Waterhouse, 1979).

24. Ian M. D. Little, "An Economic Reconnaissance," in Walter Galenson, ed., *Economic Growth and Structural Change in Taiwan* (Ithaca, N.Y.: Cornell University Press, 1979), pp. 474–480.

25. Renters News Service, Singapore, 5 March 1980.

26. Barbara Ellis, "Italy's Prosperous Anarchy," *Forbes*, Vol. 123, No. 7 (April 2, 1979), pp. 36–37; and Sari Gilbert, "Tax Avoidance: Italy's Inheritance," *The Boston Sunday Globe*, 19 November 1978, p. E-1.

27. "Swedes' Needs" in *The Wall Street Journal*, 22 January 1980, p. 1. The European study, published by Man-Power Inc., Milwaukee, Wisc., listed Sweden first among major industrial countries in absenteeism, at 16 days a year, followed by Germany (9.5), France (8.3), U.S. (3.5), and Japan (1.9).

28. Quoted in Melvyn B. Krauss, "The Swedish Tax Revolt," *The Wall Street Journal*, 1 February 1979, p. 16.

29. Jude Wanniski, "Puerto Rico and Statehood," (Rolling Hills Estates, California: A.B. Laffer Associates, 1979). See also, Bruce Bartlett, *A Walk on the Supply Side* (New Rochelle, N.Y.: Arlington House, 1981 forthcoming).

30. *The Economic Report of the President: 1978* (Washington, D.C.: U.S. Government Printing Office, 1978). See also Rudiger Dornbusch and Stanley Fischer, *Macroeconomics* (New York: McGraw-Hill, 1978), pp. 311, 315, 320, and passim. Although the tax cut is sometimes charged with contributing to the inflation of the 1970s, the inflation did not accelerate until the 10 percent tax surcharge and several other levies were imposed in 1968, followed by the new doubling of capital gains taxes in 1969 and by a vast expansion, from 120 billion dollars to 220 billion dollars, in state and local government expenditures (and taxes) for goods and services between 1969 and 1974.

31. Browning and Johnson, *The Distribution of the Tax Burden*, p. 70.

32. Irwin Garfinkel and Robert Haveman, with the assistance of David Betson, U.S. Department of Health, Education and Welfare, *Earnings Capacity, Poverty, and Inequality*, Institute for Research on Poverty Monograph Series (New York: Academic Press, 1977), p. 32.

33. See chapter 2 of this work.

34. "Inflation to Be Cut by Proposition 13, U.S. Report Finds," *The Wall Street Journal*, 7 July 1978, p. 2. See also The Congressional Budget Office, *Proposition 13: Its Impact on the Nation's Economy, Federal Revenues, and Federal Expenditures*; reprinted in Arthur B. Laffer and Jan P. Seymour, eds., *Economics of Tax Revolt*, pp. 110–113; Charles W. Kadlec and Arthur B. Laffer, "The Jarvis-Gann Proposal: An Application of the Laffer Curve," in ibid., pp. 118–122.

35. According to a Library of Congress study of projections of three econometric models (Wharton, Chase, and DRI), passage of Kemp-Roth would have increased the proportion of total revenues paid by the rich, with the share from taxpayers earning more than $200,000 rising by 13 percent. See Laffer and Seymour, eds., *Economics of Tax Revolt*, p. 29.

36. Jude Wanniski, *The Way the World Works* (New York: Basic Books, 1978), pp. 238–275; Jude Wanniski, "Inflation and the 'Arc of Crisis,' " (Morristown, N.J.: Polyconomics,

Inc., 1980). See also Jack Kemp, "The Revival of Incentive Economics," *The Ripon Forum* (January 1980). Kemp shows the destructive impact of progressive rates on the Israeli economy.

Chapter 16 / The Inflationary State

1. This Milton Friedman position, frequently espoused, was quoted by Irving Kristol in "Populist Remedy For Populist Abuses," *The Wall Street Journal,* 10 August 1978.

2. Dennis Robertson, "The Colvin Committee, the Income Tax, and the Price Level," *Economic Journal,* Vol. 37, No. 148 (December 1927).

3. Paul Craig Roberts, "The Economic Case for Kemp-Roth," *The Wall Street Journal,* 1 August 1978, p. 16; reprinted in Arthur B. Laffer and Jan P. Seymour, eds., *The Economics of the Tax Revolt* (New York: Harcourt Brace Jovanovich, 1979), pp. 57–61.

4. Michael K. Evans, "Taxes, Inflation, and the Rich," *The Wall Street Journal,* 7 August 1978, p. 10; reprinted in ibid., pp. 62–64.

5. Quoted in Scott Burns, "Why We're Selling the Future to Japan," *The Boston Herald American,* 13 March 1978, p. 11.

6. Henry Aaron, ed., *Inflation and the Income Tax* (Washington, D.C.: The Brookings Institution, 1976), p. 193.

7. David Warsh and Lawrence Minard, "Inflation Is Too Important to Leave to the Economists," *Forbes* (November 15, 1976) and David Warsh, "The Great Hamburger Paradox," *Forbes* (September 15, 1977).

8. E. H. Phelps-Brown and Sheila V. Hopkins, "Seven Centuries of Building Wages," *Economica,* vol. 22, no. 87 (August 1955) and E. H. Phelps Brown and Sheila V. Hopkins, "Seven Centuries of the Prices of Consumables, Compared to Builders' Wage Rates," *Economica,* (1956).

9. Robert Solow, "The Intelligent Citizen's Guide to Inflation," *The Public Interest,* No. 38 (Winter 1975), p. 33.

10. Robert L. Heilbroner and Lester C. Thurow, *The Economic Problem,* rev. ed. (Englewood Cliffs, N.J.: Prentice-Hall, 1979).

11. M. Panic, "The Origin of Increasing Inflationary Tendencies," in Fred Hirsch and John H. Goldthorpe, eds., *The Political Economy of Inflation* (Cambridge, Mass.: Harvard University Press, 1978), p. 137.

12. Solow, "Intelligent Citizen's Guide to Inflation," pp. 30–66.

13. Charles S. Maier, "The Politics of Inflation in the 20th Century," in Hirsch and Goldthorpe, eds., *Political Economy of Inflation,* p. 71.

14. Phelps-Brown and Hopkins, "Seven Centuries of Prices of Consumables," quoted in Warsh, "Hamburger Paradox," p. 181.

15. Warsh, "Hamburger Paradox," p. 199.

16. Ibid.

17. John W. Kendrick, *The Formation and Stocks of Total Capital,* National Bureau of Economic Research, No. 100, General Series (New York: Columbia University Press, 1976), p. 136 and passim.

18. Ronald I. McKinnon, *Money and Capital in Economic Development* (Washington, D.C.: The Brookings Institution, 1973), pp. 92–95.

19. Ibid.

20. Warren Brookes, "Lies, Damn Lies and the GNP," *The Boston Herald American,* 25 August 1978; for projections through 1981, see Brookes, "Reagan's 30 percent Tax Cut Isn't Radical—or Inflationary," *The Boston Herald American,* 24 April 1980.

21. Ibid.

Chapter 17 / The Productivity of Services

1. Barry Supple, "A Framework for British Business History," in Barry Supple, ed., *Essays in British Business History* (Oxford, England: Clarendon Press, 1977), pp. 11–15.

2. One sign of such an engorgement of the economy by relatively unproductive services was the long-growing divergence between the wholesale price index, which remained generally steady until the early 1970s, and the consumer price index, which rose rapidly throughout the industrial world. Because the wholesale index lacks the strong service component found in the consumer price index, the shift to services was said to account for inflation. More significant, though, was the fact that consumer prices had a far greater tax component than wholesale prices (until the Arabs decided to tax oil).

3. Warren Brookes, "Taxflation, Government's Windfall Profit," *The Boston Herald American,* 17 April 1979.

4. Henry J. Aaron, ed., *Inflation and the Income Tax* (Washington, D.C.: The Brookings Institution, 1976), pp. 33–80.

5. Theodore Levitt, "The Emerging Fecundity of Service," in *The Future of Productivity* (Washington, D.C.: The National Center for Productivity and the Quality of Working Life, 1978), pp. 63–72.

6. Martin Feldstein, "Consequences of Hospital Controls," *The Wall Street Journal,* 16 April 1979.

7. Dr. Reese F. Alsop and Dr. Peter Bourne, unpublished manuscript, 1977. Bourne and Alsop explain the system: "Diabetes is a condition (which) may become transformed with alarming rapidity into the life-threatening emergency of diabetic coma. Precipitating causes have long been recognized: any . . . infection (particularly of the intestinal tract), trauma, emotional upsets, dietary indiscretions or dehydration to name a few. Yet in the setting of a big city hospital none of these turned out to be critical. The determining factor in the vast majority of cases was keeping the patients waiting, the unavailability of the doctors. Dr. Miller has demonstrated that the complication of coma could be practically eliminated if diabetic patients were each assigned, urged, and instructed to call a specific telephone number day or night at the slightest symptom or deterioration in their condition. A hot line, with a special number, was established and manned by doctors in shifts around the clock so that continuous expert advice could be guaranteed. Communication and prevention were substituted for the delays which had previously so often permitted the development of coma. The 'stitch in time' principle, the immediate advice, proved to be in many cases the difference between life and death. Minor ills could no longer mushroom into major catastrophes. They simply didn't have time. Prevention had supplanted brinkmanship."

8. Donald M. Fisk, Herbert J. Kiesling, and Lynn Bell, *Privatization of Local Government Services,* unpublished report prepared by The Urban Institute, Washington, D.C., for the National Center for Productivity and Quality of Working Life.

9. Frederick W. Hornbruch, Jr., *Raising Productivity: Ten Case Histories and Their Lessons* (New York: McGraw-Hill, 1977), p. 66.

Chapter 18 / The Imperatives of Growth

1. Clarence L. Barber, "Inflation Distortion and the Balanced Budget," *Challenge,* Vol. 22, No. 4 (September/October 1979), pp. 44–47.

2. David A. Andelman, "New York's Taxi Industry Thriving on Some Controversial Economics," *The New York Times,* 13 March 1980, p. 1.

3. Peter Drucker, "Old Consumers vs. Young Producers," *The Wall Street Journal,* 18 December 1979, p. 20.

4. Peter M. Gutmann, "Statistical Illusions, Mistaken Policies," *Challenge,* Vol. 22, No. 5 (November/December 1979), pp. 14–17.

5. Although some inventory profits can be made real when inflation continues or accelerates (as many businesses have discovered to their secret delight), the taxation of earnings on the basis of historical cost accounting in both capital goods and inventories was a significant burden on some companies in the 1970s. Most of the supposed steel industry profits during the 1970s can be said to disappear if appropriate depreciation is charged. But the steel industry not only had to pay taxes on these nominal profits, it also paid dividends (which were taxed again as unearned income for their recipients). These increasing dividend payments were another effect of inflation since they were needed in part to compete with

the inflated yields of bonds (although, except for misconceived rules and taxes, inflation would not actually damage the real value of plants and equipment—the real equity of steel and other manufacturing firms—the way it destroys the principal value of bonds).

Economist George Terborgh, in a study for the Machinery and Allied Products Institute, concluded that on the basis of replacement cost accounting of inventories and depreciation, corporate profits in general during the three years spanning 1974 to 1976 were too small to cover dividend payments, and Securities and Exchange Commission (SEC) Chairman Harold Williams estimated that real depreciation of aging American steel plants was twice as great as the industry's cash flow after dividends.

These analyses raise an important alarm, but they seem somewhat overwrought for such heavily leveraged borrowing firms as the steel industry, with all its political clout and government subsidies. Large corporations have about two-thirds as much net indebtedness in bonds and other dollar-denominated notes as the government. They benefited from a similar unreported 30 billion-dollar decline in the value of their debt and were allowed to write off interest payments that largely consisted of an inflation premium to offset that decline. It was firms more dependent on equity than debt that were hurt most in the taxflationary seventies.

In addition, the argument that large businesses suffer greatly from inadequate depreciation of their equipment and facilities ignores the fact that the residual value of these assets—their value in the market, whether as an operating facility, as real estate, or even as scrap—is rising because of inflation. Because the company is writing off its equipment at the same price it paid for it in the past, the depreciation charges alone will not suffice to replace it with new equipment. But at the same time, the market value of those portions of the plants and equipment that have not been worn out or outmoded has steadily risen in many businesses. Moreover, the company is permitted to counteract inflationary effects to some extent by accelerating its depreciation costs—assigning most of them to the early years of the equipment's life. Meanwhile, the real worth of this equipment to the company has likely increased. The profitability of the use of a facility will often rise as time passes and competitors have to purchase new and more costly equipment.

The sum of these possible gains from inflation—the acceleration of depreciation charges on equipment that does not wear out, the appreciation of its residual market or sale value, the rise of the net income produced by equipment purchased in the past, the tax deductibility of interest and the destruction of the value of the debt—all these benefits usually have a total worth greater than the loss from depreciation by historic costs. Thus most big companies with substantial debt and real worth should indeed have been able to pay their taxes and dividends while at the same time replacing their plants and equipment as needed. These considerations do not answer the question of whether companies should be taxed at all, nor do they deny the claim that federal regulations and other policies have gravely damaged American corporations. But it does mean that most big companies have not been reporting false profits and that many of them have been much undervalued on the stock exchange, not because of excessive taxation of their profits, but because of excessive taxation of stockholders and potential stock purchasers.

Large corporations have suffered from a stock market that evaluates their assets at only three-quarters of book value. They have thus been forced to turn to debt to finance expansion. But they have gained by buying back their own equity at bargain rates and by buying out smaller companies at prices far below the likely costs of reproducing their assets. Rather than build a new factory at inflated prices, many corporations have been able merely to buy an existing company that possessed the desired facilities, at 25 percent off book value.

6. Roger E. Brinner, "The Anti-Inflation Leverage of Investment," in Clarence C. Walton, ed., *Inflation and National Survival*, Proceedings of the Academy of Political Science, Vol. 33, No. 3 (New York: The Academy of Political Science, 1979), pp. 149–154.

7. Hendrik Houthakker, "The Inverse Relation Between Company Growth and Price Movements," *Brookings Papers on Economic Activity*, No. 1 (Washington, D.C.: The Brookings Institution, 1979).

8. Abridged from Thomas Macaulay, *The History of England*, chapter 19, as quoted in *Challenge*, Vol. 21, No. 4, (September/October 1978), pp. 3–6.

9. W. Arthur Lewis, *The Theory of Economic Growth* (London: George Allen & Unwin Ltd., 1955), p. 405.

Chapter 19 / The Kinetic Economy

1. Jane Jacobs, *The Economy of Cities* (New York: Random House, 1969). Toward the end of this fascinating work, Jacobs writes: "The primary economic conflict, I think, is between people whose interests are with already well-established economic activities, and those whose interests are with the emergence of new economic activities." (p. 249)

2. Quoted in Arnold Heertje, *Economics and Technical Change* (New York: John Wiley & Sons, 1977), p. 75.

3. Joseph Schumpeter, *Capitalism, Socialism, and Democracy* (New York: Harper & Row, 1962).

4. William Tucker, "Of Mites and Men," *Harper's*, Vol. 257, No. 1539 (August 1978), pp. 43–58.

5. Martin J. Bailey, "Inflationary Distortions and Taxes," in Henry J. Aaron, ed., *Inflation and the Income Tax* (Washington, D.C.: The Brookings Institution, 1976), p. 302. See also note 8, chapter 15.

Chapter 20 / The Bullheaded Brewer

1. Albert O. Hirschman, "The Principle of the Hiding Hand," *The Public Interest*, No. 6 (Winter 1967), pp. 10–23.

2. John E. Sawyer, "Entrepreneurial Error and Economic Growth," *Explorations in Entrepreneurial History*, Vol. 4 (May 1952), pp. 199 and 200.

3. Hirschman, "Hiding Hand," p. 13.

4. Ibid.

5. Richard Salomon, "Seat of the Pants," *The Wall Street Journal*, 3 March 1978, p. 12.

6. Aaron Wildavsky, "Does Planning Work?" *The Public Interest*, No. 24 (Summer 1971), pp. 95–104.

7. Barbara Ellis, "Italy's Prosperous Anarchy," *Forbes*, Vol. 123, No. 7 (April 2, 1979), pp. 36–37.

8. David McCord Wright, "Mr. Keynes and the Day of Judgment, *Science*, No. 128 (1958) pp. 1258–1262.

9. John E. Sawyer, "Entrepreneurship in Periods of Rapid Growth," in *Entrepreneurship and Economic Growth*, mimeographed (Cambridge, Mass: Social Science Research Council and Harvard University Research Center in Entrepreneurial History, 1954), p. 4; quoted in Daivd C. McClelland, *The Achieving Society* (New York: Irvington Publishers Inc., 1976), p. 222.

10. McClelland, *The Achieving Society*, p. 13.

11. David E. Gumpert, "Future of Small Business May Be Brighter Than Portrayed," *Harvard Business Review*, Vol. 57, No. 4 (July/August 1979), p. 179 and J. Tom Badgett, "Will OEC and IBM Be the Final Winners?" *Kilobaud*, No. 22 (October 1978), p. 80.

12. Albert Einstein, *The World As I See It* (London: John Lane, 1935); quoted in A. P. French, ed., *Einstein: A Centenary Volume* (Cambridge, Mass.: Harvard University Press, 1979), p. 304.

13. Hirschman, "Hiding Hand," p. 13.

14. John Kenneth Galbraith, *The Nature of Mass Poverty* (Cambridge, Mass.: Harvard University Press, 1979), p. 62.

15. Ibid.

16. Michael W. Watts, "Mercantilism and the Great Chain of Being," unpublished monograph, Department of Economics, Purdue University.

17. Quoted in Thomas Sowell, "Economics and Economic Man," in Irving Kristol and Paul Weaver, eds., *The Americans, 1976: Critical Choices for Americans*, Vol. 2 (Lexington, Mass: D.C. Heath & Co., 1976), pp. 191–209.

18. John Stuart Mill, *Principles of Political Economy* (Toronto: University of Toronto Press, 1965); first published in 1848. Mill wrote: "It is only in the backward countries of the world that increased production is still an important object: in those most advanced, what is economically needed is better distribution . . ."

19. Stuart Bruchey, *The Roots of American Economic Growth, 1607–1861*, Torchbook ed. (New York: Harper & Row, 1968).

20. Nathan Rosenberg, *Technology and American Economic Growth* (White Plains, N.Y.: M. E. Sharpe, Inc., 1972), p. 14, note.

21. Marvin Harris, *Cannibals and Kings: The Origin of Cultures* (New York: Random House, 1977).

22. Leszek Kolakowski quoted by Albert Hirschman in "Hiding Hand," pp. 22–23.

Chapter 21 / The Necessity for Faith

1. Quoted in José Ortega y Gasset, *Man and Crisis* (New York: W. W. Norton, 1958), p. 14.

2. As Tom Bethell has remarked, "There are a lot of stray facts loose in the world, waiting to be corralled by a hypothesis." Response to letter in *Harper's,* Vol. 258, No. 1545 (February 1979), p. 8.

3. Charles S. Peirce, *Chance, Love, and Logic: Philosophic Essays,* Morris R. Cohen, ed., with a supplementary essay on Peirce by John Dewey (New York: Harcourt, Brace & World, 1923); reprinted ed. (New York: Barnes & Noble, 1968), p. 283.

4. Ibid., p. 74.

5. Ibid., p. 75.

6. Reinhold Niebuhr, quoted by Father Gerard Creedon, Church of the Good Shepherd, Alexandria, Va.

SELECTED BIBLIOGRAPHY

Aaron, Henry J. *Who Pays the Property Tax?* Washington, D.C.: The Brookings Institution, 1975.
_____. *Politics and the Professors: The Great Society in Perspective.* Washington, D.C.: The Brookings Institution, 1978.
_____. ed. *Inflation and the Income Tax.* Washington, D.C.: The Brookings Institution, 1976.
Anderson, Martin. *Welfare: The Political Economy of Welfare Reform in the United States.* Stanford, Calif.: Hoover Institution Press, 1978.
Bane, Mary Jo. *Here to Stay: American Families in the Twentieth Century.* New York: Basic Books, 1976.
Banfield, Edward. *The Moral Basis of a Backward Society.* New York: The Free Press, 1967.
_____. *The Unheavenly City Revisited.* Boston: Little, Brown & Co., 1974.
Barro, Robert J. "Public Debt and Taxes." In Boskin Michael, ed. *Federal Tax Reform: Myths and Realities.* San Francisco: Institute for Contemporary Studies, 1978.
_____. "U.S. Inflation and the Choice of Monetary Standard." Speech at University of Rochester, April 9, 1980.
Bartlett, Bruce. *A Walk on the Supply Side.* New Rochelle, N.Y.: Arlington House, Inc. forthcoming in 1981.
Becker, Gary. "The Effect of the State on the Family." Monograph prepared for the Mont Pelerin Society Meetings, September 1978.
Bell, Daniel. *The Coming of Post-Industrial Society.* New York: Basic Books, Inc., 1973.
_____. *The Cultural Contradictions of Capitalism.* New York: Basic Books, Inc., 1975.
_____. "The New Class: A Muddled Concept." *Transaction/Society* 16 (2) Jan.–Feb. 1979. Reprinted in Bruce-Briggs, Barry, ed. *The New Class.* New Brunswick, N.J.: Transaction Books, 1979.
Berle, Adolph. *American Economic Republic.* New York: Harcourt, Brace & World, 1963.
Bethell, Tom. "Against Bilingual Education." *Harper's* 258 (1545) February 1979.
Billingsley, Andrew. *Black Families in White America.* Englewood Cliffs, N.J.: Prentice-Hall, Inc., 1968.
Birch, David C. *The Job Generation Process.* Cambridge, Mass.: M.I.T. Program on Neighborhood and Regional Change, 1979.
Böhm-Bawerk, Eugen Von. *The Positive Theory of Capital.* South Holland, Illinois: Libertarian Press, 1959.
Boskin, Michael J., ed. *Federal Tax Reform: Myths and Realities.* San Francisco: Institute for Contemporary Studies, 1976.
Brinner, Roger E. "The Impact of Inflation on Investment." In *The Americans, 1976: Critical Choices for Americans.* Kristol, Irving, and Weaver, Paul eds. Vol. 2. Lexington Mass.: Lexington Press, 1976.
_____. "Inflation and the Definition of Taxable Personal Income." In Aaron, Henry J., ed. *Inflation and the Income Tax.* Washington, D.C.: The Brookings Institution, 1976.

_____. "The Anti-inflation Leverage of Investment." *Inflation and National Survival* (Proceedings of the Academy of Political Science) 33, (3) 1979.

Brittain, John A. *Inheritance and the Inequality of Material Wealth*. Washington, D.C.: The Brookings Institution, 1978.

_____. *The Inheritance of Economic Status*. Washington, D.C.: The Brookings Institution, 1977.

Browning, Edgar K., and Johnson, William R. *The Distribution of the Tax Burden*. Washington, D.C.: American Enterprise Institute for Public Policy Research, 1979.

Bruchey, Stuart. *The Roots of American Economic Growth, 1607–1861*. New York: Harper & Row, Pub., Inc., 1968.

Buchanan, James M., and Wagner, Richard E. *Democracy in Deficit*. New York: Academic Press, Inc., 1977.

Burns, Scott. *Home, Inc.: The Hidden Wealth and Power of the American Household*. Garden City, N.Y.: Doubleday & Co., Inc., 1975.

Cain, Glen G. "The Challenge of Segmented Labor Market Theories to Orthodox Theory." *Journal of Economic Literature* (December 1976).

Cairncross, Frances. " 'Deindustrialization'—Odd Phenomenon." *The Financier* 2 (4) April 1978.

Campbell, Colin D., ed. *Income Redistribution*. Washington, D.C.: American Enterprise Institute for Public Policy Research, 1977.

Cipolla, Carlo. *The Economic History of World Population*. Baltimore: Penguin Books, 1974.

Cloward, Richard and Piven, Frances Fox. *Regulating the Poor*. New York: Pantheon Books, Inc., 1971.

Commoner, Barry. *The Politics of Energy*. New York: Alfred A. Knopf, Inc., 1979.

De Lone, Richard H., and The Carnegie Council on Children. *Small Futures: Inequality, Children, and the Failure of Liberal Reform*. New York: Harcourt Brace Jovanovich, Inc., 1979.

Dennison, Edward F., and Chung, William K. *How Japan's Economy Grew So Fast*. Washington, D.C.: The Brookings Institution, 1976.

Doeringer, Peter B., and Piore, Michael J. "Unemployment and the 'Dual Labor Market.' " *The Public Interest* 38 (Winter 1974).

Doolittle, Frederick; Levy, Frank; and Wiseman, Michael. "The Mirage of Welfare Reform." *The Public Interest* 47 (Spring 1977).

Dornbusch, Rudiger, and Fischer, Stanley. *Macroeconomics*. New York: McGraw-Hill, Inc., 1978.

Drucker, Peter F. *The Age of Discontinuity*. New York: Harper & Row, Pub., Inc., 1969.

_____. *Men, Ideas, and Politics*. New York: Harper & Row, Pub., Inc., 1971.

Eisner, Robert. "The Outlook for Business Investment." In Shapiro, Eli, and White, William L., eds. *Capital for Productivity and Jobs*. Englewood Cliffs, N.J.: Prentice Hall, Inc., 1977.

_____. "No Tax Relief for Capital Gains." *Challenge* 21 (6) Jan.–Feb. 1979.

Eltis, Walter, and Bacon, David. *The British Problem: Too Few Producers*. Rev. Amer. ed. New York: St. Martin's Press, 1978.

Evans, Michael K. "Taxes, Inflation, and the Rich." *The Wall Street Journal*, 7 August 1978. Reprinted in Laffer, Arthur B., and Seymour, Jan P., eds. *The Economics of the Tax Revolt*. New York: Harcourt Brace Jovanovich, Inc., 1979.

Featherman, David L., and Hauser, Robert M. *Opportunity and Change*. New York: Academic Press, Inc., 1978.

Feige, Edgar L. "How Big Is the Irregular Economy?" *Challenge* 22 (5) Nov.–Dec. 1979.

Feldstein, Martin S. "The Economics of the New Unemployment." *The Public Interest* 33 (Fall 1973).

_____. "Facing the Social Security Crisis." *The Public Interest* 47 (Spring 1977).

_____. "National Saving in the United States." In Shapiro, Eli and White, William L., eds. *Capital For Productivity and Jobs*. Englewood Cliffs, N.J.: Prentice Hall, Inc., 1977.

_____. "Inflation, Tax Rules, and The Stock Market." Paper presented at the Rochester University Research Conference, October 25–26, 1979.

_____. "Social Security Hobbles Our Capital Formation." *Harvard Business Review* 57 (4) July–August 1979).

Feldstein, Martin S. Testimony before the Joint Economic Committee, July 1978, published in *Challenge* 21 (4) Sept.–Oct. 1978.

Feldstein, Martin S., and Summers, Lawrence. "Effects of Inflation on the Taxation of Capital

Income in the Corporate Sector." National Bureau of Economic Research Working Paper, no. 312. Cambridge, Mass., 1979.

Fisk, Donald; Kiesling, Herbert; and Muller, Thomas. *Private Provision of Public Services.* Washington, D.C.: The Urban Institute, 1978.

Freeman, Richard B. "Black Economic Progress Since 1964." *The Public Interest* 52 (Summer 1978).

Friedman, Milton. *Capitalism and Freedom.* Chicago: University of Chicago Press, 1962.

Friedman, Milton, et al. *Studies in the Quantity Theory of Money.* Chicago: University of Chicago Press, 1956.

Friedman, Milton, and Schwartz, Anna. *A Monetary History of the United States, 1867–1960.* Princeton, N.J.: Princeton University Press, 1963.

Galbraith, John Kenneth. "The American Economy: Its Substance and Myth." In Chase, John W., ed. *Years of the Modern: An American Appraisal.* New York: Longman, Green & Co., 1949.

_____. *The Affluent Society.* Boston: Houghton Mifflin Company, 1958.

_____. *The New Industrial State.* Boston: Houghton Mifflin Company, 1967.

_____. *The Galbraith Reader.* Ipswich, Mass.: Gambit Inc., 1977.

_____. *The Nature of Mass Poverty.* Cambridge, Mass.: Harvard University Press, 1979.

Gans, Herbert J. *More Equality.* New York: Pantheon Books, Inc., 1973.

Garfinkel, Irwin, and Haveman, Robert, with the assistance of David Betson, U.S. Department of Health, Education and Welfare. *Earnings Capacity, Poverty, and Inequality.* Institute for Research on Poverty Monograph Series. New York: Academic Press, 1977.

George, Henry. *Progress and Poverty.* New York: Robert Schalkenbach Foundation, 1955.

Georgescu-Roegen, Nicholas. *The Entropy Law and the Economic Process.* Cambridge, Mass.: Harvard University Press, 1971.

Glazer, Nathan. "Reform Work, Not Welfare." *The Public Interest* 40 (Summer 1975).

_____. *Affirmative Discrimination: Ethnic Inequality and Public Policy.* New York: Basic Books, Inc., 1978.

Goldberg, Steven. *The Inevitability of Patriarchy.* Rev. ed. London: Temple Smith, 1977.

Grace, J. Peter. "The Assault on Economic Incentive." Paper presented at the Symposium on American Capitalism, 1979.

Greeley, Andrew. "The Ethnic Miracle." *The Public Interest* 45 (Fall 1976).

Gumpert, David E. "Future of Small Business May Be Brighter Than Portrayed." *Harvard Business Review,* 57 (4) July–August 1979.

Gutmann, Peter M. "Statistical Illusions, Mistaken Policies." *Challenge* 22 (5) Nov.–Dec. 1979.

Harris, Marvin. *Cannibals and Kings: The Origins of Cultures.* New York: Random House, Inc., 1977.

Harriss, C. Lowell. "Property Taxation After the California Vote." *Tax Review* 39 (8) August 1978.

Hausman, J. A. "The Effect of Taxation on Labor Supply." Paper prepared for Brookings Conference on Taxation, October 18–19, 1979.

Haveman, Robert H., and Zellner, B. Bruce. *Policy Studies Review Annual, 1979.* Vol. 3. Beverley Hills: Sage Publications, 1979.

Hazlitt, Henry. *The Conquest of Poverty.* New Rochelle, N.Y.: Arlington House, Inc., 1973.

Heertje, Arnold. *Economics and Technical Change.* New York: John Wiley & Sons, Inc., 1977.

Heilbroner, Robert L. *Beyond Boom and Crash.* New York: W. W. Norton & Co., Inc., 1979.

Heilbroner, Robert L., and Thurow, Lester C. *The Economic Problem.* 5th ed. Englewood Cliffs, N.J.: Prentice-Hall, Inc., 1979.

Henry, James S. "Peter Drucker's Revolution." *Working Papers* (Winter 1976).

_____. "Lazy, Young, Female and Black." *Working Papers* 6 (3) May–June 1978.

_____. "The New Conservative Theories of Unemployment." *Working Papers* 6 (6) March–April 1979.

_____. "The Cash Connection: How to Make the Mob Miserable." *The Washington Monthly* 12 (4) June 1980.

Herskovits, Melville J. *Economic Anthropology: The Economic Life of Primitive Peoples.* New York: W. W. Norton & Co., Inc. 1965.

Hicks, Sir John. *The Crisis in Keynesian Economics.* New York: Basic Books, Inc., 1974.

————. *Economic Perspectives.* Oxford: Oxford University Press, 1977.

Hill, Robert B. "The Illusion of Black Progress." *Social Policy* 9 (3) Nov.–Dec. 1978.

Hirsch, Fred, and Goldthorpe, John H., eds. *The Political Economy of Inflation.* Cambridge, Mass.: Harvard University Press, 1978.

Hirschman, Albert O. "The Principle of the Hiding Hand." *The Public Interest* 6 (Winter 1967) 10–23.

————. *A Bias for Hope.* New Haven: Yale University Press, 1971.

————. *The Passions and the Interests: Political Arguments for Capitalism Before Its Triumph.* Princeton, N.J.: Princeton University Press, 1977.

Hobbs, Charles D. *The Welfare Industry.* Washington, D.C.: The Heritage Foundation, 1978.

Hornbruch, Frederick W., Jr. *Raising Productivity: Ten Case Histories and Their Lessons.* New York: McGraw-Hill, Inc., 1977.

Houthakker, Hendrik. "The Inverse Relation Between Company Growth and Price Movements." *Brookings Papers on Economic Activity.* No. 1. Washington, D.C.: The Brookings Institution, 1979.

Hume, David. *Essays Moral, Political and Literary.* Edited by T. H. Green and T. H. Gross, Reprint of the new edition London 1882. Scientia Verlag, Aalen, Germany, 1964.

Hutchison, T. W. *Knowledge and Ignorance in Economics.* Chicago: University of Chicago Press, 1977.

Hutt, W. H. *A Rehabilitation of Say's Law.* Athens, Ohio: Ohio University Press, 1974.

Jacobs, Jane. *The Economy of Cities.* New York: Random House, Inc., 1969.

Jencks, Christopher. "A New Look at an Old Tax." *Working Papers* 5 (2) Summer 1977.

————. "Why Worry About Inflation?" *Working Papers* 6 (5) Sept.–Oct. 1978. Letter in *Working Papers* 7 (1) May–June 1979.

————. et al. *Inequality: A Reassessment of the Effect of Family and Schooling in America.* New York: Basic Books, Inc., 1972.

Johnson, Harry G. *Economic Policies Toward Less Developed Countries.* Washington, D.C.: The Brookings Institution, 1967.

Johnson, M. Bruce, ed. *The Attack on Corporate America.* New York: McGraw-Hill; Inc., 1978.

Kahn, Lord Richard. "Mr. Eltis and the Keynesians. *Lloyds Bank Preview* 124 (April 1977).

Kasun, Jacqueline. *Slaughter on Main Street.* Clovis, Calif.: Valley Christian University Press, 1979.

————. "More on the New Sex Education." *The Public Interest* 58 (Winter 1980).

Kemp, Jack. *An American Renaissance.* New York: Harper & Row, Pub., Inc., 1979.

————. "The Revival of Incentive Economics." *The Ripon Forum* (January 1980).

Kendrick, John W. *The Formation and Stocks of Total Capital.* National Bureau of Economic Research, General Series, no. 100. New York: Columbia University Press, 1976.

Kenniston, Kenneth, and The Carnegie Council on Children. *All Our Children: The American Family Under Pressure.* New York: Harcourt Brace Jovanovich, Inc., 1977.

Keynes, John Maynard. *The General Theory of Employment, Interest, and Money.* New York: Harcourt, Brace & World, 1964.

Kindleberger, Charles P. *Economic Response: Comparative Studies in Trade, Finance, and Growth.* Cambridge, Mass.: Harvard University Press, 1978.

Kirzner, Israel M. *Competition and Entrepreneurship.* Chicago: University of Chicago Press, 1973.

Klein, Burton. *Dynamic Economics.* Cambridge, Mass.: Harvard University Press, 1977.

Krehm, William. *Babel's Tower: The Dynamics of Economic Breakdown.* Toronto: Thornwood Publications, 1977.

Kristol, Irving. *On The Democratic Idea in America.* New York: Harper & Row, Pub., Inc., 1972.

————. *Two Cheers for Capitalism.* New York: Basic Books, Inc., 1978.

Kuznets, Simon. *Population, Capital and Growth.* New York: W. W. Norton, & Co., Inc., 1973.

Lachmann, Ludwig M. *Capital, Expectations, and the Market Process.* Kansas City, Mo.: Sheed, Andrews and McMeel, 1977.

Laffer, Arthur B. "The Monetary Crisis: A Classical Perspective." Rolling Hills Estates, California: A. B. Laffer Associates, November 12, 1979.

Laffer, Arthur B., and Seymour, Jan P. *The Economics of the Tax Revolt.* New York: Harcourt Brace Jovanovich, Inc., 1979.

Lapham, Lewis H. *Fortune's Child.* Garden City, N.Y.: Doubleday & Co., Inc., 1980.

Lebergott, Stanley. *The American Economy.* Princeton, N.J.: Princeton University Press, 1976.

Lehrman, Lewis E. "Inflation and Civilization: Man's Fate and His Money." Article read at the Economics Club, Columbia University, January 26, 1977.

———. "Monetary Policy, The Federal Reserve System, and Gold." New York: Morgan Stanley Investment Research, January 25, 1980.

Leibenstein, Harvey. *Beyond Economic Man: A New Foundation for Microeconomics.* Cambridge, Mass.: Harvard University Press, 1976.

Lenkowsky, Leslie, "Welfare in the Welfare State." In Tyrrell, R. Emmett, ed. *The Future That Doesn't Work.* Garden City, N.Y.: Doubleday & Co., Inc., 1977.

Levitan, Sar A.; Johnson, William B.; and Taggart, Robert. *Still a Dream: The Changing Status of Blacks Since 1960.* Cambridge, Mass.: Harvard University Press, 1975.

Levitt, Theodore. "The Emerging Fecundity of Service." *The Future of Productivity.* Washington, D.C.: The National Center for Productivity and the Quality of Working Life, 1978.

Levy, Walter J. "Oil Policy and OPEC Development Prospects." *Foreign Affairs* 57 (2) Winter 1978–79.

Lewis, W. Arthur. *The Theory of Economic Growth.* London: George Allen & Unwin Ltd., 1955.

Light, Ivan H. *Ethnic Enterprise in America.* Berkeley: University of California Press, 1972.

Lindsay, Cotton Mather. "Equal Pay for Comparable Work: An Economic Analysis of a New Anti-Discrimination Doctrine." An LEC Occasional Paper. Coral Gables, Fla.: Law and Economics Center, University of Miami School of Law, 1980.

Lippmann, Walter. *The Good Society.* Boston: Little, Brown & Company, 1943.

Little, Ian M. D. "An Economic Renaissance." In Galenson, Walter, ed. *Economic Growth and Structural Change in Taiwan.* Ithaca, N.Y.: Cornell University Press, 1979.

Macaulay, Thomas. *The History of England.* 4 vols. New York: E. P. Dutton, Everyman's Library, 1953.

McClaughry, John. "Uncle Sam's War on the Independent Contractor." *National Review.* 31 (51) December 21, 1979.

McClelland, David C. *The Achieving Society.* New York: Irvington Publishers Inc., 1976.

McKinnon, Ronald I. *Money and Capital in Economic Development.* Washington, D.C.: The Brookings Institution, 1973.

Macoby, Eleanor Emmons, and Jacklin, Carol Nagy. *The Psychology of Sex Differences.* Stanford, Calif.: Stanford University Press, 1974.

Mayer, Martin. *The Bankers.* New York: Weybright and Talley, 1974.

Mayer, Thomas et al. *The Structure of Monetarism.* New York: W. W. Norton & Co., Inc., 1978.

Meigs, A. James. *Money Matters.* New York: Harper & Row Pub., Inc., 1972.

Mill, John Stuart. *Principles of Political Economy.* Toronto: University of Toronto Press, 1965.

Minarek, Joseph J. "Who Wins, Who Loses from Inflation?" *Challenge,* 21 (6) Jan.–Feb. 1979.

Mincer, Jacob, and Polachek, Solomon. *Economic Problems of Women.* (National Longitudinal Survey: U.S. Department of Labor.) Hearings before the Joint Economic Committee, 93rd Cong., 1st sess., part 1, July 10, 11, 12. Washington, D.C.: U.S. Government Printing Office, 1973.

Moynihan, Daniel Patrick. *The Negro Family: The Case for National Action.* In Rainwater, Lee, and Yancy, William L., eds. *The Moynihan Report and the Politics of Controversy.* Cambridge, Mass.: M.I.T. Press, 1967.

———. *The Politics of a Guaranteed Income.* New York: Random House, Inc., 1973.

———. "The Politics and Economics of Regional Growth." *The Public Interest,* 51 (Spring 1978).

Mundell, Robert A. *Man and Economics.* New York: McGraw Hill, Inc., 1968.

Novak, Michael. *The American Vision: An Essay on the Future of Democratic Capitalism.* Washington, D.C.: American Enterprise Institute for Public Policy Research, 1978.

Oaxaca, Ronald L. "Male-Female Wage Differentials in Urban Labor Markets." Working Paper no. 23. Princeton, N.J.: Industrial Relations Section, Princeton University, 1971.

Ortega y Gasset, José. *The Revolt of the Masses.* New York: W. W. Norton & Co., Inc., 1951.

Our Turn To Listen: A White Paper on Unemployment, Education and Crime Based on Extensive Interviews with New York City Teenage Dropouts. New York: Vocational Foundation Incorporated, 1978.

Paglin, Morton. "Poverty in the United States: A Reevaluation." *Policy Review,* 8 (Spring 1979).

Patterson, Orlando. *Ethnic Chauvinism: The Reactionary Impulse.* New York: Stein & Day, Pub., 1978.

Pechman, Joseph A. *Federal Tax Policy.* Washington, D.C.: The Brookings Institution, 1977.

———. and Okner, Benjamin A. *Who Bears the Tax Burden?* Washington, D.C.: The Brookings Institution, 1974.

Phelps-Brown, E. H., and Hopkins, Sheila V. "Seven Centuries of Building Wages." *Economica* 22 (87) August 1955.

Podhoretz, Norman. *Making It.* New York: Random House, Inc., 1969.

Posner, Richard J. "Utilitarianism, Economics, and Legal Theory." *The Journal of Legal Studies* 8 (1) January 1979.

Prothro, Laurie. "Making a Living in Subterranea—Notes from the Underground." *Taxing and Spending* 2 (2) April 1979.

Questiaux, Nicole. "Family Allowances in France." In Burns, Eveline M., ed. *Children's Allowances and the Economic Welfare of Children.* New York: Citizens Committe for Children of New York, 1968.

Rainwater, Lee, and Yancy, William L. *The Moynihan Report and the Politics of Controversy.* Cambridge, Mass.: The M.I.T. Press, 1967.

Rein, Martin, and Rainwater, Lee. "How Large Is the Welfare Class?" *Challenge* 20 (4) Sept.–Oct. 1977. Reprinted in Haveman, Robert H. and Zellner, B. Bruce, eds. *Policy Studies Review Annual, 1979,* vol. 3. Beverly Hills: Sage Publications, 1979.

Reynolds, Alan. "Fifty Years Later: What Do We Know About the Great Crash?" *National Review* 31 (45) November 9, 1977.

Roberts, Paul Craig. "The Breakdown of the Keynesian Model." *The Public Interest* 52 (Summer 1978).

———. "The Economic Case for Kemp-Roth." *The Wall Street Journal,* 1 August 1978. Reprinted in Laffer, Arthur B., and Seymour, Jan, eds. *The Economics of the Tax Revolt.* New York: Harcourt Brace Jovanovich, Inc., 1979.

Robertson, Dennis. "The Colvin Committee, the Income Tax, and the Price Level." *Economic Journal* 37 (148) December 1927.

Robison, David A. *Six Business Employment Programs, Emphasis: Disadvantaged Youth.* New York: Center for Public Resources, Inc., 1978.

Rose, Richard, and Peters, Guy. *Can Government Go Bankrupt?* New York: Basic Books, Inc., 1978.

Rosenberg, Nathan. *Technology and American Economic Growth.* White Plains, N.Y.: M. E. Sharpe, Inc., 1972.

Ross, Heather L., and Sawhill, Isabel V. *Time of Transition: The Growth of Families Headed by Women.* Washington, D.C.: The Urban Institute, 1975.

Rostow, W. W. *How It All Began: Origins of the Modern Economy.* New York: McGraw-Hill, Inc., 1975.

Rothschild, Emma. *The Decline of the Auto-Industrial Age.* New York: Random House, Inc., 1973.

Sawyer, John E. "Entrepreneurial Error and Economic Growth." *Explorations in Entrepreneurial History* 4 (May 1952).

Schiller, Bradley R. "Equality, Opportunity, and the 'Good Job.'" *The Public Interest,* 43 (Spring 1976).

Schuettinger, Robert L., and Butler, Eamonn F. *Forty Centuries of Wage and Price Controls.* Washington, D.C.: The Heritage Foundation, 1978.

Schumpeter, Joseph. *Social Classes, Imperialism.* Two Essays. New York: Meridian Books, 1955.

———. *Capitalism, Socialism, and Democracy.* New York: Harper & Row, Pub., Inc., 1962.

Sennholz, Hans F., *Death and Taxes.* Washington, D.C.: The Heritage Foundation, 1976.

Shackle, G. L. S. *Epistemics and Economics: A Critique of Economic Doctrines.* London: Cambridge University Press, 1972.

Smith, Adam. *The Wealth of Nations.* Edited by Edwin Cannan. New York: G. P. Putnam's Sons, 1904.

Solow, Robert. "The Intelligent Citizen's Guide to Inflation." *The Public Interest* 38 (Winter 1975).

Sowell, Thomas. *Say's Law: An Historical Analysis.* Princeton, N.J.: Princeton University Press, 1972.

_____. *Classical Economics Reconsidered.* Princeton, N.J.: Princeton University Press, 1974.

_____. "Economics and Economic Man." In Kristol, Irving, and Weaver, Paul, eds. *The Americans, 1976: Critical Choices for Americans.* Vol. 2. Lexington, Mass.: D. C. Heath & Co., 1976.

_____. "Ethnicity in a Changing America." *Daedalus* 107 (1) Winter 1978.

_____. *Knowledge and Decisions.* New York: Basic Books, Inc., 1980.

_____. *Markets and Minorities.* London: Basil Blackwell, forthcoming in 1981.

_____. *American Ethnic Groups.* Washington, D.C.: The Urban Institute, 1978.

Stigler, George J. *Essays in the History of Economics.* Chicago: University of Chicago Press, 1965.

Stockman, David. "The Social Pork-Barrel." *The Public Interest* 39 (Spring 1975).

Supple, Barry. "A Framework for British Business History." In Supple, Barry, ed. *Essays in British Business History.* Oxford, England: The Clarendon Press, 1977.

Thurow, Lester C. *Generating Inequality.* New York: Basic Books, Inc., 1975.

_____. *The Zero-Sum Society: Distribution and the Possibilities for Economic Change.* New York: Basic Books, Inc., 1980.

Tiger, Lionel. *Optimism, The Biology of Hope.* New York: Simon & Schuster, 1979.

_____, and Fox, Robin. *The Imperial Animal.* New York: Holt, Rinehart & Winston, 1971.

Tucker, William. "Of Mites and Men." *Harper's* 257 (1539) August 1978.

Ture, Norman B. *The Economic Effects of Tax Changes: A Neoclassical Analysis.* Washington D.C.: Institute for Research on the Economics of Taxation, forthcoming in 1980.

Tyrrell, R. Emmett, Jr., ed. *The Future That Doesn't Work: Social Democracy's Failures in Britain.* Garden City, N.Y.: Doubleday & Co., Inc., 1977.

van den Haag, Ernest, ed. *Capitalism: Sources of Hostility.* Washington, D.C.: The Heritage Foundation, 1979.

Wagner, Richard E. *Inheritance and the State: Tax Principles for a Free and Prosperous Commonwealth.* Washington, D.C.: American Enterprise Institute for Public Policy Research, 1977.

Wallis, W. Allen. *An Overgoverned Society.* New York: The Free Press, 1976.

Walters, Kenneth D., and Monsen, R. Joseph. "State-Owned Business Abroad: New Competitive Threat." *Harvard Business Review* 57 (2) March–April 1979.

Wanniski, Jude. *The Way the World Works.* New York: Basic Books, Inc., 1978.

_____. "Puerto Rico and Statehood." Rolling Hills Estates, Calif.: A. B. Laffer Associates, 1979.

_____. "Inflation and the 'Arc of Crisis.'" Morristown, N.J.: Polyconomics, Inc., 1980.

Warsh, David. "The Great Hamburger Paradox." *Forbes,* September 15, 1977.

_____, and Minard, Lawrence. "Inflation Is Too Important To Leave to the Economists." *Forbes,* November 15, 1976.

Wildavsky, Aaron. "Does Planning Work?" *The Public Interest* 24 (Summer 1971).

Wrigley, E. A. *Population and History.* New York: McGraw-Hill, Inc., 1969.

Index

Absenteeism, 145
Accelerated depreciation, 241
Advent Corporation, 61
Affirmative action, 129–130, 134, 137, 139, 143, 144, 150, 243
Affluent Society (Galbraith), 35
Aggregate demand, 34, 46, 142, 143
Aggregate economics, 228
Aggregation: paradox of, 44
Aggregative fallacy, 40
Aggressiveness: in earning superiority, 135–136
Aid for Families with Dependent Children (AFDC), 110, 111, 115, 119, 123, 157, 278n
Airlines, 210
Albany, New York, ix
Alsop, Reese F., 212, 285n
Altruism: as basis of capitalism, 22, 27, 168
American Enterprise Institute, 187
American Institute of Economic Research, xi
American Stock Exchange, 84
American Telephone and Telegraph (AT&T), 82, 84, 129
Anderson, Martin, 12, 119, 287n
Anthropology, ix, 69, 255; economic, 21
Antidiscrimination laws, 110
Antidropout campaign, 148–149
Antipoverty programs, 116, 152
Anti-Semitism, 96–97
Antitrust suits, 243
Antiviral drugs, 212
Arson, 108, 118
Asian capitalism, 184, 201–202, 229
Aspen Institute, 6

"Assault on Economic Incentive" (Grace), 280n
Assimilation: of minorities, 93–94
Aston-Martin, 60–61
Atlanta, Georgia, 132
Auspitz, Josiah Lee, xi
Automation, 211
Auton Computing Company, 60

Bacon, Robert, 193
Banfield, Edward, 70–73, 97, 99
Banks, 201, 210
Barter, 23
Barzini, Luigi, 237
Beaton, David, 119
Beinstock, Herbert, 147
Bell, Daniel, 4, 5, 7, 208
Bell, Jeffrey, x
Berkeley, University of California at, 119
Berkshire Paper Company, 52–54
Berle, Adolph A., 73
Bessemer, Sir Henry, 236
Bethell, Tom, x
Bilingual education, 125, 129
Biological differences: and male-female earnings gap, 137
Biological doom theory, 255
Biological insecticides, 239
Birth rates, 124
Black Panthers, 74
Blacks, 11–12, 83, 99, 106, 124, 127–129, 131, 133, 138–139, 141–142; in civil service, 149–150; and credentialism, 146–

Blacks *(continued)*
152; education, 145; high-school drop-
outs, 147; incomes, 132, 134–135; men,
135, 149–152; myths about, 64–74; un-
employment, 13; women, 150–151
Blue Cross/Blue Shield, 211
Bonds, 245
Boorstin, Daniel, 6
Boston, First National Bank of, 163
Boston Globe, 154
Boston Herald American, *x*
Bourne, Peter, 212, 285*n*
Bray, Tom, *xi*
Brewer, Michael, *xi*
Brinner, Roger, 179, 224
Britain's Economic Problem: Too Few Producers (Eltis
and Bacon), 193
British National Health, 155
British Protestants, *see* WASPS
British Treasury, 193
Brookes, Warren T., *x,* 163, 165, 176, 228
Brookings Institution, 18–20, 193–194, 209
Browning, Edgar K., 187
Buchanan, Patrick, 153
Buckley, William F., Jr., *x,* 4, 174
Budget balancing, 227
Bundy, McGeorge, 66
Bureaucracy, 44, 139, 238
Burns, Scott, 173, 208
Business, 154–156, 204, 236; big, 75, 140,
245, 285–286*n;* small, 78, 99–100, 143–
145, 162, 223, 241; strategy, 37
Busing, 139

Califano, Joseph A., Jr., 280*n*
California: Proposition 13, 187–188; wel-
fare, 119–121, 126, 278*n*
California Business Round Table, 187–188
Cannibalism, 255, 257
Cannibals and Kings (Harris), 21
Capital flight, 59
Capital gains taxes, 175, 183, 189, 224, 244–
245
Capitalism, 254–256; adventure and re-
demptive morality of, *x;* chance in, 254;
critiques of, 3–8, 261; and democracy, 38;
dynamics of, 23–27; golden rule of, 8, 20;
history of, 256; origins of, 21–23; rules
of, 265; vs. socialism, 24; work under, 51
Capitalism, Socialism, and Democracy,
(Schumpeter), 83
Capitalism and Freedom (Friedman), *x,* 6
Capitalist freedom, 7
Capitalist marketplace, 38
Cardiological units, 212
Carnegie Council on Children, 11, 271*n*

Carson, Rachel, 239
Carter administration, 153, 156
Carter, James Earl, 89, 244
Catholics, 88, 101
CAT scanners, 212
Census Bureau, 214
CETA, 111, 153, 156–159, 161–163, 167–
169
Chafee, John, 168
Chance, 257, 262–263, 266–268
Chance, Love and Logic (Peirce), 266–267
Chapman, Bruce, *xi*
Charity, 107, 112, 222, 267
Chesterton, G. K., 86, 180
Child allowances, 119, 126–127
Children: and the two-income family, 15–
16
Child-support payments, 121
Child-support prosecutions, 115
Chinese, overseas, 23, 73, 94, 109
Chrysler Corporation, 85, 153–154, 156–
157, 169
Churches, 222; and radical politics, 95
Civil Rights, 139, 160; HEW Office of, 129
Civil Service, 146, 149, 186
Civil suits, 253
Class conflict, 86–101
Closing circle theory, 255, 258, 260, 268
Club of Rome, 255
Coal, 63
Collectibles, 245
College professors, 90
Commerce Department, 83, 214
Commercial revolution, 229
Commodities, 176, 189, 245
Commoner, Barry, 82, 255, 260
Competition, 37–38; *see also* Perfect competi-
tion
Competitiveness: in earnings superiority,
135
Comprehensive Employment and Training
Act, *see* CETA
Computers, 81, 210
Conglomeration, 214
Congressional Budget Office (CBO), 12, 41,
153, 188
Congressmen, 44
Connally, John, 153
Conservatives, 227-228
Consumer debt, 178
Consumer Price Index (CPI), 18, 285*n*
Convergence theory: of capitalism and so-
cialism, 50
Coombs, Orde, 97
Copying equipment, 78
Cordere, Helen, 22
Cost of Living Adjustments (COLAs), 18–
19

Creative destruction, 236–240
Creative thought, 262, 265
Credentialism, 145–152
Credit laws, 177
Cubans, 168
Currency holdings, 222

Data processing systems, 210
Davis-Bacon Act, 148
Debt, 228–231
Defense, 209, 225, 238
Deficit spending, 219, 225, 226
DeLorean, John, 61, 241
Demand, 29–31, 34, 38
Demand curves, 30
Demand-oriented economics and politics,
    39–40
Democracy, 86
Demographic change, 67
Denison's law, 179
Denmark, 182
Denver, Colorado, 114, 120, 124
Dependence Effect, 35–36
Diabetes hotline, 212, 285n
Diagnostic devices, 78
Diffusion, 203
Digital Equipment Corporation, 81
Disability insurance, 111
Discrimination, 141–142, 280n; myths of,
    128–139
Distributed processing, 82
Distribution of the Tax Burden (Browning and
    Johnson), 187
Divine, Father, 73–74
Division of labor, 8
Divorces, 14–15, 18, 65
Doeringer, Peter, 140, 148
Dole, Robert, 158
Domestic services, 15
Dow Jones Industrial Index, 84–85
Downward mobility: and American gentry,
    100
Drucker, Peter, 208
Dual labor-market theory, 140–142
Dunne, John Gregory, 250
Dynamic Economics (Klein), 78

Earnings: male vs. female, 137, 151
Earnings Capacity Utilization Rates (Garfinkel and
    Haveman), 68
Earnings-capacity utilization studies, 134
Eastman Kodak Company, 79
Economica, 197
Economic anthropology, 21

Economic Anthropology (Herskovits), 21
Economic classes: and resistance to integra-
    tion, 91
Economic Cooperation and Development,
    Organization for, *see* OECD
Economic futility of war, 9
Economic growth, 265–266; and federal aid,
    165
Economic noosphere, 226
Economic opportunity: equal, 90
Economic Problem (Heilbroner and Thurow),
    197
Economic Research, National Bureau of,
    113, 175
Economics: golden rule of, 9; institutionalist
    critique of, 142; limitations of, *ix*, 10
Economics and the Public Purpose (Galbraith), 35
Economic texts, 30
Economy of Cities (Jacobs), 287n
Edelman, Peter, 11
Edison, Thomas A., 256, 268
Education, 91, 99–101, 146–149; bilingual,
    125, 129
EEOC (Equal Employment Opportunity
    Commission), 129, 137, 139, 144
Effective demand, 33–34
Egalitarianism, 30
Einstein, Albert, 254
Eisenhower, Dwight D., 7, 110
Elderly, 18
Elitism: of material progress, 259
Eltis, Walter, 193
Employment: compensatory programs, 139;
    full, 142
Employment Security, Department of, 164
Energy, 210, 242, 256
Energy, Department of, 62–63, 110
Energy crisis, 155
Energy Resources Corporation, 60
England, *see* Great Britain
Entrepreneurial accelerator, 252
Entrepreneurship, 6, 23, 25, 31, 33, 35–37,
    56, 75–85, 166, 192, 232, 245–246, 251
Entropy theory, 260–261, 263
Environmental movement, 160
Environmental protection, 225
Environmental Protection Agency (EPA), 78,
    164, 238–240
Equal Employment Opportunity Commis-
    sion, *see* EEOC
"Equality, Opportunity, and the 'Good
    Job'" (Schiller), 280–281n
Equal pay for equal work, 130
Equal rights agencies, 131, 137, 144–146,
    152
Eurocurrency market, 201, 226
Europe, 147, 169, 177–178, 182, 184, 241
Evans, Michael, 192, 193

Exports, 155
Extension services, 160

Faith, 73–74, 262, 264, 266, 269; importance in capitalism, 24, 27
False abstraction, 30
Family, 6, 69–72, 74, 91, 142, 150–152; biological differences in, 136; disruption of, 12, 14–17, 65, 72, 112, 114, 120, 126; extended, 72; female-headed, 133–134; two-income, 14
Family Assistance Plan, 119–120
Federal aid: and economic growth, 165
Federal borrowing, 162
Federal budget, 41–42
Federal Communications Commission, 82
Federal disability benefits, 110
Federal Home Loan Bank, 177, 221
Federal programs: growth of, 44
Federal regulation, *see* Regulation
Federal Reserve, 204–205, 222
Feige, Edgar, 17
Feldstein, Martin, 113, 175, 211
Feudalism, 198, 200
Filipinos, 94
First-job barrier, 147
Fiscal integrity, 227
Floating exchange rates, 243
Food and Drug Administration (FDA), 238–240
Food stamps, 123
Forbes, 82, 194, 197, 251
Ford, Gerald, 110
Ford, Henry, 268
Ford Foundation, 66
Ford Motor Company, 78
Foreign money, 45
Fortune, 55, 83, 163, 221
Foundations, 222
France, 126, 142, 182–185, 201
Friedman, Milton, x, 6, 118, 191
Fringe benefits, 220

Galbraith, John Kenneth, 5, 16, 35–38, 40, 75–79, 82, 144, 170–175, 199, 255
Galileo, 262
Gambler's ruin, 62
Gambling impulse, 253
Gambling stocks, 189
Gans, Herbert J., 11
GAO (General Accounting Office), 161, 163, 165
Garfinkel, Irvin, 16, 68, 119
General Accounting Office, *see* GAO

General Motors Corporation, 84, 110
General Theory, (Shackle), 34
General Theory of Employment, Interest, and Money (Keynes), 31, 43
Genocide, 96
Gentrification, 93
Germans, 11, 100, 202
Germany, 182–185, 201
Glazer, Nathan, x, 142
GNP (Gross National Product), 13–14, 17, 111–113, 155, 178, 192, 230
God: as foundation of knowledge, 267
Gold, 20, 42, 44–45, 107, 189, 268
Goldberg, Steven, 87, 136
Golden rule of capitalism, 8, 20
Golden rule of economics, 9, 228
Good Society (Lippmann), 7–8
Gordon, Robert, 193
Government, 37, 44, 160, 244; and blacks, 66; bureaucracies, 39; in the economy, 31; growth, 39; housing, 92; as cause of inflation, 203–205; investments, 42; jobs, 138, 148–149; productivity, 205–216; programs, 243; securities, 44–45, 219; spending, 45; and women, 138
Grace, J. Peter, 280n
Great Barrington, Massachusetts, 36
Great Britain, 49, 113, 153, 155, 169, 178, 182–185, 188, 230–231, 241, 251
Great Depression, 8–9, 73, 109, 217, 231
Greed, 30
Greeley, Andrew, 88
Greenville, South Carolina, ix
Greenwald, Douglas, 179
Griggs v. *Duke Power Company*, 137
Gross National Product *see* GNP
Group leadership: male aptitude for, 136
Growth: definition of, 235; unpredictability of, 250–251
Guaranteed income, 114, 119–120, 126
Gutmann, Peter, 17

Hansen, Alvin, 256
Harper's, xi, 239
Harris, Marvin, 21, 255, 257–258
Harvard Business Review, 169
Harvard University, 88
Haveman, Robert, 16, 68, 119
Hayden, Tom, 7
Health, Education and Welfare, Department of, *see* HEW
Health care, 210–211, 225
Health insurance, 110, 155
Heilbroner, Robert L., 5, 7, 54, 170–172, 197
Heller, Walter, 41
Herskovits, Melville J., 21–22

HEW (Department of Health, Education and Welfare), 93, 110, 119–120, 123, 125, 129–130, 150, 280n
Hiding hand principle, 249
High-school dropouts, 147
High-technology companies, 143, 166, 222, 224, 227
Hirschman, Albert O., 248–250, 252, 255
Hispanics, 124, 128, 130
History of England (Macaulay), 228
Hoarding, 41, 219
Hobby, Oveta Culp, 110
Hoff, E. H., 81
Home ownership, 18–19
Hong Kong, 49, 168, 184, 232
Hoover, Herbert, 110
Hopkins, Sheila V., 196–197, 200
Hotson, John, 193
Housing, 92–93, 107; private, 45; speculation, 176–178; subsidies, 123; welfare, 93
Housing and Urban Affairs, Department of (HUD), 93
Howe, Neil, *xi*
Hui (Chinese form of capital formation), 23
Hume, David, 9
Hutt, W. H., 274n
Hydraulic dictatorships, 257–258
Hypocrisy: function of, 86–88; of secular socialism, 95

IBM, 79, 81–82, 143; role in economy, 81, 210
Illinois, 164–165
Immigrants, 52, 93
Immigration, 67–68, 167
Immigration and Naturalization Service (INS), 144
Imports, 242; protections, 154; quotas, 241
Income: artificial maintenance of, 117; distribution, 125; escalator clauses, 18–19; fallacies of growth, 13; ways government can foster expansion of, 46
Income taxes, 185
Independence effect, 135
Indexing (linking of incomes to cost of living), 18–19
Indians, American, 67, 124
Industrial revolution, 8, 71–72, 199–200, 229
Inevitability of Patriarchy (Goldberg), *ix*, 136
Infanticide, 255, 257
Inflation, 29, 190–205, 219, 225; beneficiaries of, 220–222; definition of, 24; and government gains, 44; effect of hoarding on, 43; premium, 43; and productivity, 16;

and the rich, 18–20, 56; and small companies, 85; and women workers, 14
Inflation and Income Tax (Brookings), 209
Informatics, 77, 82
Information theory, 261, 263
Inheritance, 55–56; taxes, 59
In-kind benefits, 19
Inmos Corporation, 61
Insurance, 106–109, 113–114, 157; fire, 118
Integration: racial and economic, 90, 92–93
Interest rates, 44, 162, 173, 179
Internal Revenue Service (IRS), 16–17, 57, 252
International Business Machines, *see* IBM
International Center for Economic Policy Studies, *xi*
International Monetary Fund (IMF), 189, 193
International trade, 33, 243
Inventions, 256
Inverted hierarchy, 29
Investment, 32–36, 43, 62, 106, 172–173, 178; credits, 243; as defense against risk, 45; nature of, 24–25; and savings, 48
Iran, 48
Irish, 11, 88, 100, 138, 150
Italians, 11, 88, 100, 138
Italy, 169, 183–185, 201, 251

Jacklin, Carol, 136
Jacobs, Jane, 235, 287n
Japan, 39, 49, 147–148, 177, 178, 182–184, 201, 227, 229–230
Japanese, 11, 23, 94, 109, 113, 133
Jarrell, Randall, 216
Jarvis, Howard, 38
Javits, Jacob, *xi*
Jencks, Christopher, 18, 73, 254
Jews, 11, 88, 100, 106, 138, 146
Job-creation programs, 153–169
Job effect of production, 46
Jobs, 89–90, 140–152; guaranteed, 168
Johnson, Lyndon Baines, 110
Johnson, William R., 187
Jung, Carl, 51

Kahn, Richard, 274n
Kelley, Whitmore (Nick), 52–54
Kemp, Jack, *xi*, 181, 186
Kemp-Roth tax cut bill, 41, 186, 190–192
Kendrick, John, 113, 200
Kennedy, John F.: tax cut, 1964, 175, 186
Kennedy Institute of Politics, *xi*
Kenniston, Kenneth, 11, 271n

Keynes, John Maynard, *x,* 31, 33–35, 40–44, 166, 172, 173, 192, 273–274*n*
Keynesian school, 31, 190, 217
Khrushchev, Nikita, 7
Klein, Burton, 78–79
Knowledge technocracy, 207
Ko (Japanese form of capital formation), 23
Kodak, *see* Eastman Kodak Company
Kolakowski, Leszek, 258
Korea, 147–148, 184, 201
Korean War period, 172
Krehm, William, 193
Kristol, Irving, *x,* 5, 6, 7, 10, 50, 73, 171
Kroc, Ray, 38
Kuznets, Simon, 179
Kuznets curve, 76
Kwakiutl, 22

Labor: capitalization of, 51; elasticity of, 226
Labor Department, 15, 144, 147, 150
Labor market: and equal rights agencies, 131; restrictions, 148
Labor unions, 238
Laffer, Arthur, and Lafferites, *x,* 37, 180, 181, 185, 186, 188, 190, 192, 202, 205
Laffer curve, 179–181, 184, 187, 194
Laissez-faire, 30, 35
Land, *see* Real estate
Land-grant agricultural colleges, 160
Lasch, Christopher, 5
Lasers, 78, 83
Latin America, 189
Law, 45
Law Enforcement Assistance Administration, 166
Laws of mind, 261–265
Lawyers, 44
Left, 38, 77–78
Legalized aliens, 124
Legislators, 238
Leibenstein, Harvey, 25–26, 51, 73
Leisure, 41
Levitt, Theodore, 210–211
Lewis, W. Arthur, 231
Liberalism: impact on poor, *ix, xi, xii;* moral hazards of, 105–113
Liberals: attitudes toward poor and blacks, 64–74
Licensing, 148
Light, Ivan, 73
Limits of Growth (Club of Rome), 255–256
Linear or homogeneous time, 230
Lippmann, Walter, 7, 8, 29
Liquidity, 41, 43, 44, 47, 58, 201
Liquidity preference, 43
Loan guarantees, 156

Loeb Award, 194
London School of Economics, 195
Long, Russell, 119
Longbow, 256
Los Angeles, California, 168, 212
Love, 87, 262, 269
Lovell, Arnold, 193

Macaulay, Thomas, 228–229
McClelland, David, 252
Maccoby, Eleanor, 136
McGovern, George, 165
McKinney, Stuart, 221
Macroeconomics, 31–32, 250
Making It (Podhoretz), 87
Male and Female (Mead), *ix*
Male vs. female earnings, 137, 151
Marginal efficiency of capital, 33
Markets, financial, 106, *see also* Stock market
Market sector, 76, 140
Marriage, 70–72
Marshall, Alfred, 166
Marx, Karl, 5, 28, 40, 77
Marxism, 98, 263
Mass retailing, 213
Massachusetts, 120–121, 162–166, 281*n*
Material fallacy, 232
Material progress, 259
Material resources vs. durable wealth, 48
Mathias, Charles, *xi*
Mead, Margaret, *ix,* 136
Means tests, 111, 142
Media, 241–242; attitude toward blacks, 66
Medicaid, 123, 125, 155, 182, 211
Medical science, 212
Medicare, 155, 182, 211
Melting pot, 93–94
Men: provider role of, 88
Mercantilism, 9, 28, 199–200
Meritocracy, 90
Mexico, 168
Miami, Florida, 168
Michigan, 120
Microbiology, 77, 83
Microcomputers, 82–84
Microeconomics, 32, 250
Microprocessors, 54, 78, 80–81, 210
Midas, 48, 63, 232
Middle-class values, 93–94
Mill, John Stuart, 256, 287*n*
Millionaires, 63
Minard, Lawrence, 194
Minarek, Joseph, 18–20
Minimum wage, 148, 162
Minority workers, 145
Mississippi: black income in, 132

Monetarism, 194–195, 202, 217, 219
Money, 22–24, 31, 43–44, 217; creation of, 162, 219; and insurance, 107; social pressures of, 88; supply, 194–195; taboo, 87
Money (Galbraith), 199
Money illusion, 13, 15
Money market funds, 220
Monopoly, 37–38, 82, 243
Monopoly capitalism, 38
Moore, Gordon, 81
Moral Basis of a Backward Society (Banfield), 97
Moral hazards, 157, 161; definition of, 108; of liberalism, 105–113
More Equality (Gans), 11
Morgenthaler, David T., 193
Mormons, 73
Moynihan, Daniel Patrick, 88, 118–119, 126, 139, 150–151, 164, 167
Moynihan Report, 12
Muggeridge, Malcolm, 4
Multinational corporations, 75, 201
Multiple regression analysis, 114
Mumi (Solomon Islands tribal capitalist), 21–22, 83
Myrdal, Gunnar, 18, 185–186
Myth of immobility, 55

Nader, Ralph, 153
Napoleon I, 105
Nathan, Richard, 119
National Broadcasting Company (NBC), 130
National Enterprise Board, 61
National health insurance, 110, 155
Nationalized manufacturing companies, 241
National Laboratories, 238
National Mortgage Association, 177
National plans, 251
National Review, 4
National Semiconductor Corporation, 60
National Venture Capital Association, 193
Negative income tax, 118–119
Neighborhood Youth Corps, 158
Neoconservatives, 3, 5
Neo-Malthusians, 255
Newark, New Jersey, 168
New Deal, 109–110
New Hampshire, 164
New Industrial State (Galbraith), 35, 78
New Leader, xi
"New Right," xi
Newsweek, 130
New York, 120–121, 126, 162, 164; black income in, 132
New York City, 161, 169; riots, 1977, 97
New York Post, 66
New York Times, 66, 88, 130, 170

Niebuhr, Reinhold, 268–269
Nisbet, Robert, 5
Nixon, Richard, 110, 118, 126, 166, 244
Nonprofit concerns, 222
Northeast, 163, 164
North Sea oil, 24, 49
Norton, Eleanor Holmes, 137
Noyce, Robert, 81

Occupational Safety and Health Administration (OSHA), 144, 240
OECD (Organization for Economic Cooperation and Development), 155, 182
Office technology, 209–210
Oil industry, 84, 223
Oil-rich countries, 48–49
"Old Right," 4
On-The-Job Training (OJT), 144
OPEC, 155, 156, 201
Orientals, 11, 73, 100, 106, 109
Orphans, 18
Ortega y Gasset, José, 158
Ownership: as motivating force, 26

Panic, C., 197
Partial equilibrium fallacy, 172
Patterson, Orlando, 94
Paul, Saint, 267
Peirce, Charles, 263, 266–267
Pensions, 220, 225
Perfect competition, 30–31, 38, 260
Perks, 220
Perry, George, 193–194
Peugeot-Citroën, 169
Phelps-Brown, Sir Henry, 195–197, 200
Photography, 78
Piore, Michael, 140, 148
Planet of the Apes, 250
Planning sector, 76, 140
Podhoretz, Norman, 87
Poles, 11, 88, 100, 138
Political Enemy of Inflation, (Maier), 197
Political leadership, 29
Political marketplace, 38
Political philosophy, 29
Politicians, 245–246
Politics: egalitarianism in, 90; as insurance, 105; of persecution, 129
Populism, 259
Portuguese, 168
Posner, Richard, 168
Postindustrial age, 200, 206–207
Post Office Department, 169
Postwar baby boom generation, 15, 124

Potlatching, 22
Poverty, Institute for Research on, 16, 68, 119
Poverty and the poor, ix, xi, 64–74, 98–99, 111–112, 114–127, 137, 142, 146, 260; male, 133; misconceptions of, 89; Third World, 255; *see also* Welfare
Prejudice: racial and ethnic, 90; *see also* Discrimination
Pratt, Larry, xi
Price-level theory, 196–197
Price pyramid, 202–203
Price stabilization, 244
Primary sector jobs, 140–145
Printing: innovations in, 78
Private enterprise, *see* Capitalism
Problems: role of, 264–265, 267–268
Producing power: balance with purchasing power, 32
Productivity: decline, 14, 16, 18, 29, 160–161, 218; government, 205–216; growth, 113, 160, 230; and insurance, 109; small business, 85; x-efficiency in, 24
Product-liability suit, 253
Professional schools, 45
Progress and Poverty (George), x, 42
Progressive taxation, 41, 44
Promotion barrier, 147
Property taxes, 177, 183, 187–188
Proposition 13, 38, 187–188, 191, 215
Protection: business demands for, 37
Protestants, white, *see* WASPS
Psychological forces: in the economy, 181
Psychology of Sex Differences (Jacklin and Maccoby), 136
Public Interest, 119
Public opinion, 29
Public Opinion (Lippmann), 29
Public-service jobs, 45
Public-service unions, 159
Public works, 225
Puerto Ricans, 93–94

Quantity Theory of Money, 194–195, 217, 261
Quincy Market, Boston, 213
Quotas: in unemployment, 142

Railroads, 169, 242
Racism, 139; illusory nature of, 91, 93, 98
Rand, Ayn, x
Ranson, David, 179
Rapid depreciation allowances, 243
Reagan, Ronald, xi, 119–122, 278n

Real earnings, or *take-home pay,* 215
Real estate, 20, 42, 44, 189, 220, 221
Recession, 153
Redistribution, 94, 118
Regulation, 44, 148, 238–240, 258
Reich, Wilhelm, 30
Reification, 30
Religious beliefs and values, 258, 267
Renault: and Peugeot-Citroën, 169
Rents: for welfare housing, 125
Representative democracy, 38
Republican party, 35, 110, 153, 190, 209
Research and development, 37, 223–224
Residency rules: for welfare, 121
Resources: elasticity of, 226
Revised Sequence, 35
Revolt of the Masses (Ortega y Gasset), 29
Ricardo, David, 10
Ripon Society, xi
Risk, 45, 63, 105, 107, 243, 250, 253; in capitalism and socialism, 26; and security, 113
Rivlin, Alice, 12, 41
"Robber barons," 6
Roberts, Paul Craig, xi, 40–41, 173, 186, 191, 193, 274n
Robertson, Dennis, 192
Rockefeller, Nelson, xi, 119; family estate at Pocantico Hills, 56
Romero Barcelo, Carlos, 186
Ross, Heather L., 278n
Roth, William, 186
Rouse, James, 213
Rule-and-consent system, 214

Salomon, Richard, 250
San Diego, California, 168
Saudi Arabia, 47–49
Savings, 32, 34, 39, 48, 58, 106, 113; decline of, 20; rates, 179
Sawhill, Isabel V., 278n
Sawyer, John, 249, 252
Say, Jean-Baptiste, 32
Say's Law, 23, 31–35, 38–40, 45, 251
Schuettinger, Robert, 171
Schumpeter, Joseph, x, 5, 76, 83, 236–237
Scientific breakthroughs, 238
S-curves of growth, 78
Seattle, Washington, 114, 120, 124, 203
Secondary sector jobs, 141–145
Security, 44; and risk, 113
Segalman, Ralph, 278n
Segregation: and bilingual education, 94
Semiconductors, 54, 79, 82, 210, 238
Senate Finance Committee, 119
Services: productivity of, 205–216

Sexuality: and poverty, 70–71
Sexual liberation, 259
Sexual Suicide (Gilder), 71
Shackle, George, 34
Shockley, William, 238
Shopping centers, 213
Silicon chip, 79–80
"Silicon Valley," 80–81, 83
Singapore, 147–148, 168, 184
Sinks of purchasing power, 42, 44
Sismondi, Simonde de, 5, 256
Siuai, Solomon Islands, 21
Smith, Adam, *x,* 5, 9–10, 28–29, 37, 40, 210, 256, 266
Smoot-Hawley Tariff Act, 33
Socialism, 3, 76, 237, 255–256, 263; vs. capitalism, 24, 26–27
Social security, 19, 110, 112, 221–222; payments, 111, 113
Social theory, *ix*
Sociology: distortions of, *ix*
Sociology of despair, 247
Solomon Islands, 21
Solow, Robert, 196–197
Solzhenitsyn, Aleksandr, 4, 7
South: and civil rights movement, 160
Soviet Union, 12, 237
Sowell, Thomas, 32
Space program, 82
Spain, 47–48
Speculation, 20, 42, 176, 189; in housing, 176–178
Sprague, Peter, 60–61
Sprague Electric Company, 60
Standard of living, 61
Star Wars, 250
State college and university system, 112
Statistical distributions: illusions of, 10–20
Statistics of crisis, 242
Steel industry, 285–286*n*
Steiger, William, 83
Steiger Amendment, 175, 181
Stockman, David, *xi,* 19
Stock market, 57, 84, 174–176, 245
Studio (Dunne), 250
Subsidies, 37, 68, 154, 155, 169, 242
Suffrage: limitations on, 86
Sumps of wealth, 42–46, 50
Supply curves, 30
Supply side economics, *x,* 28–46, 192, 205, 218
Susu (West African form of capital formation), 23
Sutton, Percy, 66
Sweden, 182–185, 188, 221, 251; impact of taxes on, 17–18, 201
Switzerland, 184

Taiwan, 49, 147–148, 168, 184, 201
Take-home pay, 215
Tanamoshi (Japanese form of capital formation), 23
Tanzi, Vito, 193
"Targeted approach": to promoting investment, 245
Tariffs, 241
Tariff wars, 9
Tax brake theory, 191–193
Tax cuts: necessity for, 17, 40–41, 43, 185–189, 224
Taxes, 59, 85, 153, 170–189, 203–205, 215, 218–221, 226–227, 257–258; inflationary effects of, 190–194; and the rich, 56; and women workers, 14
Taxflation, 176, 220
Tax hikes, 40, 162
Tax policy, 46, 77, 244
Tax-push concept, 193–194
Tax rates, 43; vs. tax revenues, 181–182
Tax revolt, 167, 188, 215
Tax shelters, 20, 220
Technostructure, 75–76
Telecommunications, 77, 82, 210
Tenure, 44, 147
Texas Instruments Corporation, 79
Thatcher, Margaret, 227
Theory of diffusion, 202
Theory of general equilibrium, 40
Theory of Price Control (Galbraith), 77
Theory of value, 30
Thermodynamics, 260–261
Third World, 63, 188, 200, 248–250, 255
Thomas, Franklin, 66
Thrift, 51; paradox of, 33, 40–41
Thurow, Lester, 13, 15–16, 54–55, 57, 140, 148, 197, 254
Tiger, Lionel, 73
Time: as capital, 230; role in upward mobility, 71
Time pinch, 15
Tocqueville, Alexis de, 5
Tokenism, 141
Tolstoy, Leo, 25–26
Tong, Goh Chok (Singapore Trade Minister), 184
Topping, John, *xi*
Total capital formation, 113
Toxic Substances Control Act, 240
Trade, 9, 21, 106; international, 33, 243
Trade policies, 241
Transfer payments, 155, 182
Transgenerational welfare poverty, 278*n*
Treasury guarantees, 177
Tucker, William, 239
Turkey, 189

Underground economy, 17, 187, 218, 221–222

Unemployment, 39, 147, 157, 162, 163; male, 137; youth, 89

Unemployment compensation, 45, 110–111, 157, 163, 281*n*

United Nations, 96

United States: attitudes toward wealth, 49–50; vs. socialist countries, 50

U.S. Commissioner of Patents, 256

U.S. Steel, 110

Unheavenly City (Banfield), 70, 72

Upper classes, 100–101; impact of inflation on, 18–20; role in capitalist economy, 62

Upward mobility, 68, 73–74, 94–95, 99, 122

Value Line Composite Index, 84

Veblen, Thorstein, 5

Venezuela, 49

Vietnamese, 168

Visible Man (Gilder), *ix*

Vocational Foundation, Inc., (VFI), 146–147, 158

Von Hayek, Fredrich, *x*, 6

Von Mises, Ludwig, 6

Wage-and-price controls, 170–172, 244

Wage incentives, 214

Wages, 148, 193; minimum rates, 126

Wage Subsidies proposal, 119

Wagner, Richard E., 275*n*

Wall Street Journal, *x–xi*, 12–13, 35, 40, 88, 174, 181, 250

Walras, Leon, 40

Wang Laboratories, 81

Wanniski, Jude, *x*, 180, 181, 186, 188, 194, 215

War, 255, 257; economic futility of, 9

War and Peace (Tolstoy), 25

War on Poverty, 12, 139

Warsh, David, *x*, 194–195, 197–201, 203–204, 206, 208–210, 216, 261

Washington, D.C., 120

WASPS, 11, 88

Way the World Works (Wanniski), *x*, 180

Wealth and the rich, 47–63, 245, 259, 275*n*; attacks on, 96–101

Wealth effects, 19

Wealth of Nations (Smith), 9–10, 28–29, 40

Wedge effect of taxes, 215

Wedgewood Benn, 61

Welfare, 12, 19, 45, 68, 114, 127, 142; fraud, 116–118, 122; history, 106–107, 109–110; housing, 125; Massachusetts, 163; proper goal of, 126; recent growth, 111–112; work requirement, 121–122

Welfare (Anderson), 12

Welfare culture, 122–125, 136, 143

West Africans, 23

West Indians, 11, 23, 94, 133–134

Wholesale price index, 285*n*

Widows, 18, 56

Wildavsky, Aaron, 251

Wilson, David B., 154

Wiltshire Associates, 84; Wiltshire index, 85

Windfall profits, 84, 223

Wisconsin, 69

Wisconsin, University of, 68

Women, 88, 146, 147; black, 135, 150–151; and discrimination myths, 128

Work, 72, 74, 87, 120, 127, 152; under capitalism, 23–24; upward mobility, 69–70; *see also* Jobs

Work effort, 40–41, 68–70; male-female differences in, 16

Work incentives, 67

Working women, 14, 16

Work-training operations, 144

World economy, 200

World War II, 147, 170, 197, 230, 232, 256

Wright, David McCord, 251

Wrigley, E. A., 71–72

X-efficiency, 25, 73, 115, 131

Xenophobia, 98

Xerox Corporation, 81, 210

Yoruba (West Africans), 23

Zabian, Michael, 52, 55

"Zero-sum game": view of capitalism, 10; of income redistribution, 45, 230